European Garden Design

Ehrenfried Kluckert

European Garden Design

From Classical Antiquity to the Present Day

Edited by Rolf Toman

Photographs by Markus Bassler, Achim Bednorz,
Markus Bollen, and Florian Monheim

KÖNEMANN

FRONTISPIECE:
Salignac, Manoir d'Eyrignac
Avenue in geometrical forms

Editorial Management and Typesetting: Rolf Toman, Espéraza; Birgit Beyer, Cologne
Editors: Ulrike Weber-Karge, Dresden; Thomas Paffen, Münster
Index: Andreas Gasler
Picture Research: Stefanie Hubert, Cologne
Production: Petra Grimm, Cologne
Repro Studio: Typografik, Cologne

Original Title: *Gartenkunst in Europa von der Antike bis zur Gegenwart*

Translating and Editing: Translate-A-Book, Oxford, UK
Typesetting: Organ Graphic, Abingdon, UK
Project Coordination: Alex Morkramer and Nadja Bremse-Koob
Production: Petra Grimm

Printed in Germany

ISBN 3-8290-2289-1

10 9 8 7 6 5 4 3 2 1

Contents

Editor's Preface

This book on European gardens deals mainly with gardens in Italy, Spain, Portugal, France, England, the Netherlands, Germany, and Austria. In these countries most of the gardens shown have been newly photographed for the book. Northern Europe (Scandinavia) and Eastern Europe (Russia) have at least been touched on, whereas some European countries do not figure at all. Nevertheless the ambition of presenting a sufficiently comprehensive account, geographically speaking, of the European garden has to a large extent been achieved.

A more problematic issue arises with regard to the period of time specified in the subtitle: "From Classical Antiquity to the Present Day." In fact, almost four-fifths of the book is devoted to Renaissance and Baroque gardens along with the landscape gardens of the Enlightenment and the Classical and Romantic eras, that is to say approximately the period from 1500 to 1850. This reflects the fact that this period was the golden age of the art of the garden. But it is not the only reason why the period after 1850 is treated in such a cursory manner. It becomes increasingly difficult to classify the rich diversity of European gardens; that is to devise categories enabling them to be dealt with in separate chapters. The periodizations of art history are no longer adequate, and other conceptual approaches are suitable only to a limited extent. To speak of "forms and aspects," as in the final chapter, merely conveys the lack of usable general concepts. It would require a further volume to do justice to the considerable variety of 20th-century gardens. As in other fields of art, increased individualism may be noted. To give an account of this multifaceted development would be a fascinating task, but it is beyond the scope of the present book.

The comparative brevity of the treatment of the period from classical antiquity to the Middle Ages has to do with the fact that there is a great deal that can be said about this period, but not much that can be shown. The gardens of the Renaissance and Baroque eras are, of course, no longer preserved in their original condition. But an adequate notion of these historical gardens can be obtained from old drawings and even, in a few cases, from attempts at re-creating garden architecture.

Potsdam, Klein-Glienicke
"Natural" arrangement of clumps of trees in a landscape garden

Myths of Paradise

Scene from Paradise
Detail from *The Golden Age* (opposite)

The garden of all gardens lies in the unattainable distance of dreams and fantasies in which man's hopes and yearnings take refuge, along with his sufferings and dilemmas. Since fulfillment of Man's deepest desires is not possible in this world, it is imagined as belonging to the afterlife. But its image is portrayed and elaborated during life on earth, so the dream is never forgotten. People speak of a Golden Age, of the Elysian fields, of Arcadia, and finally of the *locus amoenus*. Paradise, a garden, is an element common to these age-old visions of a lost human bliss whose promised return is awaited.

These visions have had a decisive influence on the structures and themes of garden culture in Western civilization. This statement takes on particular significance in view of the fact that the words "garden" and "paradise" share a common linguistic root. The word "paradise" can be derived from the Old Persian *pairi-dae'-za*, meaning a fenced-in royal park or pleasure garden. The Late Babylonian word *paradisu* is simply a verbal variant of *pairi-dae'-za*. It can be translated literally as something that is walled or fenced in, or simply a demarcated area. The Hebrew *pardes* and the Greek *paradeisos* have the same meaning, and likewise denote the pleasure garden of the Persian monarch. It is interesting to note that the idea of demarcation or fencing-in also applies to "garden." The Indo-Germanic word-stem *ghordho* means both "courtyard" and "enclosure." The Latin word *hortus*, a garden, belongs in the same etymological context.

But to what extent are the ideas of "enclosure" and "garden" compatible? The answer to this question takes us directly into the realm of desires alluded to above. The place that is enclosed is at the same time a separate, thus a secret place. It is accessible only to particular people, the chosen ones who are allowed to enter it. Anyone who proves unworthy of it is expelled.

To the inhabitants of a country comprising both desert and steppe-like landscapes, the pleasure garden of the Persian monarch appeared as a place of every imaginable pleasure and delight. Because it was enclosed it was coveted. The word "paradise" refers to its being enclosed.

The earliest descriptions of the garden of paradise also come from the desert regions of the Near East. They are to be found in the Akkadian Adapa myth of the 15th century BC, in the Sumerian-Babylonian Epic of Gilgamesh from the 12th century BC and the Hebrew biblical account of paradise from the 8th century BC. The first two of these myths are concerned with Man's immortality. In them, paradise plays more of a secondary role. But it is in paradise that the decision is made as to whether Man can achieve or retain immortality. Man's life has, of course, its limits, just as the garden has its boundaries and is only accessible under certain conditions. But in the Great Flood described in the Epic of Gilgamesh the garden is spared. Paradise exists somewhere on earth, in a form similar to the pleasure gardens of the kings of Persia. To the man who finds it, it promises eternal life, that is to say immortality.

The Garden of Paradise
Treasury and receptacle for the true riches of salvation and eternal bliss, 1491

The search is worthwhile even if the hero Gilgamesh himself comes to grief.

This motif provides a link with the Old Testament account of paradise, which begins with a precise indication of its location: "And the Lord God planted a garden eastward in Eden; and there he put the man whom he had formed" (Genesis, 2:8). In Genesis, Eden is described more precisely as the area where the four rivers which water the garden have their source. These are Tigris, Euphrates, Pison, and Gihon. But the two latter rivers of paradise are not shown on any map. For this reason the attempt has been made again and again, to locate the garden of paradise on earth. It was believed that the unknown rivers could be traced in an undiscovered country, after all God had created the Garden of Eden for Man. Was the Garden of Eden a continent that was irrigated and divided by four great rivers? It may be assumed that the unknown rivers Pison and Gihon were as long and as mighty as the known rivers, Tigris and Euphrates. It was a matter of a divine continent in the hereafter. It is well known that each of the early Babylonian kings of the 3rd millennium BC called himself Lord of the Four Quarters. This title was an allusion to their symbolic rule over the world, that is to say an appropriation of the concept of the "Pantocrator." The Four Quarters denoted the four regions of the earth, from the center of which the source of life emanated, to divide itself up and give shape to the world.

Here we find the basic model describing the garden that is watered by a central fountain. This ideal-type of the oriental garden, the pleasure garden of Persian or Babylonian kings, stands in the same relationship to the ancient oriental or Old Testament kingdom of Heaven as does, later, the Christian Church to the New Jerusalem of the New Testament. The garden and the Church were, and still are today, secular images of a heavenly place where desires are fulfilled, where Man hopes to find eternal life and happiness.

The Golden Age
Painting on wood, 73.5 x 105.5 cm
(*c.* 30 x 42 in.), *c.* 1530,
Lucas Cranach the Elder
Munich, Bayerische
Staatsgemäldesammlungen

Valencia, Monforte Park
Formal garden layout with sculptures

If it is a question of rediscovering, in the concrete guise of the garden, the elements that have been defined in terms of myth, then, along with the ideas of enclosure and the headstreams – suggesting garden walls and irrigation – a further constant takes on significance: trees and plants, which inexhaustibly blossom, ripen, and bear fruit. In the 4th book of Homer's *Odyssey* the Elysian fields are bounded by the sea. They are an island in the western ocean, at the edge of the world. This island cannot be reached by mortal men, but only by heroes who are allowed to live there by the special favor of the Gods, such as Menelaus, for example. Unlike the latter, Odysseus expects death after his wanderings. One cannot as yet properly speak of a garden as such, it is more of a heavenly paradise on earth, where Man spends his eternal life in bliss and where, favored by Nature, he may partake of all the delightful fruits during all the seasons of the year. Even though Odysseus was not able to share in these delights, he was allowed to enter the earthly version of paradise, the garden of Alcinous, the Phaecian king and Nausicaa's father. In the 7th book the seafarer and hero strolls in the pleasure garden with its portal and the "fence running round," admiring its "sweet figs" and "pomegranates." In a corner of the garden Odysseus thinks that he senses the breath of heaven, for there he discovers "plots of all kinds of herbs that keep fresh all the year round."

This *locus amoenus* became a topos, that is a well-known theme, in Renaissance literature and hence a model for pleasure gardens. Garden metaphors are used to depict courtly love. Allegorical and didactic pamphlets likewise make use of this classical topos, which merges with medieval Christian garden motifs.

Whereas in Homer, Elysium, at the end of the world, is strictly separate from the garden of Alcinous, in the case of Virgil, the timeless, remote realm of Arcadia blends with the everyday rural world in a bucolic pastoral idyll: peace, harmony, and security are the attributes of an image with which to counter the dismal present of the Roman civil wars. Arcadia likewise becomes a topos of a realm of fulfillment and a metaphor for aesthetic sensitivity. Arcadian gardens are frequently intimate subdivisions within the huge grounds of the late Baroque. The romanticization of ruins, and pastoral idylls, which are part of an iconographic program at Hohenheim near Stuttgart, can also be found in early landscape gardens.

The leap from the ideas of classical antiquity, which were handed down as a tradition of garden topoi, or themes, to Renaissance gardens or to the landscape gardens of the late 18th and early 19th centuries is a large one. It is too large to provide a satisfactory answer to the question of how far these classical notions of gardens and paradise may have influenced the form taken by actual gardens. Homer's *Odyssey* and Virgil's *Georgics* may have done no more than provide poetic themes which were later the subject of further literary treatment and thereby occasionally suggested ideas for gardens. The Renaissance theory of gardens (see pp. 40) will shed some light on these matters. But it is less a matter of the complex structure of ornamental beds than the basic pattern for gardens in the West, namely beds planted in the form of a cross, with a central fountain. The model of the Four Quarters is again involved. Two aspects must be taken into account. On the one hand it was the Hellenic-Roman tradition which contributed to the adoption of the garden layout in the form of a cross, which had been developed in Persia and the Near East. On the other hand, it was Moorish-Saracen gardens which, as variations of the oriental Four Quarters gardens, determined the basic structure of early Christian monastery gardens and estate gardens. It is useful to contemplate the gardens of classical antiquity for this familiarizes us both with this basic model and with its variants, and also with the use of motifs taken from the images of paradise as Elysium, *locus amoenus*, or Arcadia.

In this sense it becomes possible to bridge the gap between the first beginnings of gardens in classical antiquity and the gardens of the period of "Sentimentality," *c.* 1800. The fantasy of an "island of hope" then took on concrete form; examples of this can still be seen in the gardens of Kassel (in Germany) or Stowe (in England). At least the decorative buildings, combined with the artificially shaped wilderness throughout which streams so pleasingly meander and ponds are scattered, were intended to present an imaginary model of those once lauded Elysian fields.

London, Hampton Court Palace
Aerial view of the Privy Garden

Florence, Boboli Garden
Central fountain of the "Isolotto"

Gardens in Classical Antiquity

Pompeii, garden of Roman villa
House of the Vettii
Peristyle with archaeo-botanically replanted garden

Proving miracles and wonders is a difficult business, particularly when they are far back in time. But this does not apply to the Seven Wonders of the World of classical antiquity, which were described authentically and credibly by both contemporaries and later scholars – with one exception: the Hanging Gardens of Babylon. Most lists of the ancient wonders of the world, including the "*Laterculi Alexandri*" or the "*Anthologia Palatina*" of Antipatros of Sidon from the 2nd century BC, do not explicitly include these Babylonian gardens. Either they refer vaguely to hanging gardens, without specifying their location, or the obelisk donated by Queen Semiramis is mentioned among the *opera miranda*. Even in the oldest description of the city, which originated in Babylon itself, one searches in vain for any statements concerning hanging gardens. Perhaps we should believe Quintus Curtius Rufus, who – admittedly not until the 2nd century AD – wrote a comprehensive biography of Alexander the Great. He referred to the oldest Greek writings, for example the "*Persicha*" of Ctesias of Cnidus from the 4th century BC, of which only fragments have been preserved. They include passages concerning Babylon, its monumental walls, and the Hanging Gardens. Rufus was evidently quoting from this:

"Close by the Palace of Babylon are the Hanging Gardens – a wonder celebrated in Greek writings [by Ctesias, the author]. They are situated at the height of the coping of the wall and give pleasure with their many tall trees which provide much shade. Pillars made of natural stone support the entire edifice, and above these pillars there is a floor made of blocks of stone for the soil which is piled high upon it, and also for the water which keeps it moist. And this edifice bears trees so massive that their trunks grow to a thickness of 8 cubits and they tower up 50 feet [*c.* 15.5 m] into the sky, and indeed even bear fruit as if they were nourished by the mother earth."

The measurements give the game away. Trees with a diameter of 8 cubits (*c.* 3.5 m or 11.5 ft.) are an impossibility for this region. Are the Hanging Gardens a product of the imagination? Anyone who reads further accounts from classical antiquity will be forced to reach this conclusion. Sometimes a garden of Semiramis is mentioned, sometimes it is the garden of a Syrian king's concubine. Then Nebuchadnezzar is brought in, with the huge palace with terraced gardens which he had built. While classical authors disagree as to who created the garden, they agree in their descriptions of the irrigation techniques. The water was moved by "worms," that is revolving screws, driven by oxen, which pump the water continuously upwards from a river. But these pumping machines, also known as Archimedean screws, had not yet been invented at the time of Nebuchadnezzar II, who lived *c.* 620 BC, or of Semiramis (8th century BC) – Archimedes had not even been born

Even for these ancient historians, Babylon, the city of wonders, lay in the dim and distant past. They took over older sources and elaborated them with the knowledge of their own age or its ideas concerning gardens. It is therefore hardly surprising that the Babylonian garden was given the features of the Homeric garden of Alcinous. In other words: in the imaginary Graeco-Roman garden of Babylon, the lost garden of paradise took on, for the first time, concrete form, and acquired high standing by being included among the Wonders of the World.

In an engraving done by Maarten van Heemskerk in 1572, the walls, the obelisk, and the Garden of Babylon with its roof garden are seen.

The city of Babylon with its Hanging Gardens
Drawing, Maarten van Heemskerk, 1572

Based presumably on the belief, handed down from classical antiquity, that the obelisk was created by a monarch, the other wonders were also ascribed to Semiramis (illustration opposite).

In the accounts of the Hanging Gardens of Semiramis, the mythical garden of paradise becomes part of the reality of garden construction in classical antiquity, but this transference would have been inconceivable without its divine associations. The Egyptian garden, for example, was defined as a kind of intermediate zone linking this world with the next. The pleasures enjoyed in the gardens of the palaces of the pharaohs or princes appeared as murals in their graves. In the newly built Amarna, in the middle of his palace, Akhenaton, the religious revolutionary of the New Empire (1550–1080 BC), together with his wife Nefertiti, had an immense complex of temples and gardens constructed, which was consecrated to the gods. The most magnificent garden was dedicated to the sun god Aton, as can be seen from the great Aton Hymn which originated *c.* 1350 BC:

"All cattle draw satisfaction from its herbs; trees and plants grow. The birds fly from their nests..."

Remains and other evidence of sumptuous gardens have been discovered in the ruins of the royal residence. The boundary between illusion and reality was a fluid one. The gardens merged into rooms where floral and animal motifs were painted on the walls and floors. In Egypt the garden was designed as a place of myth, indeed even more: as a religiously motivated expression f everything that was understood as Nature. Aton, the sun disk, was worshiped as a life-giving force, the source of the constant renewal of Nature. For this reason Akhenaton often had himself depicted in a particular situation: with his wife and two daughters, reverently offering flowers to the sun disk.

In ancient Egypt the lotus blossom was a symbol of rebirth. In the grave of Sen-Nufer in Thebes, who was the supervisor of royal gardens and parks in the 18th dynasty, under the rule of

Idyllic bucolic sacral landscape
Mural from Pompeii, 3rd quarter of the 1st century
Naples, Museo Nazionale

Garden landscape
Mural from the Villa of Livia at Primaporta
1st quarter of 1st century AD
Rome, Museo Nazionale Romano

Thutmose III (1496–36 BC), the deceased is shown sitting in the fruit-bearing tree of Heaven with his sister Merit, holding a lotus blossom.

Whereas Egyptian gardens from the era of the pharaohs have in some cases been archaeologically investigated, and are documented in grave paintings, there is hardly any evidence at all of classical Greek gardens. Scattered remarks by Aristophanes or Plutarch from the 5th century BC suggest that gardens were attached to the philosophical academy in Athens. Moreover, domestic gardens in Athens were used not only for growing vegetables but also as places to enjoy strolling among ornamental shrubbery and flowers. A municipal garden or park is hardly conceivable, given the density of development there. But a note by Plutarch may be evidence of a need for places with trees providing shade: he recorded that the Athenian statesman Kimon provided plane trees for the *agora*, and evidently also had more trees planted in the city. These were situated along the water conduits and channels leading to the pump rooms. For Plato this linking of the water system with the municipal tree and garden zones was one of the elements of an ideal city layout, as he mentioned in his "*Nomoi*" ("Laws").

The *oikia kai kepos*, the house-and-garden system, took on special significance in the suburbs and the country. Under the influence of Greek culture, the Romans took over, among other things, the house-and-garden concept. One reason for this was to achieve optimum agricultural

output. In the 8th book of his treatise *De Agricultura*, Cato wrote:

"In the vicinity of the city it is advisable to have a garden (*sub urbe hortum*) with all kinds of vegetables and flowers for wreaths, Megarian onions, wedding myrtle, white and black myrtle, Delphic, Cypriot and wild laurel trees, also with walnut trees..."

Although there is no evidence of the use of a myrtle wreath as a bridal wreath in ancient Greece, Cato appears to be drawing on the Roman cult of Venus, which prescribed myrtle wreaths for weddings. This means that decorative plants were part of the concept of a utilitarian garden. Cato's concept was taken up and elaborated by the great Roman agricultural theorists such as Marcus Terrentius Varro (116–27 BC) and Lucius Junius Moderatus Columella (1st century AD). In Columella's handbook of agriculture and animal husbandry, the 10th book is devoted to gardening. Here the Roman author abandons his somewhat sober style and resorts to the poetic form of the hexameter in order to do justice to his emotions on seeing a garden:

"But as soon as the earth is combed, its hair neatly parted,
No longer lying wild and lewdly desirous of seed,
Then lend it color with various flowers, the stars of the earth,
Plant white stock and Caltha, the golden gleaming buttercup,
Plant the feathery narcissi, the dragon's fearsome snap
Horribly gaping lilies blossoming to white chalices,
Hyacinths also, snow white and gleaming, radiantly sky-blue.
Plant violets, the one pallidly creeping, the other growing upright
Green in crimson gold – and the too, too bashful rose."

A colorful and luxuriant flowerbed is laid out before the reader's eyes, probably for the first time in the cultural history of the European garden. Columella knew full well that visual pleasure is at the same time sensual pleasure, for in the following section he not only refers to chervil and endives as "good for a jaded palate," but also to the Megara onion and the colewort which will "fire up a sluggish husband to do his duty to Venus."

Columella's poetic ambition, undoubtedly inspired by Virgil's "Georgica", written decades earlier, contrasts with his more pragmatic remarks and instructions regarding agriculture and animal husbandry. For this reason his garden poetry cannot be regarded as a theoretical basis of Roman horticulture. The important thing to remember is that Columella extended the utilitarian garden by adding an independent ornamental garden to it. The rhetorical form of his statements tempts the reader to take a walk for pleasure in a shady garden. Thus one could perhaps after all discern a theoretical approach here, especially since in imperial Rome, as population density and the attendant noise level increased, the demand for *rus in urbe*, for a small piece of countryside within the town, was made with increasing urgency.

Rome was the metropolis of the ancient world. When people spoke of *urbs*, or of municipal culture in general, they meant Rome. Marcus Valerius Martial, a contemporary of Columella and Seneca,

Pompeii, Villa of Peacocks

Pompeii, House of Loreius Tiburtinus
Well with steps

wrote epigrams describing the intolerable level of noise in the city. He fled to his country estate. His description of the garden of his friend Julius' town house above Trastevere was all the more euphoric. He was not sure whether to call this house a *villa rustica* or a *villa urbana*. At this time the importance of municipal gardens and parks as recreational areas was increasing. But the *rus in urbe* was intended not merely to encourage walking for pleasure but also to remind Romans of their rustic origins. In 12 BC, following a fire at the Forum, Augustus set aside a space at the foot of the Capitol where the soil was uncovered and had an olive tree, a vine, and a fig tree planted there. These three plants stood for the production of basic foodstuffs, and provided the initial impetus for the idea of the *rus in urbe*. They awakened the Romans' longing to bring a small part of country life into the town.

There were over eighty gardens in different places in the municipal area of imperial Rome. Some of them were the smaller gardens (*hortulus*) of simple dwellings, others were larger gardens (*hortus*) of splendid villas. Alongside kitchen gardens little paths opened up, bordered with box trees, and leading to the ornamental beds. In his letters Cicero gives fairly precise information regarding the design and make-up of the gardens. In a letter to his brother Quintus he wrote:

"I was able to praise your gardener. He has covered everything with ivy, the base of the villa and the spaced columns of the colonnade, so that the statues appear to be running a nursery for plants and selling the ivy."

Placing sculptures in the gardens was an innovation, which in the Republican era would have been condemned as oriental luxury. As a result of the conquest of the Mediterranean countries and the establishment of Roman provinces, sculptures and other works of art found their way to Rome. The erstwhile *hortulus*, a mere utilitarian garden, was replaced by the sumptuous show garden.

At the beginning of the 1st century BC, a Roman ship carrying a cargo of works of art was on its way to Rome when it was driven by a storm into the Gulf of Gabes, and sank off the east coast of Tunis. Two thousand years later the wreck was salvaged, and most of the works of art and sculptures were in 1995 put to use in the way originally intended. They were not set up in Roman gardens, however, but in the inner courtyard of the Landesmuseum in Bonn (illustration opposite). The candelabra, basins, and fountains, as well as sculptures, were integrated into the garden design of the inner courtyard. This "re-creation" gives us a very precise notion of how Roman gardens were designed in this period of historical transition. It is in accordance with the descriptions given by Cicero and other Roman scholars of the time, and with another important source which to this day enables us to see what a Roman garden looked like: the garden paintings in the towns in the Campagna that were devastated by Vesuvius. For example, the murals in the villas of the Insula Occidentalis in Pompeii show that Roman gardens were not only architecturally constructed, and planted with flower borders or high trees and bushes, but were also adorned with marble basins, Hermae, and groups of lifelike sculptures. Furthermore, the Romans had a liking for all kinds of birds, which enlivened the bushes. The paintings show that the design of some gardens included an aviary (illustration p. 14). Over and above the revealing garden paintings, the municipal gardens in Pompeii have been thoroughly investigated, enabling a typology to be drawn up which is also valid for Rome. Almost every garden was bounded by a row of columns on at least one side. At the rear of the grounds there were, in some cases, vegetable patches, fruit trees, and vines. Even less affluent artisans had a small domestic garden, which was sometimes located in the inner courtyard, and received light only through a shaft.

In the villa of Loreius Tiburtinus in the Via dell'abbondanza in Pompeii there is both a peristyle (a courtyard surrounded by columns) and a large garden. The latter is divided lengthwise into two parts by an irrigation channel with an overarching pergola. On both sides of the pergola there are beds and fruit and olive trees (illustration opposite). Their design may have resembled that of the garden which Pliny the Younger (the adopted son of Gaius Plinius Secundus, the author of the *Naturalis Historia*) visited in the Tiber valley and described as follows:

"In front of the arcades a terrace, divided up into flowerbeds of many different shapes, surrounded by box hedges. Also a gently sloping lawn into which the box tree has cut animal figures that stand facing one another in pairs."

The garden was thus closely related to the house, and therefore was part of the villa's extended living space.

The most famous Roman garden was probably that of Lucius Licinius Lucullus (117–56 BC), of whom Plutarch, in the biography which he wrote a century and a half later, said that after a life that had weathered many struggles, during which he had accumulated immeasurable wealth, he "sought the restful pursuit of philosophy." In order to enjoy the leisure of old age undisturbed, Lucullus had his villa built in the middle of Rome, on the Pincio, the steep slope at the parade ground known as the *collis hortulorum* (garden hill). The "*Horti Luculliani*" extended from the present-day Spanish Steps to the Villa Borghese. The differences in the height of the terrain were compensated for by means of terraces and flights of steps. On the central terrace, which was surrounded by colonnades Lucullus, according to ancient documents, had trees planted which – 100 years after his death grown tall and providing shade – bore unique witness to the idea of *rus in urbe*. Pirro Ligorio's engravings of ancient Rome may perhaps give us a clearer idea of the famous Roman's garden (illustration left.)

In the Republican period and the early years of the imperial age, the Palatine was the area where the Roman aristocracy most liked to live. Cicero had his villa there, as did the famous orator Hortensius, who sold his villa along with the garden to the Emperor Augustus. The Roman Emperor extended the grounds, thereby creating the nucleus of the imperial palace which was only given its final form by Domitian toward the end of the 1st century. Even in the 16th century, traces of these sumptuous grounds probably remained, for

Re-created ancient Roman garden
with sculptures from the Mahdia wreck
Bonn, Landesmuseum (installation from the exhibition *Das Wrack* [The Wreck])

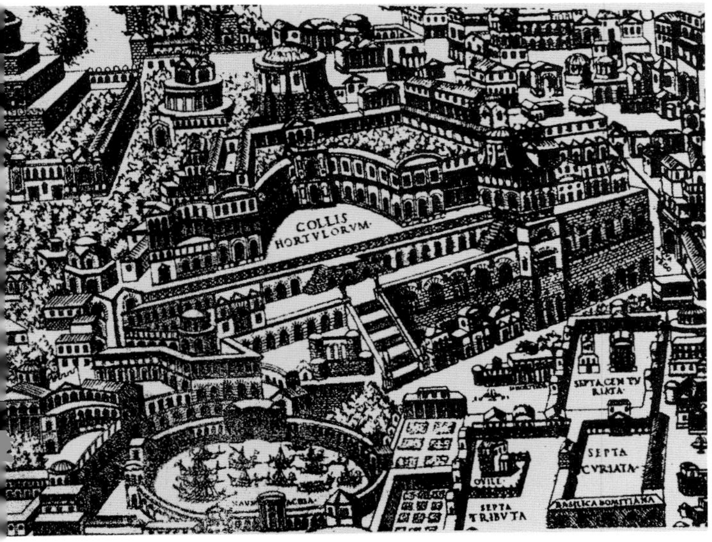

The Collis Hortulorum with the gardens of Lucullus
As visualized by Pirro Ligorio, taken from *Roma antica*, 1561

Tivoli, Hadrian's Villa
Island villa or "teatro marittimo": Ionian columns with architrave of the round temple

ILLUSTRATIONS OPPOSITE
Tivoli, Hadrian's Villa
Serapeion: columns with statues around the central basin (top)

the Farnese family, on the initiative of Cardinal Alessandro Farnese, had their gardens laid out on this spot, the Orti Farnesiani, as they later came to be called (see pp. 74–45). To this day, evidence of the essential elements of Roman garden design survives in this region. The garden path (*ambulatio)* between beds, lawns, and bush areas, links the pavilions (*dietas*) with one another. The wider paths leading around the entire complex of beds were called *gestatio*. Likewise, many ancient fountains and pump rooms, the *nymphaei*, still exist. In the yellow frieze of the house of Livia an awning (*solarium*) is depicted, the kind set up on the garden terraces to give shade during the hot season.

Hadrian's Villa in Tivoli

In AD 118, the Emperor Hadrian had a huge villa complex built at the foot of the city of Tibur (Tivoli). Following the excavations and research of the past hundred years, the areas of the "Teatro marittimo" and the "Canopus Serapeion" are particularly worth seeing today (illustrations top, bottom, and opposite). The latter has been compared to the idea of a "triclinium," or dining room. The serapeion, a complex with deliberate associations with Egyptian religious cults, comprises a grotto in two sections, an extensive basin, and a ring of columns with statues in the spaces between them.

The so-called "Teatro marittimo," also known as the "island villa," was a self-contained villa complex surrounded by a ring wall. At the center the Emperor had an island built with small living areas. Some of the "Cento Camerelle," the hundred small rooms for the servants, have been excavated and re-created. Then there were the thermae, the warm springs branching out in subterranean vaults with floor heating, water conduits, and extended spaces.

Tivoli, Hadrian's Villa
Island villa or "teatro marittimo": Ionic columns of the former colonnade with the circular watercourse

Hortulus – The Medieval Garden

Trees and birds from the *Little Paradise Garden* (detail from the illustration opposite)

No medieval gardens exist today. The few cases which are presented as such are in fact re-creations. They are based on the numerous existing written sources and vivid depictions of gardens in Gothic frescoes, panel paintings, carpets, or graphic portrayals. Seen in this light, the investigation of medieval gardens ought not to be difficult. But one still must be careful. Only to a limited degree can Gothic paintings be used as sources regarding the layout of medieval gardens. An example of this is provided by the *Little Paradise Garden* created by an Upper Rhenish master *c.* 1410 (illustration opposite). Here, a walled-in garden is shown, with flowers, trees, birds, and the Virgin Mary with the Child, an angel, and courtiers. Below the seated knight, a slain dragon is to be seen, symbolizing the conquest of Evil through the birth of Christ. The lily clearly symbolizes Mary, and the strikingly twisted tree is an allusion to the tree of knowledge. A little monkey placed next to the angel, along with robins, chaffinches, goldfinches, and other well-known native bird species (illustration left) are intended to draw the viewer's attention to the paradisial ambience. Mary is leafing through a book, and the infant Jesus is playing on a psaltery under the guidance of a lady's maid.

Thus what is important here is not the depiction of a garden, but the associations with the paradise that man has lost but which he can regain through the birth of the Redeemer. The garden and its attributes have been idealized so that it may take on a symbolic quality, and act as a foil to the religious statement. Thus the Upper Rhenish master was primarily concerned with enumerating Mary's attributes and the symbols of heavenly paradise. Understandably, therefore, such portrayals can hardly be used to re-create actual historical gardens. This also applies to the "*Minnesang*" (the

The Great Garden of Love
c. 1450
The Master of the Gardens of Love

songs of courtly love), courtly epics, or heroic sagas and the illustrations to them, and to copperplate engravings with allegories of love. It is true that such texts and pictures do provide a wealth of details, such as depictions of flower and tree species, but only in a very few cases is there any evidence regarding the layout of a garden.

Nevertheless there are some individual cases where it may be meaningful to draw conclusions regarding garden design from medieval pictures. The motif of the fountain of life was frequently used. In a miniature from the Saint-Medard Gospel Book, which originated *c.* 800 in a workshop of the palace school in Aix-la-Chapelle, the fountain of life, or paradise, is shown in front of an imposing exedra and on the ground of a terrain richly endowed with plants (illustration top p. 22). The landscape is populated with numerous animals: deer, dogs, and birds. The architectural design of the fountain can on the one hand be derived from the canonical tables which often precede a gospel book; on the other hand the curved architrave suggests the semicircular colonnades of ancient villas, as seen for example in the villa of the Emperor Hadrian (117–138) near Tivoli. Here, the so-called Great Dining Room was surrounded on three sides by semicircular colonnades (illustration p. 22 center), while on the fourth side there was a large rectangular pool, likewise enclosed by colonnades. The colonnade, along with the other architectural features of the villa, was an expression of the Romans' cultural refinement. Scholarship sees a connection between such architectural motifs from Roman villas and the

The Little Paradise Garden
Wood, 26.3 x 33.4 cm
(*c.* 10 x 13 in.),
Upper Rhenish master, *c.* 1410
Frankfurt am Main, Stadelsches Kunstinstitut

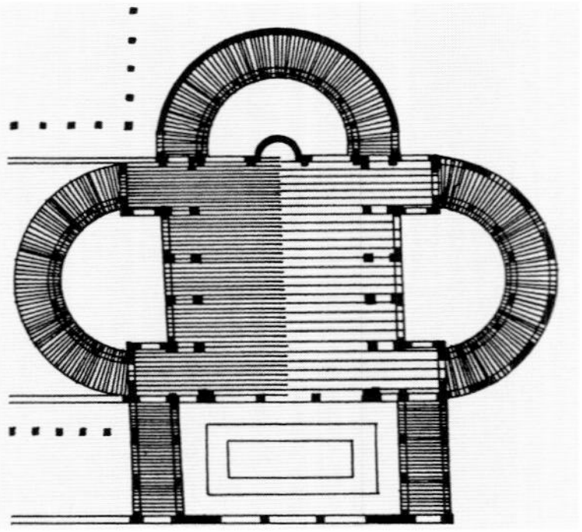

design of the first great Christian religious buildings of the Middle Ages. The paradise of the St. Gall monastery plan is similarly designed, even though it was also conceived specifically for liturgical purposes (illustration below). In the St. Gall monastery plan, the term "paradise" is given to the semicircular antechambers which, either open or roofed, were situated in front of the main church, to the east and west. This layout may be compared to the forecourts of early Christian basilicas, such as, for example, in the design of the old St Peter's Church in Rome dating from the early 4th century. In medieval churches, the concept of "paradise" denotes an architecturally designed antechamber in front of the church, in which the faithful would assemble in order to prepare themselves for the church service. Here they cleansed themselves in a fountain. According to existing documents, these forecourts were either paved or had plants growing there. In the Middle Ages the German translations of *Paradisus*: *wunnigarto* or *ziergarto*, begin to appear. The term *Rosenhag* (rose hedge) shows that heavenly paradise was also visualized as a rose garden. In the St. Gall plan, the antechamber on the west side of the main church is described as a "paradisiacum," that is to say, as a paradisial field. It may be assumed with a degree of certainty that plants grew in this field.

Linking the depiction of the fountain of life in the Carolingian miniature from Saint-Medard on the one hand, with the Hadrian's Villa and the St. Gall monastery plan on the other, may appear a risky enterprise. But if one takes into account the fact that the Carolingian era unambiguously saw itself in relation to classical antiquity, then such cultural connections are possible. Alcuin, Charlemagne's teacher, incorporated the bucolic motifs of the ideal landscape of the late classical period into his own landscape descriptions. The *amoenus locus*, the place of pleasure, or the pleasure garden, was composed of rose bushes, herbs, lilies, an untroubled brook, and a shady grove. Images such as these continued to have an effect on the art and literature of the early and high Middle Ages and must certainly also have influenced conceptions of the garden.

Monastery gardens

Apart from speculations as to whether there were plants in the St. Gall paradise, this earliest monastery plan, along with associated contemporary documents, gives us more concrete clues as to medieval garden design. Various gardens are indicated on the plan, including a medicinal herb garden and a kitchen garden, as well as plants growing in the graveyard and in the cloister

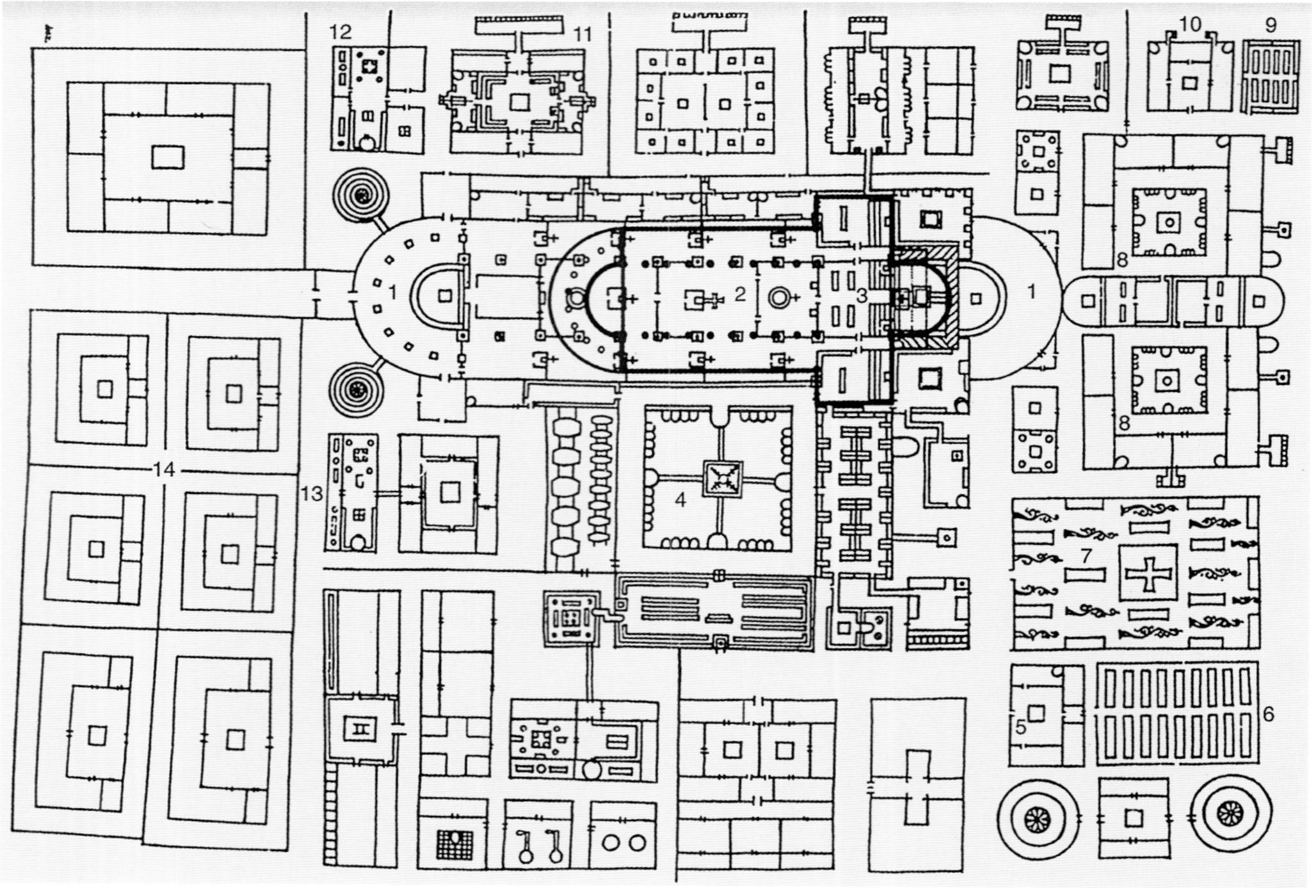

Fountain of Life
Book painting from the Saint-Medard Gospel Book, *c.* 800

Hadrian's Villa
Ground plan of the Great Dining Room

Plan of the St. Gall monastery, *c.* 820
1 Paradise
2 Monastery church
3 Choir
4 Cloister
5 Gardener's house
6 Vegetable garden
7 Graveyard
8 Cloisters of the novices' school and the hospital
9 Medicinal herb garden
10 Doctor's and apothecary's buildings
11 Guest house
12 Countinghouse
13 Brewery and bakery
14 Stables

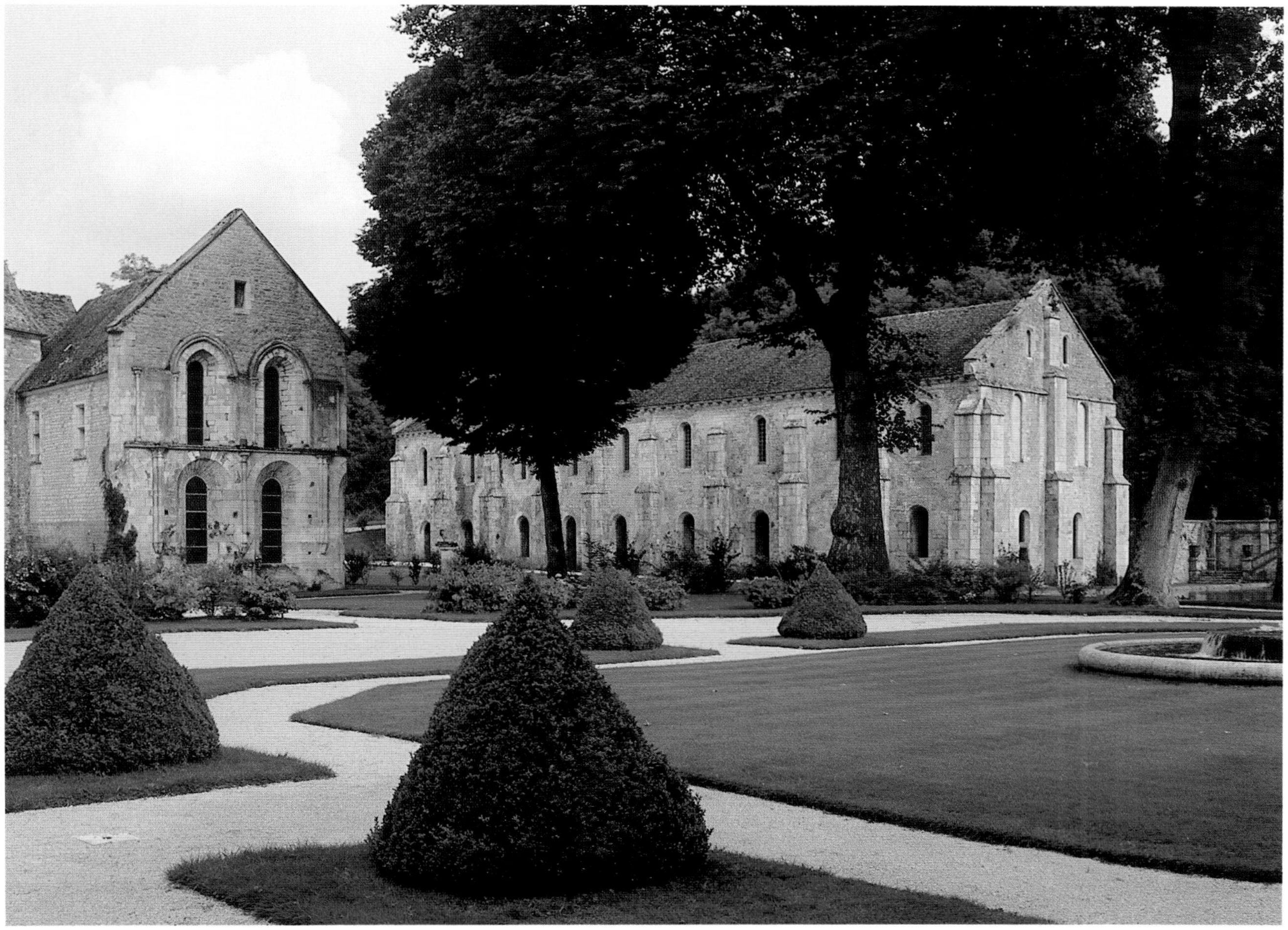

Fontenay (Burgundy), former Cistercian monastery
Cloister garden (above); garden layout to the south of the monastery buildings (left)

Santes Creus (Catalonia)
Cistercian abbey: cloister garden (detail)

garth. "*Herbularius*" was the name given to the medicinal herb garden behind the complex of doctor's and apothecary's buidings. The structure is as simple as could be, and conceived purely in terms of usefulness. In a rectangle enclosed by narrow borders there are two four-bed rows with medicinal herbs. Sage, rue, and caraway are there, as are fennel and lovage. Mint, poppy, wormwood, and other herbs were grown in the herbaceous borders. There the rose and the lily are also to be found, the flowers of the Virgin and indispensable for a monastery garden. We may be sure that their religious associations did not restrict the utilitarian nature of the garden. Quite the contrary: the juxtaposition of herbs and flowers is typical of the synthesis of medical science, religion, and aesthetics in medieval thinking. It was a matter of divine salvation and the medical process of healing that depended on it.

Walahfried Strabo's poem *Hortulus*, dating from the first half of the 9th century, is probably the first comprehensive statement in Western Christian civilization concerning garden design. It is connected with the St. Gall monastery plan – at least the layout described and the kind of plants concerned correspond to the "*Herbularius*" in many details. The first three of the twenty-seven verses of the poem describe the work of the gardener, while the remaining verses describe the individual plants, beginning with sage and ending with the rose.

The medieval herb gardens can be proved to derive from medical pamphlets of late antiquity. Strabo studied the writings of the statesman and scholar Cassiodor (487–583), who had founded a monastery at Scyllaceum near the Messina Straits. There he had also set up a vivarium (fish-breeding pond), an animal enclosure, and a herb garden. In his main work, the *Institutiones*, he refers to both Roman and Greek culture. His pharmacological studies were based on the herbal of Dioscurides Pedanios, a 1st-century Greek doctor. This herbal was re-issued at the beginning of the 6th century, and provided with illustrations in a Byzantian workshop in Constantinople. Today, the codex is kept in Vienna and is therefore known as the "Vienna Dioscorides." It contains a herbarium with illustrations of 435 plants.

It is questionable whether the plants grown in the graveyard as shown in the St. Gall monastery plan can be interpreted as an arboretum. Certainly, even the area for the burial of the dead was consciously designed as a garden. The idea of presenting the graveyard as an arboretum, that is to say not simply to plant trees there, likewise goes back to classical antiquity. Archaeologists in Athens have discovered that the Kerameicos cemetery was clearly conceived as a sacred grove where the departed were to repose in pleasure. In the 12th book of the "*Nomoi*," Plato explicitly emphasizes that a man who has contributed to public life has earned the privilege of being buried in a burial mound where there are trees. These customs may possibly have been handed down and appropriately reinterpreted in the Middle Ages so that a cemetery with trees can be considered as a special kind of monastery garden.

In fact, as far as the cultural history of gardens is concerned, the herb garden and the graveyard garden are the most interesting parts of a medieval monastery. Scarcely any information exists regarding plants grown in the cloister garth. The axes, oriented toward the central fountain, provided the structure for four smaller or larger beds enclosed by box trees or wooden boards. But it must be pointed out that this simple structure determined the basic shape of later ornamental gardens, which,

Maisonnais (Cher),
Prieure Notre-Dame-d'Orsan
The abbey was founded in the 12th century. The present-day building dates from the 16th and 17th centuries. The special feature of the Prieure d'Orsan is its re-created medieval garden: raised beds enclosed by wattle fencing (above); round wattle bench (left).

Maisonnais (Cher), Prieure Notre-Dame-d'Orsan
Raised beds enclosed by wattle fencing (above); cabbage patch (bottom) in the Prieure garden

as Dieter Hennebo emphasizes, has been preserved down to the present day in the peasant gardens of the Munsterland in Germany.

The universal knowledge of classical antiquity, revived during the Carolingian era, set its stamp until well into the high Middle Ages on the scientific studies which likewise served as a basis for garden design. In addition to the *Institutiones* of Cassiodor, one other work acquired importance for medieval garden construction, the *Geoponica*, a 10th-century encyclopedia compiled by anonymous authors in which many scientific texts of late antiquity, some of which were by then no longer extant, were reconstructed and collected. Books 10–12 are concerned with gardens and based on the agricultural treatises of the Romans Cato, Varro, and Columella. Their recommendations regarding the arrangement of plants from an aesthetic point of view, the mixture of herbs and flowers, and the alternating arrangement of plants and trees became permanent features of medieval gardens. Aesthetic elements were put at the service of religion. What was beautiful was what pleased God. The lily and the rose were pleasing to look at because they reflected the purity of the Virgin Mary and her role as the mother of God. It was precisely the contrast between herbs and roses, which was seen as something positive, and which down to the present day is still deliberately employed, that was intended to point to the healing powers of the herbs. Lavender and rosemary, with flowers whose blue color symbolized the Virgin Mary are, incidentally, among the few plants which, from a botanical point of view, are compatible with roses. Was then the symbolism of the Virgin Mary inseparable from the herbal essences when it was a matter of curing illnesses?

Prieure Notre-Dame-d'Orsan

Not far from Saint-Amand-Montrond in the Departement of Cher, in the hamlet of Maisonnais, one can travel back in time to the Middle Ages. Here, in the grounds of the 12th-century abbey – the buildings to be seen there today date from the 16th and 17th centuries – a medieval garden lies before us such as is probably not to be found anywhere else. We owe this minor miracle to the architects Sonia Lesot and Patrice Taravella along with the gardener Gilles Gillot, who, with a delight in

minute detail, have brought the medieval grounds back to life amid the ancient masonry. The kitchen garden, the herb garden, the vegetable garden, and the rose bed were laid out in accordance with accounts and descriptions of medieval gardens. The secret garden of love and delight is set apart by a pergola. A turf bench supported by stakes and boards, similar to that recommended by Albertus Magnus, has been designed, as have wooden trellises to support rose trees. Here the garden of Mary, or the Little Paradise Garden, takes on the form that we know from medieval paintings.

The medieval garden of the Prieure Notre-Dame-d'Orsan also fully matches the image of a castle garden as we know it from the descriptions of the medieval poets. It is not difficult to visualize the appropriate scenery: the lady of the castle sits in the garden, amid the serenity of nature, turning the pages of a book, while the child plays at her feet and a lady-in-waiting plucks cherries and puts them into an elegant wicker basket.

The Courtly Pleasure Garden

Albertus Magnus (Albert the Great) was born *c.* 1200 in Lauingen (Swabia), and died in Cologne at the age of eighty on November 15, 1280. He taught for example Thomas Aquinas and was an all-round scholar of the high Middle Ages: scientist, philosopher, theologian. In his scientific and philosophical writings, in which, among other things, he dealt with the design and construction of gardens, he made a contribution to the development of scholarship that went beyond his own day. On the various types of garden he wrote:

"There are certain places which are given over less to usefulness and a rich harvest than to pleasure." He called these gardens *viridantia*, that is green pleasure gardens, a term derived from the Roman tree and pleasure gardens. It is clear that in the herb gardens he deliberately avoided the strict pattern of beds, embellished with flowers, as it was familiar from the example of St. Gall. As a medieval humanist he was concerned not so much with physical health as with spiritual edification. Accordingly, Albertus Magnus emphasized that this garden was intended to appeal to two of the senses in particular: sight and smell. For this reason the ground was to be poor and the grass

ILLUSTRATIONS ABOVE AND BOTTOM
Maisonnais (Cher),
Prieure Notre-Dame-d'Orsan
Details of the garden

Detail from a late medieval rose picture
In classical antiquity the rose was frequently used as a symbol of the approach of spring. In the Roman garden it was associated with the "Rosalia," the everyday rose festival connected with the remembrance of the dead. Perhaps this is the source of its Christological significance. The rose becomes the symbol of paradise, which is why it was frequently planted in monastery gardens and gardens of love. But this flower, with its many thorns, is also associated with the martyrdom of Our Lord, and for this reason it sometimes appears together with the Madonna and Child in representations of the Little Paradise Garden.

was not to grow too high. Herbs were also desirable, but only in close association with flowers. The scholar's instructions on this point are unequivocal:

"Between these herbaceous borders and the lawn there is to be a raised section of turf full of delightful flowers and suitable at its center for sitting down, for the recuperation of the senses and the delight of repose."

Herb, tree, and pleasure gardens are described as a single unified area of experience without any strict distinction between them. They are linked by the raised section of turf, which acts as a kind of miniature protective wall.

The medieval depictions do show ornamental gardens, herb gardens, and pleasure gardens as surrounded by a common wall, but they are separated from one another by low fences with open gates (illustration opposite). The garden of love presented a monastic aspect, although the subject was unambiguous: musicians, dancing courtiers, and attractively dressed women met for merry rendezvous on colorful turf benches, beneath trees in bloom, by a sparkling fountain. There were useful and ornamental plants, along with songbirds, pheasants, or hares. Just as the monastery garden presented a courtly aspect, so vice versa the courtly pleasure garden appeared in a monastic setting. By the 15th century the people involved had become interchangeable. Not only court society frequented the pleasure garden, but also the Holy Family – though with the difference that in this case it was a Little Paradise Garden.

Was the rose bed in the medieval monastery garden something like a nucleus of the courtly pleasure garden? This may appear to be jumping to conclusions, but Albertus Magnus shows in his conception of the garden that he defined beds of ornamental plants as independent aesthetic elements. In so doing he brought new ideas into the art of garden design. The result was the pleasure garden, or at least the conceptual preconditions for the garden of love of courtly society.

Paradise now takes on a new quality. The garden is the suitable place to secularize this heavenly zone. The paradise garden is transformed into a garden of love and pleasure, and acquires its highest status in the knightly society of the high and late Middle Ages. Love and reverence for the Virgin Mary acquired its secular equivalent in courtly love. It was often a very short path from the ardor of faith to the ecstasy of high courtly love. The rose garden, likewise a symbol of both the Virgin Mary and the noble lady, the one loved with the spirit, the other with the passions, became the heart of the gardens of courtly society. The religious symbols of the Virgin, the rose and the lily, were transferred, and were declared in courtly poetry, along with the garden, to be the symbol of woman's earthly beauty. The lines by Walther von der Vogelweide are well known:

"*ir wangen wurden rot, same diu rose, da si bi der liljen stat.*" [Her cheeks turned red, like the rose beside the lily.]

What is beautiful is now no longer exclusively what pleases God, but also what appeals to the senses. The garden serves, as Albertus Nagnus had demanded, the pleasure of the senses. In the high Middle Ages worship of the Virgin Mary and courtly love were closely connected.

The French epic, the *Roman de la rose* not only presents this state of affairs, it also makes a distinction between the different spheres of the sacred and the profane. (The first part was written by Guillaume de Lorris *c.* 1235, the author of the second part, written forty years later, was Jean de Meun.) The thematic interface is the garden, which is presented as a medieval monastery garden, and hence a projection of the longing for heavenly paradise, and at the same time as a *locus amoenus* in the classical sense. With this dual significance, the garden is the scene, and at the same time the symbol, of an allegorical game of love played out before the backdrop of reality and illusion. Amant, the principal character and at the same time the author himself, enters a garden outside the city gates, and dreams of the virtues and vices which appear to him as allegorical figures. Nature opens the gateway for him. He becomes acquainted with the garden as a place for the delights of dancing, but also as a utilitarian garden with herbs and fruit trees. He encounters Venus, Minerva, and Juno to perform Paris's task, as can be seen in an illustration to the *Roman de la rose*: Venus, standing under a tree unclothed and holding a mirror, the symbol of vanity, may possibly be an allusion to the Fall. Juno, Jupiter's wife, is chastely dressed. Deduit, the pleasure for whom the garden was designed, hides behind her. Minerva, in contrast, remains at the rear of the garden, feeding a bird.

The ambivalence conveyed by this configuration is unmistakable. The allegorical garden of love could be interpreted as the Garden of Eden – even if not in the strictly biblical sense. The question of choosing between the virtues and the vices does not arise. What matters is to accept Eros (Venus) and revere science (Minerva). The world unfolds between the poles of spiritual and sensual love. Here, in outline, a view of the world emerges which already points far into the future, to the humanism of the 14th and 15th centuries.

Whereas Jean de Meun in the second part of the *Roman de la rose* concentrates on the allegorical,

Garden of Love, miniature from the *Roman de la Rose*
Parchment, 20.5 x 19.5 cm (*c.* 8 x 8 in.)
"Master of Prayer Books," Bruges (?), *c.* 1490–1500
London. British Library, Ms. Harley 4425, fol. 12v.

Pair of lovers playing cards in a tent
Unknown Swiss master, *c.* 1495

philosophical issues, Guillaume de Lorris gives a pragmatic account of the form of the garden: a square layout enclosed by walls, with herb beds and ornamental beds with exotic trees.

The medieval monastery garden which can be re-created with the aid of documents, the dissertations of Albertus Magnus, and the detailed descriptions of the garden in the *Roman de la rose* have inspired painters and graphic artists to make the garden of love their subject. All this creates a complex image of the medieval tree or pleasure garden. It was usually situated close to the women's quarters. This is true of both castle gardens and municipal grounds, as can be seen from a painting dating from the period *c.* 1470. The eye moves from the house of a wealthy family, through a loggia to a terraced garden with low beds enclosed by bricks. The beds are probably herb beds, while ornamental plants are to be seen by the castellated wall. A footpath may possibly have led from here out into the landscape and to another, larger garden, a tree or pleasure garden as was customary on large estates during the high Middle Ages.

Allegorical Garden of Love
Les échecs de l'amour: the author in the garden of desires, *c.* 1500

The type of the arboretum was probably derived from the medieval utilitarian or graveyard garden. In the utilitarian garden fruit trees, regularly spaced, grew in a meadow. It was thus a tree-and-meadow garden. These ideas possibly go back to depictions of landscapes from classical antiquity with flower-filled meadows and glades such as those we are familiar with from Pompeii, for example.

In the *Roman de la rose* we read of a little brook, a fountain, and a spring which bubbles out from under a tree. The brook, which flowed past the lady-in-waiting's chamber, could be used for passing messages, as can be seen in the miniatures of the Munich manuscript of Gottfried von Strassburg's *Tristan*. Brangane, Isolde's loyal lady-in-waiting, discovers the wood shavings as they float past and informs her mistress, who hurriedly leaves her chamber and goes into the tree and flower garden where Tristan awaits her:

"*und sleich durch bluomen und durch gras, hin da buom und brunne was.*" ["and crept through flowers and grass to where the tree and fountain were."]

The tent and the arbor were also among the important elements of the garden of love. The tent was put up on the occasion of court festivities. It was used for playing cards (illustration above) or for amorous rendezvous. The arbor was particularly suitable for the latter. The basic features of the pleasure garden also included rose bowers, trellises with rose s and trellised pathways

constructed from latticed wood densely covered with plants, for which no further explanation is required.

This garden frequently also had an animal park attached to it, a menagerie. Thus the lord of the castle could proudly show his guests strange and exotic animals. Moreover it is recorded that in these enclosures animal fighting took place for the entertainment of courtly society.

When Duke Christoph of Württemberg had a new pleasure garden built at his castle in Stuttgart in the 16th century, he included an animal park. He took pleasure in stags, does, and peacocks. At other castles in his domain he designed larger animal enclosures, which were used for hunting. This tradition, of which hunting books provide evidence, goes back to the 14th century. It continued well into the 18th century. In the 19th century the princely animal park developed into the bourgeois zoo.

The above gives an outline of the typology of medieval gardens as they developed from the simple monastery garden to the tree and pleasure garden. The symbolism associated with the Virgin Mary had a decisive influence on garden design, particularly as courtly love, in its loftiness, encompassed both sacred and profane aspects which could scarcely be separated from each other. Similarly, introverted meditation goes directly hand in hand with the quest for sensual pleasures as described by Albertus Magnus. The garden fulfilled all these functions.

There is one important aspect which up to now has only been hinted at: the inspiration drawn from Byzantine and especially Islamic gardens. The manifold oriental influences made themselves felt not only regarding exotic plants, but also in the art of collecting and chaneling water.

Medieval literature tells us of wondrous oriental gardens. Crusaders, pilgrims, and merchants told of trees and animals from southern lands. The boom in trade with the Levant strengthened the economic and political power of the Italian maritime and trading cities. It may be assumed that intensive trading allowed ideas of Arabian garden design to enter Italy and the countries north of the Alps. But the waterworks and fountains, the intertwined branches of adjacent trees, or the sophisticated use of water channels which could flood whole areas of the palace courtyards and their gardens were not only known from travelers' reports but could be admired in the Moorish part of Europe, on the Iberian peninsula.

Pair of lovers in a medieval garden
1462–1470, Renaud de Montaubon, Bruges
Paris, Bibliotheque National de France, Ms. 5072

Islamic Gardens in Spain

Anyone who today strolls through the gardens of the Alhambra above Granada can easily feel that he or she is entering a fairy-tale world. Whether one walks across the terraces to the east of the palace down to the Torre de las Damas, or visits the various architectural sections of the old city of the Moorish rulers, one always feels the harmonious unity of gardens and architecture which is created by water. Water channels were laid from the garden courtyards, which are provided with pools, to deep inside the residential areas. Thus there are channels leading out from the fountain basin of the famous Court of the Lions – an erstwhile garden of magical design – into adjoining rooms, where more gardens are watered (illustration opposite). Still water, flowing water, water that comes bubbling out of fountains – these were the paradisial elements of Islamic gardens.

Large wall mirrors created an illusion of space, and skillfully planned window apertures brought selected scenes from the outside world into the dining rooms or living rooms. But the pool brought heaven down to earth: the loggia of the Partal Palace, for example, is reflected, along with the hedges, bushes, and palm trees, in the scarcely moving surface of the water in the rectangular pool. But the greater part is filled by the blue of the sky (illustration below).

News of such magical gardens reached northern Europe at an early date and stimulated fantasies of gardens in the minds of the medieval courtly poets. A popular narrative subject of oriental origin was the story of the love of two children, a pagan prince and the Christian daughter of a slave, Floris and Blauncheflur. The Floris Romance first appeared in the mid-12th century, on the Lower Rhine, and was then reworked by Konrad Fleck *c.* 1220. At the heart of the romance is the magical garden of Amiral, a blend of medieval pleasure garden and oriental magic garden. We are told of

Granada, Generalife
Garden with pool

Granada, Alhambra, Palacio del Partal
The Palacio del Partal is probably one of the buildings of Muhammad III (1302–09) and thus the oldest preserved palace of the Alhambra.

ILLUSTRATION OPPOSITE
Granada, Alhambra
View of the Court of the Lions, 2nd half of the 14th century. The rectangular courtyard used to be a garden. On the short sides there are protruding fountain pavilions, from which channels take the water to the central Fountain of the Lions.

Seville, Crucero
The Crucero is a 12th-century garden. It already shows the characteristic features of all later Spanish-Islamic garden architecture, which was to survive for centuries in Morocco.

noble trees which Amiral had brought from far away. Imports of this kind were somewhat unusual for the North, but not for oriental desert oases that had water but no trees. Plants were imported in both classical antiquity and the Middle Ages. It can be proved that the Moors brought with them from the eastern Mediterranean area plants which they needed for their gardens in southern Spain.

It is possible that Konrad Fleck had access to accounts of travelers to the Orient telling him of eternally flowering trees and plants that never faded. He describes a magic tree with branches that spread out over a fountain like a canopy. The magic is transferred to the fountain, whose water changes color whenever anyone comes near the edge of the basin.

For the inhabitants of northern latitudes such accounts were bound to sound magical. But the magic can be explained. Travelers told of the waterworks of the famous imperial palace in Constantinople. In a fountain basin, whose shell was lined with black and white marble, there stood a column of colored marble, making the water, as it flowed in and out, refract the light into a variety of colors. Another fountain was topped with a golden pine cone from which sweet drinks, sometimes even wine, flowed on festival days. Colored water was therefore not the result of magic powers drawn from mysterious trees from paradisial regions, but of the effective use of technology. So Konrad Fleck's descriptions depict the exotic plants and sophisticated waterworks of oriental and Byzantine gardens. Today, the sentimental love story in conjunction with the charming description of the magic garden may put the visitor to the Islamic gardens of Spain in the mood for their long-ago magic.

What, in passing, has remained of the old magical gardens of Moorish Spain? The earliest Spanish gardens are to be found above Granada. They are the gardens of the Alhambra and the Generalife. Both originated during the final phase of Moorish rule. The garden of Alcazar in Seville should also be mentioned; it was laid out even earlier than the gardens of Granada. But since it was rebuilt a number of times in the 14th and early 16th centuries, there are hardly any oriental traces left to be discovered.

The Crucero in Seville and Madinat al-Zahra'

To the south of the Alcazar in Seville this garden from the 11th-century Abbadid period is to be found. The low beds and water conduits can still be discerned, as can the water basins and the remains of a portico. Over them, the "Crucero" has been built, a 12th-century Almohadic palace garden (illustration on left). The system of topped footpaths forms rectangular coordinates, and today still creates a charming effect with the central fountain and the water basins in the center of the courtyard.

In the middle of the 10th century, Caliph Abdal-Rahman III had had a palace built near Cordoba for his favorite wife, Zahra. Archaeological investigation of the site, which has long since been destroyed, has been in progress since 1910 (illustration below). Immediately in front of the so-called "Rich Hall," the "High Garden" is spread out, at the center of which a pavilion surrounded by pools once stood. The "Low Garden" can be reached from here. Both gardens are divided by alleys in the form of rectangular coordinates.

Madinat al-Zahra'
Of the city laid out in the shape of terraces in the Sierra de Cordoba, only a field of ruins remains. Here too, it has been possible to establish the existence of gardens in front of the so-called *Salon Rico* (Rich Hall).

With the conquest of the Spanish peninsula at the beginning of the 8th century, the Moors had begun to influence the way of life in the castles and cities. In the first decades, the conquerers were still subordinate to the Caliphate of Damascus, until Abd ar-Rahman I established the independent emirate of Cordoba in 756. The Moorish conquests also resulted in the Reconquest, the "*reconquista.*" With the decline of the Caliphate of Cordoba in the 11th century, the rise of Granada began under the rule of the Almoravids from North Africa. When the Christians finally reconquered Cordoba in 1236, the Moors fled to safety in Granada, and extended the city's fortifications. Two years later Muhammad ibn al-Ahmad founded the Nasrid dynasty. His skillful diplomacy enabled him to consolidate his rule. He acknowledged the sovereignty of Ferdinand III, the Holy, the most successful monarch of the Reconquista. He thus inaugurated a cultural heyday in which the city flourished unmolested by the Christian overlords. Granada survived until 1492 as the last Moorish bastion. It was a tiny oriental enclave surrounded by southern Spain which had been reconquered two centuries previously.

The Alhambra in Granada

The Nasrid palace, the main complex of the Alhambra, a typical Islamic palace with a courtroom, public assembly halls, the royal palace, and the women's quarters, dates from the early 14th century. Even today, its four main courtyards and the architectural elements linking them reveal, albeit in a reduced form, the Moorish garden system. Unfortunately there are no plants in the Court of the Lions with the imposing Fountain of the Lions, part of the Harem, which was begun in 1377 under Muhammad V (illustration p. 33). As can be seen from a romanticized 19th-century engraving, there were originally plants in the rectangular spaces between the cross-shaped channels. The engraving shows plant beds. But it is also conceivable that potted plants were once set up there. To the west it is adjoined by the so-called Court of the Myrtles in the official palace reception area, which has been preserved almost entirely in its original form (illustration above.) A wide channel-like basin with small fountain exedras on the short sides fills the courtyard. The basin is flanked on both sides by dense myrtle hedges. If the accounts given by medieval travelers and the novels of courtly love in in the style of Konrad

Granada, Alhambra
The Aberca or Court of the Myrtles is to a large extent taken up by a long pool bordered with myrtles reflecting the courtyard facades.

Granada, Generalife
Patio de la Acequia, 1st third of 14th century
This extended garden also shows the rectangular coordinates of topped footpaths with a central basin to be found in the Crucero and the Court of the Lions.

Fleck are to be believed, courtyards of this kind were adorned with luxuriant vegetation, headily scented flowers, and exotic birds. The pool reflects the dignified Comares tower with its battlements and front portico. It seems to plunge down like an erratic block, to dissolve in the rippling surface of the water and the deep blue of the sky.

It is an interesting conception, reminiscent of the Roman garden-house system. An architecturally conceived garden area in front of the building, with water basins at the center, is also to be found in the peristyle houses of Pompeii. The footpaths, halls and courtyards formed a unity with the living and reception areas and were open to the garden by way of loggias. The forecourts of early Christian buildings were similarly conceived. The antechamber, or "paradise," where there was often a large fountain, was situated in front of the main church. The villa culture of the Romans and the structures of early Christian buildings may possibly have influenced the development of Islamic gardens.

The complex of a cloister-like channel-fountain system in the Court of the Lions and the villa-like layout of the Court of the Myrtles with the Comares tower continues in the Lindaraja courtyard, which with its central fountain, its cypresses, orange trees, and box trees, still exudes an oriental atmosphere today.

Nearby, to the east, the Torre de las Damas with the Partal Palace, which has already been mentioned, rises up (illustration p. 32). In front of the portico the courtyard stretches out with a rectangular pool in the manner of the Court of the Myrtles. It may be supposed that the portico was conceived in conjunction with a garden layout intended to create a link with the outside, the adjoining extensive park of the Alhambra.

The Generalife in Granada

A mere 50 m (164 ft.) above the Alhambra hill the rulers of Granada had a pleasance built *c.* mid-13th century: the Generalife. In 1526, only a few decades after the expulsion of the Moors by the Christians, a Venetian nobleman by the name of Andrea Navagero visited Granada and the Alhambra. He also found the Generalife, the grounds of which, as he wrote, he entered "by the back door of the surrounding wall of the Alhambra." It is to this observant Venetian that we owe a unique description of the castle and the gardens:

"This castle, though not very large, is an excellent building with wonderful gardens and waterworks, the most beautiful thing that I have seen in Spain. It has several patios, all with an abundant supply of water, but in particular one

Generalife, Granada
Detail of the Patio de la Acequia

with a flowing channel in the center and full of splendid orange and myrtle trees. There is a loggia there with a view of the outside, below which there are towering myrtles so high that they almost reach up to the balcony. Their foliage is so dense and their tops are all at the same height so that they seem like a green meadow. Water flows through the entire palace and, if one wishes, through the rooms as well, some of which are suitable for a delightful summer stay."

The Italian visitor spent many hours in the gardens of the Generalife and tells of exotic trees and marvellous water conduits which can suddenly flood the lawn on which one is standing. He too soon discovered the source of the inexhaustible water supply:

"On the highest part of these castle grounds, in one of the gardens, there are broad steps leading up to a small terrace, where the entire mass of water comes out of a cliff to be distributed throughout the palace. The water is held back with many screws there, so that it may be allowed to gush out at any time and in any way and in whatever quantity is desired."

Since then, centuries have passed the gardens by. The once magnificent grounds have gone to ruin, and have been rebuilt and restored. Further buildings have been added. Hardly anything is left of what Navageros saw and what inspired his exuberant description – only his account of it. But that is a great deal, for with its help the Moorish Generalife can be restored to life in our mind's eye. What the present-day visitor sees is a main courtyard with dense vegetation, where the myrtle rises up toward the sky and the space is elegantly divided up by globular box trees. The water channel runs along the central axis, and from its stone surrounds filigree jets of water emerge to fall back in an arc into the channel. The main garden hall is reached via a gate with twin columns. From there you walk to the viewing balconies, including the ivy-covered terrace with a view of the Darro valley as described by Navagero in another literary work.

Back to the main courtyard, the central channel leads to buildings that were added in the 16th century. Walking through these, one comes to a beautiful water garden with a small basin flanked by slender cypresses and colorfully blooming potted plants. Nearby there is the "water staircase" (Escalera del Agua) described by Navagero, leading to the 19th-century Belvedere. To the side of the steps there are ascending terraces on which there probably used to be hedges and flower beds.

The construction of water steps is unusual within the style of Islamic gardens. For classical antiquity, on the other hand, in Roman as in Hellenic culture, there is evidence of water steps. This tradition of irrigation might have been adopted in Byzantine gardens and handed on to Islamic garden designers. But it is also conceivable that when they conquered the Iberian peninsula the Moors found Roman villa gardens and adopted certain irrigation techniques for their own gardens. The water tricks, based on a sophisticated installation system of water conduits, certainly go back to Hellenic techniques involving water pressure. Navagero, on whom one such trick was played, describes the experience with some

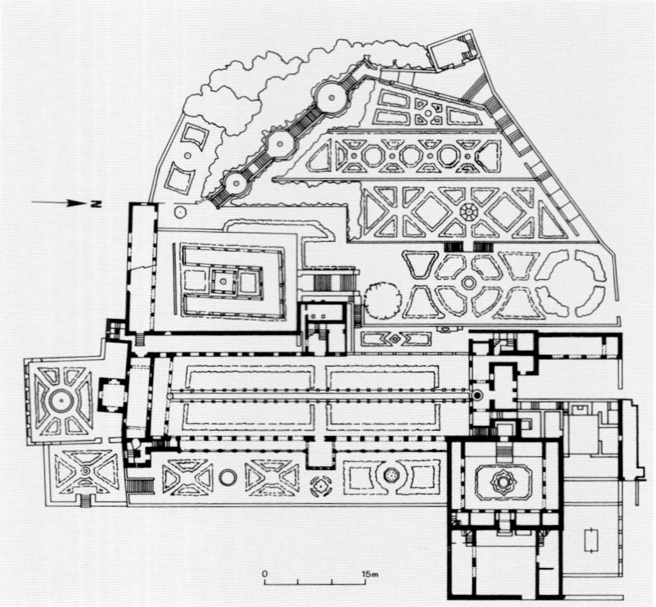

Generalife, Granada
Ground plan of castle and gardens before the 1958 fire

admiration for the technical ingenuity of the garden designer.

We also learn from this Italian that the Nasrid rulers had further pleasances with gardens built above the Alhambra. But they had been destroyed and lay in ruins by the time the Venetian traveler visited them. For him – as for us today – the Generalife signified the apogee of Islamic architecture and garden design on European soil.

After the completion of the Reconquista, the Christian Spaniards either let the gardens and palaces fall into ruin, or adapted them to their own aesthetic and social requirements. The result was frequently a fusion of Moorish and Christian stylistic features. This so-called Mudejar period began as early as the mid-12th century, and ended in the 16th century. It included the extension of the Alcazar in Seville. Of the pure Moorish Almohada building of the early 13th century only fragmentary remains have been preserved. The greater part dates from the Christian period. More than seventy years after the fall of Moorish Seville, between 1350 and 1369, Pedro the Cruel, the King of Castile and Leon, had his palace built by Moorish builders. The Alhambra was taken as an example. But the harmonious interplay of the groups of buildings and the rhythmic alternation of garden and architecture, which had such an enchanting effect in the Generalife, were lacking. What emerged was a series of rectangular garden terraces with ponds and pavilions. The layout was modified under Charles V, and the usual features were added in the Baroque period, so that the Moorish or Mujedar style disappeared almost entirely. In Seville there was nothing at all of the elaborate water system that was so typical of Islamic gardens.

Thus there are in fact only two Islamic gardens left in Spain that deserve to be singled out as such: the Alhambra and the Generalife in Granada. If in Seville the imagination, with the aid of literary testimony, is unable to restore the magic of bygone Moorish gardens to life, in the gardens of the Alhambra and the Generalife it can do so with the greatest delight. There is the added fact that in these gardens one's attention is drawn to interesting traditional aspects which on the one hand link the Islamic garden with Western culture, while on the other hand revealing their differences. It is certainly meaningful to compare Moorish gardens in Spain with Roman villa gardens or Byzantine palace gardens (to the extent that these have been preserved), and with the sacred sites of early Christianity, since in the course of the 7th century Islam took over the legacy of Byzantium in Asia Minor, thereby coming into close contact with classical and early Christian culture.

Granada, Generalife
View of the garden layout

But what distinguishes the Islamic gardens of Spain from other European gardens is the overwhelming prime significance of water. According to the teachings of the Koran, water in its clarity and purity is an image of paradise. Furthermore, the garden that is kept alive by water becomes a symbol of the earthly paradise created by man. In the Islamic garden water is omnipresent, whether in the form of the bubbling jet of water from a fountain pipe or the dignified calm of a pool.

Renaissance Garden Theories

Frontispiece of *L'architettura*
by Leon Battista Alberti. The first print appeared in Florence in 1485.

The history of gardens is closely bound up with the history of garden theory. This connection is both interesting and problematic. Garden theories refer to both art and nature. In their spectrum a wealth of tensions unfolds between the contemplation of nature and the contemplation of art, tensions that are intended eventually to lead to a garden design. It has been architects, artists, philosophers, theologians, and, if you like, gardeners with a pragmatic approach who have attempted to formulate their knowledge and visions of gardens. They have been guided by various fundamental ideas: should the garden be presented as an earthly paradise or as a utilitarian garden? Was it primarily a matter of giving concrete form to an idea or of carrying out agricultural tasks? Was it even possible to unite both aspects in a single garden?

With the humanism of the 14th and 15th centuries, scholars began to reflect anew on the world. The task was to combine the legacy of classical antiquity with modern ideas concerning politics and religion. Aesthetic aspects were also involved: they were no longer the exclusive concern of faith, but had to do with individual interests and needs. A work of art gave pleasure to the senses, educated the mind, and provided spiritual edification. Does this cultural pattern also apply to gardens? Garden theories can shed light on this complex issue.

In the Renaissance three principal types of garden theory can be distinguished. The first type largely considers and describes gardens from classical antiquity and the Middle Ages, without, however, producing new design ideas. In contrast, the second type develops imaginative visions, many elements of which were put into practice in Renaissance and Baroque garden construction. The third type, finally, combines various pragmatic theories. It is concerned with concrete design suggestions, some of which were still being followed in the late 18th and the 19th centuries.

Leon Battista Alberti (1404–72)
Leon Battista Alberti, a humanist and an architect, wrote the *Ten Books on Architecture* (*De Re Aedificatoria*) between 1443 and 1452. The first print appeared in Florence in 1485. In the 9th book Alberti deals with private buildings, and in this context also turns his attention to garden design. His reflections are of the first type, being borrowed exclusively from ancient writings. He is concerned with classical villas and their gardens, which he takes as models for gardens in his own age. He distinguishes between the town house, the country house, and the villas in the vicinity of a town. In his opinion – for which he had Cicero's backing – the villa with a garden, close to a town, was preferable to all other types of villa. Even though the solitude of an isolated country house appears tempting, "the vicinity of the town is advantageous, with a hiding place that is easy to reach and where one can do whatever one wishes."

The fulfillment of individual needs is paramount. For this reason, according to Alberti, a garden should be conducive to health and enjoyment. He underlines this requirement with a quotation from Martial:

"If someone asks what I do in the country, I reply: not very much. I breakfast, drink and sing; I play, bathe and eat. Then I rest and read. I awaken Apollo and tease the Muses."

As in the villa architecture of classical antiquity, Alberti also establishes a close connection between the garden and the villa or the town house. The dwelling house itself should contain elements of the garden, in the form of still-life pictures on the

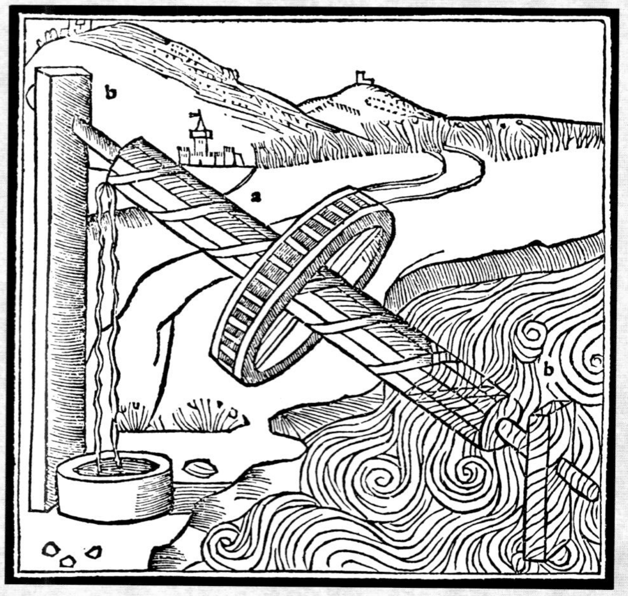

Drawing of a hydraulic device from Fra Gioconda's work
"M. Vitruvius per Iocumdum Solito castigatior factus cum figuris et tabula ut iam legi et intelligi possit, Venice, 1511"

walls, indicating the plants outside. To these should be added sections of wall with quite large window apertures giving views of the garden, concrete garden pictures, so to speak. Finally there are the loggias giving access to the outside. Still-life pictures, windows, loggias, and pergolas bring about the interpenetration of the garden and the house.

As regards plants, Alberti also took his bearings from the ideas of antiquity. He suggests box, myrtle, and laurel trees. He sees cypresses covered with ivy, and recommends creating geometrical shapes from the bent and interlaced branches of closely adjacent lemon and juniper trees.

Alberti also set store by an arboretum. The rows of trees are to be arranged in a quincunx. By this he meant a pattern produced by one tree at each corner of a square and one in the center. Alberti evidently also had ornamental decorative forms in mind which could be given shape by means of herbs and box trees, which are easy to trim:

"A pleasing effect is created by what gardeners used to do in ancient times in order to please their masters: writing their names on the meadow in box or aromatic herbs."

For Alberti, a garden was primarily a pleasure garden. The utilitarian garden was for him part of a country estate; he gave it no place in his private villas. It should, however, be remembered that in his deliberations Alberti had medieval gardens in mind. The task was to improve or rearrange them. The gardens of classical antiquity were known to him only from the writings of Vitruvius or Cicero. From them he developed an ideal. He detached the medieval pleasure garden from its overall context and tried to establish it as an independent entity by envisaging new elements such as, for example, ornamental box trees or quincunx tree arrangements. In so doing he created, on the basis of ancient writings, important preconditions for the Renaissance garden.

Desiderius Erasmus of Rotterdam (1469–1536)

The ideas of Desiderius Erasmus of Rotterdam concerning gardens are also of the first type. He

Caprarola, Villa Farnese
Garden near the Casino del Piacere

Florence, Villa Gambereia
The villa garden from the 1st half of the 18th century was "restored" at the beginning of the 20th century.

of Albertus Magnus are reborn. Erasmus, with his humanistic education, gave greater emphasis to the emotional dimension when he spoke of the pleasure to which the garden was to be dedicated. He also adopted elements that had been handed down from classical antiquity: paths for walking, with marble columns at intervals, and pergolas to encourage meditation. Erasmus may, like Alberti, have thought of linking house and garden. His description of painted walls and floral mosaics on the floor probably refers to an atrium. Erasmus emphasized: "For things for which we lack the means, we substitute art. On the first wall a grove with rare wild birds and quadrupeds is painted…"

What matters here is, unmistakably, visual pleasure, for he writes later: "A garden does not contain all kinds of plants. Moreover, our pleasure is doubled when we see a painted flower in competition with a living one. In the one case we marvel at the artistry of nature, in the other at the painter's ability, and in both cases at God's goodness in bestowing all this on us for our use." Erasmus was still influenced by the medieval principle of illustrating God's omnipotence by aesthetic means. But the classical promenade, the painted walls, and the indisputable paramountcy of pleasure are reminiscent of the concept of the modern garden in Alberti's manner.

Francesco Colonna

Unlike Alberti and Erasmus, Francesco Colonna included concrete design specifications in his garden visions. To this day, it is not known with certainty who is concealed behind this author – a monk, a prince of the same name, or an authorial collective with Alberti as its secretary. Colonna's essay *Hypnerotomachia Poliphili* – roughly translatable as "Poliphil's Dream of Love" – is seen as belonging to the genre of the allegorical novel and may be compared to the French *Roman de la rose*. It first appeared, illustrated with over 200 woodcuts, in Venice in 1499. It is concerned with the development of classical culture as seen by the Renaissance. The decorative quality of classical architecture and its gardens takes up a very large amount of space. Many later garden architects were stimulated by its detailed descriptions of complex labyrinths, ivy-covered rows of arcades, or pruned trees, and parts of the garden embellished with sculptures.

Again, the medieval garden is the starting point. It is specifically located on the island of Cythera, and consists of the obligatory vegetable and herb garden cum orchard and arboretum. However, there are also a "pleasant shrubbery" and a "winsome pleasure garden." On closer inspection,

too envisaged a combination of ancient and medieval ideas of the garden, which he described in his *Colloquia*, including his *Convivium religiosum*, published in 1522. In contrast to the humanist Alberti, Erasmus wanted to present the garden as an image of divine truths. To this basic idea he subordinated such elements as naturally accorded with the medieval garden. A herb garden, an orchard and "…an open meadow with nothing save the green of the grass…," that is to say a pleasure garden, make up the garden site, which is enclosed by a wall. In this conception the ideas

the island is divided into three zones: a copse ring, a meadow ring, and the central section, which, to use later terminology, might be called a "parterre." In his description, the meadow ring seems like a Renaissance garden. The individual areas are enclosed by pergolas, with pavilions at their points of intersection. Each consists of four Ionic columns supporting an entablature with a red architrave on which are placed cupolas adorned with yellow roses. Then the author describes the artistic boxwood topiary. The giant carrying the towers, the six-column colonnade and the water-spouting serpents are spectacular features (illustration top right).

The central parterre can be identified by its beds with knot ornaments, each of which has a kind of marble altar at its center, which in its turn bears pruned spruces or box trees. The patterns of beds, interlaced ribbons, and acanthus leaves are made of flowers or are laid out, like the square or diamond-shaped ribbons, as white marble strips. The enclosure for this area is made up of citrus trees cut to a round shape, box trees cut like a sickle moon, and conical juniper bushes and myrtle hedges.

Even though Colonna's book *Hypnerotomachia* is an allegorical novel, not a theoretical treatise on gardens, it proved to have very great value with regard to concrete garden planning. Francis I, King of France (1494–1547), who was so enthusiastic about Italian gardens, had his garden in Fontainebleau laid out in accordance with Italian ideas. He was fascinated by, among other things, Colonna's idiosyncratic tree and bed figures. An abridged French version of the *Hypnerotomachia* appeared in 1546, a year before his death. About half a century later, Colonna's book was translated into English and given the title *The Strife of Love in a Dream*. The English landscape garden architect William Kent (1685–1748) is said to have owned a few copies of it.

Bernard Palissy (*c.* 1510–*c.* 1590)

Colonna's work is thus best regarded as an example of the second type of garden theory, as are the ideas of Bernard Palissy, who elaborated a comparable garden vision in his "*recepte veritable*" of 1563. In opposition to customary practice in France, he had his garden adjoining a mountain to the north and west. He divided it by means of alleys into four sections of equal size. At the center, following Colonna's example, he placed an amphitheater. At the corners of the garden he

TOP LEFT AND ABOVE
Woodcut illustrations from Francesco Colonna's *Hypnerotomachia Poliphili*, Venice, 1499
Grave of Adonis (top left); topiary variations (above)

Florence, Villa Medici la Petraia
View of the parterre from above

Bagnaia, Villa Lante
Grotto pool

placed grotto-like "cabinets," and also made the alleys lead likewise into small cabinets. Palissy gives a very detailed account of this garden's design and contents:

"The first 'cabinet' lies to the north, in the corner of the garden, right up against the mountains. I built it from fired bricks shaped in such a way that the aforesaid cabinet is like a cliff which has been hollowed out *in situ*. Inside some recesses for sitting have been cut into the brickwork."

Palissy likewise gives a very detailed account of the alley cabinets. They are made entirely of elms, and have the shape of small classical temples. Herbs and mosses grow inside them.

Palissy's descriptions seem grotesque and, in accordance with the age, mannered. The garden appears to be determined solely by the crossed alleys, for he has nothing to say about other design aspects. Instead, he regards the grottoes and cabinets, some of which are multistoried and include promenades, as the most important components of the garden. In some late Renaissance and Baroque gardens, traces of his imaginative ideas may be found, for example in the Boboli gardens in Florence or the Villa Orsini in Bomarzo.

Sebastiano Serlio (1475–1554)

We have the Italian master architect and theoretician of architecture, Sebastiano Serlio, to thank for the most significant stimulus with regard to ornamentation of beds. His knot and spiral ornaments laid out with symmetrical axes influenced the parterre design not only of the Renaissance but also, and especially, of the French Baroque. They were modified to produce many variations. Serlio's voluminous theory of architecture, *Tutte l'opere d'architettura*, which was intended to comprise eight volumes, appeared in 1537. The 8th volume was not completed. In the 4th book he published his ground plans for beds (illustration opposite bottom left.) A German translation of the first five volumes was published in Basel in 1609.

Charles Estienne and Johann Peschel

During the 16th century there was a gradual move away from invoking visions of gardens. Instead, people turned their attention to the practical tasks of gardening. For the successful Paris publisher and medical expert Charles Estienne (1504–64), a garden was primarily a place of production. His *L'agriculture et maison rustique* appeared in Paris in 1564. A German translation also appeared eleven years later.

Estienne distinguishes three types of garden: the kitchen or herb garden, the flower or fragrant herb garden, and the arboretum/orchard/pleasure garden. He situates the whole walled-in garden to the north of the house from which a wide central path leads to the exit. The house is directly adjoined by the flower garden to the east of the central axis, and by the kitchen garden to the west. These are followed on both sides by one square each of the arboretum. All parts of the garden can be irrigated by fountains situated along the central paths.

Estienne allocates a primarily aesthetic function to the flower garden. He suggests enclosing the flower garden with a trellised walkway to be made up of box, juniper, cypresses, and cedars, with climbing jasmin and roses. The garden is to be divided into two equal parts and to include a small maze and a bench for sitting on, with turf or herbs planted on it. For his parterre Estienne also explicitly requests exotic plants to adorn the beds and the trellised walkway, such as laurel, myrtle, or pines, but he also envisages palms, citrus, olive, and fig trees. Some of his parterre designs, showing original knot ornaments (illustration right) were published after his death, in the 1600 edition of Estienne's work.

Estienne took his cue from contemporary gardens with their customary division into squares. The design and arrangement of beds, and the trellised walkways, were in line with typical 16th-century gardens. His contribution was the fact that he was the first person to describe a garden as a system and to attempt to create a relationship between the garden and the house along with the associated areas for cultivation.

Johann Peschel, a vicar from Thuringia, developed even more thorough and detailed design principles for a pleasure garden than Estienne. His treatise, published in Eisleben in 1597 with the cumbersome title [in translation]: "Garden arrangement, containing an orderly, truthful account of how, based properly on geometry, one may produce a useful and decorative garden" describes a pure pleasure garden, in which neither economic utility nor religious edification is foremost.

The dimensions of the garden are determined by the existing terrain. For a councilor in Erfurt, for example, he designed a small town garden, but he also gave thought to large-scale gardens outside the town gates. The garden boundaries, according to Peschel, take the form of a wall. Within this enclosure there are various garden arrangements, namely beds, mazes constructed of trellises as tall as a man, and trees arranged *ad quincuncem*. For the latter area, trees planted in a quincunx, Peschel designed four slightly differing square patterns,

Parterre designs Posthumous illustrations for Charles Estienne's *Maison Rustique*, 1600 edition

BOTTOM LEFT
Ground plans for beds Engraving from the 4th book of Sebastiano Serlio's tract *Tutte l'opere d'architettura*, 1537

BELOW
Villa Lante, Parterre

Simple (upper) and complex (lower) bed arrangements according to Johann Peschel's *Garden arrangement…*, Eisleben, 1597

each with a fifth tree at its center, somewhat in the manner of the arrangement of the five dots on dice:

"For it is always a pleasure to look at an arrangement in which, if the trees are placed in an orderly fashion, they can be seen from anywhere in the entire garden without any impediment."

The trellises or palings (Peschel calls them "Staketen") for the maze should bear hazelnuts or filberts:

"But at the two outer pathways one would customarily place thorny plants such as roses, barberry, Vua crispa, and suchlike."

For the center of the maze Peschel envisages a pavilion or a fountain. He gives particularly lengthy treatment to the ornamentation of the beds. He develops a variety of different bed designs from simple patterns. His basic form is the square enclosing a circle broken by diagonals or cross shapes. Thus, for example, T-shapes and hook shapes are created, along with the segments of the circle thereby left free. Peschel designed a kind of set of building blocks for beds to enable the sections, with their various designs, to be put together in ever fresh combinations (illustration left). He recommended that footpaths and walkways should be paved. For the garden owner who dislikes grass in the cracks he recommended sandy paths.

Johann Peschel's garden theory is conceived in strictly two-dimensional terms. In his reflections he takes into account neither the nature of the terrain nor the arrangement of the site as a whole. He includes neither terraces, nor watercourses, or pools. Instead he sketches the design of a garden step by step, explaining precisely how the studio designs can be transferred to the terrain.

The theories of Estienne and Peschel, different though they are, are both of the third, pragmatic type. Both authors take medieval gardens as their starting point, but with their new ideas and designs they lay the basis for a multitude of design possibilities for the Renaissance garden. Estienne's imaginative grotto designs and Peschel's bed patterns deserve special emphasis.

Olivier de Serres (1539–1619)

Olivier de Serres, Sieur du Pradel, was probably the first theoretician to bring the garden into the sphere of courtly art, by elevating *bon sens* to the sole criterion of evaluation. This may reasonably be regarded as the decisive step from the

Johann Schwind's garden in Frankfurt
Colored copperplate engraving by Matthäus Merian the Elder, in *Florilegium renovatum et auctum*, 1641
Frankfurt am Main, Historisches Museum

Renaissance garden to the Baroque garden. In his work *Le Théâtre d'Agriculture et Mesnage des Champs* (Paris, 1600), which was reprinted nine times during the author's lifetime, de Serres compares designing a parterre to a painter's artistic activity. Among the four garden types he highlights in particular – along with the garden for root vegetables, herbs, and fruit – the *bouquetier* as a pleasure garden "according to the master's imagination and ingenuity more for pleasure than for utility." The four gardens are separated from one another by alleys or trellised walkways. Of the *bouquetier* de Serre writes:

"...it must be situated at the main entrance to the gardens, for it is the first thing that one encounters, with its parterres and beautiful compartments, and the sight of it gives much more pleasure than that of the more distant parts."

The author distinguishes between "compartments," "quarters," and "parterres." A compartment is a quite large bed unit with ornamental plants. A number of compartments, separated by footpaths or alleys, together make up a quarter (*quarreau*). Finally, a unit of several quarters is called a parterre. De Serres recommends larger, more robust plants at prominent points, for example to frame the quarters or to line the alleys. Small, delicate plants, on the other hand, should be used to enclose the compartments and other finely wrought sections of the parterre:

"This proportional distribution gives the entire parterre a very pleasing appearance, like a dress that is adorned with broad edging or a picture with a decorative frame, its beauty enhanced by this impressive setting."

As enclosing plants de Serres favors box trees, because they can easily be shaped to a wide variety of figures such as pyramids, human figures, animals, or columns. In developing these ideas he must have been helped by the imaginative box tree figures from Colonna's *Hypnerotomachia*.

It must be remembered that de Serres and other theoreticians still took their bearings from the medieval concept, comprising the various garden types. But one is struck by their clear inclusion of garden design as one of the visual arts. The *bouquetier* is gradually detached from the sphere of agriculture and acquires a new significance as a castle garden, its design being seen in terms of exclusively aesthetic criteria.

Giardino Giusti, Verona
The Giardino Giusti from the 1570s is one of the oldest Renaissance gardens in northern Italy. Goethe praised its "excellent position" and its large cypresses.

PAGES 48-49
Hilly landscape in Tuscany
To this day, numerous views of the landscape as depicted in Renaissance paintings are to be found in Tuscany.

The Italian Renaissance Garden

Villa dell' Ambrogiana
Painting, *c.* 1600
Giusto Utens
Florence, Museo Topografico
"Firenze com'era"

Florence, Villa Palmieri
Sculpture in the garden of the villa

The Villa Palmieri in Florence
"At the top of this hill there stood a palace with a large and beautiful courtyard at its center, with a wealth of open walkways, halls and rooms, which, taken both together and separately, were of exceptional beauty and impressively adorned with colorful paintings. Roundabout there were meadows and charming gardens with fountains filled with cool water and cellars rich in fine wines, that seemed more appropriate for experienced drinkers than for modest, temperate girls."

These lines from Giovanni Boccaccio's *Decameron*, begun in 1348, sketch, in a few words, a typical Italian Renaissance garden. The word "palace" denotes an estate or a villa on a hill close to the town – "only two short miles" away, as the poet writes elsewhere. Meadows and gardens surrounded the building. The fountains which he mentions, the meadow covered with flowers, or the pergola entwined with vines, may be reminiscent of medieval pleasure gardens. If, in addition, one also studies Boccaccio's depiction of gardens in his *Amorosa Visione*, written in 1342, it is like looking at late medieval paradise gardens as they were painted by the early Dutch masters or the artists of the Cologne School. But Boccaccio's description of this Italian Renaissance garden is already geared to the contemporary garden, since it is intended to serve both the owner's leisure and the courtly entertainments of his guests.

Boccaccio's charming descriptions are based on one specific garden, that of the Villa Palmieri in Florence. Unfortunately, this garden no longer exists. It was completely converted into a Baroque garden in 1697 and extended in the 19th century by the addition of extra garden areas. Boccaccio's descriptions of the garden can, however, be visualized with the aid of a unique piece of evidence, the series of paintings by Giusto Utens. This painter, of Flemish descent, was commissioned by Ferdinando I de' Medici at the end of the 16th century to create a record of the villas of the famous ducal family in the form of landscape paintings. Utens painted the views on the ceiling of the banqueting hall of the Villa La Ferdinanda built by Bernardo Buontalenti. Today the fourteen lunettes are housed in the Museo Storico Topografico in Florence (illustration above). A bird's-eye view of the villas and their gardens is shown, hence the architecture and garden design can be studied in close detail. One is thus given vivid insight into the development of the Tuscan villa garden from the mid-14th century on.

Villa Cafaggiolo

Above the village of Cafaggiolo, to the north of Florence, in the hereditary lands of the Medici, there stands the Villa Cafaggiolo, which was built as a fortification in the 14th century, and, under Cosimo de' Medici, enlarged to create a grand country residence by Michelozzo di Bartolomeo in 1451 (illustration right). Today, the fortified villa above the Sieve valley stands before an impressive forest backdrop. Four hundred years ago, however, the projecting towers in the upper story and the living quarters with their flat broach roofs, rose up before an expansive cultivated landscape, as is shown in Utens' lunette fresco. The fortified defensive walls are surrounded by a moat, across which a drawbridge leads to the gateway tower. Parts of the villa and garden area are enclosed by fences or walls, bordered in some places by elegant fruit trees, in others by dense shrubbery. To the left of the villa parts of the farm buildings such as stables, granaries, and living quarters for the servants have been preserved to this day. The areas that are in front of the fortified villa and to the sides were put to agricultural use. Vineyards, fields, and orchards surrounded the grounds of the villa.

Florence, Villa Cafaggiolo
Detail from a painting by Giusto Utens, *c.* 1600
Florence, Museo Topografico "Firenze com'era"

Present-day view of the villa and the garden

Florence, Villa Medici in Careggi
Michelozzo di Bartolomeo was commissioned by Cosimo de' Medici in 1457 to build the villa.

The rebuilding carried out by Michelozzo can be retraced both in Utens' fresco and, in places, in the present-day building. He covered the gateway tower and the massive keep with flat broach roofs, and widened the embrasures to create windows. At this time the fortified villa was transformed into the summer residence of the Medici. It was probably also when the garden was laid out or extended at the rear of the villa grounds. On the fresco a parterre can be discerned, divided by a central axis and two lateral axes. It contains six square bed compartments, which do not show any ornamentation, but are evidently enclosed by a low box hedge. The central alley leads up to a fountain which is flanked by pergolas. On the left, separated by a fence, more small beds can be identified. This is probably the herb garden.

One cannot as yet speak of a typical Renaissance garden. The pergola, the fountain, and the large bed areas enclosed by box hedges – let us assume that they were covered with flowers – bring Boccaccio's descriptions to mind. At this time the garden was beginning to be established as a place for leisure, meditation and social gatherings. Its specific artistic forms and characteristics developed only gradually during the course of the 15th and 16th centuries.

A final note: the garden of the Villa Caffagiolo was replaced in the 19th century by a large lawn with tall cedars and weeping willows imported from England.

Villa Medici in Careggi/Florence

Leon Battista Alberti recommended a country villa on a hill near a town. Following this advice, in 1457, that is five years after the publication of Alberti's work "*De Re Aedificatore*," Cosimo I de' Medici had a *casa di signore* in Careggi to the north-west of Florence, which he had acquired decades previously, redesigned and extended. He commissioned the work from his house architect Michelozzo. Toward the end of the 15th century, lower side wings based on plans by Antonio de Sangallo the Elder (illustration above) were added to the west facade.

In the Villa Careggi above Florence the humanists Marsiglio Ficino, Pico della Mirandola, and Angelo Poliziano, along with artists and architects such as Donatello, Michelangelo Buonarotti, and Leon Battista Alberti, met at Cosimo's invitation to discuss Plato's philosophy and to celebrate the ancient philosopher's birthday on November 17.

An expansive invitation by Cosimo in the following words has been preserved: "Yesterday I

Cosimo il Vecchio
Wood 86 x 65 cm (*c.* 34 x 25 1/2 in.), *c.* 1518–19 Jacopo Pontormo
Florence, Galleria degli Uffizi

arrived at the Villa Careggi, in order to concern myself not with my fields but with my soul. Come and see us as soon as possible, Marsiglio! Bring Plato's Book *On Supreme Happiness* with you!"

There, stimulated by Leon Battista Alberti's ideas, the position of the garden between the villa and the countryside, may possibly have been discussed at length. From then on this topic was to dominate the layout of contemporary gardens. The villa and its garden became an integral part of Humanistic philosophy, in which a new conception of life emerged: Man creates his own *locus amoenus*, his paradise. Just as God created nature and Man, so Man, by cultivating nature, repeats the process of creation. Within the nature that he had thus adapted to himself, Man was at liberty to determine his feelings and to attempt to live a life in accordance with his individual needs.

The longitudinal axis of the garden points toward the villa. The sloping terrain is offset by terraces which originally had ornamental beds and fountains. Today, of course, nothing of this survives, yet, apart from the tall deciduous trees, one can still sense in the structure of the garden an echo of the former Renaissance garden. The front parterre of the southern main garden is separated by a little wall and adorned with small terracotta pots. It may be supposed that, as in Cafaggiolo, there were pergolas in this part of the garden. The leafy bowers with benches, which today surround the water rondel, may possibly likewise date back to the original garden design. One of the most exquisite items in the garden was the fountain putto by Andrea del Verrocchio, which was created *c.* 1465 and which today stands in the courtyard of the Palazzo Vecchio in Florence.

In the upper story the side wings added by Sangallo formed a loggia. The loggia in the southwest corner was open on three sides, that is open also to the garden. A comparable ensemble of house and garden had, of course, been described by Boccaccio in his *Decameron*. The loggia of the Villa Careggi with its relationship to the garden set an example for many villas that were built in the 16th century.

Fiesole, Villa Medici
Garden terrace below the villa and the adjoining main terrace

Villa Medici in Fiesole

The "Platonic Academy" later moved into the Villa Medici in Fiesole, which had likewise been rebuilt by Michelozzo. Despite the changes that have come about over the centuries, its Renaissance garden is still quite well preserved (illustration above). The garden terrace in front of the villa was used, so to speak, as a natural living space. The parterre which spreads out below this terrace may possibly have originally been an orchard and kitchen garden. Along the supporting walls there is said to have been a pergola entwined with grapevines. The adjoining main terrace, with a little *giardino segreto*, a secluded area of the garden provided the members of the Academy with a particularly agreeable place to spend time (compare pp. 90–99). There, with a view of the Arno valley and the city of Florence, Plato's philosophy was discussed – just as Cosimo had desired it.

Not much has survived of the design of the parterre, but the overall layout of the garden terraces has been preserved. Today, the balustrades adorned with statues and columns, the cypresses, and the compartments with their ornamental box hedges and boxwood globes, along with the sandpaths edged with terracotta bowls, still give a good impression of the original design. The two Medici villas with their gardens in Careggi and Fiesole are among the earliest examples of their kind which still remain.

Villa Medici in Castello

Of the Renaissance garden of the Villa Castello, just as little has been preserved in its entirety to the present day. But care has been taken to retain the old garden structures. Castello, situated not far from Careggi, was acquired by the Medici in 1477. It was a 13th-century fortified villa which they had rebuilt as a grand villa. The villa owes its present form to Cosimo de' Medici, who in 1538 had the building rebuilt and the garden redesigned by Niccolò Tribolo (illustration below). The parterre in Giusto Utens' lunette fresco agrees, regarding design, with its present-day form. Even the Fountain of Hercules, designed by Tribolo, on the central alley, which continues the central axis of the building, has been preserved. One will look in vain, however, for the adjoining dense copse with the Fountain of Venus. A mosaic in the ground where the alleys cross is a reminder of the erstwhile location of the fountain. The Venus was a work by Giovanni da Bologna from the second half of the 16th century. In the 18th century the statue was taken to the Medici Villa La Petraia. The copse is said to have been a maze constructed from tall cypresses, laurel, and myrtle trees. The intention was that visitors walking through this maze should be taken by surprise at the abrupt appearance of 16th-century Venus.

The bed compartments are artistically laid out with box hedges. They form triangles, leaving circular spaces free with boxwood globes in them. The main alley leads to the enclosing wall of the parterre and to a grotto with animals who appear as if they had just been put into the world by God (illustrations pp. 58–59). The manneristic animal groups in stone and colored marble are thought to be the work of Antonio di Gino Lorenzi. The idea of the so-called second creation as discussed by the philosophers of the Academy takes on visible form here. Hints of this grotto can also be discerned in Utens' lunette fresco. Behind it, on the other side of a little brook, there is a copse in quincunx form. After walking through it one arrives at a large pool in the middle of which a rocky island rises up. Here the river god Apennines, created by Bartolomeo Ammannati in 1565, crouches (illustration opposite).

Grottoes, mazes, and little mountains, the so-called mountainettes, pools with rocks and fountain figures, sophisticated waterworks – these were all part of the permanent inventory of a grand Renaissance garden. Rarely however were they all found together in a single garden.

Villa Medici La Petraia in Castello/Florence

The little village of Castello, which has now been incorporated into Florence, offers another typical Renaissance country villa. The one-time *casa di signore* La Petraia dating from the 13th century

OPPOSITE
Florence, Villa Medici in Castello
Fountain figure of Apennines in the garden of the villa. The sculpture created by Bartolemeo Ammannati in 1559 adorns the center of a great pool in the higher part of the copse-like garden.

PAGES 56–57
Florence, Villa Medici in Castello
Close-up photograph of the villa's long garden facade and the parterre in front of the villa. The main fountain on the right was designed by Niccolo Tribolo, and was originally crowned by Bartolomeo Ammannati's bronze statue of Hercules in battle with Antaeus (1560).

Florence, Villa Medici in Castello
Aerial photograph of the villa with the garden behind the building, as it appeared after being redesigned at the end of the 18th century.

became the property of the wealthy Strozzi family in the 15th century. The Medici took over the villa in 1530. After inheriting the estate from his father Cosimo in 1591, Ferdinando de' Medici decided to transform the site into a summer residence. He commissioned the work from the engineer and theater director Bernardo Buontalenti. It is to him that we also owe the design of the garden alongside the existing building. Today, the former Renaissance garden of the country villa, with its original terraces and parterre structure, can still be very clearly visualized.

Below the villa the main parterre opens up with two flights of steps leading up to it. The layout is divided into two areas, with box hedges joined up to form typical Renaissance ornamentation. The fountain with its three basins, at the center of the central axis, dates from the 18th century. Utens' lunette, incidentally, shows that the structure of the site has hardly been changed at all. The parterre to the right of the villa was turned into a "figure garden" in the 18th century. A fountain was installed at the center bearing the bronze figure of Venus created by Giambologna. Where formerly one of the side casinos stood, there is now a pavilion from which there is a splendid view of the Tuscan hills to the east of Castello.

PAGES 58–59
Florence, Villa Medici in Castello
The manneristic animal groups in the garden grotto were made by Antonio di Gino Lorenzi using stone and colored marble.

Florence, Villa Medici La Petraia
Aerial photograph of the villa and the formal parts of the garden

Pratolino (Villa Demidoff)
Painting *c.* 1600
Giusto Utens
Florence, Museo Topografico
"Firenze com'era"

Pratolino (Villa Demidoff)
Fountain figures of the Renaissance can still be found here today.

Villa Demidoff in Pratolino

The unique garden of Pratolino, situated a few kilometers north of Florence must have seemed to contemporaries like a miracle, for to be on this site was like being in paradise. The resplendent and imaginative plants, sculptures, and technical installations from the Medici era have vanished. Only scant remains are left for the visitor's seeking eye. At most, the park which now belongs to the Villa Demidoff, named after its 19th-century owners, is able to surprise us, with its 100-year-old trees and its broad meadows. But we have the good fortune to possess the detailed description by the German engineer, architect, and garden specialist Heinrich Schickhardt, who visited the villa and the garden shortly after its completion. During his second trip to Italy in 1600, the master builder from the Württemberg court stopped off at Pratolino together with Duke Friedrich von Württemberg. In order to embellish his dukedom and enhance its architecture, the Duke commissioned his master builder to carry out detailed studies in the "land of miracles." Schickhardt kept a detailed diary, which was published in Montbeliard in 1602. Along with his detailed descriptions, it also contains numerous sketches of individual elements of the garden and particularly of the waterworks. With the aid of his notes and Utens' lunettes (illustration above), we can today form a fairly exact picture of this Renaissance garden, which in its day was one of the most famous gardens in Europe.

"Bratelino. This is a magnificent, beautiful, well-adorned pleasure garden, the like of which is hardly to be found in the whole of Italy. It is the property of the Grand Duke of Florence and to be seen primarily as a princely palace. Outside this palace there is a balcony with two places, near the ponds, from which one can descend into the garden using spiral stone steps (shaped like a worm-screw) with banisters."

Thus Schickhardt begins his diary entry on Pratolino. From 1561, Francesco I de' Medici began to buy up land and buildings in this region and, until *c.* 1581, had villas built and gardens laid out by the engineer and theater director Bernardo Buontalenti. Here the Medici prince wanted to create a pleasurable and intimate refuge for himself and his mistress Bianca Cappello. Schickhardt's description can be matched to the lunette. From the projecting central area of the villa one steps out onto a balcony, from which two curved flights of steps and a further double flight lead down into the park. If from there one turns back toward the house one comes to a grotto by which the Württemberg engineer and master builder was amazed:

"One steps into a vault, or a grotto, as they call it, under the palace, in which there are many splendid waterworks, most artistically arranged, the like of which is scarcely to be seen anywhere else in Italy. This grotto has a good six different vaults or chambers, in which large parts of both the walls and the ceiling are lined with melted amber, with various sorts of seashells, strange snails, coral chips and other beautiful kinds of stone in between. There is water everywhere, and it is all very wild and strange to behold."

Schickhardt produced a ground plan showing the construction of the grotto, which extended beneath the balcony and in some places beneath the villa. The large grotto is called the *grotta del diluvia* because it can be put under water. Steps arranged in a semicircle lead on to a passage which takes one to the next grotto. This is called the Galatea grotto after a sculpture showing the Goddess of the Sea being pulled along by dolphins. The six further chambers mentioned by Schickhardt are equipped with pipes and hydraulic contrivances to make the figures move, to produce music, and to cause water to gush out from the fountains. These waterworks were new to Schickhardt, and it is easy to appreciate the fascination which this "advanced" technology held for him:

"On the walls around there are many indentations in which there are many figures of different kinds, some of them, for example, made of brass, some of marble and some solely of seashells, and almost all of them yielding water. There are many among them that move and perform some kind of work: one using a grindstone, another driving oxen, two ducks drinking from a little brook and stretching their heads up afterwards. Many lizards, frogs, snakes, and such little creatures sometimes sit on the rough stones, sometimes spout water, and there is also a globe driven around by the water."

Around 1600 German spelling was still very inconsistent, even among of scholars. One is struck by the fact that in the original German, Schickhardt chooses capital letters for verbs and nouns which appear very significant to him. Mechanical moving ducks which drink, or a stonegrinder, appear sensational to him. He made sketches in order to clarify the technological mechanisms. Thus, for example, he drew a wheel occupied by animals driven by water power, intended to suggest a hunt. The "walking maiden" was moved by means of a system of chains (illustrations top right):

"...there is a maiden made out of copper, about two foot [*c.* 60 cm] tall who walks up and down carrying a little kettle."

As Utens' lunette shows, the main alley leads from the grotto exit in a southerly direction through the park to a large pool. Here, on the right, a hill rises up amid compartments with trees:

"In addition to the waterworks just described, an artificial hill is also to be seen, approximately 20 foot [6 m] high consisting of many, rugged, rough stones piled on top of one another, with grass and hedges growing between them, on top of which there is a jumping white horse with two wings, and just below this, next to a little door, there sit nine Muses with Apollo, hewn in stone, and there are many other figures sitting and standing on this hill."

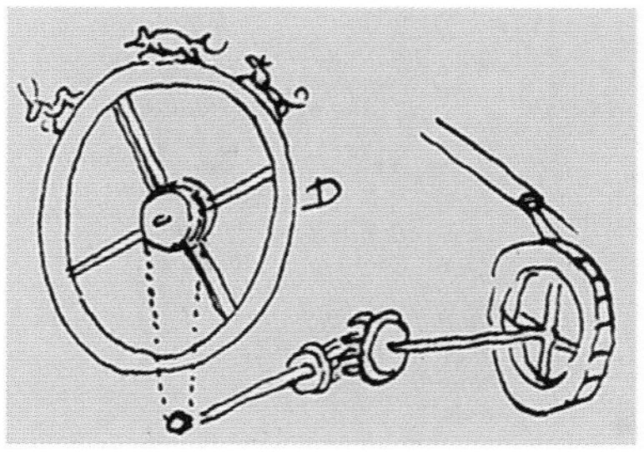

Drawing by Schickhardt, Villa Pratolino garden
Animal hunt

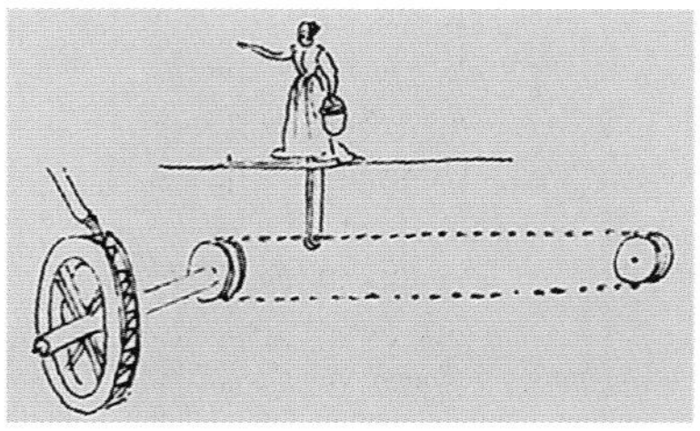

Drawing by Schickhardt
Walking maiden

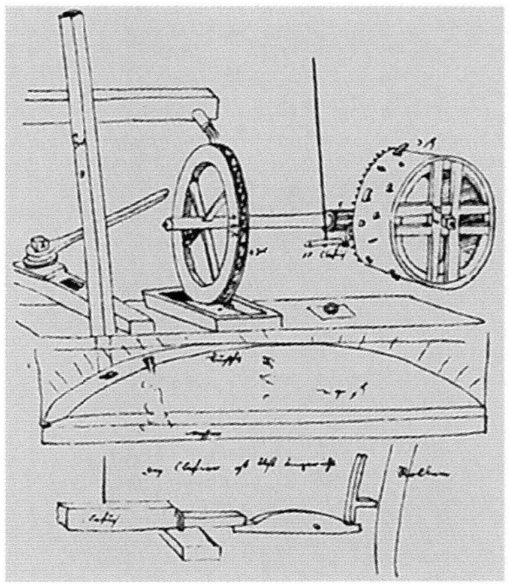

Drawing by Schickhardt
Organ machinery

Pratolino, Villa Demidoff
Head of the huge figure of Apennines, *c.* 1580, Giovanni da Bologna

This *Montagnetto*, or artificial mountain, is presented as a Parnassus with Apollo, the Muses and the winged horse Pegasus. A more detailed drawing by Giovanni Guerra, dating from 1604, conveys the precise appearance of this hill. Such "little mountains" were popular in late 15th-century gardens – especially, of course, where the landscape was flat. The Este family, for example, had a relatively high hill built in the garden of their castle in Ferrara, with trees planted on it, creating a "bosquet hill." In Pratolino the theater, which was in the vicinity of the mountain, was used for entertaining performances – inspired, as it were, by Apollo and the Muses. But the mountain was not only a backdrop for the theater, it was also a kind of vast musical instrument:

"Inside the mountain there is a water-driven organ; it has two stops, a principal and an octave, with a very artistic effect. When the organ is started and one is walking in the garden it is as if one were hearing music coming from the Muses that sit on the mountain."

And again Schickhardt investigated the mechanisms, entering the mountain by a round arch. The drawing which he made speaks for itself and hardly requires any explanation (illustration left). Schickhardt also visited the northern part of the park, which cannot be seen on the lunette, but which can be seen on a woodcut by Bernardo Sanzone Sgrilli dating from 1742. A parterre extends uphill to a semicircular pool. There, the court master builder from Württemberg saw "...kneeling on a very large pedestal an extremely large stone figure, beneath which the water gushes down into the pond with a loud rush." This is one of the few pieces of monumental garden sculpture which still survive today, the personification of Apennines (detail on the left and illustration on p. 65 top). The figure, which is *c.* 12 m (40 ft.) high, dates from *c.* 1580 and was probably the work of Giovanni da Bologna. Behind this colossal figure there was a hill, with grottoes that have not been preserved, which according to Schickhardt's notes were also equipped with waterworks, including an elegant fountain. In Sgrilli's woodcut a circular maze can also be identified, situated behind the grotto hill. The stylized depiction of the maze can hardly have been faithful to the actual plants involved. Sgrilli probably consulted the book on mazes by Lelio Pittoni, widely read at the time, which was published in Mantua in 1611 and became the standard authority on Italian Baroque gardens. We shall deal later with Sebastiani Serlio's maze designs in connection with the Renaissance gardens in Rome and Latium. The maze at Pratolino, like the one at Castello, probably used high cypresses and myrtle trees. Many of the gravel

ILLUSTRATION OPPOSITE
Pratolino, Villa Demidoff
Landscape park with view of the villa

Pratolino, Villa Demidoff
Pond, in the background the colossal figure of Apennines by Giovanni da Bologna, *c.* 1580 (top)
Male figure with eagle in the coppice area (right)

paths led to little garden "cabinets" with stone benches or concealed arbors to enable those caught in the maze to take a rest.

Villa Medici in Rome

Scholars do not agree as to which of the villa gardens should be regarded as the first Renaissance garden. Is it the garden of the Medici Villa in Careggi, its successor garden in Fiesole, or the gardens in Rome, which were laid out soon after the popes had returned, in 1377, from their "Babylonian imprisonment" at Avignon? Since nothing of these gardens has been preserved, the question must perhaps be asked somewhat differently: which is the first typical Italian Renaissance garden? This question is probably best discussed against the background of an untypical Roman Renaissance garden, of a garden designed, let us say, in the Florentine manner, from which the new revolutionary Roman art of garden design resolutely dissociated itself. This is the garden of the Villa Medici, which Cardinal Ricci da Montepulciano had designed along with the new villa by the master builder Annibale Lippi in 1544 (illustrations pp. 66–70). The design elements can be very clearly distinguished in the engraving by Giacomo Lauro (illustration right). The main parterre is surrounded by a box hedge. The pattern of the individual beds follows Sebastiano Serlio's parterre designs of 1537 (illustration p. 45). Adjacent to the main parterre there is a quarter with beds in a regular arrangement on which low fruit trees are planted. Above this, in the immediate vicinity of the villa, a smaller quarter with small beds can be identified, where herbs were probably grown. In all probability, two areas of the garden must be distinguished here, planned separately and at successive stages. The parterre laid out above the central axis of the villa's facade was probably already included when the villa area was planned. The obelisk, the fountains, and the box hedges are spatially related to the elevation of the facade. This also applies to the ornamentation of the beds, which was intended to reflect the architectural ornamentation of the facade. It is quite probable that, starting at the right-hand wing of the villa, a tall cypress hedge separated the main parterre from the right-hand garden area. The neighboring zone was probably originally a separate utilitarian garden which was later incorporated into the overall layout.

As has been pointed out, the overall conception is somewhat untypical for a Roman garden. It is conceived in two dimensions and, clearly, in relation to the villa, so that it could not develop an architectural life of its own. These are precisely the characteristics of the Florentine garden.

The Cortile de Belvedere in the Vatican

The contrast with a typical Roman garden, which originated at the same time and not far away, is very clear. The Cortile de Belvedere in the Vatican is considered to be a typical Renaissance garden, which set an example far beyond Italy's frontiers. This was initially not so much a matter of the design of the parterre as of the solution of an architectural problem which Giorgio Vasari described as follows:

"This Pope [Julius II] had conceived the idea of developing the space between the Belvedere and the Palace into a square, theater-like site, thereby enclosing the little valley which lay between the old Papal Palace and the building which Innocent VIII had decided was to be the new papal residence."

ILLUSTRATION OPPOSITE
Rome, Villa Medici
Detail of the main parterre with the terrace wall in the background, which can also be identified on the engraving from G. Lauro's *Antiquae urbis splendor* (see bottom).

Rome, Villa Medici
Engraving showing the Villa Medici and its garden from G. Lauro's *Antiquae urbis splendor*, Rome, 1612–14.

Obelisk in the main parterre of the garden

PAGES 68–69
Rome, Villa Medici
Group of sculptures in the garden of the villa with Parnassus, Pegasus, and Muses

Rome, Villa Medici
Male figure on reliefed pedestal adjoining the main parterre

The "little valley" was the main problem if a link was to be created between the Vatican, that is the Papal Palace, and the Belvedere, which was situated *c.* 300 m (*c.* 1,000 ft.) away, the villa of Innocent VIII (illustration opposite, top). In 1503 Pope Julius commissioned the master builder Donato Bramante to carry out the work. His solution to the problem was a stroke of genius. There is probably to this day no one who has described this site better than the contemporary eyewitness Giorgio Vasari:

"For the lower floor he [Bramante] built two very beautiful arcades, one above the other, in the Doric style. On top of these, the upper floor was formed by a closed colonnade with windows in the Ionic style, leading from the topmost rooms of the Papal Palace to the ground floor of the Belvedere. Thus on each side of the valley a loggia was created measuring more than four hundred paces, one with a view of Rome, the other facing the copse at the rear. The intention was to level the floor of the valley itself and channel all the water down from the Belvedere in order to put up a beautiful fountain there."

Bramante introduced an innovation which was decisive for the development of garden design: he built steps in order to exploit the optical dimension of the terrain. This increased not only the depth and breadth of the garden, but also its height. The composition, on a lavish scale, with double flights of steps and balustrades linking the terraces, created what was to become a basic model of Italian garden architecture. Following this, the gardens of the Villa d'Este in Tivoli or the Palazzo Farnese were planned as three-dimensional architectural complexes. Heinrich Schickhardt, the master builder at the court of Württemberg, also stood in the courtyard of the Belvedere, admiring the site. Rome was to give him decisive inspiration for his later garden project in Leonberg near Stuttgart.

When Bramante died in 1514, building work on the Cortile de Belvedere was as yet unfinished. It was completed under the supervision of Pirro Ligorio by 1563.

In Rome, Bramante's architectural garden quickly became a model to be copied. An immediate successor to the Belvedere garden was the monumental layout of the Villa Madama on Monte Mario, high above the Eternal City. Two years before Bramante's death, Raphael was commissioned by Cardinal Giulio de' Medici, the later Pope Clement VII, to draw up plans for a villa. Raphael submitted designs which followed Bramante's example by incorporating the topography of the terrain in the villa design. Together with the brothers Antonio and Battista Sangallo, Raphael planned to divide the slope of the hill into terraces, thereby integrating it with the villa at the top of the hill. In front of the garden Raphael situated an extended terrace, from which a double flight of steps in the style of the Cortile led down to a rectangular terrace and the first garden parterre. From there a further garden terrace was reached via a semicircular arrangement of ramps. This in turn was linked by ramps to an oval situated below (illustration right). Completion of the site was prevented by the pillaging of Rome by the troops of Charles V in 1527 and the banishment of Pope Clement VII. By now it has been largely destroyed. Raphael's idea of conceiving the garden as a dynamic architectural entity and integrating it with the architecture of the villa, was new and unique, but it was not without precedent. He was inspired not only by Bramante's Cortile but also by the study of classical antiquity. In 1515 Raphael had become the chief supervisor of classical buildings in Rome,

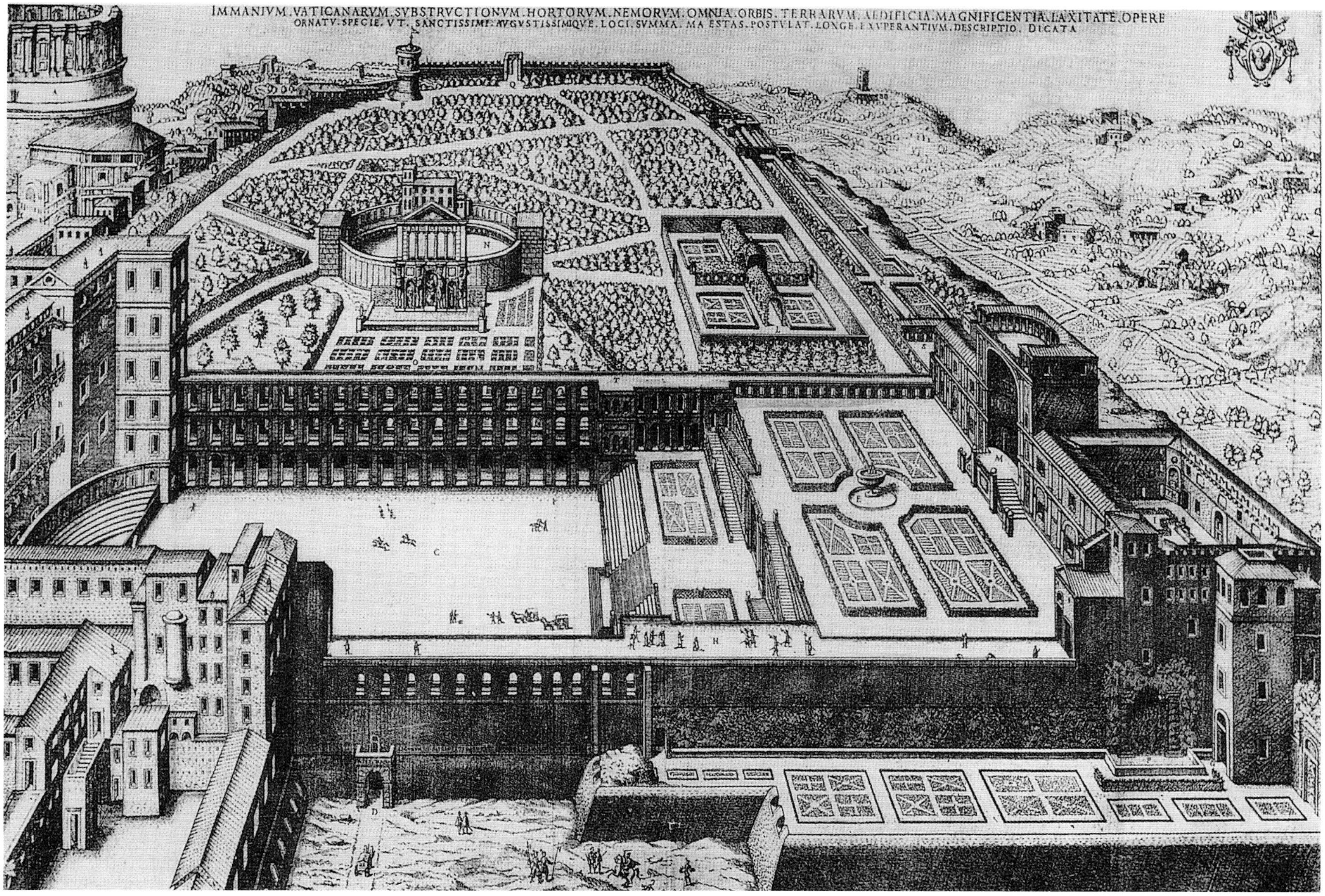

responsible for the care and study of the antiquities. The classical monuments on the Palatine, which he had seen with his own eyes (to the extent that they had been excavated by that time), and his knowledge of the books of Vitruvius, with his ideas on town villa gardens: these were to be the inspiration for his extraordinary design on Monte Mario.

IMMANIVM.VATICANARVM.SVBSTRVCTIONVM.HORTORVM.NEMORVM.OMNIA.ORBIS.TERRARVM.AEDIFICIA.MAGNIFICENTIA.LAXITATE.OPERE
ORNATV.SPECIE.VT.SANCTISSIMI.AVGVSTISSIMIQVE.LOCI.SVMMA.MAESTAS.POSTVLAT.LONGE.EXVPERANTIVM.DESCRIPTIO.DICATA

Casino for Pius IV in the Garden of the Vatican

A rarely visited gem amid the Vatican gardens is the elegant garden villa of Pope Pius IV. If, after leaving the Sistine Halls, one makes one's way to the gallery of Urban VIII one can see, from the west windows, the resplendent garden site, to which a picturesque element is added by the Casino Pio Quarto (illustration opposite). The architect Pirro Ligorio was occupied with the extension of the Vatican Palace site at the very time when, *c.* 1560, he was commissioned by Pope Pius IV, who appreciated the pleasures of the senses, to build this garden villa "in between" his other

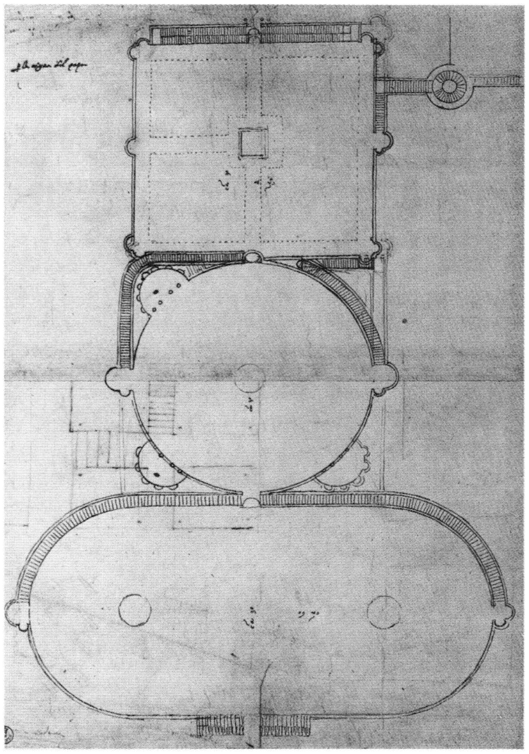

Belvedere court in the Vatican
Engraving by H. van Schoel, 1579

Rome, Villa Madama
Raphael's plan for the terraces of the villa and garden

PIVS IIII MEDICES MEDIOLANEN PONT MAX
HANC IN NEMORE PALATII APOSTOLICI AREAM
PORTICVM FONTEM AEDIFICIVMQVE
CONSTITVIT VSVIQVE SVO ET SVCCEDENTIVM
SIBI PONTIFICVM DEDICAVIT ANN SAL M D LXI
PIVS IIII PONTIFEX OPTIMVS MAXIMVS

work. For the supreme pontiff of Christendom, this little ocher-colored pleasance was to be a sort of hermitage. Here he wished to recuperate from the pomp and public duties of his office. The papal Academy of Science was later housed in the villa.

Villa Farnesina in Rome

Agostini Chigi was one of the most dazzling personalities in Rome during the Renaissance era. As a banker he earned a fortune, which he generously donated for the advancement of the arts. In private he devoted himself to literature and astrology. In 1509 he commissioned a plan for a palace in the Trastevere district. Baldassare Peruzzi designed a two-story palace. He divided up the facade with pilasters and large, robust projecting cornices. For the wall zone of the roof cornice he envisaged a frieze of sumptuous garlands of fruit. He gave the garden hall the form of a pillared loggia flanked by projecting tower-like wings.

The building was finished by 1511. The patron commissioned paintings from the most famous artists in Rome. In the vault of the loggia, Raphael painted what is probably his most beautiful series of frescoes, narrating the story of Cupid and Psyche, a magical tale whose atmosphere must have extended into the intimate garden in front of the loggia.

In 1580 the villa came into the possession of the Farnese family, from which it took its name. In 1731 the Palazzino was inherited by the Neapolitan line of the Bourbon monarchy. Today it houses the Academy of Science.

Orti Farnesiani in Rome

Raphael died in 1520. His colleagues, above all Antonio Sangallo, continued work on the Villa Madama on Monte Mario. A few years later Cardinal Farnese decided to carry out his ambitious project of laying out terraced gardens on the slope of the Palatine. In 1525 he commissioned from the architect Giacomo Barozzi da Vignola designs for what were later called the Orti Farnesiani, the Farnese gardens, which were to be constructed there over the remains of classical Roman structures such as palaces, gardens, and

Rome, Villa Chigi (Farnesina)
View of the garden facade and the garden. The so-called Farnesina was the first work by Baldassare Perruzi. Built in 1509–11 it is at the same time the first suburban villa of the Cinquecento in Rome.

ILLUSTRATION OPPOSITE
Rome, casino for Pius IV in the garden of the Vatican
The garden villa with its decorations in the classical manner is the work of Pirro Ligorio.

temples (illustration below). The work was completed by 1573. Terraces and flights of steps, box hedges, balustrades adorned with terracotta pots, grottoes, and smaller buildings were combined in a homogenous garden site, which impressively followed the course of the slope. Geometric flower beds, smaller bosquets, fountains, and water stairways created a new type of garden resembling the stage of a theater. Today, unfortunately, only a very few remains have been preserved (illustrations top and opposite) The only thing worth seeing today is the aviary, which was not envisaged by Vignola himself but was added later. It was Girolamo Rainaldi who extended the site at the beginning of the 17th century.

Villa d'Este in Tivoli

The tradition of the Roman Renaissance garden as an architectural spatial entity is impressively continued in the garden of the Villa d'Este in Tivoli. It is very closely linked with the Cortile de Belvedere, especially since Pirro Ligorio, who completed the Belvedere complex, developed the conception for Tivoli. Ligorio had probably been commissioned back in *c.* 1550 by Cardinal Ippolito II d'Este, with his love of ostentation, to submit

Rome, Orti Farnesiani
View of the garden layout (top)
Engraving from G. Vasi, *Magnificenze di Roma*, 1747–59 (left)

ILLUSTRATION OPPOSITE
Rome, Orti Farnesiani
Flower beds in the upper part of the terraced area

ILLUSTRATION OPPOSITE
Tivoli, Villa d'Este
Details of the neptune Fountain above the large water organ

designs for the villa and the garden site. At that time Bramante's brilliant architectural composition in the Vatican, comprising terraces, open stairways, ramps, and exedras, was very close to completion. Ligorio too envisaged these elements for the Villa d'Este (illustration opposite).

The two parts comprising the garden can still be clearly distinguised today. The sloping garden to the north-east is built into the mountainside, with breathtaking steepness, by way of a system of terraces, ramps, and steps. The central axis, which is indicated by architectural recesses, leads down from the upper palace terrace to the level lower garden area and directly to the main garden, the Giardino delle Semplici. Here the open main alley changes into a closed trellised pathway which half way down is crossed by another trellised pathway and topped by a pavilion. Medicinal herbs and utilitarian plants were envisaged for the beds. As can be seen from an engraving by Etienne Dupérac dating from 1573 – a stylized view made shortly before the completion of the site – this part of the garden is flanked on either side by two mazes. Of the four mazes originally planned, only the two in the south-west area of the garden were actually constructed (illustration right). Ligorio, following the fashion of the time, was evidently guided by Serlio's maze patterns. The designs by the Italian architect and theoretician of architecture were in vogue at the time, even outside Italy. Copies of his work reached the French court, where the Italian's sketches and architectural ideas were greatly appreciated. This was probably the reason why in 1542, five years after the publication of his *Regole*, his first reflections on architectural theory, Serlio became a royal master builder at Fontainebleau.

Tivoli, Villa d'Este
Fount of nature, with many-breasted female figure as a provider of water (right)

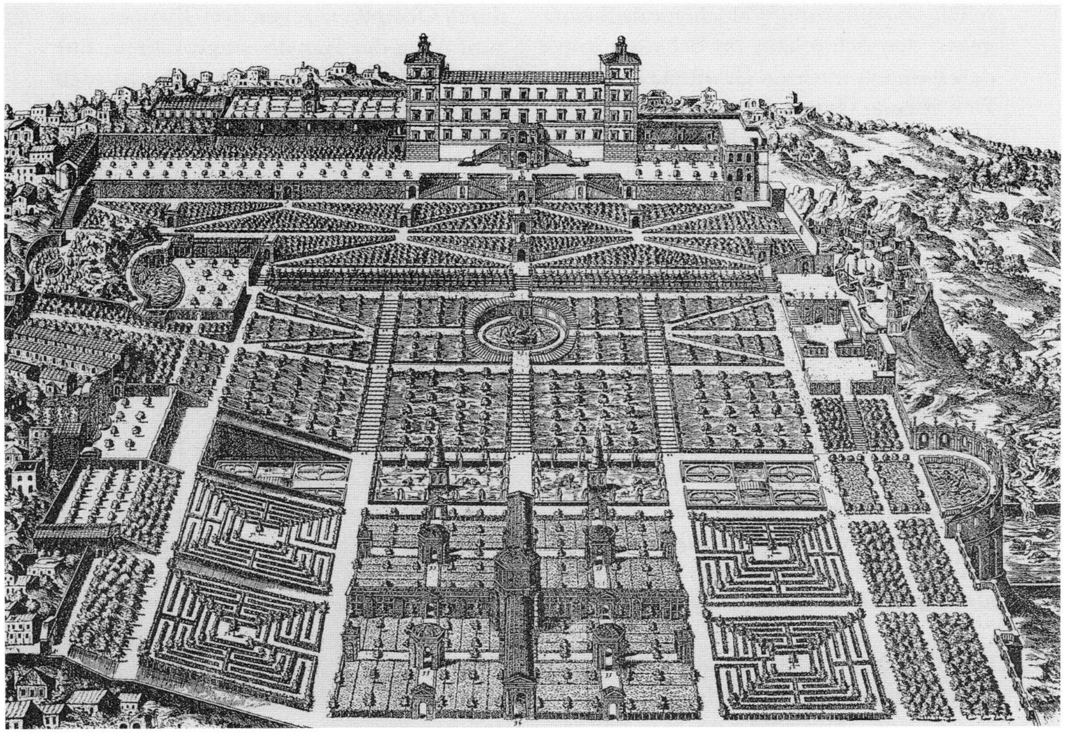

View of the overall layout
Engraving by E. Dupérac, 1573

At a right angle to the main axis linking the Giardino delle Semplici with the sloping garden and the villa, four staggered fishponds, three of which were actually constructed, were to indicate the beginning of the slope. The last of them cuts into the north-west hillside, and ends at a double terrace above which the imposing architectural spectacle of the water organ rises up. To offset this, Ligorio chose an exedra projecting like an apse from the supporting wall at the south-west border of the garden. Here a marine fountain with a figure of Neptune was planned but never constructed.

Walking in the direction of the villa along the main alley up the hill, which rises gently to begin with, one comes via the cypress rondel, that was added later, to the wonderful Channel Path, also known as the Alley of a Hundred Fountains, probably the most ambitious of the cardinal's projects (illustration p. 78, top). At both ends of the

art of bringing water to Rome from the Tiber regions, the Alban mountains, is here interpreted symbolically as a fundamental precondition of the cultural efflorescence of the Eternal City. According to contemporary reports it was possible at the time, when standing on the terrace of the Fontana di Tivoli, to look beyond the Fontana di Roma and the backdrop of the Rometta and see the buildings of Rome in the distant haze. (One could still see over the whole garden site, which was not as overgrown and hidden from view as it is today.)

The garden of the Villa d'Este was designed with the view from bottom to top in mind, as can also be seen in the engraving by Etienne Dupérac. The visitor, whether walking in the evergreen mazes or stepping out of the trellised pathway in the central axis, was presented with diverse and interesting views of the sloping garden, of the rising and falling paths, ramps, and doors that crossed one another with great artistry, and finally of the facade of the villa. In addition to this "aesthetic" aspect of the garden, the visitor on the terrace of the Fontana di Tivoli was also offered the mythical-metaphorical aspect mentioned above. The water gushed out of the artificial mountain, flowed along the channel pouring into one fountain basin after another, and finally reached the Rometta. Thus the garden becomes an allegory of culture which, with its roots in prehistorical myth, develops in accordance with the dynamism of nature.

In the engraving by Dupérac one is struck by the clear, indeed almost rigid geometrical division of the garden site. In this sense the garden is an unambiguous product of the Renaissance. This also applies to the many classical statues and those elements of the garden that follow classical

Tivoli, Villa d'Este
Alley of a Hundred Fountains (above)
Detail of one of the water dispensers (right)

ILLUSTRATIONS OPPOSITE
Tivoli, Villa d'Este
Dragon or fire-wheel fountain (top);
Ovato fountain (bottom)

channel a monumental fountain was installed, the Fontana di Tivoli and the Fontana di Roma. At the Tivoli fountain, the garden's main reservoir, a branch of the river Aniene emerges via a subterranean channel and is conveyed underground again to the channel path where it feeds the fountain and the many overflow basins. Above the Tivoli fountain an artificial hill with grottoes rises up. It is crowned by Pegasus, who, according to myth, made the stream of Hippocrene spring up on Parnassus. The channel, whose fast-flowing waters gush out over three terraces, leads to the statue of Roma enthroned high above the Tiber. Behind it is the backdrop representing the city of Rome with its most important buildings. This Rometta, the greater part of which was demolished *c.* 1855, forms with the Fontana di Roma a companion piece to the artificial hill of the fountain. The

practice. The many mythological allusions and the playful deployment of historical and archaeological knowledge have a manneristic effect. The latter point is particularly applicable to the Rometta constructed of background buildings. On the other hand, the alleys and paths laid out according to particular systems of axes of vision, that is in terms of a "point of view," should already be regarded as Baroque design elements.

Villa Lante in Bagnaia

While the Cortile de Belvedere can be described as belonging to a fundamental type of Italian Renaissance garden, the conception of which developed to a unique apogee of garden design in Tivoli, the garden of the Villa Lante in Bagnaia near Viterbo is regarded as the most beautiful Renaissance garden in Europe (illustrations

Bagnaia, Villa Lante
View of the main parterre (above), the water steps (top right), and the fountain with the winged horse Pegasus (below)

pp. 80–83). This is the verdict of travelers who have visited the Villa Lante in our own day, and it is surely correct, since the garden has to a large extent been preserved in its original condition. This can easily be verified in the villa itself from the fresco in the loggia of the Casino Gambara, which shows a view of the villa from the 16th century, and hence the original appearance of the garden. The large four-part basin with the central round fountain, surrounded by enclosed bed compartments, can be seen, apart from a few details, just as it was about 400 years ago (illustration opposite, top).

The architectural history of the Villa Lante goes back to 1477, when Cardinal Raffaele Riario had his first palace built. A bare hundred years later, Cardinal Giovan Francesco Gambara da Brescia decided to have the grand country residence rebuilt as a villa under the supervision of Giacomo Barozzi da Vignola. A short time previously Vignola had rebuilt the Villa Capraro, which was only 15 km (*c.* 9 miles) away, for Alessandro Farnese, a relative of Cardinal Gambara's. The site was finally completed under Cardinal Alessandro Montalto between 1585 and 1590, and came into the possession of the Lante family in 1656.

The villa complex consists of two pavilions of the same design, the Casino Gambara with the above-mentioned fresco, and the Casino Montalto. The main parterre with the Moor's Fountain in the middle of the pool is framed by bed compartments, the design of which has been altered a number of times over the years. Today they are planted with low box hedges forming geometric shapes in the Baroque fashion. The center of each bed is marked by a circular box hedge and the corners are emphasized by boxwood cubes with plants growing out of them in terracotta bowls. The garden continues on the other side of the casinos with more fountains and sophisticated watercourses. The Dolphins' Fountain, linked via steps with the Giants' Fountain, deserves to be singled out. The fascination of the garden lies in these waterworks, which are already to be categorized as manneristic, and in its grottoes and groves. The Giants' Fountain is flanked by two colossal statues personifying the Tiber and the Arno (illustration p. 82–83). The fountain is fed via water steps laid out with great artistry and consisting of interlocking voluted forms (illustration above) The structure resembles a crab's shell – an allusion to Cardinal Gambara's heraldic beast (Ital. *gambero* means crab). The central axis of the garden site is a water axis (illustration on the right). It comprises the sequence: Dolphins' Fountain, water steps, Giants' Fountain, Fontana di Quadrato (also known as the Moor's Fountain or the Fontana delle Peschiere.) Between the water steps and the last-named fountain there is yet another curiosity, which is the so-called Cardinal's table with a gutter along its longitudinal axis.

What distinguishes the garden of the Villa Lante from all other gardens in Latium and Rome, is the superabundance of water and the proximity of natural forests. The site is an early example of the symbiosis of the natural and the cultivated landscape, of forest and garden – a feature of the transition to the Baroque garden. The fact that the garden is no longer conceived as an architectural artifact points in the same direction. The moderate hillside location did not require massive construction of terraces. Hence steps, balustrades, and fountain enclosures are to be understood as features of the garden landscape and as an architectural framework for the garden sculptures. Here we see the beginning of the transition to the sculpture garden that was so decisive for Baroque garden design.

As a result, the garden of the Villa Lante cannot be unambiguously classified: this is probably precisely what constitutes its charm. Its intermingling of nature and culture already sets it apart from the typical Renaissance garden. Nor can it be regarded as a purely manneristic garden, since any suggestion of eccentricity conflicts with the geometric design of the parterre. Nonetheless, it does point in the direction of mannerism. The path out of the ordered world of the parterre via the water steps to the Giants' Fountain provides a metaphor for the path from Bagnaia to Bomarzo.

Sacro Bosso, Bomarzo

The Garden of Monsters in Bomarzo is a unique and bizarre fantastic garden from the Mannerist period. Vicino Orsini made it the task of his life to create a realm of the grotesque. Scholars distinguish three phases in which the garden, the sculptures, and the architecture came into being.

Bagnaia, Villa Lante
Aerial photograph of the garden layout with a view of the main parterre and the Moor's Fountain, the two casinos and the central water axis with the water steps

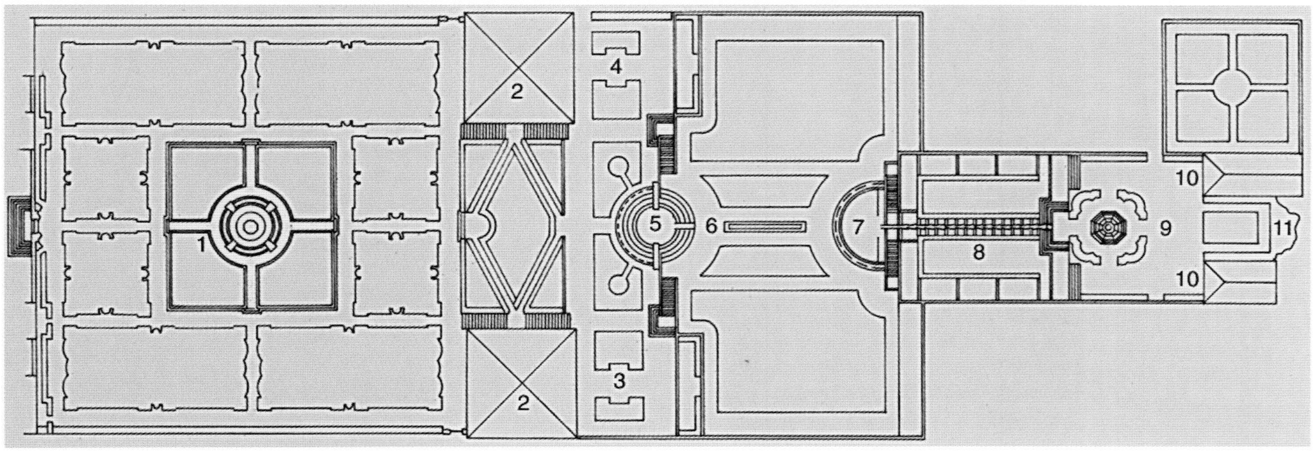

Bagnaia, Villa Lante
Plan of the garden site:

1. Moor's Fountain
2. Montalto casinos
3. Venus grotto
4. Neptune grotto
5. Grotto or Light Fountain
6. Cardinal's table
7. Giants' Fountain
8. Water steps
9. Dolphins' Fountain
10. Muses' Pavilions
11. Fountain of the Flood

Bagnaia, Villa Lante
Giants' or River Gods' Fountain

Bomarzo, Sacro Bosso
Sleeping nymph (right)

Oriental dragon battling against dogs; elephant crushing a Roman soldier with its trunk (below)

During the first period, 1548–52, the so-called Teatro d'Amore, the Theater of Love with its concave-convex steps was built, along with the piazza with the fountain and waterworks. The waterworks were not, however, completed until after 1558, the beginning of the second building phase. Along the axis which begins there, the artificial lake, the Pegasus Fountain, the Ships' Fountain, and the fishpond had been created by 1564. After that, by *c.* 1580, the upper plateau with the monumental vases was laid out, the piazza of Persephone was designed and the Tempietto was built. And finally the monsters were created, which Vicino Orsini had painted in vivid colors during the last years of his life.

The garden of the Villa Orsini cannot be viewed in its entirety. It was deliberately laid out like a maze for the fantastic architecture and the monsters to make their full impact. A characteristic of Mannerism is its conscious avoidance of proportionality. The distortion of human proportions and the displacement of elements from their architectural context create the illusion of a cosmos gone awry and put question marks over the existing and hitherto accepted view of the world. In Bomarzo the rules of the world are no longer valid – it is as if this garden wished to escape from the laws of nature.

When one enters the weird Crooked House, which Orsini, incidentally, dedicated to his friend Cardinal Madruzzo, one's sense of balance deserts one (illustration pp. 86–87) The horizon tips upwards, the trees and bushes begin to move. To visit the park is at the same time to visit another world, and the visitor must first adjust his senses to its natural laws. Just as the building in which he finds himself is out of plumb, he also feels as if he himself is "out of kilter," crazy. After he has gradually become accustomed to the crookedness and is amazed at the atmosphere and the new views of the park with its sculptures, then the world goes out of joint once again when he leaves the house. Thus the monstrous figure of *Orlando furioso*, tearing an Amazon to pieces with brute force, seems almost like a familiar feature of his new world. Nearby, the Pegasus Fountain rises up, representing Parnassus and indicating the power of literature, which is acted out using the example of the above-mentioned Orlando figure and other monsters. One encounters giant fruits and pine cones in stone.

Then suddenly one is standing on the brink of Hell, a monumental grotesque ornament. But inside, the situation becomes relaxed, in an almost jocular way, for here the visitor finds a little dining room. Nearby there is a noteworthy temple, which Orsini had built by Giacomo Barozzi da Vignola, and dedicated to his deceased wife Giuilia Farnese as a kind of temple cum mausoleum.

The park with its monsters, figures of gods, grotesque architecture, and literary allusions, along with the many coded inscriptions, was intended as a place of illusion and amazement. Orsini, the learned aristocrat, wanted to rival the Seven Wonders of the World of classical antiquity, by presenting new wonders: the enigmatic goings-on of mythology, the deception of the senses by means of distorting perspective, the shaping of nature in the form of a maze. He thereby created a counter-world to the rationalistic philosophy of his time. The garden of the Villa Orsini in Bomarzo cannot be compared to any other garden. It works with elements of the Renaissance, but distorts the proportions of its artistic products and presents them in an exaggerated form, as illusions.

Comparisons with later Baroque gardens can also be made, but only if one imagines Bomarzo as disentangled, ordered and as a large-scale site, the whole of which can be seen. But then the Bomarzo garden would no longer be what it is.

Bomarzo, Sacro Bosco
Seated nymph (above);
Aphrodite or Amphitrite (left)

Bomarzo, Sacro Bosco
Nature Theater and Crooked House

Verona, Villa Giusti
Grotesque mask on the balcony frontage

Villa Giusti in Verona

"...the Giusti garden, with its excellent situation and enormous cypresses each standing upright and straight as an arrow. The taxus cut to a point in Nordic garden design are probably an imitation of this splendid natural phenomenon. A tree whose branches, from the bottom to the top, the oldest and youngest of them alike, all strive upwards towards heaven, and which lasts for three hundred years, is surely worthy of our veneration."

Thus Goethe paid homage to the garden of the Villa Giusti in Verona, which he visited during his Italian journey. The garden terrain which, to the north of the River Etsch, extends up the hillside in the manner of terraces, was laid out back in the 15th century. At that time the Giusti family, Florentine by birth, came to Verona to settle. They had a charming Renaissance pavilion built on the upper hillside plateau. Unfortunately only the general layout of the Renaissance garden can now be discerned. Toward the end of the 18th century, it was redesigned in what was then the modern style of the English landscape garden. It is unlikely that Goethe saw it in this condition, since if faced with a construction site he would not have found such poetic words.

During the Second World War the garden was devastated by air raids. Many of the cypresses, which were more than 100 years old, and a large number of taxus trees fell victim to the bombs. In the 1950s an outline plan for the lower part of the garden was submitted which adopted the style of the Italian Baroque garden. If one stands today in front of the entrance, flanked with obelisks and recessed fountains, and looks up the cypress alley, then one may perhaps imagine the garden's bygone splendor (illustration below). Allegorical figures in wide flower bowls, fountain figures, gravel paths, lawn, and bed compartments enclosed by box trees, and the grotesque mark on the balcony frontage (illustration above) have once again conjured up a piece of Italian garden culture. The parade of cypresses described by Goethe and the venerable taxus can today be admired once again, even if not in their former splendor.

Verona, Villa Giusti
Garden entrance with view of the central cypress alley

ILLUSTRATION OPPOSITE
Verona, Villa Giusti
Parterre with sculptures and cypresses

Woman with Unicorn
Tapestry of the Five Senses:
La Vue
Wool and silk, 300 x 300 cm
(*c.*10 x 10 ft.), *c.* 1500
Paris, Musée de Cluny

The *giardino segreto*

In the Italian Renaissance, the secret or secluded garden, the *giardino segreto*, denoted a small area within the overall layout of the garden or park. It acquired popularity because the master or lady of the house liked to withdraw to this retreat in order to be alone or to relax in a small group. The location of the *giardino segreto* took this into account. Either it was situated directly outside the bedchambers or private apartments of the palace or villa, or it was spread out in an open area to give spectacular vistas of the landscape.

But before looking at these varieties, a brief look at the tradition of this type of garden is needed. The name is an allusion to the medieval *hortus conclusus*, which appears in the thematic context of the Garden of the Virgin Mary, the rose garden and the Little Paradise Garden. The motif of "The Virgin Mary with the Unicorn" often played an important part (illustration above). According to the *Physiologus*, a "sacred bestiary" from late antiquity, the oldest German translation of which dates from *c.* 1070, the unicorn was considered to be a wild animal that could only be captured in the presence of the Virgin. It lays its head in the Virgin's lap and is thereby tamed – a reference to Christ growing in the Virgin's womb. The hunter, who is represented as the archangel Gabriel, the confidant of God with his dogs *spes* (hope) and *fides* (faith), drives the animal toward the Virgin. This scenario unfolds inside and outside a garden with a protective wall, as shown on an early 16th-century pewter model in the Germanisches Nationalmuseum in Nuremberg (illustration below).

The castle, the gate, and the garden wall also identify this type of garden as a medieval variant of the pleasure garden. Associations may arise with courtly love developing in the summery, open space of the garden, to the accompaniment of musical pleasures and far removed from all the constraints of the court. The inclination to acquire a secluded area of the garden as one's personal space, where there were no public duties, eventually contributed to the emergence of the Italian *giardino segreto* as a genre. During the 15th and 16th centuries this kind of garden was discussed by theoreticians, and appreciated by the owners as an idyllic counterpart to the palace study. The *giardino segreto* is associated not only with motifs specific to gardens; one also encounters themes from cultural history that are loosely connected with the subject of gardens. The *Fountain of Youth*, for example, is a pictorial subject which developed independently of any garden ambience, frequently appearing in the context of the bathhouse or of curing and healing. On the other hand the *Fountain of Youth* was also used as an aspect or motif in connection with the subject of love. In an Italian codex with the title *De Sphaera* three motifs are combined (illustration opposite). The *giardino segreto* turns out to be a garden of love in which a Fountain of Youth has

The Virgin Mary in the *hortus conclusus*
Pewter plate, early 16th century
Nuremberg, Germanisches Nationalmuseum

Fountain of Youth, bathing scene
Miniature painting from *De Sphaera*
Modena, Biblioteca Estense

been installed. The secret garden, laid out adjoining a palace complex and surrounded by a high wall, is being used for festivities by the lords and ladies. Flautists, a horn-player, a lutanist, and a drummer are accompanying a trio of singers who have sat down on a little bench. Servants with carafes, glasses, and little bowls are walking toward a fountain in whose basin naked women are cavorting; they welcome the refreshments. A young man has also just undressed in order to climb into the water from the edge of the basin. The amoretti crouching and dancing in the column of the fountain proclaim the delights of communal bathing. A direct allusion to the *Fountain of Youth* can be assumed with certainty, as the rejuvenation therapy increases the attraction and potential use of the Garden of Love, which is without doubt what we have here.

The planning and construction of the *giardino segreto* of Mantua is a typical example of the need for privacy and tranquillity. After the death of Francesco II Gonzaga, his widow Isabella d'Este

Florence, Villa Medici in Castello
Giardino segreto

had the ground floor of the Corte Vecchia of the Palazzo Ducale in Mantua refurbished, between 1519 and 1523, as new apartments for herself, probably by Battista Covo. Along with a *studiolo,* she also arranged for a secluded garden to be laid out, to which she had sole access from her living or sleeping quarters. The little garden, most charmingly laid out in geometrical forms, the private nature of which is directly evident to the visitor, is bounded on the courtyard side by an arcade with Ionic columns.

The type of garden directly adjoining the living area became popular, at least in Mantua. Federico II Gonzaga, Francesco's successor, who commissioned the Palazzo del Tè before the gates of Mantua, had the palace, which had been built by Giulio Romano for ceremonial purposes, extended by adding a private area. Undoubtedly inspired by Isabella d'Este's personal sanctum in the inner-city Palazzo Ducale, he instructed his master builder to build a casino as a summer retreat in the north-east corner of the great parterre. It took from 1532–4 to carry out the work. An antechamber gives access to the two living rooms and a tunnel-vaulted loggia adjoined by a little garden with a grotto pavilion and a fountain with bizarre decorations and recesses (illustration right).

In contrast to the secret garden in Mantua, which directly adjoined the living quarters, the *giardino segreto* of the Villa Medici in Castello is walled off from the villa building and from the main garden (illustration above). Access had been provided, it is true, from both the villa and the garden, but the noble owners set store by seclusion. The small garden plot, planted with box hedges and shrubs, and provided with an arbor or a pavilion, was to be nothing other than a retreat.

The Castello Ruspoli goes back to a 9th-century castle which had been pulled down in the 13th century, to be replaced by a castello in the style of the early Renaissance. By then, toward the end of the 15th century, the Renaissance garden had probably also been laid out. Around 1538 Count Sforza Marescotti, who was married to Ortensia

Mantua, Palazzo del Tè, Casino
View of the *giardino segreto* through the loggia

Vignanello, Castello Ruspoli
Giardino segreto

from the house of the Farnese, commissioned Antonio Sangallo the Younger to furnish and decorate the rooms.

The garden area which, though laid out lengthwise, is not large and gives more of an impression of intimacy, is divided by two axes. Three "quarters" can be identified, divided in their turn into a number of compartments. They give access to the *giardino segreto*, which is situated further below the main garden (illustration above) and to which a concealed pathway leads down. Visitors standing on the upper parterre will have difficulty in finding the garden, and that, of course, was the clear intention.

The present-day design suggests that this was formerly a Garden of Love or a pleasure garden. The elegantly arranged flower beds are enclosed by box hedges laid out with geometrical regularity. There was probably once a pavilion at the center and perhaps also little orchards at the sides, separated from the central part by trellised pathways. That, at any rate, is how Italian Renaissance secret gardens or gardens of love are preserved in engravings and frescoes in the garden villas and palaces. It may be supposed that even in the 15th century this garden was laid out at a certain distance from the castello, but was linked with the main parterre in later centuries.

The *giardino segreto* of the Castello Ruspoli can thus be considered as representing a new genre. It does not adjoin the apartments of the garden palace, but is deliberately set apart from the villa in order to remain, indeed, secret.

We encounter yet another conception of the secluded garden in the Villa Medici in Fiesole. The garden layout was intended for use as a kind of natural living space. The *giardino segreto* was reached via the main terrace. It was to this place that the members of the Philosophical Academy withdrew in order to discuss Plato's philosophy in

Florence, Villa Gambereia
Terraced garden with terracotta pots (top)
Tuff walls with sculpture recess (far left)
Lion sculpture in a hedge (left)

ILLUSTRATIONS OPPOSITE
Florence, Villa Gambereia
Giardino segreto (top)
Bow-shaped end of the *giardino segreto* (bottom)

total seclusion and with a grandiose view of Florence and the Arno valley.

Villa Gambereia near Settignano

Not far from Florence, near Settignano, a comparable conception of a garden was made reality. In 1610 Zanobi di Andrea Lapi acquired the Gambereia country estate, which had belonged to the Benedictine Order since the 14th century, and had a large-scale villa with gardens and farm buildings built there. On the south side of the Villa Gambereia the upper story is adorned with a charming loggia. Beneath it, at the top of a mountain ridge, the garden extends like the bows of a ship in the direction of the Arno valley. The ship-like effect is further reinforced by the exedra-shaped end, fashioned from box trees, which seems to stretch into the sky. This relatively large area of the garden is the former *giardino segreto* (illustrations top and right).

Neither sketch plans nor documents of the site have been preserved. The present design of the garden goes back to Martino Porcinai and Luigi Messeri, who were commissioned by Princess Giovanna Ghyka to design the grounds, which they did between 1905 and 1913. The strict symmetrical division of the main parterre with hedges, conical trees and hemispheres of boxwood is derived from garden motifs of the late Renaissance. The wide-surface pools where one would customarily expect ornamented bed compartments, have a somewhat strange effect. They would be more in keeping with a late Baroque approach, were it not, that is, for the untypical dense boxwood growth. Be that as it may, the garden of the Villa Gambereia, with such a wealth of enchanting views over the olive groves of the Tuscan hills, illustrates the former owners' need for seclusion amid the great natural theater of their homeland.

Villa Farnese in Caprarola

In Caprarola the visitor encounters what is probably one of the most unusual villas in Latium (illustrations pp. 96–99). This applies not only to the pentagonal Palazzo Farnese but also to the

ILLUSTRATIONS OPPOSITE
Caprarola, Villa Farnese
Fountain sculptures at the Casino del Piacere (top)
Fountain with river gods below the Casino del Piacere (bottom)

Caprarola, Villa Farnese
Entrance facade (right)
Grotto fountain in the Casino del Piacere (bottom)

garden site and especially the *giardino segreto*. In 1558 Cardinal Alessandro Farnese the Younger commissioned the man who at the time was probably the most sought-after master builder, Giocomo Barozzi da Vignola, to develop a castello that had only recently been designed and begun by Antonio da Sangallo, into a sumptuous ceremonial building (illustration above). The busy architect saw that he faced a special challenge. Not long before, *c.* 1550, the ambitious and ostentatious Cardinal Ippolito II d'Este had begun to plan and build his villa in Tivoli. It was the declared goal of the Farnese cardinal that Caprarola should surpass the Tivoli villa in brilliance and splendor. Vignola designed a unique and impressive palace which was more like a monumental fortress than a country garden villa. The unusual five-cornered ground plan of the palace had a decisive effect on the layout of the gardens. The upper gardens, which were laid out after Vignola's death, from 1573, by Giovanni Antonio Garzoni and Girolamo Rainaldi, were completed by *c.* 1580.

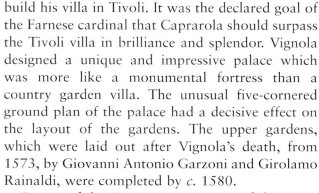

In one of the picturesque grottoes of the secret garden there is a Shepherds' Fountain flanked by river gods. This pastoral theme hints at the nature of the *giardino segreto* as a garden of love and pleasure. The theme of love is taken up again, at least in part, in the iconographic program in the Casino del Piacere. The pavilion was probably begun by Vignola but built after his death, by Garzoni. The maiden with the unicorn, familiar from the garden of love, is to be seen in the vault fresco of the lower loggia. The Hermae carrying baskets on the side terraces of the casino – one is carrying a little dog, another is playing the panpipes – can be included as incidental motifs in the subject of the garden of love that is touched on here.

An area situated somewhat to one side with the Casino del Piacere and the Piazzale delle Cariatidi was not laid out until 1620 by Cardinal Odoardo Farnese under Rainaldi's architectural supervision. This latter complex is a splendid *giardino segreto*

(illustrations top and opposite). This summer garden hideout was very welcome to the cardinal with his desire for quiet and solitude when faced with the urgent business of politics. He had a refuge designed which provided recreation and distraction. The garden area was surrounded by grottoes and rusticated walls. On the casino forecourt a fountain rises up, besieged by river gods, from whose basin water comes cascading down. The cascade, formed by intertwined dolphins, also called Catena d'Aqua or Catena dei Delfini, goes back to a design by Jacopo del Duca. The *giardino segreto* of Caprarola exceeds the hitherto customary dimensions of this genre. One can call it an isolated villa layout within a sizeable garden area with a palace.

The examples quoted convey the most important motifs and design variants of the *giardino segreto*. This type of garden soon became a popular element of upper-class gardens in other European countries. In France in particular the *giardino segreto* soon became, under the influence of Italian architects and garden designers, an indispensable element of the spacious garden layouts of the Baroque.

Caprarola, Villa Farnese
Giardino segreto (top)
Sculpture: Judith (left)
Detail of the *giardino segreto* (opposite)

Renaissance Gardens in France

From the end of Hohenstaufen rule in the mid-13th century, there were very intensive political relations between the French crown and Italy. Following the end of the disputes between France and England in the second half of the 14th century, the House of Anjou once again turned its power-hungry gaze toward Italy.

A hundred years later, in 1494, the empire of Naples entered the political limelight when the thirteen-year-old heir to the throne, Charles VIII, took an army to Italy in order to assert, by force of arms, the ancient claim of his dynasty to Naples. He achieved little, however, being forced to yield to an alliance of Pope Alexander VI, the Habsburg Emperor Maximilian I, and the Duke of Milan, Lodovico il Moro, and to retreat. Although Charles returned to his homeland to the castle at Amboise on the Loire without any political trophies, he did not come back empty-handed. Evidently he had had sufficient time when he was in Naples to take a detailed look at its many palaces, villas, and gardens. He wrote enthusiastically to the Duke of Bourbon:
"My brother, you cannot imagine what beautiful gardens I have [seen] in this city. Truly. It seems that only Adam and Eve are lacking to make an earthly paradise, they are so beautiful and full of good and strange things."

Château de Villandry
View from the east of the garden and the castle
The Villandry garden is one of the most frequently visited gardens in France.

Château d'Amboise
Garden near the castle
Today nothing remains of the one-time Renaissance garden.

The Castle Gardens of Amboise, Blois, and Gaillon

The passage above adds to the evidence of the transfer of culture that was beginning between Italy and the other European countries. Italian art, hence the Renaissance garden, took root in France, and soon in the other countries north of the Alps as well. Charles VIII engaged a number of Italian artists at his court in Amboise, including the garden designer Pacello da Mercogliano, a Neapolitan priest. Although there is no documentary evidence relating to his activity in Amboise, he is nevertheless considered to be the creator of this first Renaissance garden in France. Sadly, Charles, who was so enthusiastic about Italian gardens, did not live to enjoy Mercogliano's artistry, for he died in 1498 as the result of an accident. His successor, Louis XII, completed the project, which we know from the splendid detailed engravings by Jacques Androuet Du Cerceau (illustration below). These, however, show the garden as it was many decades after its creation. In his engravings, which were first published in two volumes in the 1570s, Du Cerceau brought together all the important castles and gardens of the age in France, an age which began with the reign of Charles VIII, blossomed during the reigns of Louis XII (1498–1515) and Francis I (1512–47), and came to an end with Henry IV (1589–1610).

Du Cerceau's engraving shows the garden parterre in Amboise on a terrace high above the bank of the Loire. In a note, Du Cerceau criticized the proportions of the garden, and the plant bed compartments do, indeed, extend lengthwise in only two rows, making the layout resemble a narrow strip. The spatial proportions, which were determined by the layout of the medieval castle above the high supporting wall, set severe limits on the extent of the garden. A harmonious relationship between the castle and the garden was therefore impossible from the outset. Just as individual Renaissance wings had been added to the medieval castle buildings, so an attempt was made to realize the new formal ideals in the castle garden, which

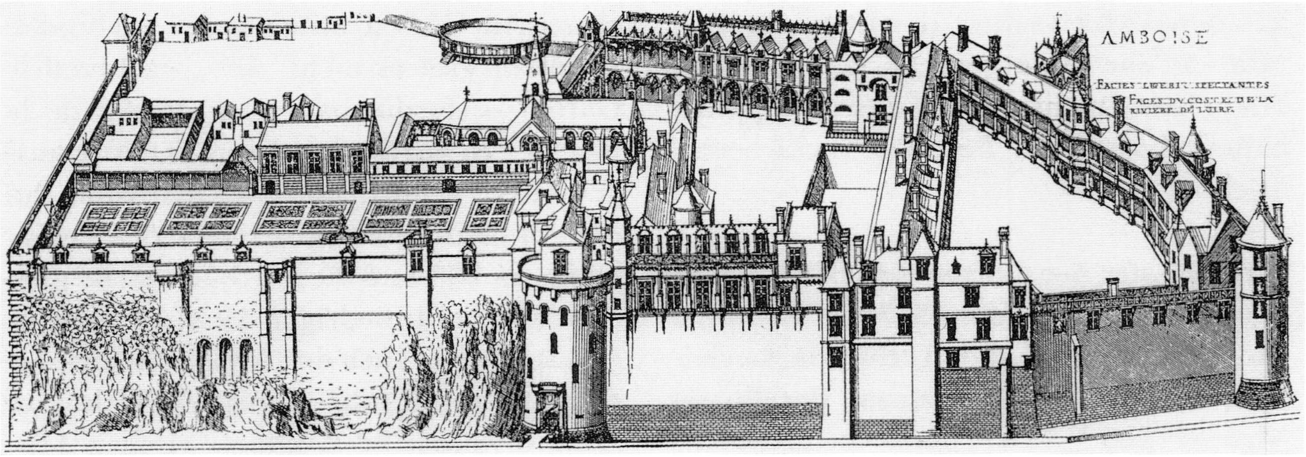

Chateau d'Amboise
View of the castle and its garden as depicted by J.A. Du Cerceau, 1607

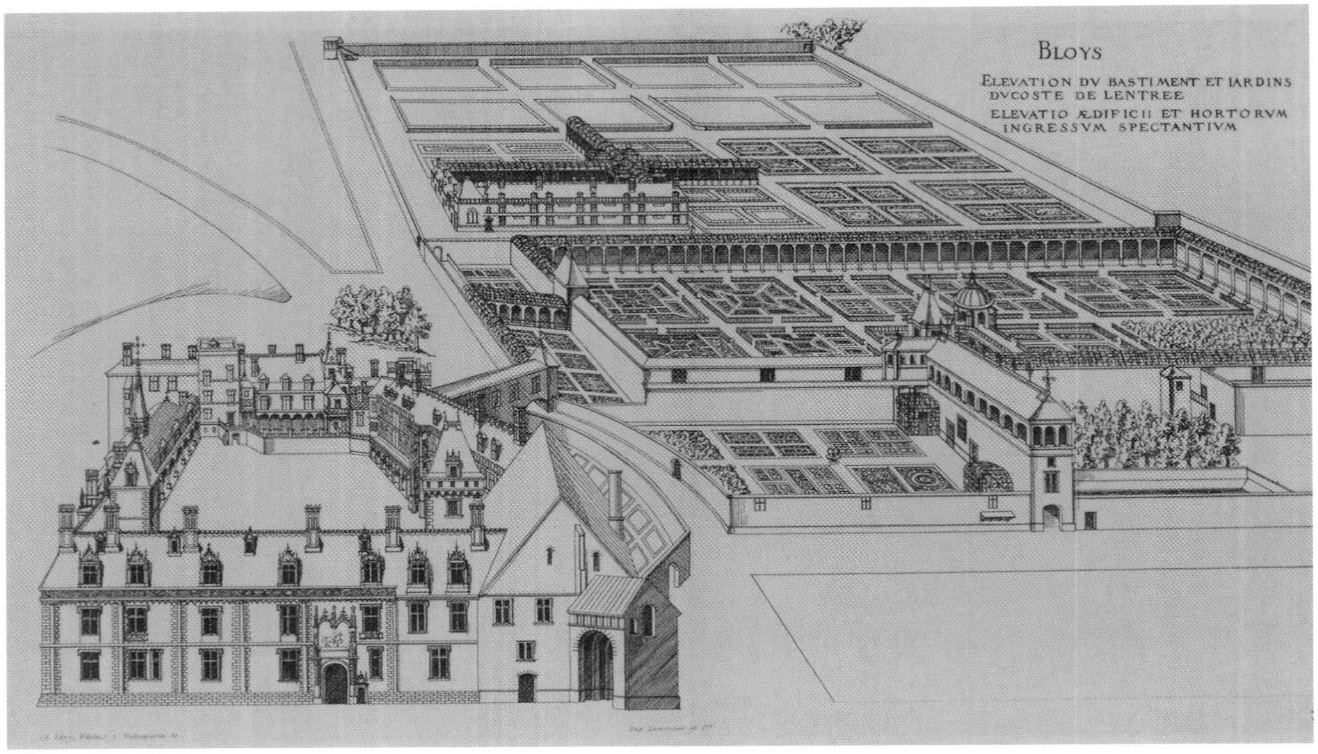

Blois, castle, and garden
View of the overall layout according to J.A. Du Cerceau, 1607

Flower bed detail

had now been enlarged and changed into a Renaissance garden.

Louis XII was as enthusiastic about Italian garden design as his predecessor Charles had been. He commissioned his minister, Charles of Amboise, to acquire Italian marble fountains, which he had installed not only in Amboise but also in Gaillon and Blois. The characteristic features of Amboise also apply to the gardens of Blois and Gaillon. The parterres were laid out without any specific architectural relationship between the garden and the buildings. Great store was set, however, by the ornamentation of the beds in the Italian Renaissance style. The gallery on the river side of Amboise makes it clear that – in contrast to Italian practice – the landscape had not as yet been taken into consideration when the garden was laid out. Instead of giving a free view of the imposing panorama of the Loire valley, the wall was raised, with nothing more than the addition of windows. This shows that the medieval notion of the *hortus conclusus*, the intimate and secluded garden area, was still dominant.

The gardens of Blois were also laid out under Louis XII. Planning and supervision were again entrusted to the Neapolitan priest Pacello da Mercogliano. Work began *c.* 1500. The gardens were separate from the castle buildings, and accessible only via a bridge, the Galerie des Cerfs (illustration above). The tendency to conceive the castle and the garden together, as an overall architectural concept, or at least to attempt to integrate the garden into the existing castle grounds, had not as yet made itself felt in Blois either. It can be seen from Du Cerceau's engraving that the garden was made up of three parts situated on three terraces at different levels. They were not linked by either steps or ramps. The greatest attention was evidently paid to the center garden, the *jardin bas* or *jardin de la reine*, with the other two gardens being regarded as more in the nature of secondary areas. Here, in the upper *jardin du roi*, a herb and kitchen garden in conjunction with a pleasure garden may have been envisaged. In the lower garden there were probably also useful plants and small decorative beds. It took up only a third of the length of the main garden.

The ten plant bed compartments of the *jardin de la reine*, described as "*parquets*" in the account books, were laid in pairs along the longitudinal axis. Using ten plant beds prevented symmetrical rectangular coordinates: the intersection of the axes, highlighted by a pavilion, was displaced to the right. The luxuriant ornamentation of the beds followed Italian patterns, symmetrically laid out in individual compartments. Each compartment was separately designed, creating a lively variety. Except for the front left corner, the entire area was surrounded by a "*treillage*," a trellised latticework pathway. Treillages were in vogue at the time, and remained so until the Baroque era. These trellised pathways were often interrupted by pavilion-like structures with the appearance of triumphal arches at the access points of the main axes. But in Blois only one such structure was to be found, and that was at the point where the short treillage running at a right angle to the castle bridge, the Galerie des Cerfs, adjoined the main garden of the chateau.

Around 1500, Louis XII had a garden casino with an adjoining orangery, built for his wife Anne de Bretagne, at the place where the lower and center gardens adjoined each other. Beyond the elongated building a fruit tree plantation opens up with two *jeux de paumes*, or courts for ball games. The garden casino has been preserved to the present day.

Cardinal Georges d'Amboise, a minister of Louis XII, may have studied the castle-garden layout of his king, and deemed it worthy of improvement. From 1506 to 1509 he had a garden laid out, probably also under Mercogliano's supervision, for his castle at Gaillon, close to the episcopal city of Rouen. In Du Cerceau's drawing of 1576, one is struck by the relationship between the castle and the main garden (illustration below). Although a bridge from the main area over the moat leads first to a walled-in courtyard, and is only there adjoined by the garden, one can see a clear relationship between the axes of the castle and the garden.

To judge by Du Cerceau's drawing, the east side of the overall layout was given prominence as the display side, for the arcades of the east wing of the castle continue in the courtyard arcades. These are adjoined by the garden wall with its massive supporting pillars on which there is a window gallery with towers at the corners and in the center. The supporting wall was necessary because a steep terrain had to be terraced for the garden. The magnificent gateway tower in the center of the garden gallery that runs parallel to the main castle building gives access to the garden, a parterre comprising twenty-six ornamental beds. In 1517 a contemporary, Antonio de Beatis, gave a detailed account of the artistry of the ornamental beds. It was, he said, above all a matter of blossoming herbs, along with box and rosemary, creating imaginative figures such as riders, ships, or birds. The royal coat-of-arms was also to be seen. It was designed, Beatis wrote, "*molto artificiosamente.*" In general his account is in line with the reflections of the theoretician Olivier de Serres.

The latter took the view that the ornamental beds should be enclosed with herbs such

Blois, castle garden
View of the alleys by the castle (detail)

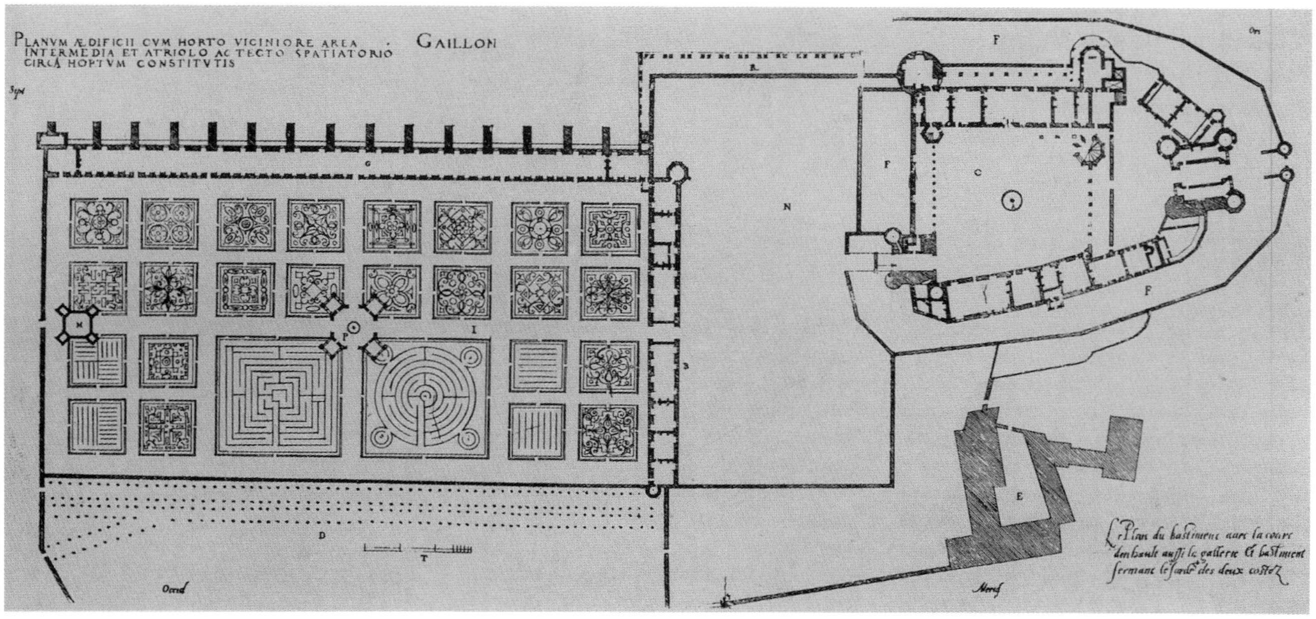

Gaillon, castle and garden
Ground plan of the site according to J.A. Du Cerceau, 1607

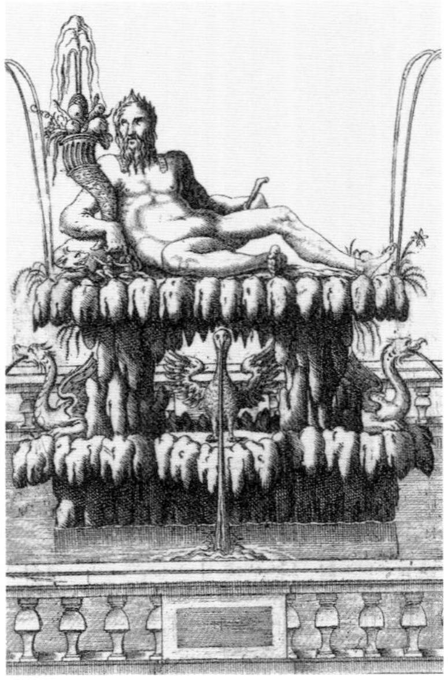

Fontainebleau
Tiber Fountain (detail)
Engraving by A. Francini

as lavender, thyme, mint, marjoram, and rosemary. To create patterns in the beds he recommended planting, among other plants and flowers, violets, stocks, pinks, or pansies. And finally, he suggested that box was to be clipped in the imaginative, artistic shapes to which it is so well suited.

The symmetry of the parterre is interrupted by two mazes which break up the strict pattern of the rows of compartments. A garden house set at the end of the central axis provides a companion piece to the gallery tower at the entrance to the parterre. This structure repeats the forms of the gateway tower on a smaller scale, thereby creating a link between the garden, its architecture, and the castle building itself.

Away from the castle, the cardinal had a hermitage set up, with a miniature garden and a rock face with space for a grotto. We recall what Palissy had to say concerning grottoes, which were inspired by Italy and became very popular in France in the 16th century. The hermitage at Gaillon is one of the earliest examples of this type, which subsequently, in the Baroque gardens of the 18th century, became established as a fixed element of garden design.

The specifically French quality of the garden at Gaillon lies in the connection between the garden and the architecture of the castle, although the building is spatially separated from the parterre. The courtyard in particular functioned as an architectural link between two elements, the architecture and the parterre.

Fontainebleau, castle and garden
View of the overall layout *c.* 1565
according to J.A. Du Cerceau

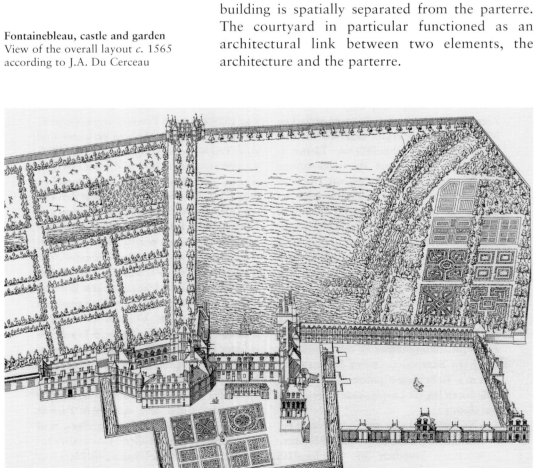

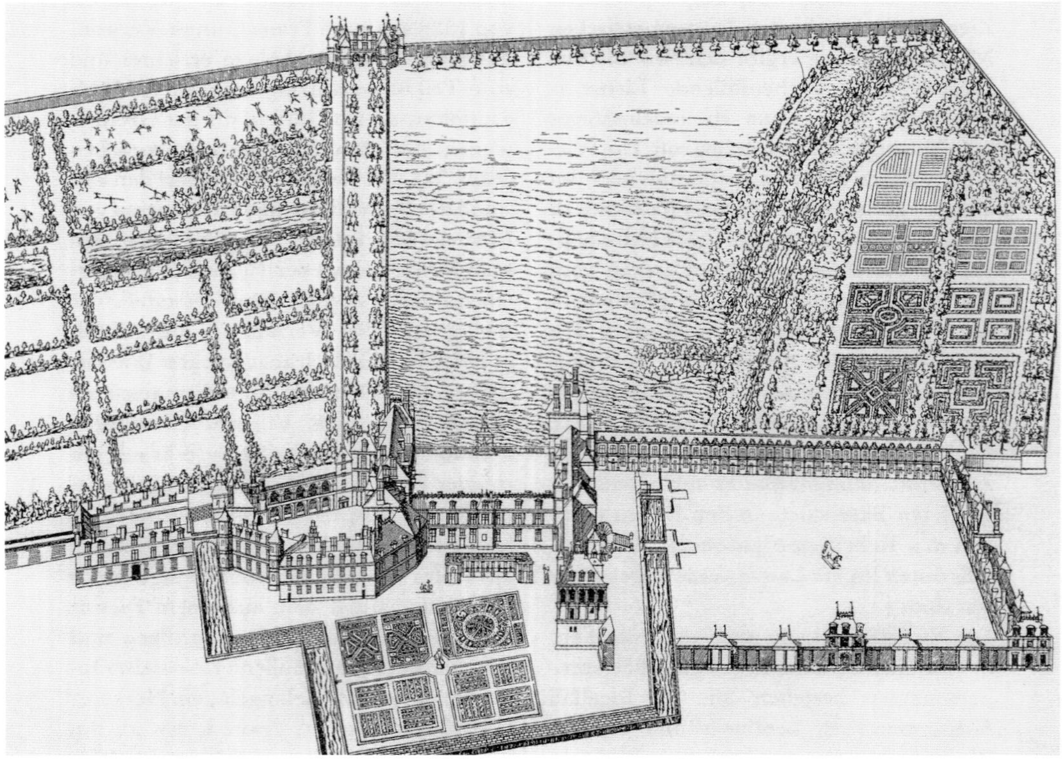

The Garden of Fontainebleau Castle

The gardens of Fontainebleau and Anet mark the next, and the decisive stage, in the evolution of the specifically French type of garden, which developed into its unusual size and variety in the 17th and 18th centuries. From 1528 onward, Fontainebleau Castle was enlarged under Francis I to become a hunting seat (illustration pp. 106–107). The incorporation of older buildings produced an irregular layout. The site as a whole did not present an architectural unity, but it did offer interesting opportunities of designing the courtyards as gardens or of contrasting them with spacious garden areas and – similarly to what had been done in Gaillon – finding specific solutions to the contrasts between the castle, the garden, and the court (illustration left).

What the ruler had in mind was the idea of a garden combining the traditional layout of the intimate garden, closely associated with the castle building, and a garden extending away from the castle into the landscape. Hence in the corner

formed by the castle chapel, the transverse wing, and the main building, he had an ornamental garden laid out consisting of four bed compartments. Where the axes crossed he placed an antique marble statue, the so-called *Versailles Diana* which today is in the Louvre in Paris. This area of the garden was called the *jardin de Diane* after her. The garden, the castle courtyard, and the castle buildings were enclosed by a channel of water. This was a private garden which could only be reached from the royal apartments. Under Catherine de' Medici the garden was named the *jardin de la reine*, the queen's garden. Bronze copies of famous statues from antiquity were placed there, including the Laocoön group, the Belvedere Apollo and the Sleeping Ariadne. Today these sculptures are also housed in the Louvre.

On the other side of the transverse wing, the Galerie de François I as it is called today, the Cour de la Fontaine, the Fountain Court, stretched out, bounded in its turn by a large lake which had been created when a swamp was dug out. To the west of the lake was another ornamental garden along with an orchard and a utility garden. Today visitors to this spot can take a walk through the *jardin anglais* that was laid out in 1812. On the opposite side, the lake was bounded by an alley of four rows of trees adjoined by a large garden area. Here Francis I had included an orchard cum meadow garden and a playground, which Du Cerceau indicated by people romping about and by swings. A broad, tree-lined channel coming from the lake flowed through this area.

Water played a dominant part in this extensive garden layout, which was not completed until *c.* 1565, in the time of Catherine de' Medici. Marie Louise Gothein was thus right to speak of Fontainebleau as the "French Renaissance water-channel garden."

The idea of using water surfaces and channels as a structural principle was of decisive importance for the development of the French Baroque garden. The last-named section of the Fontainebleau garden was redesigned between 1661 and 1664 by

Fontainebleau, castle garden
View of the landscape park with an 18th-century stone pavilion

PAGES 106–107
Château de Fontainebleau
View of the castle and the large pool

Fontainebleau, castle garden
View of the great channel (top)
Conical trees (above)

ILLUSTRATION OPPOSITE
Château d'Anet, castle garden
Water landscape with ancient trees

the creator of the Versailles gardens, André Le Nôtre (illustrations above and pp. 106–107). Le Nôtre extended the channel in the area in front of the castle to create a square pool, which he surrounded with four large compartments. He bordered this parterre with terraces planted with clipped trees, with the intention of concealing the asymmetrical overall layout and the irregular line of the castle buildings facade. What Le Nôtre had to work on was not, however, the garden of Francis I but that of Henry IV. The latter had already, shortly before 1600, had the utility garden redesigned as a *parterre de broderie*, a complex of ornamental beds based on Italian models. Beyond this parterre he had planned a large park, which was laid out in 1609. The channel from the period of Francis I was then enlarged to form a a spacious pool. With these carefully planned alterations, the external landscape was for the first time purposefully included in the conception of the garden at Fontainebleau.

It was perhaps in Fontainebleau that the landscape was consciously discovered for the first time in France as part of the visual experience of walking in a garden. The king now saw his garden as a kind of model of his territory, symbolizing the structure and extent of the area ruled by him in reality. He was able to connect the plant-bed compartments, alleys, channels, and pools that belonged to the castle with the panoramic landscape he saw before him, and thus a metaphor for the scope of his power. There was, however, still no satisfactory connection between the castle and the garden. The courtyard area in front of the castle did not adequately meet this need. Le Nôtre had also felt this deficiency in Fontainebleau when he was redesigning it, and he now resolved to conceal the irregular line of the facade by means of terraces and trees.

Château d'Anet

In Anet, one of the most enchanting Renaissance castles in France, Philibert de l'Orme, who at the time was the most famous master builder in the country, developed a new solution to the problem of the relationship between the castle and the garden. In 1546 he was commissioned by Diane de Poitiers, Henry II's mistress, to plan and build a castle and garden for use as a hunting lodge. Although de l'Orme integrated older parts of a previous building into his conception, he succeeded in his aim of creating a perfect harmony and symmetry between the castle and the garden (illustrations pp. 109–111)

The gateway, built like a triumphal arch, and still preserved today (illustration p. 110), led across an inner courtyard directly to the main building, the *corps de logis*, which was flanked by side wings. Beyond the main building the expansively laid-out garden came into view. The ceremonial courtyard and the side of the garden appeared now as having equal status. De l'Orme laid an axis through the entire complex, which ran across the gateway building, the central gable of the main building, and the garden's central alley.

The gateway is crowned by a technical wonder: a group of animals, comprising two hunting dogs and a stag at bay, connected to the mechanism of the portal clock, described by de l'Orme as follows:

Château d'Anet
Castle and garden (right)
Terrace at gatehouse (bottom)

"Although it is hardly in the nature of a stag to stamp its hoof when it hears dogs barking, things have been arranged so that when the aforesaid dogs strike the bell on the quarter, the stag stamps its hoof for the hour to be heard."

Wilfried Hansmann emphasized the witty and sophisticated play on the fact that the lady of the house had the same name as the Goddess of the Hunt, Diana, a theme which could be perceived in the architecture and the design of the garden. A double flight of steps in the shape of a half moon, the symbol of Diana, led down from the garden side of the main building to the parterre, which was surrounded on three sides by a rusticated gallery. The ornamental beds are said to have been planted in heraldic patterns relating to Diana's ancestry and royal lineage. They were replaced in 1582 by a *parterre de broderie* designed by Etienne du Pérac and planted by Claude Mollet, one of the first famous royal gardeners in France.

Today there is unfortunately nothing left to be seen of the Renaissance garden. It survived for just over a hundred years. Louis-Joseph de Vendôme, its later owner, commissioned André Le Nôtre in 1681 to redesign the site in the contemporary style.

The rusticated walls were removed and the garden of Diana became part of the vast grounds

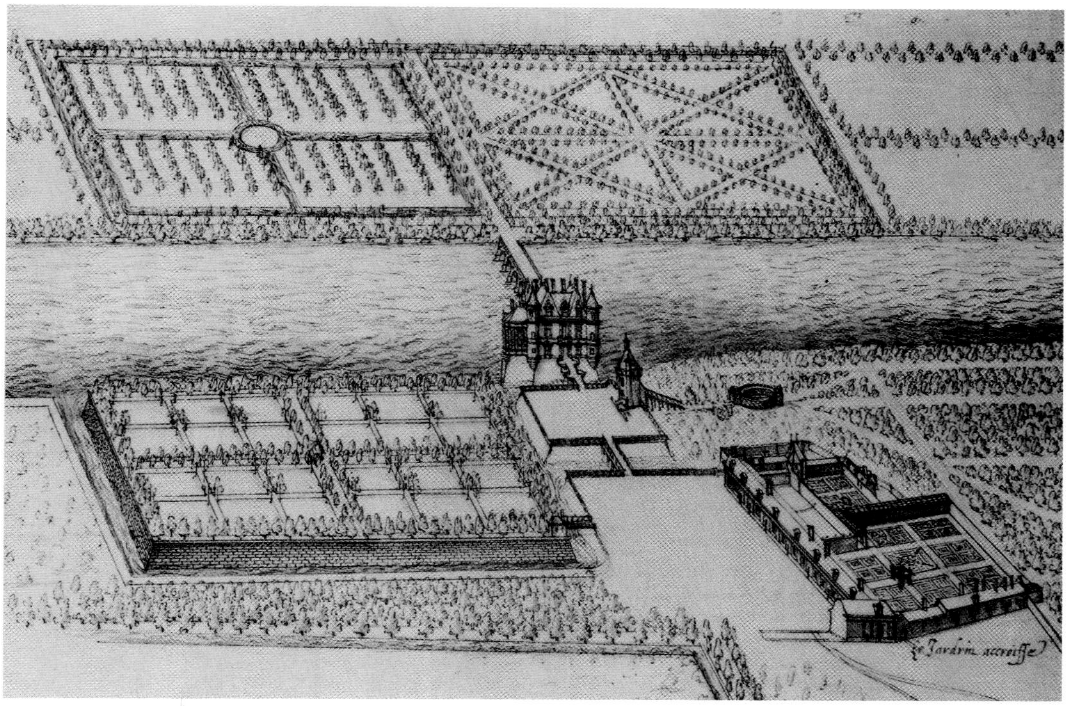

Château de Chenonceaux
Detail of a drawing by J.A. Du Cerceau of the castle and its garden

five times its size. Water from the River Eure, which flowed past to the west, was channeled off, and soon another Baroque garden adorned the countryside; but this too went to ruin during the following century. After the castle had been destroyed and partially reconstructed at the beginning of the 19th century, the new owner, Adolphe de Riquet, Comte de Caraman, had an English garden laid out on the site *c.* 1840.

Château de Chenonceaux

There is an unusual but exceptionally appealing relationship between the garden and the castle of Chenonceaux on the River Cher near the Loire. The Renaissance castle extends across the river like a noble bridge. To the east of the castle complex, and with no wholly compelling connection with the castle itself, the great parterre stretches out, its southern flank bounded by the Cher (illustration left). A channel drawing water from the river encircles this impressive garden area. The river is thus treated as an aesthetic link between the castle and the garden – an arrangement that is unique in all of France.

The castle and garden were built and laid out between 1551 and 1555 for Diane de Poitiers as a gift from the French king Henry II. In 1560 the site became the property of Catherine de' Medici. She had the grounds to the west of the castle made fit for planting. The small parterre constructed on the bank of the Cher to the west of the ceremonial courtyard of Chenonceaux was also of her making (illustration p. 114).

At the beginning of the 20th century the site was restored to its former condition by Henri

Chateau de Chenonceaux
The east garden, *jardin de Diane de Poitiers* with the large parterre

Château de Chenonceaux
The design of the west garden, *jardin de Catherine de Medici* is less lavish than that of the east garden. It consists of a round pond and lawns between narrow beds.

ILLUSTRATION OPPOSITE
Château de Chenonceaux
Detail of the large parterre of the east garden (*jardin de Diane de Poitiers*)

Duchêne, who has re-created many historical gardens in his country, so that we can experience and study this Renaissance garden, with its particular tensions between castle, garden, and river. The arrangement is similar to the view handed down by Du Cerceau.

The parterre is symmetrically subdivided in the form of a cross and along the diagonal, creating trapeze-shaped and triangular beds. These adorn asymmetrical gravel paths and strips of lavender which have the effect of ornamental loops. The edging strips are planted with boxwood globes and small, low-growing Seville orange trees, and with flowers that change according to the season. At the center a circular lawn bed is laid out, which must once surely have had a fountain.

On the opposite side, that is to the northwest of the entrance to the Château de Chenonceaux, is the parterre of Catherine de' Medici, the dimensions of which are, however, much smaller. This parterre resembles the main parterre in its layout, and is linked with the extensive adjoining garden layout to the north.

During the reign of Henry IV (1589–1610) garden design came under the influence of courtly art. *Bon sens* now became the one and only yardstick. The theoretician de Serres visited Fontainebleau, Saint-Germain-En-Laye, Blois, the Tuileries, and also, of course, the Jardin du Luxembourg in Paris in order fully to report on the layout of the parterres and the ornamentation of the beds at these outstanding sites.

Château de Chenonceaux
Temple-like ornamental architecture with reliefed columns (caryatids)

St-Germain-En-Laye
Castle and garden layout according to an engraving by A. Francini, 1614

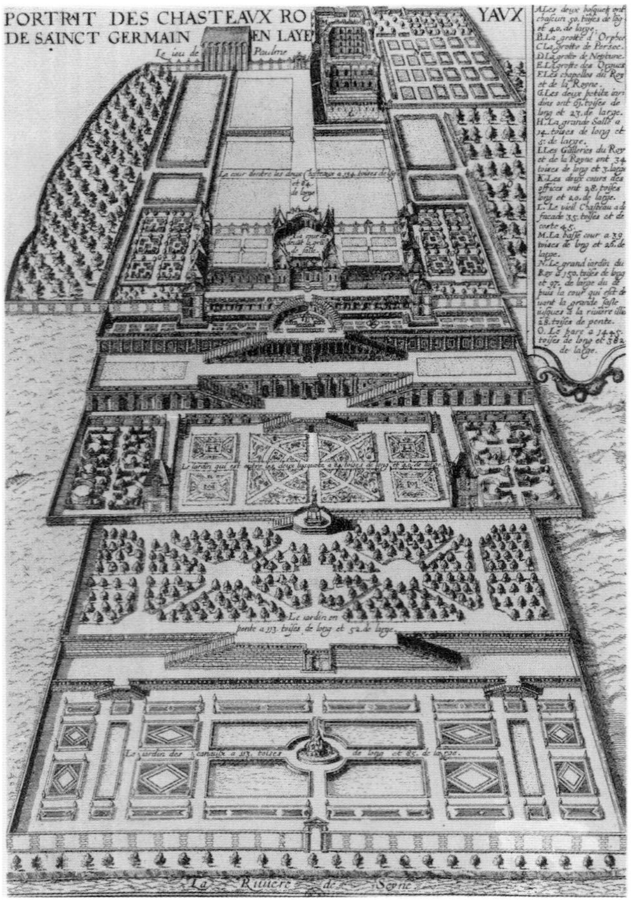

The Gardens of Saint-Germain-en-Laye

There are euphoric contemporary reports concerning the gardens of Saint-Germain-en-Laye. The monumental site was regarded as the Eighth Wonder of the World. Henry II commissioned the first designs from Philibert de l'Orme *c.* 1557, and, as the account books show, they were implemented immediately. The king died two years later. It was only under Henry IV, toward the end of the 16th century, that the layout was completed. The engraving of 1664 shows the magnificent garden site descending to the Seine via six terraces (illustration left). It has a very pronounced architectural quality. The castle on the upper terrace consists of a group of pavilions interconnected by flat stretches, some of them designed in the shape of exedras. On the other levels there are more pavilions, the starting points of galleries which enclose the bed compartments. They are bounded by walls with plants growing on them, which in turn lead toward smaller or larger garden pavilions or toward the main building. The entire site creates the impression of a theatrical stage with sumptuous scenery. Claude Mollet, mentioned above in connection with Anet, submitted the parterre designs, which are varied and imaginative.

The numerous water features are the work of the brothers Thomas and Alexandre Francini. The latter was also responsible for supervising the fountains and waterworks at Fontainebleau. His brother Thomas was elevated to the rank of a *gentilhomme servant du roi* under Louis XIII. His son, François de Francine, was the creator of the fountain at Versailles. While semicircular steps lead down to the first terrace, the next two terraces are reached by two double flights of ramp steps. Directly in front of the main parterre the grotto areas with their waterworks open up, leading backwards, including the famous Grotto of Orpheus (illustration below). The main parterre, formed in box, is divided into two smaller bed compartments at the sides, and four larger ones at the center, which are subdivided diagonally and radially. The smaller side beds are decorated with the initials of the royal couple, Henry IV and Maria de' Medici. The parterre is flanked by two bosket zones. Half a century after the garden was completed, the terraces collapsed, but they were rebuilt under Louis XIV.

Paris, Jardin du Luxembourg
Steps adorned with sculptures, leading up to an alley.

The Jardin du Luxembourg in Paris

When Henry IV was murdered by a Catholic fanatic in 1610, his widow Maria de' Medici fled from her apartments in the Louvre across to the other side of the Seine. There, *c.* 1612, she acquired a site from François de Luxembourg, on which she had a castle and a garden laid out, the Jardin du Luxembourg, which, though much changed, is still famous (illustration above). Here the regent wanted to make her native land of Italy blossom, taking the Boboli garden in Florence as her model. But the site did not entirely match her ideas. The attractiveness of a Tuscan terraced garden could scarcely be created on the flat site by the Seine. In addition, in French garden design the *parterre de broderie* had departed from its original Italian form and developed in ways of its own. When Jacques Boyceau de la Barauderie, the most famous parterre designer of Henry IV and Louis XIII submitted his first designs in 1612, Maria de' Medici was enthusiastic even though she could identify only one single "Tuscan feature": the great alley ran not in the direction of the central axis of the castle but at a right angle to it, as in the Boboli garden. Before the main facade the parterre with its unique bed patterns opened out. Boyceau chose the acanthus leaf as his basic motif, with its rich potential for variation. He transformed it imaginatively in ever new filigree forms, including the queen's monogram. Boyceau did not use flowers, but used box to create ornamentation.

St-Germain-en-Laye, Grotto of Orpheus
Engraving by A. Francini, 1614

Château de Villandry

The Renaissance gardens of France have either gone to ruin or have been transformed into Baroque gardens, which in turn became English landscape gardens. In this form many have survived to the present day. But there is one place which has preserved all the enchantment and the splendor of the Renaissance parterre, even if not uninterruptedly, and in the guise of the unique re-creation that it is.

In Villandry, near Tours, one encounters a strange but noteworthy configuration: a 12th-century medieval castle and another castle from the Renaissance era, along with an 18th-century terraced garden, which was in ruins until the beginning of the 20th century.

The garden was re-created, and is today one of the most beautiful Renaissance gardens in France. To re-create not a Baroque garden, for which there was secure evidence, but the more speculative form of a largely unknown Renaissance garden, was a brave act, and a desirable one in view of the dominance of Baroque gardens in France.

We owe it to the Spaniard Joachim Carvallo, who between 1906 and 1924 redesigned the 18th-century terraces using Du Cerceau's record as a basis, and together with other Spanish artists created a typical French Renaissance garden. To the south of the castle there is the kitchen garden decorated with artistic bed patterns (illustration pp. 120–121). Box tree compartments may be admired in the *jardin de musique* to the east and in the *jardin d'amour* to the southeast of the castle (illustrations opposite and right). The main axis of the garden, an alley, separates the ornamental garden from the kitchen garden and the water garden. The water garden has a channel through it that leads from a pool to the castle moat.

Joachim Carvallo set conscious store by strict symmetry, offset by playful and imaginative ornamentation. He was primarily concerned at Villandry to create an alternative to the English landscape garden, which in his opinion had destroyed the fascination of the French Renaissance and Baroque garden, and was preventing the traditional resources of garden design from making their rightful effect.

The French Renaissance garden was based on the Italian garden. From their initial enthusiasm for Italian garden culture, the French gradually evolved concepts of their own, which, with artistry and imagination, led to further development of the Italian models.

Whereas in Italy the castle and the garden were in most cases planned and executed as a homogenous whole, in France the castle and garden areas remained separate entities for a long time. It was not until the end of the Renaissance era that the two finally came together, when they became, with incomparable splendor, the garden complexes of the Baroque period. The Italian element within the French garden – from plant bed patterns via grottoes to terracing – was to remain a separate adornment.

Château de Villandry
Hedge and small ornamental trees in the *jardin d'amour*

ILLUSTRATION OPPOSITE
Château de Villandry
View of the castle from the southeast across the *jardin d'amour*

Château de Villandry
Steps leading up from the lower level of the kitchen garden (*potager*) to the terrace of the ornamental garden (*jardin d'amour*).

PAGES 120–121
Château de Villandry
View of the castle from the south across the kitchen garden (*potager*)

ILLUSTRATION OPPOSITE
Château de Villandry
Detail view of the water garden with pond and fountain

Château de Brécy
Brécy Castle, situated not far from Caen in the province of Calvados, dates from the early 17th century. The garden is from the same period, and has been preserved, apart from slight alterations, to the present day. Its charm lies in the lavish use of steps, balustrades, terrace walls, and gateways with many Manneristic ornaments and sculptures. In its overall structure it is like a monumental theater with a stage comprising several settings staggered upwards. A central gravel path with four flights of steps leads across the four terraces to a monumental gateway with an ornamented grid in the Mannerist style (illustration top p. 126). From the top one can see the whole garden site at a glance. Boxwood cones and low box hedges adorn the terraces. One's gaze travels far beyond the castle with its gable windows ornamented in the Baroque manner, to the gently undulating hills of Calvados (illustration left).

Even though the characteristic Renaissance ornamentation of the plant beds is missing, the typical conception of a garden from *c.* 1600 can be discerned in the structure and the organization of the individual terraces. Only the compartment situated in front of the castle displays impressive knot patterns composed of box hedges. Furthermore, the balustrades decorated with pine cones and the Manneristic lions' heads (illustration above and left), along with other imaginative sculptures, give the garden the look of a French Renaissance garden.

Château de Brécy
View of the castle-like mansion and the garden site (left)
Ornamental balustrade elements: lion's head (top) and pine cone (bottom)

ILLUSTRATIONS OPPOSITE
Château de Brécy
A parterre extends in front of the castle with very beautiful boxwood ornaments (bottom), while on the higher terraces little trees cut to shape and stone sculptures determine the image of the garden (top).

Château de Brécy
View from the castle of the gently rising garden on four staggered terraces

Renaissance Gardens in Germany, Austria, and England

Leonberg, orange orchard
Bed detail with small corner pavilion

Germany and Austria

In Germany, Italian Renaissance garden design not only set an example, it also set standards, since there was hardly anything of an indigenous tradition. The medieval type of monastery garden was no longer sufficient for the ceremonial requirements of princes and dukes. Due to the close political and economic contacts between south German principalities and dukedoms and Italy, knowledge of both theoretical treatises and the concrete concepts of Italian garden design quickly traveled north. North of the Alps the idea of the Renaissance garden spread not only in the large capital towns but also in the provinces, where learned counts cultivated political and economic contacts with the princely families of Italy.

Neufra near Riedlingen on the Danube (not far from its source) presents us with a special case. In the second half of the 16th century Count Georg von Helfenstein had a "hanging garden" designed for his second wife, Apollonia. The terrain to the north of Neufra's parish church of St. Peter and St. Paul, and to the west of the castle building, slopes down toward the village. Here, huge supporting walls were built, with vaulted substructures, in order to create level terraces for the castle garden. A painting in Schloß Heiligenberg by Meinrad von Hüfingen dating from 1688 shows a view of Neufra (Neiffern) in which these supporting walls and the massive supporting pillars, tapering upwards, can be clearly seen (illustrations below). The walls and the site have been preserved, apart from some slight alterations, to the present day. In order to withstand the lateral pressure of the vaulting, the walls were reinforced by three semicircular towers alongside the supporting pillars. Today only one half-tower on the north wall can be visited. But by way of compensation two corner pavilions at the northeast corner and the castle side remain.

For his site, Georg von Helfenstein had probably been inspired by Schloß Ambras near

Neufra, Schloß Heiligenberg
Detail from a painting by Meinrad von Hüfingen (right)

Ambras, princely castle
View of castle and garden
Engraving by M. Merian, *c.* 1650 (bottom, center)

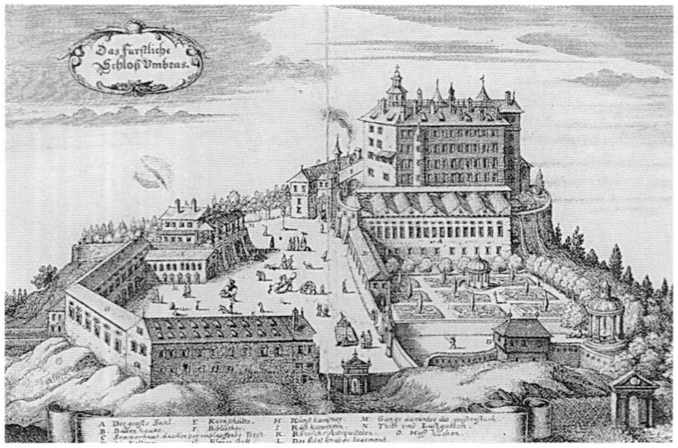

Hechingen, town pleasure garden
Detail from an engraving by M. Merian, *c.* 1640 (far right)

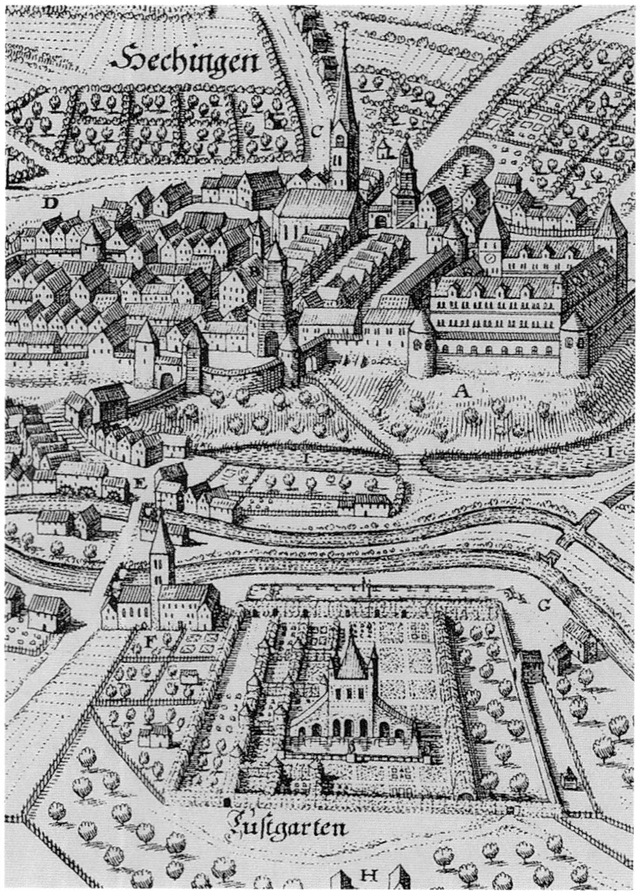

Public garden outside the town
Early 17th century, from *Horti Ankelmanniani*
Berlin, Staatliche Museen Preußischer Kulturbesitz, copperplate engravings collection

Innsbruck, where he had spent considerable time. There, in the 1560s, a *giardino segreto*, a form of secluded private garden that had originated in Italy, had been built for Philippine Welser, the wife of Archduke Ferdinand of Tirol (illustration opposite, bottom left). As the garden was to adjoin the women's apartments of the castle, it had to be created on top of a base. Today, evidence of a vaulted construction for the former garden can still be found at the supporting wall surrounding the eastern part of the castle.

A pleasure garden was also laid out below the town hill in Hechingen, to the south of Tübingen, where Count von Zollern had his residence. This is preserved only in an engraving by Merian dating from 1640 (illustration opposite, right). Under Count Eitelfriedrich IV (1576–1605) Hechingen was transformed into a Renaissance town. Evidence of this can still be seen in the lower gateway dating from 1579 and the round tower in the Rabengasse. They indicate the location of the former town fortifications. The pleasure garden was laid out near the River Starzel in the vicinity of the Spittelkirche, probably between 1577 and 1595, when the town castle was rebuilt. The garden was surrounded by stables, a cattleyard, the gun room, and the race track.

In those years the Stuttgart gardens were also laid out, which, along with Heidelberg, Amboise, and Fontainebleau, were regarded as the most splendid Renaissance gardens north of the Alps. The gardens of the medieval and Renaissance counts and dukes of Württemberg followed their Italian models particularly closely. This was probably more than anything else a consequence of Swabian marriage policy. In 1380 Eberhard III, the Mild, married Antonia Visconti, the daughter of the Prince of Milan. Very soon after her marriage, Antonia had a garden in the Italian style laid out in Stuttgart adjoining the old castle, on the site of the present-day Karlsplatz. This garden was first mentioned in an official document in 1393. It may

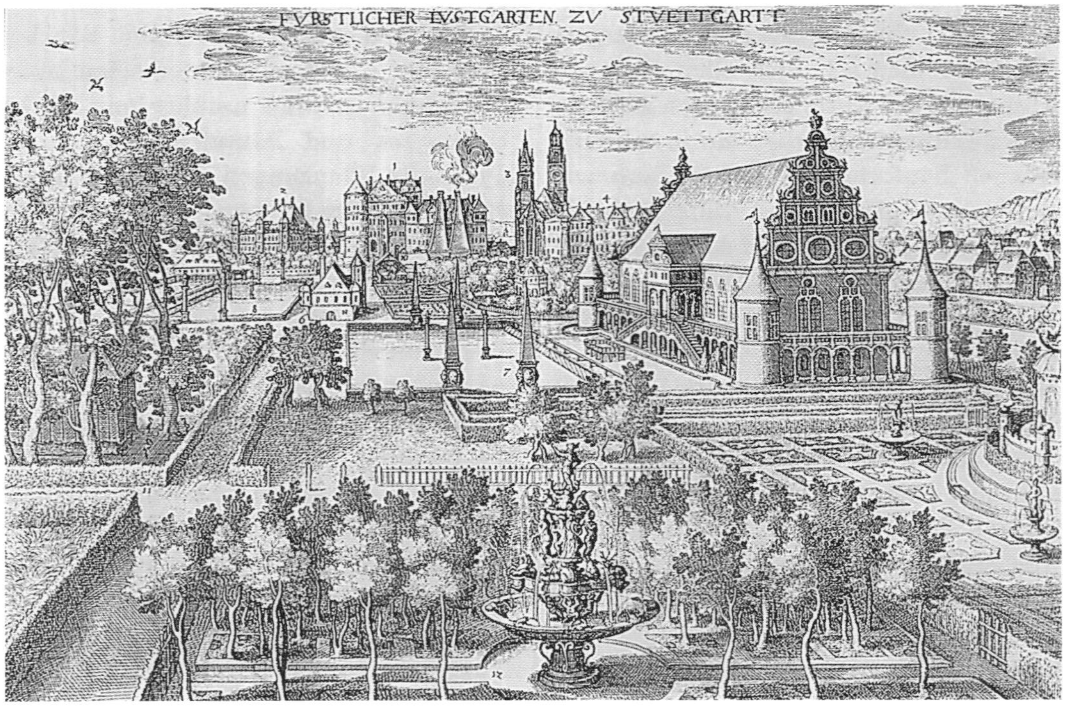

Stuttgart, princely pleasure garden
Engraving by Merian, 1616

ILLUSTRATION OPPOSITE
Leonberg, orange orchard
View of the castle from the garden site

be pointed out in passing that it was Antonia Visconti who, for the first time, brought Italian music for lute and viola da gamba to Stuttgart, and hence to the area north of the Alps. Almost a hundred years later, on September 12, 1491, Elisabeth, the wife of Count Ulrich the Much Loved, sold the garden in question for 260 florins to Barbara Gonzaga, the daughter of the Prince of Mantua and wife of the later Duke Eberhard the Bearded.

It may be assumed that this first Stuttgart pleasure garden was a typical Italian garden. A contemporary description, drawn up in connection with the sale, now in the main state archive in Stuttgart, conveys a very good impression of the "Italian style" of this site. At its center there was a spacious garden house. Here there were "...all manner of animals carved in stone and painted in their natural colors to make them the easier to identify." Visitors walked between rectangular beds enclosed with low hedges. On the lawns flowers bloomed and herbs grew, along with "strange plants," that is to say exotic plants, among them the Seville orange tree.

It was not until the end of the 16th century that a pictorial impression of this garden was preserved. This is an etching by Jonathan Sautter dating from 1592, probably the earliest illustration of the garden. This site, known in the 16th century as the "Duchess's Garden," had a pavilion at its center with a garden house to the left of it. The pavilion was a summerhouse built of wood, on pillars, an aviary which had been built in 1558. In the garden house, the so-called "Little Pleasure House," there were pictures of hunting scenes and various views of Stuttgart along with court festivities. The four flower and plant beds, divided geometrically around the central pavilion in a partly radial, partly irregular arrangement, are each enclosed by a hedge. Somewhat apart from them, and therefore not to be seen on the etching, is said to have been a maze and a pond enclosed by arcades.

The "New Pleasure Garden" to the northeast of the castle, where today the "Schloßplatz" and the upper castle garden are situated, was commissioned by Duke Christoph in 1550. It was not

Leonberg, orange orchard
View of the garden site from the castle

long before this garden came to be considered the most beautiful in Germany, not least by virtue of Georg Beer's Great Banqueting House. The well-known engraving by Matthäus Merian dating from 1616 conveys the best impression of the layout of this garden (illustration opposite, top). From the gallery of the Banqueting House there was a splendid view of the site. In the foreground the orange orchard with the fountain can be identified. This was laid out by Heinrich Schickhardt, the master builder at the court of Württemberg (who we have already encountered in Pratolino). Behind it is the new race track with the obelisks and higher up, in the direction of the Old Castle, as it is known today, the old race track, and a house where the prey for the falcon hunt was kept. Schickhardt produced an exact plan of this site. It is not dated but may be assumed to have been made in 1608–09.

The Leonberg Orange Orchard

At that time the court master builder was already occupied with laying out the Leonberg orange orchard commissioned by the widowed Duchess Sibylla of Württemberg, the one-time mistress of the Stuttgart pleasure gardens (illustration opposite, bottom and right). The garden was laid out parallel to the main castle building on an oblong terrace in the former moat. Schickhardt put little pavilions at the four corners. The two plant bed compartments were subdivided into four square beds each and separated by two fountain pools. The beds were designed to lie symmetrically along an axis in the Italian ornamental manner, and were dominated in some places by cruciform and angular shapes, in others triangles and circle segments were prominent.

This garden was re-created in an exemplary fashion in 1976–80, using the wealth of available historical documentation. So today we can have a precise idea of a German Renaissance garden in the Italian style.

Schickhardt had visited the Cortile de Belvedere in Rome and wanted to build a comparable arrangement of terraces in Leonberg by providing the casing wall with a double flight of steps and integrating a fountain grotto in three sections at that point. There is no evidence of decorative figuration, so one might assume that it was a natural layout in line with the ideas of Alberti, who also regarded grottoes to be "a piece of wild, rugged nature."

Schickhardt produced many design patterns for individual beds and parterre sections (illustration p. 132 bottom). In this he was guided by Serlio's designs; even so, there are conspicious differences. The Württemberg master builder had a more

Heidelberg, castle garden
This sculpture of Father Rhine is all that remains of the former *Hortus Palatinus*.

Leonberg, orange orchard
Heinrich Schickhardt's parterre design

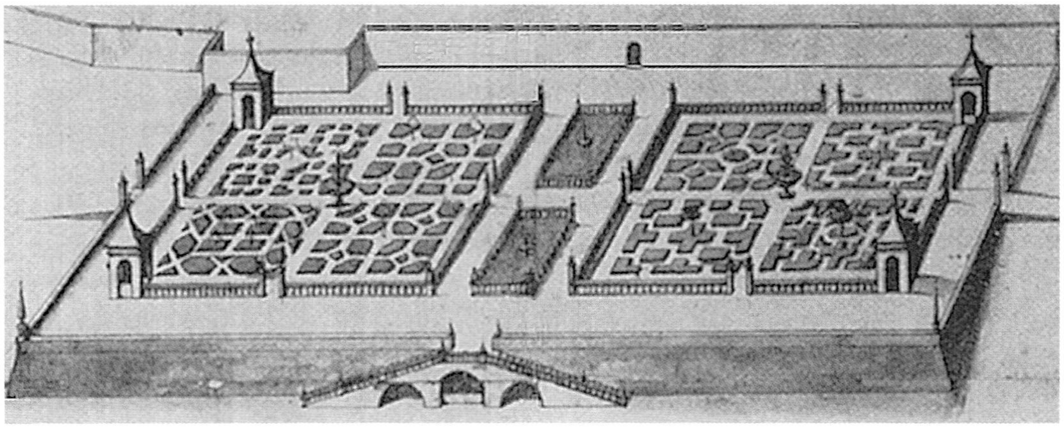

rigorous conception of geometric patterns, and gave greater profile to the bed sections, thereby giving the ornaments a clear, easily recognizable shape. Serlio's designs, in contrast, are marked by a strenuous smallness of scale. He shaped tiny rondels and piazzas looking like miniatures. His bed sections take on the shapes of gateways, angles, and segments that have moved far away from the basic geometric forms. Schickhardt, on the other hand, gave variety to his circles, rectangles, and triangles without losing sight of these basic forms. At the time, his geometric bed shapes acquired great importance in the southwest German area. They even rivaled the famous garden designs for the Heidelberg *Hortus Palatinus* by Salomon de Caus.

The Heidelberg *Hortus Palatinus*

The French engineer and garden designer Salomon de Caus who made lengthy study trips to Italy, was employed as an engineer at the court of Archduke Albert in Brussels in 1605, and went in 1610 to the English court, where he constructed water features, wrote a treatise on perspective, and designed the gardens of Somerset House and Greenwich along with Robert Cecil's garden in Hatfield. When Elizabeth, daughter of England's James I, married the Prince Elector of the Palatinate, Frederick V, in 1613, and thus went to Heidelberg, the engineer followed his noble lady to the Palatinate residence where he began to plan the huge garden layout. In 1620 de Caus published the lavishly illustrated treatise with the title *Hortus Palatinus*, in which he gave a vivid account of the parterre design and the motifs of the ornamental beds. De Caus was unable to complete the garden because unfortunate political developments summoned his master from Heidelberg to the court in Prague. There Frederick was elected King of Bohemia in 1619. The battle of the White Mountain, with its unhappy outcome for him, compelled Frederick, the "Winter King" to eke out the last years of his life in exile in the Low Countries.

De Caus's intensive garden studies in Italy had given him the necessary knowledge to have the comprehensive earthworks to the east of the castle precincts in Heidelberg carried out. In his treatise, which he dedicated to his patron Frederick, he described the transformation of the sloping terrain into a terraced garden. Some parts of the long since vanished Renaissance garden, individual sections of which were re-created in the 1970s, can still be visited. The terraces with their elegant bed patterns, a few remains of grottoes, and the Elizabeth Gateway built in 1615, leading to the section of garden to the south of the "Fat Tower," are worth seeing. The painting by Jacques Fouquières, a grandiose panorama of the garden, the castle, and the town of Heidelberg with the River Neckar and the distant Rhenish Plain, along with the engravings by de Caus bring the garden back to life in its earlier form (illustration opposite).

De Caus modified Serlio's parterre designs with great ingenuity, and in the knot compartments

Heidelberg, *Hortus Palatinus*
Oil painting *c.* 1620
Jacques Fouquières
Heidelberg, Kurpfälzisches Museum

with the intertwined ribbons he was surely also inspired by Colonna's *Hypnerotomachia*. The ribbons are formed of miniature hedges of thyme, majoram, rosemary, and lavender. On the right-hand side in the foreground of Fouquières's painting a maze can be discerned, bounded to the west by a orange grove. The Seville orange, a Mediterranean fruit, was protected by a wooden fence during the winter. Adjoining the maze to the north there is a sumptuous compartment with corner pavilions and plant beds decorated with knot ornaments. The beds surround a splendid floral rondel, which is divided up and planted in such a way that in the course of the year the processes of flowering and fading can be continuously observed, making it comparable to the hand of a clock, depending on the species of flower.

Regarding the construction and installation of the grottoes and water features, de Caus proved to be an outstanding engineer. On the upper part of the slope, at the great avenue, he cut a grotto hall into the mountain where he intended to install a water machine to operate an organ. He also had the idea of a satyr playing the pipes. Along with artificial waterfalls and fountains, he planned to install a heatable bath. Although there is no evidence, it is conceivable that, like Heinrich Schickhardt, Salomon de Caus had also studied the engineering of the waterworks in Pratolino for reference on subsequent projects. But because of the political reasons given above, these fascinating water features did not materialize.

In addition to the *Hortus Palatinus*, de Caus also wrote a treatise on hydraulic techniques. His work, *Les raisons des forces mouvantes*, was first published in 1615, and a second impression appeared in 1624. For a long time this work remained the basis for Baroque waterworks in Europe, underlining its author's importance.

At around the same time as de Caus was working in Heidelberg, Duke Heinrich Julius of Braunschweig-Wolfenbüttel had the Prince Braunschweig pleasure garden laid out at his water castle in Hesse, to the north of Halberstadt. The court gardener, Johann Royer, was engaged for the work; his detailed descriptions of the garden site still exist. In addition, the engraving by Matthäus Merian, probably made *c.* 1650, illustrates the layout (illustration below).

Starting at the water castle, the garden site, which is divided into an ornamental garden, an orchard, and a kitchen garden, is reached by several bridges. The ornamental garden is enclosed by an arcade, except for a short section where it is bounded by the moat. There an arch may be discerned, underneath which Royer arranged a water feature representing Diana, her escorts, and Actaeon. The garden architect did not have anything further to say regarding the water installations; it may be supposed that at the time he had not yet heard of the artistry of Salomon de Caus. The fountain drawn in by Merian resembles one of the basin fountains on a raised base that were customary at the time. But anyone walking up to the fountain needed to be careful, because it had one of the "water tricks" that were so popular at the time (as in Granada): a mechanism built into the steps activated jets intended to take the visitor by surprise.

The ornamental compartment comprises eleven beds with different ornamentation which – as far as can be seen – follow Serlio's models. The bed plants come as a surprise, with carnations, herbs, and bulbous plants. The individual beds are surrounded by low paling fences on which, among other things, roses, juniper, and red currants grow. The creepers have a playful effect, as Royer notes, as they are tied up to form imaginative figures. Outside the ornamental compartments, each with an obelisk in its central bed, "all manner of hedges and little trees are planted" – the latter in the quincunx arrangement. This garden has vanished, as have so many other great Renaissance sites in the immediate vicinity of towns where princes and dukes had their residences, or where there was a pleasance or a hunting lodge. Other Renaissance gardens were subsequently transformed into English landscape gardens. In fortunate cases, a few minor remains have survived, as in Heidelberg. The Leonberg orange garden, which can be seen today in its re-created Renaissance splendor, is one of the happy exceptions.

Gardens and castles have sometimes suffered a tragic fate. Schloß Neugebäude, formerly situated outside the gates of Vienna, was built by the Emperor Maximilian II from 1569 as a summer residence following the pattern of Italian suburban villas. In the 19th century the castle had to make way for a powder magazine to be built. Some architectural and decorative components such as

Leonberg, orange orchard
Detail of bed layout

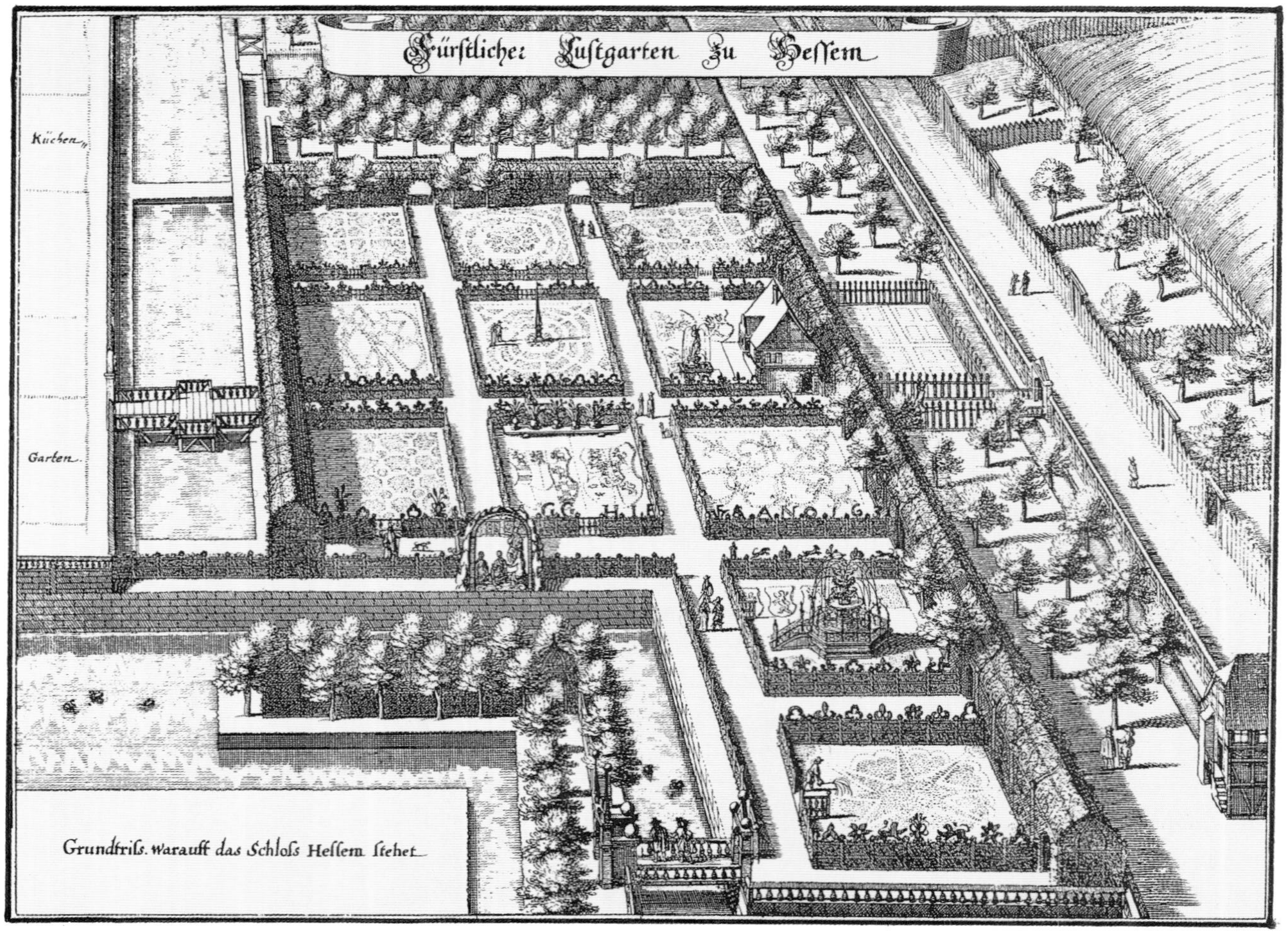

Braunschweig-Wolfenbüttel
Princely pleasure garden
Ground plan of the site, engraving by M. Merian, *c.* 1650

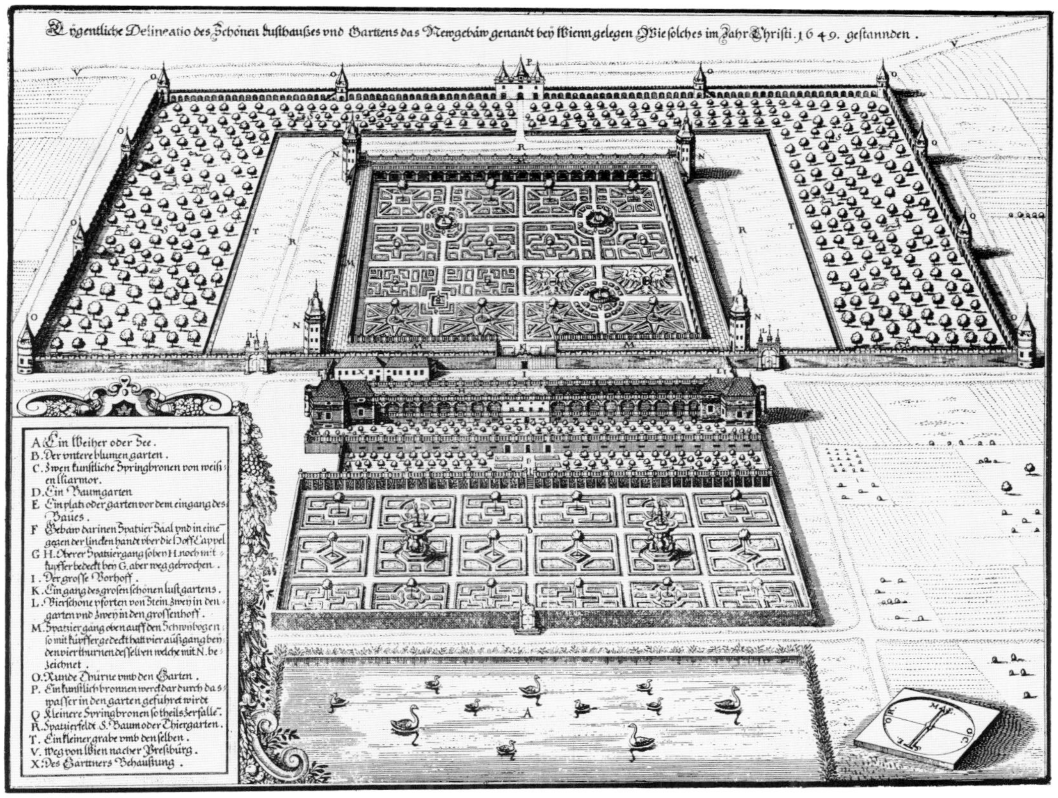

Vienna, Schloß Neugebäude and garden
Engraving by M. Merian, *c.* 1650

columns, capitals, pilaster decorations, and candelabra had already been made use of in Schönbrunn when the Glorietta and the Roman Ruins were designed.

The garden site, long since disappeared, must have been an impressive project. The emperor, so convinced of the merits of garden culture, had sent for graphic illustrations from Italy which gave him a picture of the great art of Mediterranean horticulture. According to one document, Cardinal Ippolito d'Este even sent him a plan of his own villa and garden.

After the emperor's death in 1576, his son Rudolf II set about constructing and completing the garden. There is a detailed description of the splendid site by Jacobus Bongarsius, which dates from 1585. It loosely agrees with the view shown in the Merian engraving dating from *c.* 1650 (illustration right).

The garden began to go to ruin soon after being completed. In a report dating from 1607 the site is described as "quite desperate." When Merian visited Neugebäude Castle and its garden, the individual design elements could still be clearly distinguished. The final decline set in during the second half of the 17th century.

The castle extends between the upper pleasure garden and the lower flower garden, its side wings lined by galleries with the central section. In front of it there are orchards laid out on two terraces. The castle is architecturally related to the pleasure garden, which is likewise surrounded by a gallery. The caps of the four high corner towers are said to have been covered with gilt copper. It was possible to stroll on the gallery roof, and contemplate the attractions of the garden, such as the parterre, which was divided into four plant bed compartments, each with a fountain at its center. The individual compartments in their turn were divided into quarters and each displayed different ornamentation, which included the double eagle of the Habsburgs.

The Turks must have been very impressed by the garden when they besieged Vienna for the second time in 1683, for the site was left intact by them after the Viennese had retreated from the suburbs before the advancing Ottoman army, to take refuge within the secure walls and fortifications of their city.

Compared with the sophisticated layout of Italian Renaissance gardens, the gardens north of the Alps give a somewhat forbidding impression. The basic concept of the medieval monastery garden incorporating a pleasure garden was retained to a considerable extent. Only the ornamentation of plant beds and the waterworks, that were installed on a modest scale, were taken over from the Italians and modified. In the Heidelberg *Hortus Palatinus* the concept of the architectural garden, with its use of terraces to create space, may be discerned, even if in a greatly reduced form. The Leonberg orange orchard – hardly more than a miniature terrace when compared with Italian examples – can also be regarded as an architecturally defined garden if the double flight of steps, the terrace wall, the balcony, and the simple castle premises are taken into account. This also applies, of course, to the hanging garden in Neufra, which is, however, to be considered an exotic, exceptional case.

Even though the Heidelberg *Hortus Palatinus* is considered the main example of the Renaissance garden in Germany, mention should be made again that, in addition to Salomon de Caus, there was yet another outstanding garden designer.

He was Heinrich Schickhardt, the master builder at the Württemberg court. He had already created the Renaissance garden genre in Stuttgart, with grottoes, fountains, water features, parterres, elegant ornamental beds, and the obligatory maze, along with boskets and fig sheds, before work in Heidelberg began.

Furthermore, Schickhardt turned his attention to the building of orangeries. At the duke's command he constructed a kind of building-block system, enabling buildings to be put up in winter and taken down again in summer. To achieve this, the buildings were mounted on rails on which they could be pulled to their appointed places.

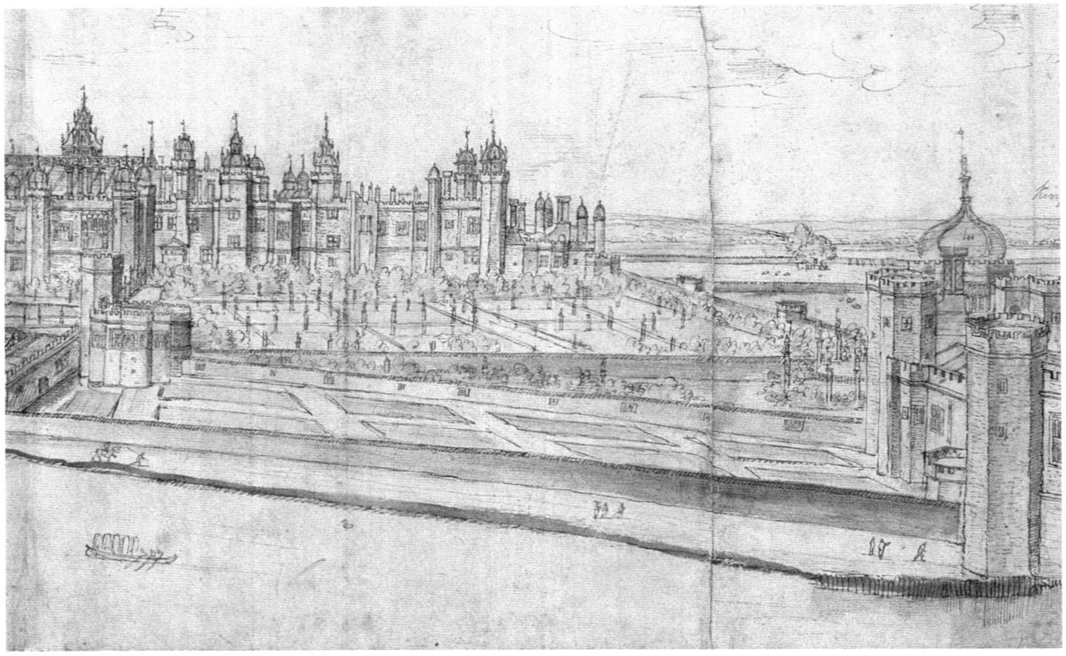

London, Hampton Court Palace
Privy Garden and Mount Garden of Henry VIII
Drawing by Wyngaerde, *c.* 1655

Renaissance Gardens in England

The history of the English garden can be traced back to the Romans. But until the specific form of the landscape garden emerges, it parallels, to a considerable extent, the development of garden design in other European countries.

The ideas were supplied by Italy and France (more precisely, the 15th-century Burgundian court), when it was a matter of transforming the medieval monastery garden, the *hortus conclusus* into a pleasure garden. The phase of the English Renaissance garden began with the early Tudor style. The first important gardens were created under Henry VIII, who saw himself as a direct cultural rival to Francis I: Hampton Court Palace (illustration above), Whitehall Palace, and Nonsuch Palace (illustration right, bottom).

At Hampton Court Palace the king had an artificial mountain (the Mount) built where he could look at the palace and the garden from a so-called gazebo (from the verb "to gaze"), that is a pavilion with a vista. Such gazebos or belvederes – in Spain they were called miradors – were popular in the Tudor period. An elegant brick gazebo has survived at Melford Hall in Suffolk. The hill at Stoneleigh in Warwickshire is likewise crowned with a gazebo, with a view of a most picturesque part of the Avon valley.

At Hampton Court Henry VIII – pragmatically and in the medieval garden tradition – also provided a kitchen garden and a splendid ornamental garden, where his daughter Queen Elizabeth I was said to have been particularly fond of spending time.

Such ornamental gardens were often knot gardens, which acquired prominence as a special feature of the English Renaissance garden. Inspired by Italian models, including Colonna's *Hypnerotomachia* and by French examples, English garden designers developed a knot style of their own, a style which was cultivated and refined down to the 17th century. The patterns in Thomas Hill's books, *The Profitable Art of Gardening* of 1568, and *The Gardener's Labyrinth* of 1577, are well known. As can be seen from a woodcut in the latter book of 1577, the parterre has a high fence in the style of a late medieval garden (illustration below, center).

This was also how the garden of a country house in Denbighshire (Wales) appeared. The garden itself is no longer in existence, but the design of the Renaissance layout can be clearly seen in a 17th-century painting. The garden areas, with portals, pavilions, and waterworks, are separated from one another by fences or high

Parterre of a small Renaissance garden
Woodcut from Thomas Hill's *The Gardener's Labyrinth*

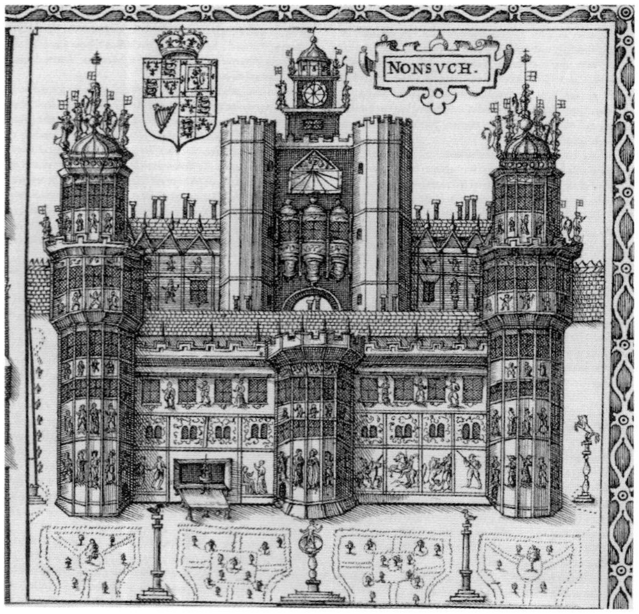

Nonsuch Palace, Privy Garden
Drawing by Hondius

walls. The main parterre consists of ornamental beds with their corners planted with thuja, a kind of cypress. A wall with a gateway leading to another terrace is flanked by two small corner towers with broach roofs. This section of the garden is reached via a curved flight of steps with a fountain at its center. This terrace is also linked by two steps to a lower compartment. There are orchards, vegetable gardens, and herb gardens throughout the entire layout.

The English Renaissance garden, unlike the French Renaissance garden, remained strikingly close to its Italian models with the conception of the garden as an architectural structure. It was not so much a question of a symmetrical relationship with the castle, palace, or country house, as of the garden's own architectural structure, comprising walls, portals, pavilions, and steps. This architectural structure was the basis of the terracing and the stately appearance of the garden site as a whole.

Another example of the architectural ambitions of English garden designers is the "sunken garden." This is a parterre on a lower level than the surrounding garden terraces, and hence is surrounded by embankments or casing walls.

This type, still very popular in English gardens, first appeared during the Renaissance period. The painting by an unknown master of the English school shows the sunken garden of Pierrepont House in Nottinghamshire (illustration below). A balustrade adorned with flower vases, interspersed on each side with flights of stairs, surrounds the rectangular garden area. There is a raised terrace in front of the country house. The parterre, with its symmetrical design and rich ornamentation, has an eye-catching effect on the guests at this grand mansion, as they stroll around the site. There was also

Pierrepont House, Nottingham
Oil on canvas, 92 x 122 cm
(*c.* 36 x 48 in.), 1708–13
Painter of the English school
Yale Center for British Art,
Paul Mellon Collection, USA

Packwood House, Warwickshire
16th-century gabled house fronted by a sunken garden

a particularly good view of the site from the courtyard terrace, as well as from the country house itself.

There are many more sunken gardens to be found in England and Scotland, and some of these do manage to emanate something approaching a "Renaissance atmosphere."

The sunken garden of Packwood House near Hockley Heath in Warwickshire is enclosed by brick walls with a planted pathway around the garden between them. At the sunken level there is the parterre with beds of bushes and a pool surrounded by a box hedge.

Packwood House

An important component of the aristocratic garden was the "mount," an artificial hill put up solely to provide a view. At Packwood House this mount has fortunately been preserved and can still be seen. A narrow path leads between the box hedges, twisting up the hill to the viewing platform.

In addition to the mount, topiary is one of the specialties of Packwood House (illustration opposite). Along with Levens Hall in Cumbria, Packwood is numbered among the famous 17th-century topiary gardens. The clipped yew trees and box bushes were not only popular in the gardens of stately homes, but were also to be found in smaller cottage gardens, and they can still be seen in many places throughout England, and perhaps most especially in the Cotswolds in Gloucestershire.

The closeness of the stately home garden to the simple cottage garden lies in the charming combination of flower beds, bushes, and vegetable gardens or orchards. Vegetable beds were laid out not only for economic, but also for aesthetic reasons. They add a subdued element to the colorful flower beds, so that the color spectrum of the entire garden has a balanced effect, without glaring contrasts.

ILLUSTRATION OPPOSITE
Packwood House, Warwickshire
Tall, shaped yew trees – the so-called "apostles" lead to another group of shaped trees, known as the "crowd."

Hatfield House, Hertfordshire
Plan of the Elizabethan garden, *c.* 1608

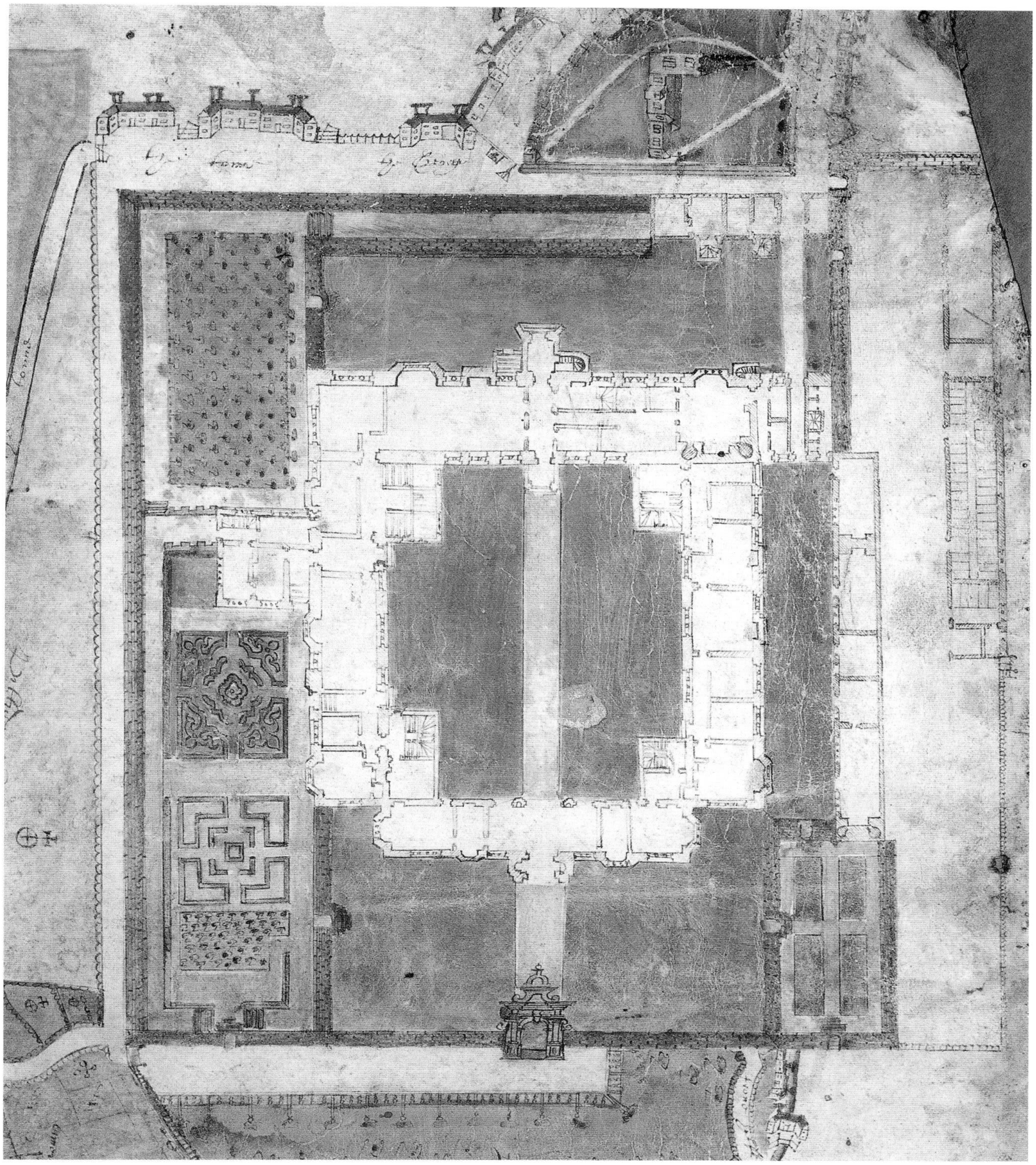

ILLUSTRATION OPPOSITE
Hatfield House, Hertfordshire
View of the facade of the Old Palace fronted by the formal part of the garden

Hatfield House, Hertfordshire
When the French engineer and garden designer Salomon de Caus was summoned to the English court in 1610 to construct waterworks, he found time to redesign Robert Cecil's garden at Hatfield House in Hertfordshire. He retained the terracing and the steps of his predecessor, Thomas Chaundler, but enlarged the fountain, and installed a cascade leading down to an artificial water garden. Planting was the responsibility of John Tradescant, who made many trips to Holland and France in order that orchards and continental flowers might take root in England. Many of his notes are kept in the Hatfield archives and in the Bodleian Library at Oxford. A work with the title *Tradescant's Orchard* contains sixty-five drawings of fruits which he grew at Hatfield. The garden has undergone many changes over the centuries, including the obligatory redesigning as a landscape garden. Much of the geometric garden structure has survived at Hatfield House, for example the plant bed compartments of the large terrace with their striking Renaissance patterning (illustration p. 142) and a maze situated to the east. Thus, the

traces of Salomon de Caus can be identified at Hatfield with relative precision. This should be of great value for an assessment of the *Hortus Palatinus* in Heidelberg, which has now unfortunately disappeared.

The beds laid out as links between the different areas of the stately home or between garden pavilions are a specific feature of de Caus' design work, which is also preserved in old views of the Heidelberg garden. Today the formal garden and the wooded parkland form a harmonious unity. Tree-lined avenues lead through the spacious park. In a small copse created only in the 19th century there are many rhododendrons and azaleas, so that the extensive park is rhythmically divided by the different plants in its various sections.

Hatfield House is one of the rare examples of traditional conceptions of the English garden, the formal and the romantic conception, unfolding in a site that is full of contrasts. Here it becomes clear that the Baroque garden was not necessarily doomed to fall victim to the landscape conception. Again and again there were those among the English landed aristocracy who appreciated the formal garden, while at the same time looking for ways to incorporate the new ideas of the landscape garden. The fact that even modern aspects of garden design have not proved in any way harmful to the basic overall structure may be regarded as a further sign of the strength of tradition where English gardening is concerned.

It was undoubtedly Salomon de Caus, the creator of the Heidelberg *Hortus Palatinus* who introduced the Italian architectural garden to England. From his trip to Italy, he brought back inspiration and concrete plans to the English court when he was employed by Anne of Denmark and Henry, Prince of Wales, to develop their gardens. Those at Somerset House and Greenwich Palace were created in 1609, and de Caus completed the Richmond Palace gardens three years later. When he left England in 1613 to start work on his masterpiece in Heidelberg, his son Isaac took over subsequent commissions. In the years until he died,

Hatfield House, Hertfordshire
Parterre layout of the sunken garden on the south side of the new house

in 1648, Isaac designed many gardens and grottoes, including the layout at Wilton House in Wiltshire for the 4th Earl of Pembroke. Perhaps the ancient cedars which are still there date back to Isaac's work on the garden. The garden has been altered several times in each century, most recently in 1971 by David Vicary.

The culture of the English Renaissance garden comes to an end with the work of Inigo Jones, who incidentally also worked on Wilton House alongside Isaac de Caus and André Mollet, the son of Claude Mollet, the first famous royal gardener in France, already encountered at Anet.

André Mollet, the author of the popular work *Le Jardin de Plaisir*, 1651, did a great deal of work in England. His theoretical and practical ideas appealed to the Court in London and to Inigo Jones. The latter had returned from his second extended study trip to Italy in 1614, and had begun to implement the architectural ideas of Andrea Palladio in England. What was later called Palladianism set its stamp on English architecture until 1800.

Inigo Jones designed garden gateways and parterres, and worked a great deal with the Frenchman, for example on St. James's Park (*c.* 1630) and Wimbledon (*c.* 1640). Then Mollet returned home to France where he lived in his house near the Tuileries as *premier jardinier du roi* under Louis XIV.

In 1660, five years before his death, he was again summoned to England. Charles II wanted a new garden design for St. James's Palace. Mollet designed a *patte d'oie*, a "goose-foot" layout. From a rondel three avenues radiated in different directions, and were intersected by two semicircular rows of acacias. The remaining areas were ornamented with box. This pattern was taken up a short time later in Baroque garden architecture, not only in England but especially in France. Mollet held the office of gardener-in-chief in London until his death.

With their designs and theoretical writings the Mollets threw the doors to the Baroque garden wide open. Many aspects of the Baroque garden are already to be found in Claude Mollet's *Théâtre des plans et jardinages*, which was published posthumously, in 1652. The first theoretical and practical basis was set out by his son André Mollet in his above-mentioned book, *Le jardin de plaisir* of 1651. In it, the principles of the classic French garden are expounded. André and his brothers Pierre and Claude II all worked at the Tuileries in Paris.

The last-named created the *parterre de broderie* in Versailles *c.* 1630. While Renaissance gardens inspired by Italian and French models were being laid out in England and Germany, and in individual cases even in Scandinavia, in France itself the first Baroque garden complexes were being created. The transition from the French Renaissance garden to the Baroque garden was a fluid process. At first there was a lack of clarity with regard to the axial relationship of castle and garden, and this subsequently led to confusion in the matter of perspective.

Nevertheless, the dominance of the French Baroque garden could be felt in Europe as early as the 17th century. But what form did the transition from the one era to the next take in the other countries of Europe? The answer is awaited with particular eagerness in the case of Italy.

Hatfield House, Hertfordshire
Fountain in the privy garden

Baroque Gardens in Italy

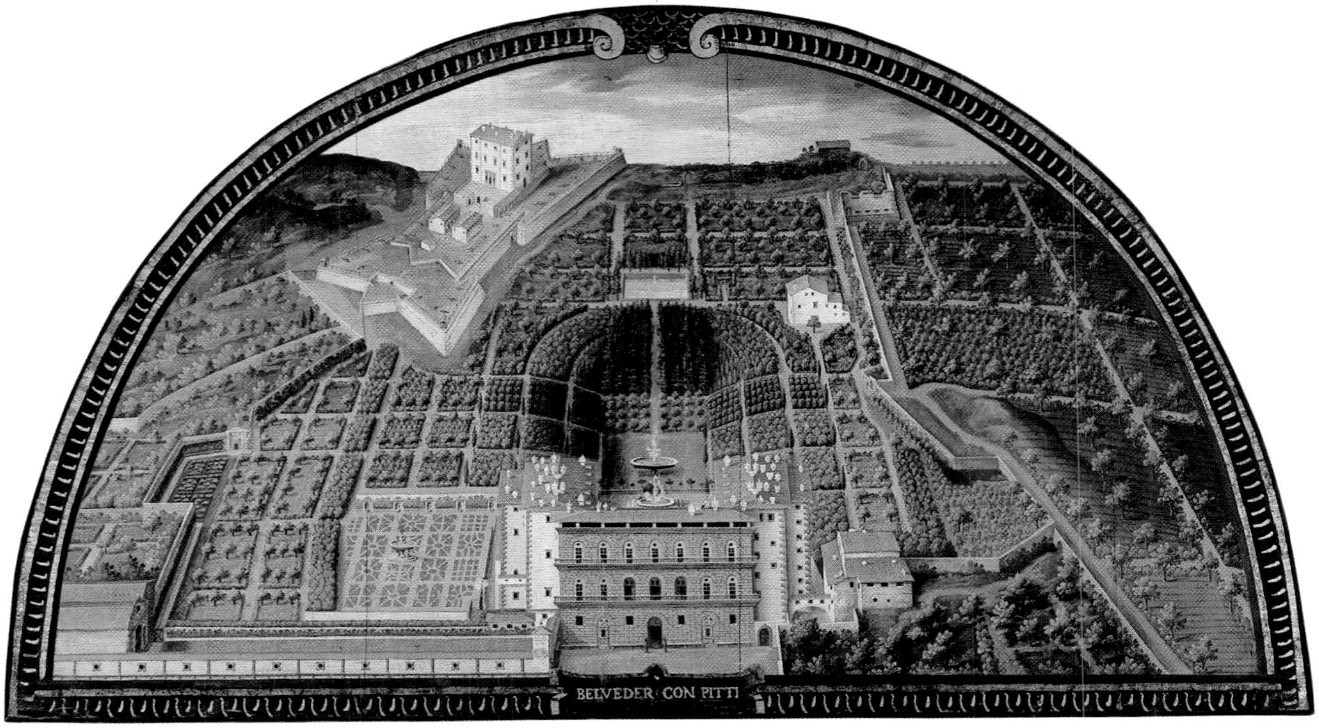

ILLUSTRATIONS OPPOSITE
Florence, Boboli Garden
Ocean Fountain on the Isolotto (left)
Neptune Fountain (top right)
Sculpture on the Isolotto (bottom right)

Florence, Boboli Garden
(Belvedere and Palazzo Pitti)
Painting by Giusto Utens, *c.* 1600
Florence, Museo Topografico
"Firenze com'era"

In Italy too, the transition from the Renaissance to the Baroque garden cannot be precisely determined. Many typical features of the Renaissance garden, for example the water features which took on the quality of theatrical spectacles, the spacious terraces integrated into the landscape, or the art of symmetrical plant bed ornamentation, were taken over in the Baroque garden, their expressive quality heightened and finally, in the French garden, enlarged on a monumental scale.

The Boboli Garden in Florence

Different assessments of the Boboli Garden in Florence are to be found in the literature. It is usually presented as a Baroque garden although work on it, commissioned by Eleonora of Toledo, the wife of Cosimo I de' Medici, had begun as early as 1549. After the death of the garden architect Niccolò Tribolo in 1550 his work was continued by Bartolomeo Ammannati. Thus the basic concept was still that of a Renaissance garden. Tribolo made use of the little valley behind the Palazzo Pitti, giving it the shape of an amphitheater without defining it as an architectural feature. From the central axis of the palace the main alley led to the valley, cut it into two equal parts, and ended at a water basin at the top. This axis determined the symmetrical structure, that is to say the system of pathways, illustrated in the lunette fresco by Giusto Utens (illustration above).

The site changed its shape over the years, and was gradually transformed into a Baroque garden. The amphitheater formed by planted slopes was stripped of its covering of plants and architecturally defined. The main axis lost its importance when a new garden site, dominated by the Piazzale Isolotto, was created to the west. Above the amphitheater the new main axis now runs almost parallel to the palace facade, to the so-called Isolotto, designed by Alfonso Parigi in 1618 (illustrations opposite, bottom left and right). Parigi designed an oval pool with an artificial island. On this island stands the Ocean Fountain of Giovanni da Bologna.

The transformation into a Baroque garden took place when the site was extended and its strict symmetry abandoned as a consequence of its new dimensions. "Optical terracing," the creation of far-reaching optical axes, became a new element to be experienced, and an aesthetic factor to be taken into account when the Boboli Garden was reassessed and rearranged.

Florence, Boboli Garden
One of the numerous sculptures (groups) along the alleys

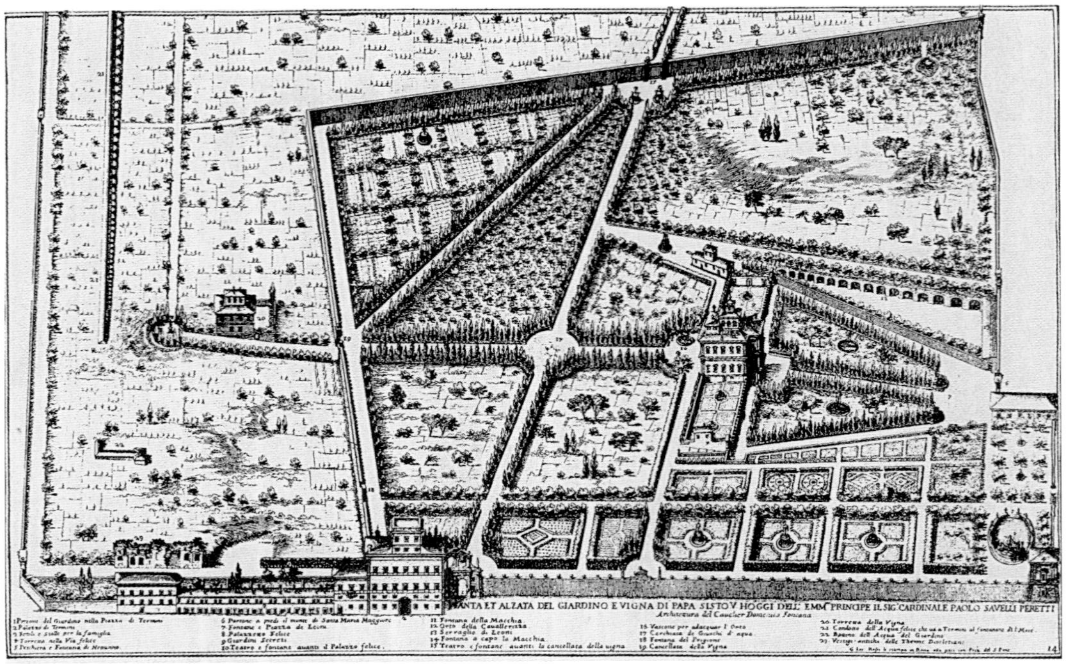

Rome, Villa Montalto
Engraving from G.B. Falda, *Li Giardini di Roma*, Rome, 1683

Villa Montalto in Rome

At this stage of development there was mutual influence between garden designers and town planners. There was a very special example of this in Rome. When, in 1585, Pope Sixtus V first announced his idea of bestowing a new system of main axes on the Holy City, and commissioned the master builder Domenico Fontana to implement the idea, he had already, when he was a cardinal, had the garden of the Villa Montalto laid out on the Esquilin. The overall plan of this garden (illustration above) is amazingly similar to the concept of the system of alleys which was intended to link the seven most important churches in Rome with one another. In accordance with the Pope's wishes, Fontana planned to run a main axis from one end of the city to the other, from the Piazza del Popolo to the Church of Santa Croce in Gerusalemme. At the center was the Pope's favorite church, Santa Maria Maggiore. The alleys were to radiate outward from both the Piazza del Popolo and Santa Maria Maggiore in order to open up the other districts of the city with their piazzas and churches. And this is the arrangement shown in the plan of the Villa Montalto. Behind the main entrance gateway there are three alleys radiating outward, similarly to the Piazza del Popolo. The central alley led to the casino. On the garden side of the building a semicircular area with a water basin was laid out. From there, an alley of cypresses led through the garden grounds, crossed half way by another alley. Where the alley met the pathway leading alongside the garden wall, there was a fountain with another alley leading to it at an angle. In this garden, for the first time, it was not so much the architectural design or the regular division of the plant beds into squares that had a dominant role, as the importance of the visual axis and the point of view – as was also the case in the Pope's ideas regarding town planning. The garden of the Villa Montalto has long since disappeared; today the main railway station (Stazione Termini) stands on its site. But it can be regarded as a kind of model of the Pope's conception of the reshaping of Rome, and thus of the layout of the capital city of the world. In order to view this model of the city, one should proceed to the Pincio, from which there is one of the most beautiful views in Rome, above the Piazza del Popolo. One can today still see Pope Sixtus V's idea of the city. The streets radiating outward in the direction of the Tiber, the Capitol, and the Quirinal, and via St Trinita dei Monti to St Maria Maggiore on the Esquilin can be clearly seen.

Villa Borghese in Rome

The creator of the park of the Villa Borghese, Cardinal Scipione Caffarelli Borghese, a nephew of Pope Paul V, evidently took as his model the system of alleys at the Villa Montalto when, between 1613 and 1616, he had a park and a casino laid out in his family vineyards outside the Porta Pinciana (illustrations below, and up to p. 149). From the main portal, a wide alley led not to the casino (as one might expect), but straight to the large rock grotto fountain located in front of the garden wall. The old garden wall was removed when the garden was developed into an English landscape garden, and today the Fontana dei Cavalli Marini (the Fountain of the Sea Horses) stands on this spot. It was created in 1770 by the German painter and

Rome, Villa Borghese
Detail view of the parterre with numerous sculptures lining the pathway

garden architect Christoph Unterberger (illustration p. 148, bottom left). About half way along, at a large rondel, the alley met a lateral axis leading to the facade of the casino. Further axes ran parallel to these two, likewise creating vistas of fountains and pavilions. Thus the casino clearly had a subordinate role, attention being directed principally to the system of visual axes within the layout of the garden. Pavilions, fountains, aviaries, and, finally, the casino, were regarded as elements of equal status within the experience provided by the garden. The park was dominated by the boskets, which were enclosed by clipped hedges. Pines, cypresses, myrtle, and laurel trees were planted.

The casino, the work of the Flemish Vasanzio Fiamingo, was built in 1613–15 (illustration above). The elevations are similar to that of the neighboring Villa Medici. Two projections at the sides emphasize the facade that is set back, with a double flight of steps leading to the portal. From the rear side of the villa two towers rise up above the building, on the axis of the side wings. Ornamental gardens were laid out behind the casino, and, to the side of them, the *giardini segreti* for oranges, herbs, and rare plants. The casino was planned for festivities and ceremonies and as an art gallery, rather than as a building to live in. The spacious area in front of it provided guests at the festivities with a ceremonious driveway for their coaches. Extensive parts of the site were made into an animal park, with cages for wild and exotic animals, ponds with fish, and fenced areas for poultry.

This lavish park, with its designed forest areas, rock grottoes, and pavilions, situated directly outside the city, required a huge amount of water. The Villa Borghese would scarcely have come into being had it not been for the grandiose achievement of Pope Paul V, the uncle of the Borghese cardinal, who gave Rome its largest aqueduct, the Acqua Paola. Giovanni Fontana took charge of the construction of the aqueduct, while Flaminio Ponzo designed the sumptuous display wall on the Gianicolo (illustration bottom right). The exceptionally sumptuous Early Baroque display facade

Rome, Villa Borghese
Main facade of the villa with double flight of steps

Rome, Villa Borghese
Two sphynxes at the edge of the parterre

of the fountain resembles the facade of a palace with gateways in the manner of triumphal arches. It underlines the importance of water for Rome and at the same time the ambition of the popes to have the splashing, gushing sound of water audible throughout their city, knowing full well that Rome itself had no natural springs at its disposal. In the 17th century Rome had the reputation of being the city with the greatest abundance of water anywhere in the world, and many a traveler was amazed by the way this vital element was squandered, while at the same time admiring, on the piazzas and in the gardens, the fascinating spectacle provided by the fountains with their festoons of water, their jets, and cascades.

But this does not mean that the Roman popes were also the inventors and engineers of the aqueducts. The ancient emperors had already had fresh drinking water brought from the lakes of the Alban mountains, or from the Lago di Bracchiano, by means of costly aqueducts. The water converged in the city in a "Nympheum," a monumental well-house. The Acqua Vergine, the classical Aqua Virgo of Agrippa, appears today in Baroque costume as the famous Trevi Fountain. Today the Aqua Marcia, restored by Sixtus V, flows out of the Acqua Felice Fountain on the Piazza S. Bernado. But the Acqua Paola on the Gianicolo was thought to be the most plentiful source of water. From the triple triumphal arch masses of water came gushing forth, in the words of a contemporary description.

The Fountain Palace of Acqua Paola was completed in 1612, a year before work began on the garden on the Pincio. Boskets and ornamental gardens could now thrive without impediment. The Villa Borghese was never actually private land without public access. The cardinal was generous enough to allow anybody free entry to his territory. There is an inscription bearing witness to this spiritual dignitary's noble-minded attitude:

"Whoever you are, be a free man, do not fear the shackles of the law here! Go wherever you wish, pluck whatever you wish, depart whenever you wish. Everything here is at the disposal of the stranger, more even than of the owner. In this golden age with its promise of general security, the master of the house does not wish to lay down iron laws. Let decency and free will make the laws for the guest. But let anyone who maliciously and intentionally violates the golden rule of civilized behaviour, fear that the angry watchman will burn before him the sacred emblems of hospitality."

In the 18th century the old park, many parts of which had already gone to ruin, was acquired by Marc Antonio Borghese. He commissioned the German painter and architect Christoph Unterberger, who had created the above-mentioned Fontana dei Cavalli Marini, to redesign the park as an English landscape garden. Thus today one walks through a park which has little left in common with Cardinal Borghese's Baroque site. But the Classicist monuments, the temple of Aeskulapius dating from 1787 (illustration opposite), the Piazza di Siena, the Casino dell'Orologio, built by Domenico Fagiuli in 1791, and the above-mentioned Fountain of the Sea Horses are well worth seeing. A word about the casino, which

Rome, Villa Borghese
Fountain of the Sea Horses

Rome, Acqua Paola
Fountain Palace on the Gianicolo of 1610–14

Rome, Villa Borghese
Monopteros (temple of Aeskulapius) in an alley in the garden area of the villa

today enjoys a worldwide reputation as one of the most splendid private galleries. Bernini's *Apollo and Daphne* is certainly one of its most famous works. But the *pièce de résistance* of the collection used to be the *Farnese Hercules*, which was still there for Johann Wolfgang von Goethe to admire when he stayed in Rome in 1787. But he lamented not only the imminent loss of the *Hercules*, but also of much more: "At present Prince Borghese is bringing himself to make a gift of these precious remains to the King of Naples." He was referring to the ancient legs of Hercules, which had been found on Farnese territory, and were being replaced at the time by replicas. "If only," said the poet, who was so enthusiastic about classical antiquity, "at least the ancient fragments had remained in Rome..."

A park with a layout that was in many respects comparable to the Villa Borghese was created by Ludovico Ludovisi, the nephew of Pope Gregory XV, shortly after the completion of the Villa Borghese. The gardens were situated where today the Via Veneto curves elegantly up to the Pincio and the lavish Palazzo Margherita, built at the end of the 19th century, stands. Here, as at the neighboring Villa Borghese, there were bosket compartments enclosed by clipped hedges. The site of the villa slopes very steeply, so that a terrace had to be built in front of the building. A large area with a fountain, flanked by an ornamental garden, provided a driveway for guests at festivities. Today nothing remains of the park except for a small piece of garden with very old trees, which may possibly date back to the time of Ludovisi. The Casino dell'Aurora with Guercino's ceiling painting *Triumph of Aurora* in the entrance hall of 1621, also dates from this period and is still to be found in its old place. If one walks from the Palazzo Margherita to the casino, which is situated between the Via Ludovisi and the Via Lombardi, one is walking through the former garden site of the Villa Ludovisi.

Rome, Villa Doria Pamphili
Villa with terrace fronted by oblong parterre site

ILLUSTRATIONS OPPOSITE
Rome, Villa Doria Pamphili
Fountains in the garden (top)

The amphitheater in the garden of the Villa Pamphili according to a drawing by Perelle, 1685 (bottom)

Villa Doria Pamphili in Rome

In the endless series of nepotistic projects by ambitious popes to build spacious parks with casinos and villas above the rooftops of Rome, the Villa Pamphili on the Gianicolo outside the Porta S. Pancrazio occupies a special position (illustrations above and opposite). In 1644 Prince Camillo Pamphili, a nephew of Pope Innocent X, commissioned Alessandro Algardi to plan and construct a large park measuring 9 sq km (*c.* $3^1/_2$ sq. miles) and an aristocratic villa. This, the largest park site in Rome, which must surely have been laid out to rival the Borghese park, was to share the fate of the other Roman gardens presented here. The entire site was transformed into an English landscape garden *c.* 1850. Two engravings by Simon Felice show the Baroque garden and the villa. Similar to the Villa Borghese, the house with the living quarters is not situated at the point of intersection of the two axes, but somewhat to the side, inside the park, which is dominated by boskets. After passing through the entrance gateway one comes to a small area from which two alleys start, at a right angle to each other. One of them leads, as at the Villa Borghese, to a fountain, behind which the cupola of St. Peter's towers up in the distance – a spectacular view. Following this alley one goes past the villa, possibly without having seen the building. But only a few steps away from the fountain a garden site comes into view with a broad main axis interspersed with rondels and larger areas, leading to the richly ornamented *parterre de broderie* and the garden facade of the villa (illustration above).

The parterre, which is cut into the hill on its short sides, is surrounded by a wall adorned with recesses containing sculptures and a balustrade decorated with flowers. One might almost take this to be a *giardino segreto*, but its location indicates otherwise. The area with a fountain immediately in front of the central projection of the villa, and the open stairs adjoining the side wings indicate that it was a place for festivities. The guests must have relished descending the steps into the adjoining ornamental garden, and making their way to the theater along the main axis. Adjoining the ornamental garden to the north is an area that was probably used as a playground. A wide alley leads through the boskets to a rondel with a fountain (illustration right). From there one comes to a semicircular area with a little summerhouse, the Casino della famiglia, which in turn adjoins a *giardino segreto*. The casino was destroyed in 1849 when Garibaldi defended the Republic of Rome against the intervention of French and Bourbon troops. Ten years later the architect Busiri Vici erected a triumphal arch at this point, which today serves as the entrance to the park.

Villas in Frascati

Frascati, the ancient Tusculum, was highly regarded as a summer residence even by aristocratic ancient Romans. Cicero, Lucullus, and Caesar kept country seats there, with extended garden layouts. The town was destroyed in the Middle Ages. Its inhabitants were driven out, and later founded the town of Frascati somewhat below the ruins. The luxurious lifestyle of the Roman nobility was revived under Cardinal Alessandro Ruffino when, in 1548, he decided to have a villa built. Other cardinals followed his example, with the result that in the course of the 16th and 17th centuries more than ten villas were built on the picturesque northern slopes of the Alban Mountains.

There were two stages in this process. The most important sites were created during the first stage, 1548–1607, while during the second stage, 1600–50, many owners had their country seats enlarged. Many sites went to ruin in the 19th century. Some of them were restored or re-created in the 20th century. Rows of villas can be seen in a bird's-eye view dating from 1620 (illustration pp. 152–153, top).

The Villa Falconieri began as the property of Cardinal Alessandro Ruffino, who had the casino built on the site of an ancient villa close to the little church of St. Maddalena. About a hundred years later the site was acquired by the Falconieri family, who had the casino enlarged to create a stately villa with four corner towers. The work was taken on by Francesco Borromini, and proved to be a lengthy business. This applied to both the interior furnishing and decoration of the villa and the terracing of the garden, where planting was not completed until 1729. The relationship of the villa to the garden appears distorted and complicated. This is due on the one hand to the terrain and on the other to the conception of the villa, whose shorter northern side faces Rome, while the valley

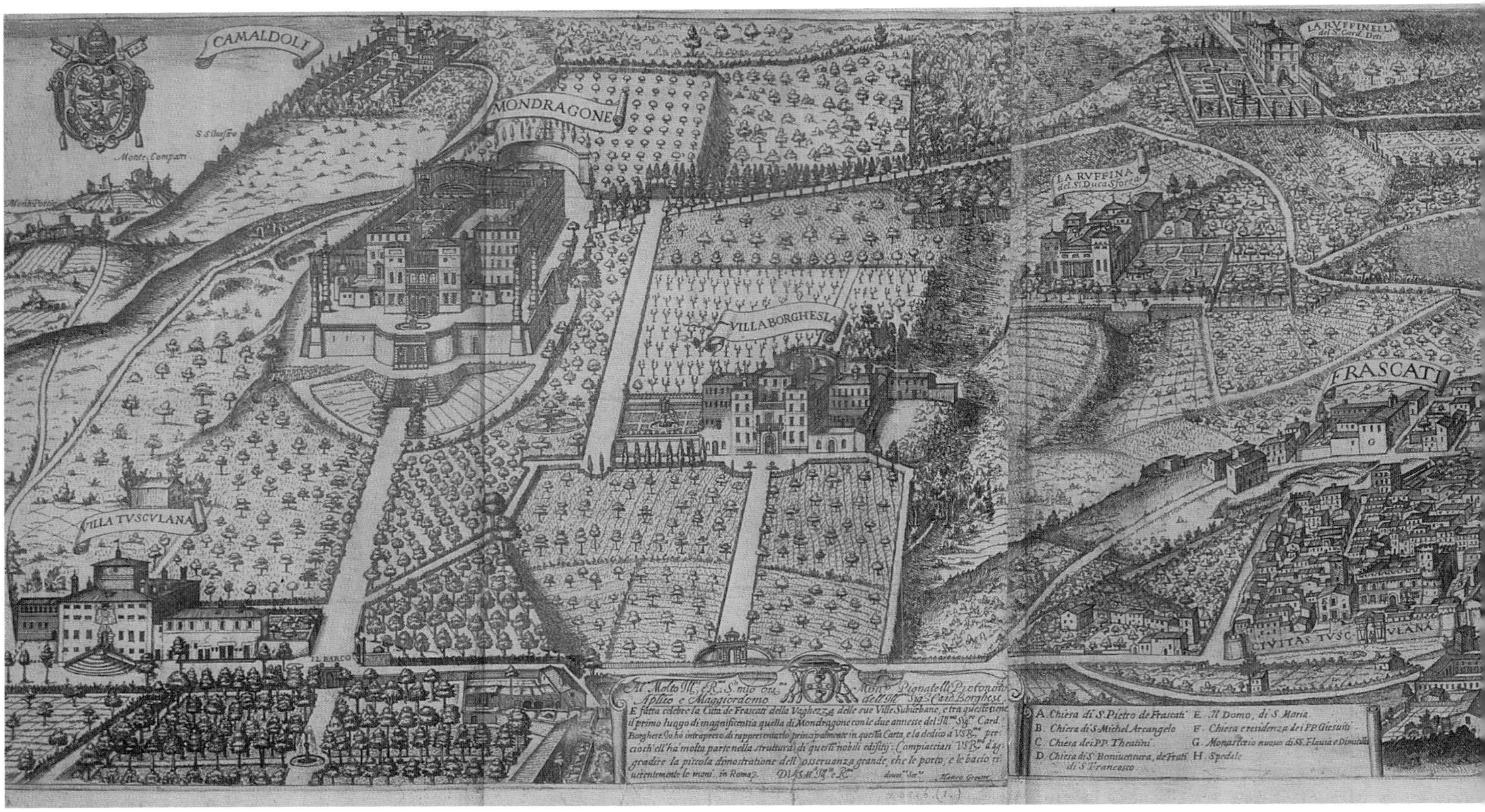

Frascati, town with villas close by
Bird's-eye view by Matthias Greuter, 1620

Pines and cypresses have always been the trees most frequently encountered in Mediterranean gardens, as can also be seen in the old view of Frascati above. Where it is a matter of vertical lines being incorporated in the design, cypresses are especially suitable because of their tall, slender form. Sometimes entrance gateways are flanked by them like doorkeepers, or else they form an eye-catching framework for a facade, or a line of sight. The ones shown here, however, at Blenheim Palace in England, are perhaps only intended to add to the variety of trees to be found there.

frontage faces east, but the garden extends westwards. The garden terraces have been reconstructed, so that today the Baroque layout can be easily imagined. Visitors will find the Baroque Falcon Gateway, dating from 1729, on the road leading up from Frascati to ancient Tusculum, and which gives access to the site. In front of the garden facade is a flower parterre. The Lion Gate, probably built by Borromini, leads to a double ramp and thence to a small lake surrounded by cypresses.

Opposite the Villa Falconieri on the northwestern slope is the former property of Cardinal Mark Sittich of Hohenems. He gave his villa the name of Mondragone, Mount Dragon, in honor of Pope Gregory XIII, whose coat-of-arms featured a dragon. The building, which the Cardinal used as a casino, was built by the architect Martino Lunghi the Elder between 1573 and 1575. Two years later work began on the Palazzo della Ritirata, a building of great length.

In 1613 the property passed to Cardinal Scipione Caffarelli Borghese, who in the same year also acquired the site of the Villa Montalto in Rome. He had an extra wing added linking the casino with the palazzo. Famous architects such as Carlo Maderna, Girolamo Rainaldi, and Giovanni

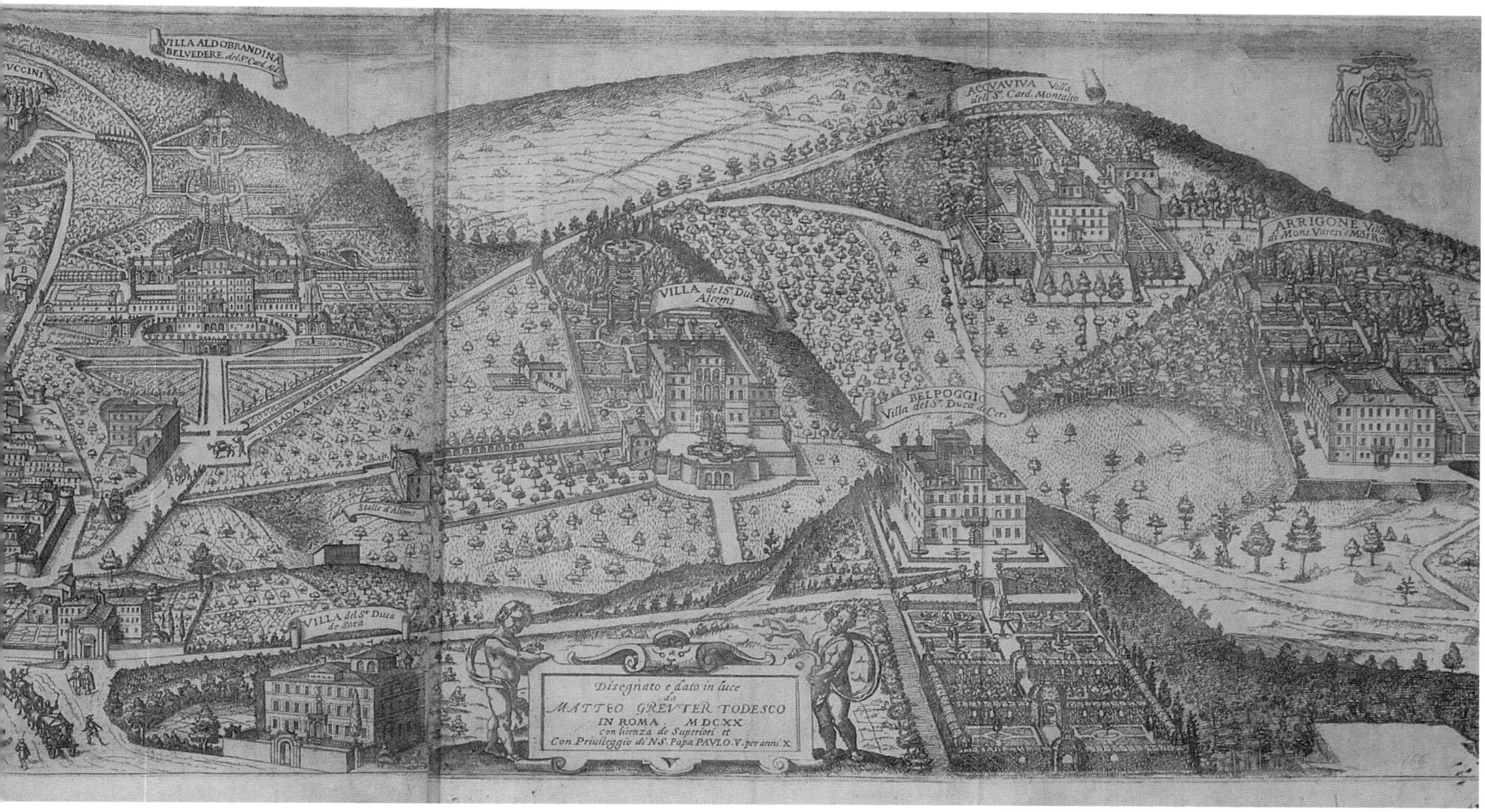

Fontana were employed in his service and gave the complex of buildings its final appearance.

To the east of the large supporting wall which, along with the Palazzo della Ritirata and the linking wing, formed the boundary of the great casino with the parterre, Giovanni Fontana constructed a "water theater," which at the time was one of the most famous of its kind; today only the large exedra and the double flight of steps remain. The plant bed compartments enclosed by box hedges and the fountains installed there no longer exist.

The Villa Grazioli, as it later came to be called, built by Cardinal Aquaviva *c.* 1590, was acquired by Cardinal Paretti di Montalto in 1616. He had the casino and the garden redesigned. Little remains of the layout today, from which one might infer that it was a Baroque design. However the villa, named after its present-day owners, the Grazioli family, does contain unique frescoes by Domenichino, Annibale Caracci, and the Zuccari school, making a visit worthwhile. A fresco in the Stanza di Eliseo gives an interesting view of the casino and the garden parterre. This fresco was probably the work of a pupil of Caracci's at the beginning of the 17th century. The fresco shows the following: two side wings projecting a long way out surround the central area, which is topped by a tower, forming a courtyard from which the garden stretches out in an uphill direction. In front of the ground floor of the main area there is a loggia with a terrace in front of it, on which people can be discerned. There are two fountains in front of the side wings. Deciduous trees and pines are distributed over the site, which shows no sign of having been professionally designed, but rather creates the impression of an open landscape, an impression reinforced by the people present. Two women are squatting in front of a white cloth with a jug and two loaves of bread, while another woman, holding a child by the hand and carrying an amphora on her head, approaches the building. A man carrying a heavy sack is walking up to a donkey which is tethered to the trunk of a pine tree. According to various 17th-century engravings, parterres with ornamented bed compartments and fountains were laid out to the side of the villa and toward the valley. It is therefore quite conceivable that little or no design work went into the rear part. On the other hand, one should take into account the standard subject-matter of painting at the time, which was frequently centered on pastoral themes. Be that as it may, there is a pre-echo here of the landscape garden.

Frascati, Villa Aldobrandini
Main facade of the villa and large forecourt with access ramp
Engraving by Specchi

Villa Aldobrandini in Frascati

One of the most famous Frascati villas is that of Pietro Aldobrandini, a nephew of Pope Clement VIII. This country mansion with its unusual architectural structure was created by Giacomo della Porta from 1598. After Porta's death, Carlo Maderna was commissioned to continue the work, which was completed by 1604. The basic concept, or dominant design feature, of the facade is a monumental broken pediment with a tympanum crowning the raised central part of the building to complete the roof (illustration left). Above the lower side wings the trimmed corner shapes of a triangular pediment rise to the height of the roof ridge. The oblique line leads the eye to the beginning of the roof or pediment. These sophisticated architectural games, which include the alternation of square and oblong windows along with the divided portal pilaster, are typical features of a distinctive variant of Mannerism.

The striking building is enthroned on a huge terrace base approached by curved double ramps (illustration left). On the garden side, in contrast, the terrain rises steeply. As a supporting wall, an elegant exedra structure, the famous water theater, is let into the hillside, to great effect (illustrations pp. 156–157). The plans for this site go back to Giacomo della Porta, and were executed by Carlo Maderna. Five round-arched recesses framed by pillars are let into the large semicircle. In accordance with the structural concept of a triumphal arch, there are rectangular recesses in the sections of wall between the pilasters, above which framed relief areas are to be seen. Above these, in the arch area, there are rotundas with busts which imitate the classical style. In the recesses there are mythological figures, including a Polyphemus playing the pan-pipes (illustration p. 157). At the center, Atlas rears up carrying the

Frascati, Villa Aldobrandini
Area between the villa and the water theater on the garden side

globe on his shoulders. He receives water from the cascade above the exedra, and directs it into the pool in front of him. To the side there are adjoining wings with the garden salon as well as the chapel of St. Sebastian.

Above the water theater comes the magnificent park, dominated by the cascade. Its starting point is framed by two pillars. These emit jets of water directed downward via convoluted festoons. There is a cunning relationship between these pillars of Hercules and the palace. If one stands in the reception hall of the projecting central section directly in front of the gateway arch, and looks up past the courtyard and the exedra, then the pillars of the arch frame the central section of the water theater, the cascade, and the festooned columns on the upper plateau. This line of vision can also be reversed to a certain extent. From the upper vantage point, in front of the pool, there is a most attractive panoramic view. The pillars of Hercules frame the central projecting section of the palace, and create a relationship between the villa and the foreshortened copse to the side, the central cascade, and the balustrade of the exedra. If one then turns one's gaze in the opposite direction, one has a view of the extensive park.

According to old engravings, the cascade was bordered by tall hedges, undoubtedly following the example of the Villa Lante in Bagnaia. To the side, pathways lead to a fountain higher up, the *Fontana rustica*, where, between two recesses with peasant figures, streams of water pour down into a basin. A curved flight of steps with a balustrade in the form of a huge scroll leads around it and up to the next terrace, the *Fontana natura*. This natural tuff grotto receives the gushing streams of water via cascades further up.

It is this incomparable water axis which determines the overall conception of the park. In contrast to the Roman villas, the casino (which in this case ought to be called a palace) is, with its dominant position, central to this site. If the pillars of Hercules are a metaphorical allusion to the limits of this world, then it is beyond this place that paradise is to be sought, unfolding up the slope beside the river of life. In this attempt at an interpretation, the villa and the water theater are the gateway and courtyard of paradise. The front facade of the palace with its splendid driveway and the alleys leading to it refer unmistakably to this world, to the broad plain of the Tiber valley and the sea, visible despite the distance – and of course to Rome, the center of the world.

The outside world of the Villa Aldobrandini is paralleled in the Stanza del Parnaso of the palace. Everything that unfolds on a large scale outside, in the water theater or along the steps and cascades, reappears here on a smaller scale on the ceiling and walls of the Great Hall. The vaulted ceiling with its frescoes suggests a Mediterranean pergola with creepers, branches of fruit trees, and dense foliage, goldfinches, nightingales, partridges, wood-pigeons, and many other birds perch or fly around in the branches. At conspicuous corners there are an eagle-owl, a falcon, a peacock, and a tawny owl. On the walls there are idyllic fantasy landscapes, and on the floor a large mosaic echoing the

Frascati, Villa Aldobrandini
Parterre with box ornamentation near the villa (top)
Plane tree copse adjacent to the water theater (above)

structure and motifs of the ceiling. But the principal attraction must be the water organ, housed to great effect in an apse framed like a triumphal arch. There is a representation of Parnassus, with Pegasus dashing forth from the rock. At his side the Muses have sat down on the stone, and up at the top Apollo sits beneath a laurel tree holding the kythara.

Here, then, there are analogies everywhere. The paradise of antiquity, the Mount of the Muses with Apollo, corresponds to the earthly paradise that has evolved around the palace, and is understood as a pointer to the eternity of Heaven, the true Elysium.

Perhaps it was this boundary between this world and the next world that Cardinal Aldobrandini wished to fathom, with the aim of coming very close to the next life, with its promise of eternal bliss, in an anticipation of paradise. It is interesting that the imagery and motifs of the inner world reflect those of the external world, being, so to speak, an enhanced form of that world.

In a letter dating from 1601, Silvio Antoniano made suggestions to the cardinal concerning the decoration of the inside rooms. He recommended subjects such as "hunting, fishing, catching birds, working in cornfields, vineyards and olive groves, the life of shepherds, beekeeping, horsebreeding and the maintenance of courts and orchards." They were evidently pastoral idylls derived from the agrarian literature of Roman antiquity. But the advisor also added:

"One could also think of other subjects such as green grass, meadows with flowers, fruit trees in bloom or hung with ripe apples, green cornfields and sheaves of corn."

Castello Ruspoli in Vignanello

Before proceeding to the Baroque gardens of Italy in the more northerly parts of the country, we must take our leave of Latium, with its wealth of Baroque villas, in Vignanello. Here, not far from Viterbo and in the neighborhood of such famous gardens as Lante, Caprarola, or Bomarzo, a hidden gem awaits us. The country seat of the Ruspoli is today still in the possession of the family to whose commitment we owe the reconstruction of the parterre, edged with box hedges, in the Baroque style, and its painstaking maintenance down to the present day (illustration opposite). Two cross-axes divide the extended grounds into three quarters, each consisting of several compartments. Low-growing box hedges are shaped in ornamental patterns, some forming the monogram of the Ruspoli family.

Count Francesco Marescotti, who took the name of his mother, a certain Countess Ruspoli,

Frascati, Villa Aldobrandini
Semicircular water theater

ILLUSTRATION OPPOSITE
Frascati, Villa Aldobrandini
Detail view of the water theater: Polyphemus playing the pan-pipes in the left-hand grotto recess

POTESTATEM · SEDIS · APOST ·

Vignanello, Castello Ruspoli
View from the castello of the large parterre with box ornamentation (above)

View of the garden facade of the castello from the end of the parterre (right)

designed this garden at the beginning of the 18th century. Pope Benedict XIII stayed at the palace in 1725, enjoying the cuisine and a walk through the garden, where he admired the alleys adorned with statues. These unfortunately have not been preserved. But in the villa one feels the presence of past centuries, and may be taken back in spirit to the almost medieval origins of the site. The decorations of the *piano nobile* consist of ornamental ribbons interlaced with great artistry, with convoluted creeping vines and heraldic *monti*, stylized mountain forms, and the Ruspoli coat-of-arms. At the beginning of the 17th century, Ottavia Orsini, the daughter of the famous Vicino Orsini from Bomarzo, was the owner of the mansion. At her prompting, a wall with recesses was built around the park during the years 1610–15. The beds were richly ornamented with flowers, and they were designed after the fashion of Mannerist patterns.

Not quite a hundred years earlier, Count Sforza Marescotti had commissioned the architect Antonio da Sangallo the Younger to restore the Castello Ruspoli, which had been built in 1491. Today, the forecourt with a Renaissance fountain, and the entrance hall adorned with pilasters and topped with a small vault, still bear witness to this original building.

Florence, Villa la Pietra
Columns, statues, a fountain, and an exedra formed by a colonnade conclude the line of vision of the garden to the south.

Villa la Pietra in Florence

On the northern edge of the city of Florence, near the former Porta San Gallo, is the entrance to the park of the Villa La Pietra.

The site is noteworthy because Arthur Acton took over the villa at the beginning of the 20th century. He took the park, which had been designed in the style of an English landscape garden, and laid it out freely in the manner of a 17th-century Baroque site. Taking his bearings from the central axis starting at the main portal of the villa, he reterraced the slopes to create three levels, on which he built pergolas, fountains, and pools. Finally, we have his passion for collecting – and that of his son, Sir Harold Acton – to thank for the fact that it was possible to adorn the park with numerous Baroque sculptures and architectural fragments. He laid out lines of vision and erected, with great artistry, fragments of columns and architraves to create effective vistas. He composed groups of sculptures and fountains in harmony with pines, pruned cypresses, and box hedges, creating a quasi-theatrical setting.

The crowning achievement of his garden design is the lower terrace, where he had a box compartment planted in concentric rings, at the center of which he placed a pool with an elegant fountain. A bright, pergola-like colonnade going round the outer box ring in the form of an exedra, completes the ensemble (illustration above). Acton had the upper terrace laid out so as to surround the villa. This level is bounded by a wall at half height, with sculptures.

From here there is a splendid view of the lower terraces. Box hedges of different heights, pools with fountains, and sculptures on high pedestals give the garden of Villa la Pietra a varied and lively appearance.

The villa and the garden have a long history to look back on. A country seat is known to have existed back in the 14th century. The first owners for whom there is documentary evidence were the Sassetti in the 15th century, wealthy bankers in the service of the Medici. It may be supposed that a garden was laid out even then. There are, however, no pictures or documents to provide information regarding its appearance. Cardinal Luigi Capponi acquired the site in the 17th century, and had it rebuilt in the Baroque style. This affected not only the villa, which Carlo Fontana redesigned together with Giuseppe Ruggieri, but also the garden, which was laid out to the right of the villa as a classic box parterre with antique sculptures.

Florence, Villa la Pietra
This corner of the garden, adorned with balustrades and statues and rounded off with an arch, is like verdant stage scenery.

ILLUSTRATIONS OPPOSITE
Camigliano (Lucca)
Villa Torrigiani
Villa facade with entrance, richly adorned with sculptures (top)
Views of the garden (bottom)

Villa Torrigiani in Camigliano

Most Italian Renaissance and Baroque gardens were transformed into English landscape gardens in the 19th century. While the garden of the Villa la Pietra, thanks to the initiative of its former owner, Arthur Acton, was restored in its entirety to its Baroque form, at other sites it has proved possible to restore at least smaller areas of the garden to their Baroque form.

The Villa Torrigiani, situated to the northeast of Lucca, is to be seen today in the middle of a typical English park. This is all the more regrettable in view of the fact that it was probably the great French garden architect André Le Nôtre who designed the parterres following his return from Rome in 1679. Today nothing is left except the elliptical pool. However, in one of the ground-floor rooms of the villa there is a plan of the old site that can be inspected.

The building, which goes back to the 16th century and was only slightly modified in the 17th century, is enclosed, so to speak, by the two parterres. Here, there is a parallel between the ornamentation of the *broderie parterre* and the wealth of sculpture adorning the main facade. The ornamentation of the beds with box patterns filled with colored pebbles, that had been customary in France since *c.* 1620, was probably used for the first time in Italy at the Villa Torrigiani. The elevation of the central projection, constructed in accordance with Serlio's model – two round arches placed one on top of the other, each flanked by two rectangular apertures – combined with the rusticated facade of the lower story and the monumental recessed figures that are housed there, has a Manneristic effect. By virtue of its dynamic structure, the entire building unit takes on an aesthetic life of its own that can only be appreciated at a certain distance. For this reason le Nôtre probably also envisaged extensive undesigned turf areas between the villa and the parterres in order to present the architecture in an effective setting. The English landscape garden encourages this approach, particularly the tall trees adjacent to the villa which make the facade look almost like a picture (illustration opposite, top).

On the old garden plan there is also an area of the garden to be seen, situated to the side and surrounded by a wall. It is a *giardino segreto* of the kind popular during the Baroque period, especially in Italy. This garden has fortunately been preserved. A visitor coming from the summer pavilion, and traversing a flower parterre, is led along a round-arched passageway into this closed garden where he or she is surprised to find a plant bed layout (illustration p. 162 bottom). Low-growing box hedges enclose colorfully planted flowerbeds. The central main pathway, flanked by large boxwood globes, leads to a grotto. Two ferocious monsters have taken up their positions to the left and right of the entrance to give the new arrival a fitting welcome. Anyone undeterred enters the grotto, and immediately finds him or herself in semidarkness exposed to the Gods of the Winds, who perform their duties with full, round cheeks, and pursed lips (illustration p. 162 top). Visitors are in the Grotto of the Seven Winds, who punish excessive inquisitiveness. Water spurts up from the floor when the threshold is crossed, and Flora, the wife of the Wind God Aeolus, sends down a shower of rain from the cupola onto the visitor. These water tricks, which we are familiar with from Spain, were used very frequently in grottoes with a similar theme. They are among the main attractions of the Villa Torrigiani.

On the opposite side, the garden is bounded by two opposing flights of steps whose balustrades are adorned with figures. Adjoining them is a large pool which acts as a reservoir for the waterworks in the Grotto of the Seven Winds and in the labyrinthine series of grottoes below the steps. Beneath the steps are two entrances to an incomparable grotto gallery with stalactites hanging from the roof and numerous monsters and animals carved in tuff.

The *giardino segreto* with its grottoes and waterworks, its lavish flights of steps, and sumptuous decorative figures, all concentrated in such a small area situated somewhat to one side, enables the visitor to form an idea of the former Baroque splendor of the whole site, with the stately villa rising proudly at its center.

Segromigno (Lucca), Villa Mansi
Pool with surrounding balustrade by Filippo Juvarra in the garden of the villa

Villa Mansi in Segromigno near Lucca

Not far from Camigliani, close to the town of Lucca, is Segromigno with the Villa Mansi, and this villa was once also surrounded by a Baroque garden layout.

The villa was commissioned by the Countess Felice Cenami and built in 1634–5 in the Mannerist style by the architect Muzio Oddi. Having recently been restored, its unaccustomed elegance is striking. Oddi found a villa dating from the 16th century.

He built a completely new two-story facade, put a double flight of steps in front of it, and gave the raised ground floor a splendid portico with three arcade arches designed in Palladio's manner. The pairs of Tuscan columns supporting the arcade entablature are graced with charming statues. This motif is repeated in the middle of the upper story. The side wings project only a small way. They are topped by pediments, each of which has a blind arch with a monumental bust. A typically Mannerist impression is created by the broken pediments of the ground-floor windows, likewise adorned with busts.

In the 18th century the property passed to Ottavio Guido Mansi, who succeeded in engaging Filippo Juvarra, master builder at the court of Victor Amadeus II of Savoy, for his garden projects. He designed two gardens with pergolas, fountains, espalier sections, and an elegant little clock tower.

Today hardly anything remains of this splendor. The Baroque garden layout was ousted by the English lawn in front of the villa and newly planted trees. Only Juvarra's two pools have survived. One walks along the former great alley, flanked by laurel hedges, accompanied by silent stone figures of girls rising up out of boxwood hemispheres, to one of the water basins. It is surrounded by a curved balustrade adorned with bowls of geraniums and sculptures (illustration above). A little way off, in a copse, the visitor suddenly comes across *Diana Bathing* before a delapidated arcade structure lined with seashells.

ILLUSTRATIONS OPPOSITE
Camigliano (Lucca), Villa Torrigiani
Grotto of the Seven Winds (top)
giardino segreto (bottom)

Collodi (Pistoia), Villa Garzoni
The "summer palace" designed by Filippo Juvarra links the village with the garden site.

Villa Garzoni in Collodi

The trio of villas in Lucca includes, of course, Garzoni – surely the greatest surprise in this region with so many villas. The palace was built only a few kilometers to the east of the Villa Mansi on the outskirts of the village of Collodi. The park, impressively crowned by the villa (illustration above), was laid out in the corner of a wood in an almost breathtaking hillside site. The first impression is overwhelming. Whether one looks down onto the site or, from below, up at the villa, one's eye is caught by the great variety of fountains, terraces, and steep steps cut into the hillside. Although the garden design was strictly symmetrical, the entire site is crisscrossed by a network of pathways that have the effect of a maze. The Marquis Romano Garzoni, the owner of the site, took a personal interest in the project, and was probably involved in the details of design. Work lasted from 1633 to 1692. In the following century Romano's great-grandson took over the further development of the garden site, and commissioned the architect and engineer Ottaviono Diodati to draw up plans for the hydraulic installations which had become necessary for the extensive waterworks.

The garden has survived to the present day. The Baroque site can thus be studied in detail and enjoyed while walking around it. The main axis, laid down in an uphill direction, consists of rhythmically laid out steps, two flights extending over three terraces. At the foot of the steps is a plant bed enclosed by tall box hedges clipped to the shape of waves, and adorned with imaginative ornamental plants (illustration p. 167). The architects did not include the classical plant bed compartments but planted large areas with free, dynamic swathes of flowering plants in different colors such as lavender, rosemary, heather, or pinks. Miniature lemon trees in pots, little boxwood globes, and larger box trees cut to spiral shapes indicated the general approach. The entrance area with two circular pools is located in front of the plant bed, which itself is in front of the steps. Waterlilies grow in one of the basins. The entire area is laid with gravel, ensuring that the splendor of the flowers in bloom, with all their color, makes its full impact (illustration opposite, bottom left).

Ascending the magnificent steps with their decorative mosaics and brick-red balustrade, one comes, half way up, to Neptune's Seashell Grotto. Numerous small fountains accompany the visitor along his or her way. This and the following terrace are crossed by two alleys. While the lower one is planted with palms, the upper Pomona alley, which borders the forest, is enhanced by sculptures. Alongside the cooling cascade a ramp leads steeply upward to the final *Fama* basin.

ILLUSTRATIONS OPPOSITE
Collodi (Pistoia), Villa Garzoni
Plan of the site in 1692 (top)

View from the large stairway to the two round pools in the lower parterre region (bottom left)
Terracotta figure by the stairway (bottom right)

There, on an arcade structure designed in the shape of an exedra, above a basin with water lilies, the goddess *Fama* stands, proclaiming the fame of the Garzoni family (illustrations opposite and p. 169). The short climb is worthwhile. If one now turns around and looks down, one's eye passes over the water splashing downward and the upper stairway landing, to the lower terrace where two swans can be seen near the right-hand pool (illustration below).

Today, if one travels in Italy in order to familiarize oneself with Baroque garden culture, then Garzoni, along with Bomarzo, must surely be one of the unforgettable impressions. Bomarzo offers the surprise of its imaginative and playful features and its unusual perspectives. But Garzoni welcomes the visitor with special gaiety and exuberance, without forfeiting its dignity or its elegance. That its first owner, Romano Garzoni, was concerned exclusively with the garden and not with any overall conception of villa and garden, can be seen from the position of the palace, somewhat to one side (plan, right).

Seen from the lower terrace, the facade high up the hill does not seem to be part of the site, since the stairway does not lead to the central axis of the building but runs at an angle of about 40 degrees to it. Thus it was not primarily a matter of professionally designed surroundings for the palace. The garden itself was developed as an independent aesthetic organism, and imbued with lasting vitality. Romano Garzini's descendants have succeeded in doing this to the present day.

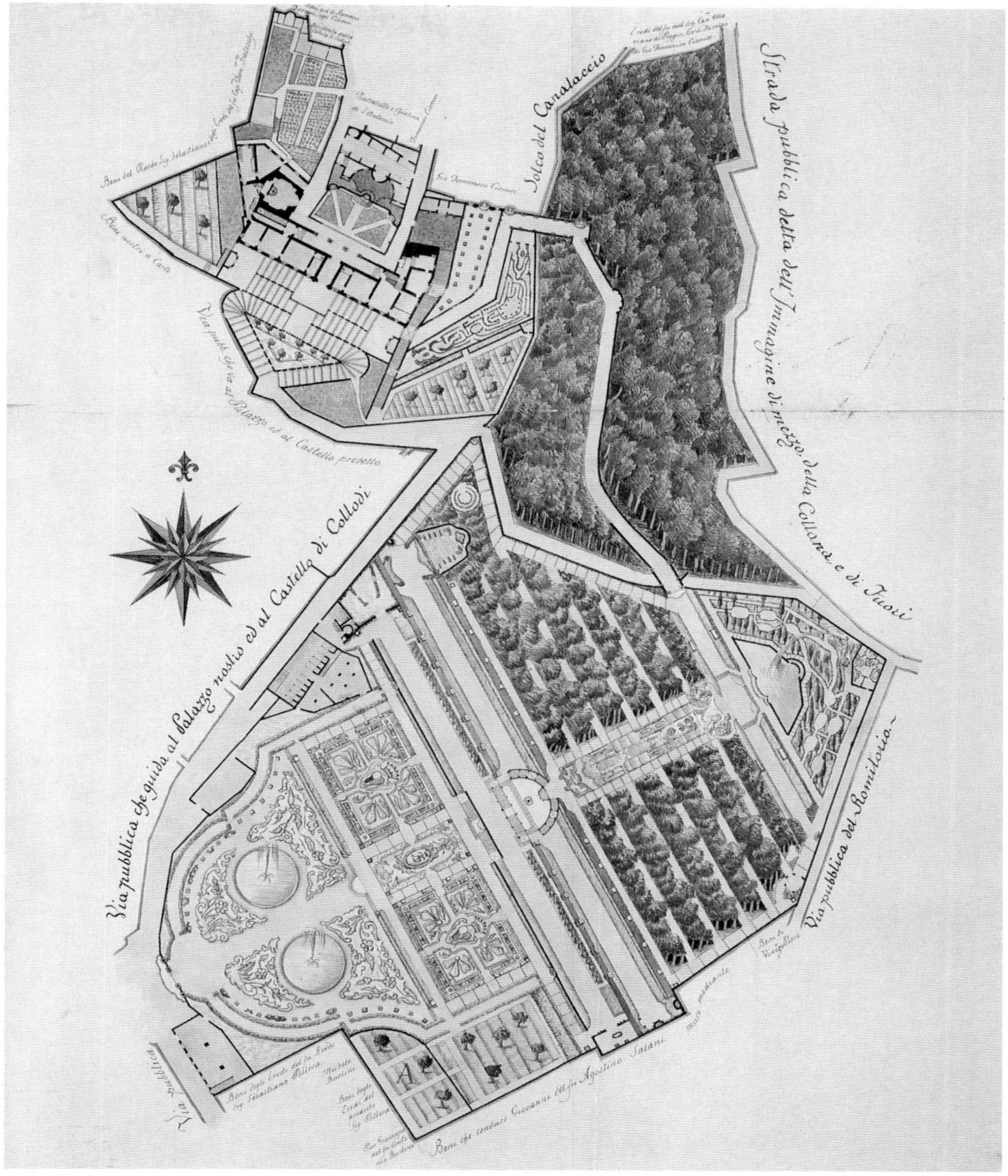

Collodi (Pistoia), Villa Garzoni
Terracotta statue of *Fama* at the upper end of the cascade. The figure is attributed to Paladini, a sculptor who was born in Lucca.

ILLUSTRATION OPPOSITE
Collodi (Pistoia), Villa Garzoni
View of the double-flight stairway extending over three levels. In the recess below is the terracotta statue of the *Peasant with the Barrel.*

Collodi (Pistoia), Villa Garzoni
Statue of a headless woman holding a man's head

ILLUSTRATIONS OPPOSITE
Collodi (Pistoia), Villa Garzoni
The personification of the town of Pescia near Lucca at the beginning of the cascade (top)

Walled pond below the *Fama* at the top end of the cascade (bottom)

ILLUSTRATION OPPOSITE
Cetinale (Siena), Villa Chigi

Behind a wrought-iron grille a light gravel path edged with box hedges leads up to the facade of the Villa Chigi in Cetinale. Cardinal Flavio Chigi, the nephew of Pope Alexander VII, had his villa built to the west of Siena by the Baroque architect Carlo Fontana. The master builder adopted the tried and trusted elevation system, conceived by Peruzzi, of the Villa Farnesina in Rome. Two projections at the corners, creating the effect of towers, flank a narrow central area with a loggia opening onto the garden. Many parts of the garden, which is dominated by box trees, cypresses and lemon trees, have retained their Baroque structure.

Cetinale (Siena), Villa Chigi
Pathway edged with cypresses in the villa garden, with a view of the Tuscan landscape

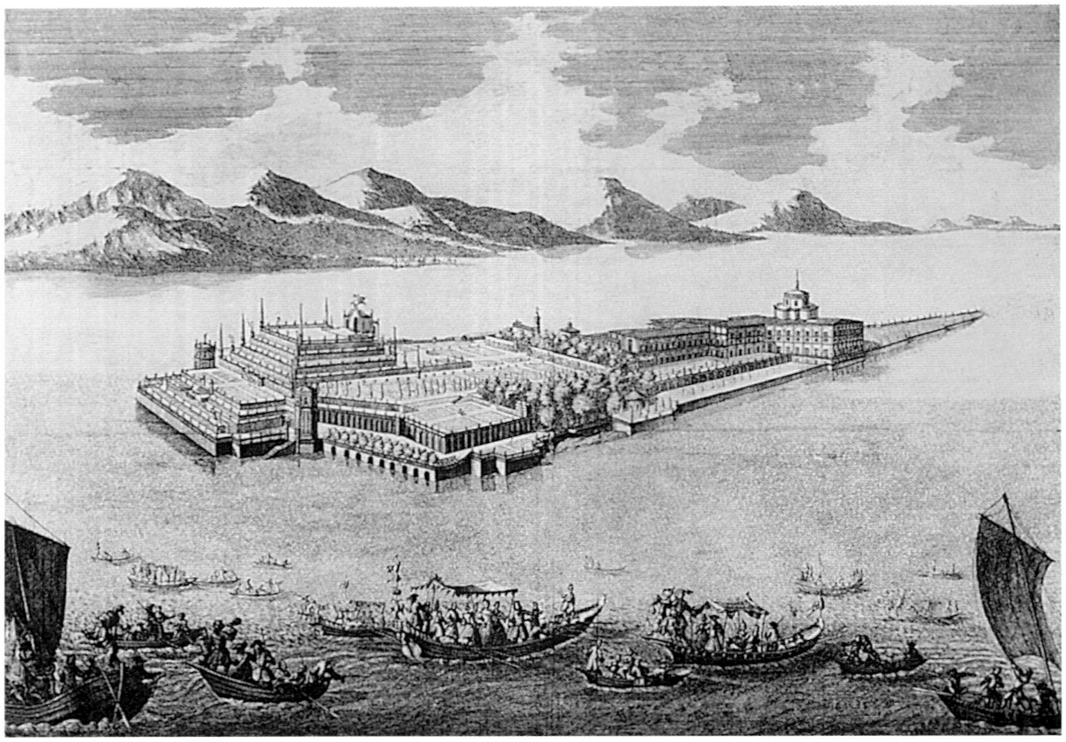

Lake Maggiore, Isola Bella
The terraced garden island, 18th-century view; engraving by M. dal Re (top)
Parterre site below the terraces (above)

Baroque Gardens in Northern Italy

The gardens of northern Italy are not fundamentally different from the country's other Baroque gardens. But they do occasionally display divergences. The system of lines of sight geared to a *point de vue* does not appear to be so important. Manneristic playfulness, which plays an important part in many Baroque gardens, is a more sparingly used item in the garden repertoire. Although Baroque culture may – to a far greater extent than that of the Renaissance – be regarded as a European phenomenon, and although French influences can be detected in almost every Baroque garden, this factor was of less crucial importance for the gardens of northern Italy. The reasons for this special position are probably to be found primarily in the topography of the country. Whereas the landscape of central Italy has, to a considerable extent, a homogenous structure, in northern Italy contrasts predominate: the plain of Lombardy changes abruptly to the foothills of the Alps, which are divided by rivers and lakes. Steep terracing, twisting paths, and intimate parterres were preferred, as appropiate to the nature of the terrain. Moreover, in this region we encounter an unusual special case, the island garden of the Isola Bella on the Lago Maggiore, probably the most famous garden in northern Italy. But we ought also to take a look at the equally paradisial islet of Isola Madre, which has been unjustly overshadowed, aesthetically speaking, by its big sister. Both islands are part of the archipelago of the Borromean islands off the village of Stresa. The Counts of Borromeo also had a summer residence on the Isola Madre, but rarely used it. Only a few remains have survived of the 16th- and 17th-century garden site. But they make an intimate and idyllic impression. The garden villa with the projecting side loggia and the terrace with the Dolphin Fountain by the wall of the house, still give one a sense of the Baroque character of the site. Today the whole island has been transformed into a picturesque botanical garden.

The Island Garden of Isola Bella on Lake Maggiore

Like a mute on a musical instrument, the Isola Bella sits on Lake Maggiore, not far from the shore, in front of the much-vaunted Alpine backdrop (illustration top left). An island off the village of Stresa has been transformed into a castle. That at least is the effect made by the castle and garden layout of Isola Bella which was designed for Count Carlo Borromeo and his son Vitaliano *c.* 1630. The French ethnologist Charles de Brosse announced enthusiastically, in his *Lettres familières* of *c.* 1770: "This work really is like nothing else in the world except for fairy-tale castles." Theodor Fontane, in contrast, noted, with Prussian succinctness: "A part of Sanssouci, only with the difference that the Isola Bella hill has been terraced not on one side but on all four sides."

At the western end of the island, at lake level, the master builders constructed the stately palace. The building juts out into the lake like the bows of a ship, thereby giving the entire island an element of artificiality. This impression is strengthened by the gardens, which are laid out to the east of the palace and which, in accordance with the topography of the island, stretch upward in the shape of a pyramid on ten terraces at different levels

(illustrations left and above). At the highest point, a spacious garden terrace, there is always a cool sea breeze in summer. One can imagine how up there, intoxicated by the view, there were festivities and performances.

The terraces rise up elegantly from the lakeside at the end of the island, facing the palace. Before the arcades of the terrace walls low hedges run wild today but which in former times must have been clipped. Lemon trees grow beside the pilasters. At the top is a three-story grotto, richly adorned with sculptures. The peak of this mount is crowned by the heraldic Borromei unicorn.

Its special position makes the Borromeo garden one of the most attractive Baroque gardens in Italy. But the site itself hardly shows any typical features of the Italian Baroque garden, and the garden has long since lost its original form. It is no longer possible to discern the broken axis, concealed by parterres, between the garden terraces and the palace, which once constituted the peculiar charm of the entire garden ensemble. Today, with the tall trees that grow there and the rampant proliferation of bushes in some parts of the terraces, the site cannot be seen as a whole, and its Baroque structure can scarcely be identified any longer.

Lake Maggiore, Isola Bella
Garden layout in the terraced area with a view of the lake and the mountains

Villa Trissino Marzotto

In the second half of the 15th century, the Marzotto family's fortified castle in Trissino near Vicenza was transformed into a country villa. More buildings were added in the course of the following centuries, so that by the 18th century a sizeable villa complex had evolved, surrounded by a garden site laid out on a generous scale. Actually, there are several gardens distributed between the terraces and linking the individual building units. The architect of the villa was the Lombard Francesco Muttoni, a Palladian who had the skill to ring the changes on the architectural approach of his great exemplar. Shortly before his death in 1747, incidentally, he published a new impression of the works of Andrea Palladio. The terrace walls with their gates adorned with scrolls and candelabras, seem like pieces of scenery in a Baroque stage play.

The hanging gardens and the water basins framed by profiled stone pedestals, with sculptures on high pedestals, also go back to Muttoni. The entire site is like a maze. Again and again one strays into intimate garden niches, then abruptly finds oneself walking along a long cypress alley stretching away into the distance. Or one finds oneself in front of the Baroque villa again, steps out onto the southern terrace and enjoys the unforgettable panorama before one of the soaring Montecchio mountains.

ILLUSTRATION OPPOSITE
Trissino (Vicenza)
Villa Trissino Marzotto
Pool in front of the lower villa with sculptures by Marinali

Trissino (Vicenza)
Villa Trissino Marzotto
Pillars of the belvedere by Francesco Muttoni in the garden in front of the villa

ILLUSTRATION OPPOSITE
Strà (Venice), Villa Pisani
Channel edged with sculptures in front of the villa
The complex of buildings built to mark the enthronement of Doge Alvise Pisani in 1730 is also known as the "Doge's Villa."

Strà (Venice), Villa Pisani
Interior view of the portico on the garden side of the villa

Villa Pisani in Strà

Villegiatura, the glorification of country life in Veneto, was based on the "Villa books" that had been popular since the 16th century. In them the authors argued for the fusion of agricultural and humanist studies. Their goal was a life lived close to nature and in agreement with the corresponding philosophical principles concerning the conduct of life. The books were aimed at the upper bourgeoisie of the capital, Venice, and the country towns of the *Terraferma*, the Venetian hinterland. Many Venetian villas were created against this background, and especially those that were situated on the Brenta.

But the assumptions soon changed. The agricultural aspect lost its interest, and the philosophy of life, with its moral approach, gave way to the villa owners' desire to cut a stately figure. One of the Brenta villas, the Villa Pisani, can serve as an example of this change of paradigm in Venetian villa ideology (illustration opposite).

The villa (in this case more of a castle, since it was built for one who aspired to the dimensions of French royal castles) was commissioned to mark the enthronement of Doge Alvise Pisani in 1730. The architect Girolamo Frigimelica, a nobleman from Padua, not only designed the grand villa but also laid out parts of the huge garden, for example the maze and the spacious arcade. The garden pavilions and the belvedere were also built to Frigimelica's designs.

Frigimelica was very strongly influenced – and this is to be seen as an exception in north Italian architecture – by 18th-century French garden design, laying out elaborate *broderie parterres* that were designed with great artistry. He also revealed a preference for straight alleys cutting far into the wooded area of the park, which measured over 4 km ($2^1/_2$ miles).

But the most explicit French touch is the wide channel which starts at the central axis of the villa, and ends at an oval pool. The channel is enclosed by a wall adorned with figures, and catches the eye with its calm, almost motionless surface reflecting the sky of the Veneto – surely an unusual sight for Italian eyes. The Mediterranean delight in lively, sparkling water surfaces could not be gratified at the Villa Pisani. Many of the French elements were eliminated in the 19th century. The loss of the *broderie parterre* will probably be felt to be particulary painful.

After the architect's death in 1732, the owner entrusted the commission to Maria Pretis, who redesigned the facade of the villa in strict accordance with Palladio's approach, with a projecting portico and divided by monumental pilasters. The work was completed by 1740.

One is taken by surprise by the sumptuous interior decoration of the villa. Paintings that deserve to be singled out here are those by Francesco Zuccari, Sebastiano Ricci, Giuseppe Zais, and Fabio Canal, to name only the most famous of the artists.

But the crowning glory as regards painting is undoubtedly the great Tiepolo fresco in the central salon. Here the artist has painted an allegory of the *Fame of the Pisani Family,* and has employed an unusual artistic device. In the lower part of the fresco one can see a small boy in his mother's arms. This arouses involuntary associations with the Madonna-and-Child theme, making this motif the center of interest. The central character in the fresco is indeed the boy, Almorò Pisani, the owner's son, who was later to be so zealous a supporter of the arts.

Strà (Venice), Villa Pisani
Artificial mount with a garden house as a *point de vue*

Gargnano, Villa Bettoni
Parterre in front of the villa with a view of Lake Garda

Villa Bettoni in Gargnano

Gargnano has an idyllic location between steep cliffs and the wide stretch of water that is Lake Garda. Given this topographical location, one would not expect to find one of the most enchanting gardens of northern Italy laid out there, but one is. The Villa Bettoni goes back to *c.* 1760, and the garden was laid out at the same time.

The Bettoni family had the sloping site terraced in the form of an amphitheater to make room for the parterres. Behind a wrought-iron gate a central gravel path edged with low box hedges leads to a fountain basin surrounded by a two-story exedra (illustrations opposite).

To the left and right, ramps and flights of steps can be seen leading up from one terrace to the next, past little grottoes and recesses with figures, to the upper parterre that ends at a balustrade. The top terrace is flanked by two gateways, both of which are topped with pediments and divided by pilasters; these gateways bring the exedra to a harmonious end.

In Upper Italy one often comes across gardens laid out across several terraces on a steep slope, and most especially in the Alpine lake region. The designers looked for the *point de vue*, and then tried to create an appropriate composition of steps, ramps, and arcades.

ILLUSTRATIONS OPPOSITE
Gargnano, Villa Bettoni
Views of the two-story flights of steps in the garden of the villa (left) and two of the rococo figures in the wall recesses (right)

Vanvitelli's Baroque Buildings in Caserta.

"It takes the splendor of what is French to complete Italy's fairest crown." Those were the words of Elizabeth Farnese, the mother of Charles IV of Bourbon, the great-grandson of Louis XIV, and from 1734 King of the Two Sicilies. Of all the Neapolitan kings, it was he who created the most monumental building: Caserta, popularly known as "La Reggia," the castle.

In 1750 Charles IV summoned the master builder Luigi Vanvitelli to execute his ambitious plans for a castle. Vanvitelli did not by any means look to Versailles or the Louvre for inspiration in creating the desired French splendor, but rather took his guidance from traditional Italian notions regarding palace building, which, however, he magnified to monumental dimensions. Vanvitelli published an engraving of his design in 1756 (illustration p. 182 top left). The layout, with its dimensions exceeding those of the castle and gardens of Versailles, was built approximately as envisaged by the architect in the engraving. Only the roof terraces planned for the corner projections, which were intended to serve as a belvedere, and the central octagonal cupola did not materialize.

Building work began in 1752 with a spectacular ceremony as the foundation stone was laid. Two

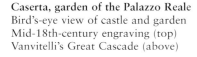

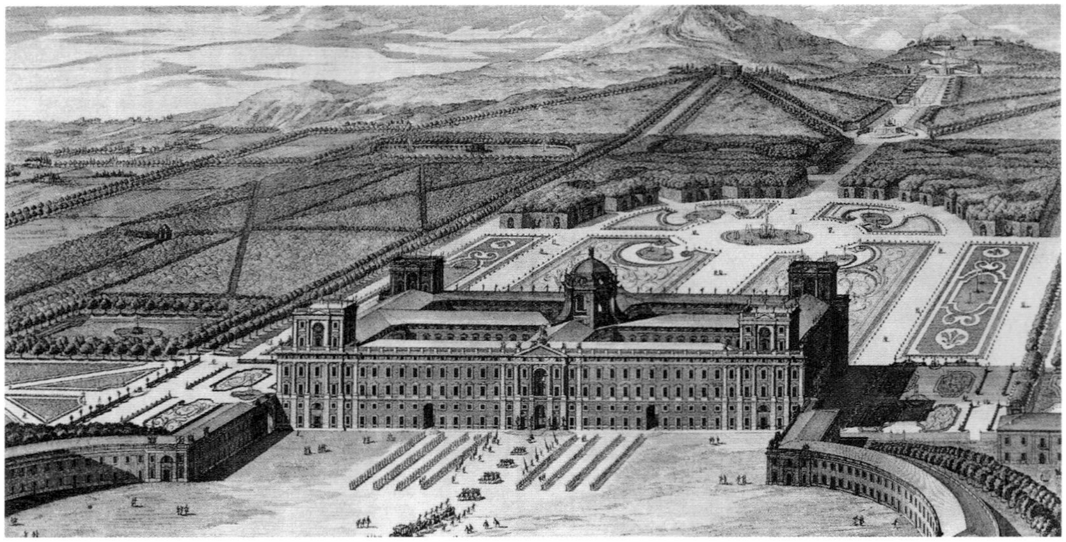

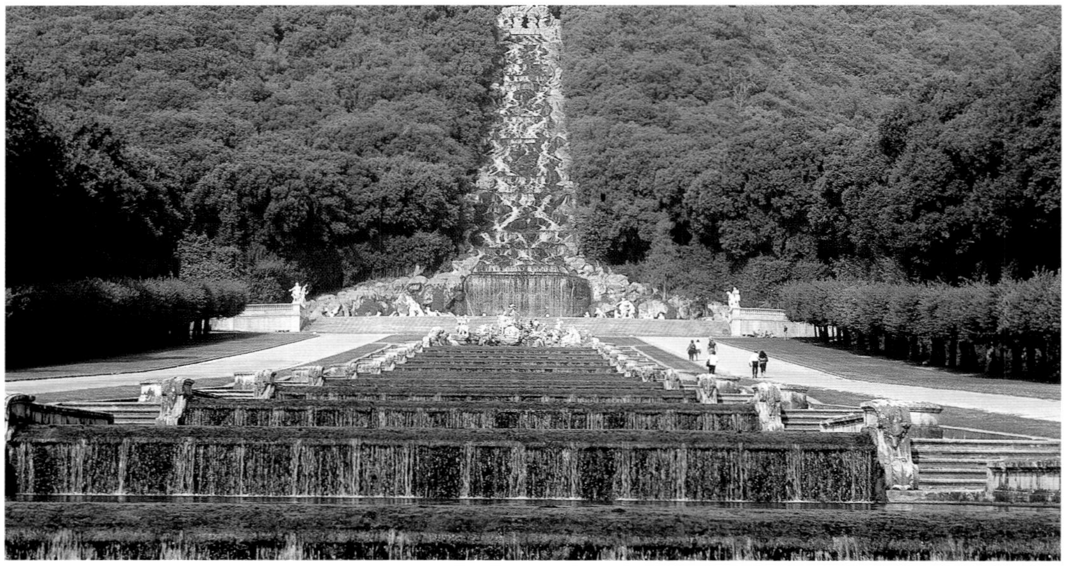

Caserta, garden of the Palazzo Reale
Bird's-eye view of castle and garden
Mid-18th-century engraving (top)
Vanvitelli's Great Cascade (above)

regular army regiments and two cavalry squadrons were drawn up so as to mark out the ground plan. Vanvitelli died in 1773, only a year before his work was completed.

Goethe visited Caserta in 1787 and noted: "The new castle, an enormous palace, like El Escorial, square-shaped, with several courtyards, truly regal ..., did not seem to me sufficiently animated, and the likes of us cannot feel comfortable in the enormous empty rooms."

When laying out the garden site Vanvitelli had to solve three fundamental problems. Firstly, large quantities of water had to be obtained, not only for the cascades but also to meet the castle's requirements. To this end he looked for known ancient Roman springs in the area of Monte Taburno to the east. The Acquedotto Carolino, an aqueduct 41 km ($25^1/_2$ miles) in length, was built in a mere twelve years – an extraordinary achievement. One of its most spectacular sections, the Ponti della Valle near Maddaloni, can still be seen today. The bridge, measuring 528 m (*c.* 1,732 ft.), is constructed of three rows of arcades one on top of the other and spans the valley at a height of 58 m (*c.* 190 ft.). The foundations of the central pillars were sunk *c.* 30 m (*c.* 98 ft.) into the ground.

Vanvitelli wished to solve the second problem, the designs for the parterres, by taking as his model the park of La Granja near Madrid, where Charles of Bourbon had spent his youth. Plant bed compartments with elegant rococo patterns and pathways laid out symmetrically with fountains and statues, were to remind the king of his homeland, while at the same time reflecting the predominant French taste of the time. These plans were too expensive to be implemented. Instead they had to settle for a spacious lawn, which one can still walk across today, while flanked with boskets of oak and holm oak.

The third problem, the design of a comprehensive range of fountains and sculptures, was solved by Vanvitelli with the aid of specialists in iconographic inventory design, and fountain engineers. The so-called Canalone cuts through the

park forming a central axis. The water from the distant mountain springs flows along it, passing through a series of fountains, pools and cascades where the waves lap, gush over steps or flow smoothly in a steady stream toward the castle. At the Fontana Margherita the realm of the ancient gods begins. The inventory of figures was drawn up by Porzio Lionardi, a friend of Vanvitelli's. At the Cascata dei Delfini huge water-spouting dolphins tower up from an artificial rock. Further up, the realm of Aeolus follows, where the allegories of the Winds are to be seen. Then one comes to a basin, which is soon followed by seven steps. There Ceres Trinacria, the goddess of Sicily and the allegorical embodiment of the granary of the Empire, sits enthroned, surrounded by nymphs and amoretti. This group of sculptures was created by Gaetano Salomone, as were the Venus and Adonis on a terrace higher up. Finally, an open stairway takes one to the Great Cascade, the realm of Diana. The sculptures, full of vitality, are the work of Paolo Persico; they present the myth of Actaeon and Diana (illustration above). The hunter Actaeon comes by chance on Diana while she is bathing, and is punished by being changed into a stag. His own hounds tear him to pieces.

By the time Vanvitelli died in 1773, the age of the great Baroque gardens was basically long since at an end. Maria Carolina of Austria, the wife of the Bourbon Ferdinand IV, took up residence in Naples in 1768 and requested for Caserta a landscape garden in the English style that was modern at the time. In 1782 the court summoned the English botanist Giovanni Andrea Graefer. As a result of Graefer's efforts the English garden was created on the eastern slope of the Canalone. Work lasted until well into the 19th century.

In the park and the castle the royal Bourbons wished to create an artificial universe, the impression of an Arcadian, utopian world to be created in a park that was bounded only by the distant mountain range. The Kings of the Two Sicilies wished their power to be symbolized in "boundless distance" and control over nature.

Caserta, garden of the Palazzo Reale
Group of figures at the Fountain of Diana by Paolo Persico, 1785–9
Diana and her retinue startled while bathing by the huntsman Actaeon.

The French Baroque Garden

Maincy, Château de Vaux-le-Vicomte
Golden crown in one of the pools near the castle

PAGES 184–185
Maincy, Château de Vaux-le-Vicomte
View of the castle across the garden

The Gardens of André Le Nôtre (1613–1700)

In 1679 André Le Nôtre set off on his long desired journey to Italy. He visited Rome and the Vatican, where he was granted an audience by the Pope. During a visit to the gardens that were so celebrated in Europe, he was moved to comment that in matters of garden design the Italians were absolutely inexperienced. How could such a verdict be uttered, when it was precisely the kings of France who courted Italian architects, sculptors, and painters in order to bestow on their country an art which was regarded throughout Europe as the crowning glory of artistic skill? Furthermore, Le Nôtre was considered by his friends and by his king, Louis XIV, to be a modest man, so that in this respect too his harsh verdict remains incomprehensible. Le Nôtre, who for over twenty years had held the office of Director-General of Royal Buildings in France, was known in all the countries of Europe as the most significant garden architect, and hence scarcely needed to denigrate the standard of gardens in another country in order to give greater luster to his own abilities.

Le Nôtre's reasons were purely objective. The wonderful gardens of Italy were conceived in terms of space, and hence also of height, and not merely in terms of surface and size, as was the French approach. There, Le Nôtre tried to design something like a monumental natural painting, with at most some relief features. In Italy, sculpture, architecture, box tree, and bosket, all came together, concentrated in space. As regards plant bed ornamentation, Serlio's patterns were still of central importance, whereas in France new and unusual kinds of planting were being carried out, as in the *broderie parterre* or the *parterres de pièces coupées pour des fleurs*, patterns composed of flower beds in conjunction with small ornamental trees and shrubs. France had moved to the forefront of Europe in garden design, and the Italian Baroque garden, particularly during those years, was taking its cue from the new model. The parterre of the Villa Torrigiani to the north-east of Lucca, for example, is said to have been designed by Le Nôtre while he was on his way back to France from Rome.

During the reign of Louis XIV (1643–1715), the French garden, on which André Le Nôtre had decisively set his stamp, developed into an imposing work of art, of a brilliance which outshone all other gardens in Europe. The incomparable gardens of Vaux-le-Vicomte, the Tuileries in Paris and finally – as the undisputed crown – Versailles, were at least predominantly created by Le Nôtre (illustrations pp. 184–196).

André Le Nôtre (illustration below) was born into a family of gardeners in Paris in 1613. His father, Jean Le Nôtre, held the rank of a *jardinier en chef du roi* and was employed for a long time in the Tuileries. He also owned a house nearby in which his son André grew up. In 1637 André, by then twenty-four years old, took over his father's post, and likewise began work in the Tuileries. It was there that his design principles took on their first tangible form. His conception was based on a clear structure: a central axis divides into two quarters that consist of individual closed compartments with differing patterns. The lower area is filled by two dominant *broderie parterres* with pools at the center. Adjoining this, in the central axis, there is a larger round pool which matches

Portrait of André Le Nôtre, the gardener-in-chief to the king
Painting, oil on canvas, 112 x 85 cm (*c.* 45 x 34 in.), 1678
Carlo Maratta
Versailles, Musée du Château

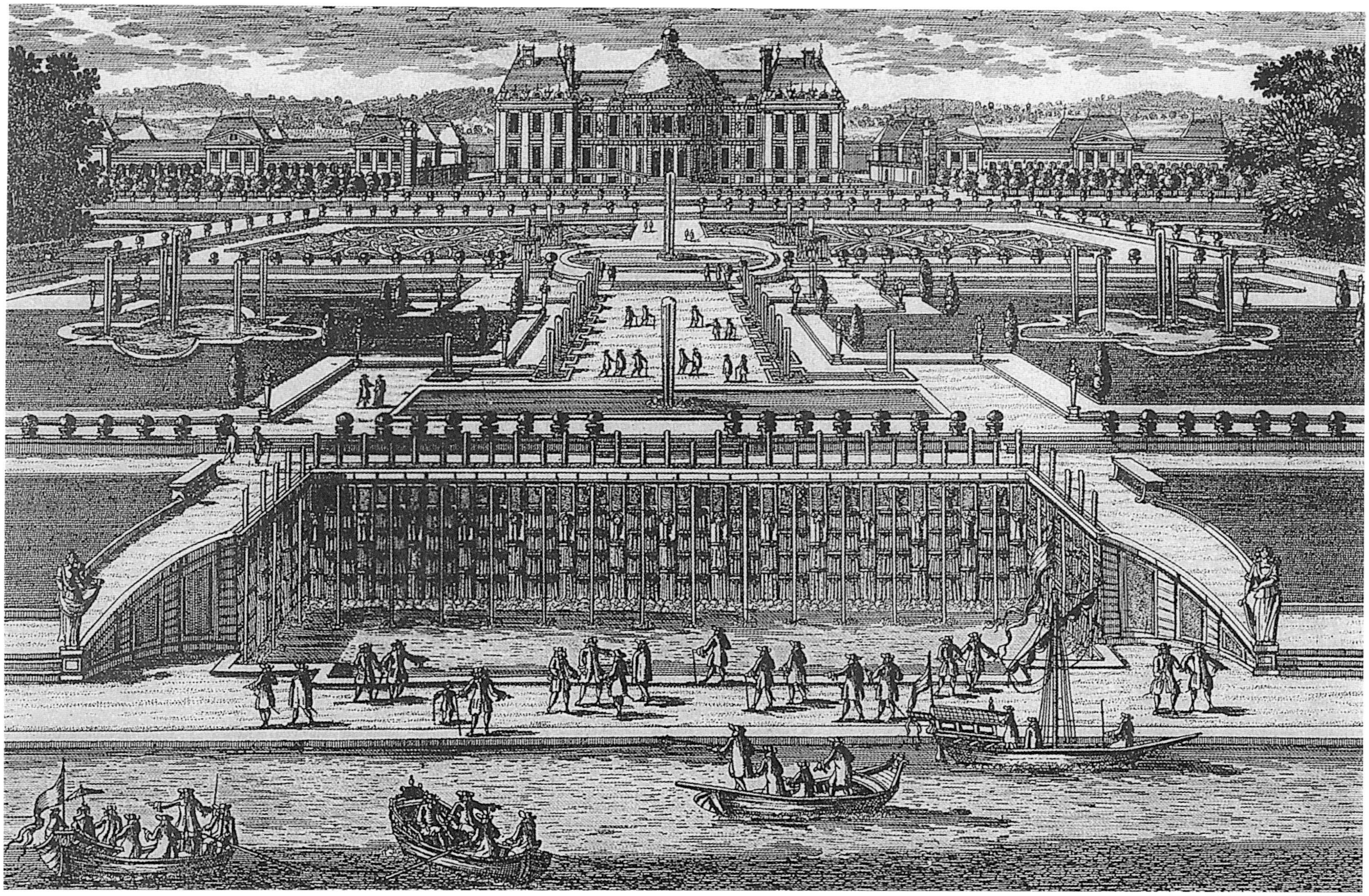

the octagonal pool at the end of the garden. As is shown by wage sheets, Le Nôtre was still working at the Tuileries in 1649, probably involved in laying out and tending boskets. In 1642 he entered the service of Gaston d'Orléans, and worked in the Jardin du Luxembourg. Three years later he submitted a design for the orangery compartment at Fontainebleau, the first of his designs of which evidence is extant. The artist had caught the attention of the French nobility. But his great moment came in Vaux-le-Vicomte in 1656.

The Castle Garden at Vaux-le-Vicomte

For the castle of the royal minister of finance, Nicolas Fouquet, which at the time surpassed even the castles and gardens of Louis XIV, le Nôtre was to lay out a truly regal garden. Fouquet summoned the most famous artists in France for the building work and the interior decoration. The plans for the building were drawn up by the court architect Louis le Vau, who was later to work at Versailles. The interior decoration scheme was the work of Charles Le Brun, who had been trained alongside Le Nôtre in the studio of Simon Vouet, the forerunner of French Classicism. The splendid castle was built within a mere year, at considerable expense (illustrations on pp. 184–185, 188–189). An oval salon opens onto the garden; it has a cupola and a facade formed by a two-story portico topped by a pediment. The high roofs of the adjoining side projections reappear in the counting houses, which seen from the garden are slightly set back and are flatter than the castle itself. In this way Le Vau gave a rhythmic shape to the architecture in the alternation of lengthy areas and topped corner and central projections, creating, so to speak, a melody in the building, which rises to a crescendo in the central main building and culminates in the cupola with the lantern. At the same time, this defined the central axis of the entire site, which was of crucial importance to Le Nôtre, who at the time was still largely unknown. Along this axis he laid out a wide central alley on a slightly tilted plane, leading into the depths of the landscape and hence to the distant horizon. He thereby created an unexpected spaciousness, the

Château de Vaux-le-Vicomte
Great Cascade, garden and castle
Engraving by Aveline

effect of which he was able to enhance still further by moderate terracing. This meant that for the first time a garden had been consciously laid out using perspective to create an extraordinary effect of distance. The two two-part *broderie parterres* located one behind the other are separated by a transverse alley, and at its point of intersection with the main alley a pool with a fountain can be seen. The huge compartments transform the landscape into a filigree ornament. Le Nôtre accentuated the inward curves of the first two beds by means of two fountains corresponding to the larger fountain mentioned above on the central axis of this terrace. By these means one's gaze is concentrated on the distance. He likewise made the boskets contribute to the long-distance effect. They flank the parterres, and this acts as a kind of frame. In this way the eye was consciously discouraged from wandering sideways. For Le Nôtre, Vaux-le-Vicomte offered gigantic scope for experiment. From various European gardens, including – indeed especially – the Italian gardens of which he later spoke so contemptuously, he took over motifs such as the channel, the pool, the open steps, or the ramp. His artistry and his new conceptions were the result of a brilliant combination of all these elements.

What must the young King Louis XIV have felt when he visited Vaux-le-Vicomte for the first time? He was indubitably enthusiastic about this spacious and unusually sumptuous garden layout. He himself at the time boasted only a modest little hunting lodge in the grounds of Versailles. At the opening ceremony on August 17, 1661 the guests walked to the distant hill with the monumental copy of the Farnese Hercules – an obvious allusion to the master of the house. From this height there was a unique view of the entire site. People at the time even spoke of "the most splendid view in the world": "All the leaping water, the channels, the parterres, the cascades, a seedling forest on one side, a copse of clipped trees on the other, the alleys peopled with ladies and courtiers adorned with ribbons and feathers, all this produced the finest view that could be imagined, and there was a superabundance of such magnificent things that there are no words to describe."

Thus exclaimed an enthusiastic guest at the ceremony. The king, who later thought that he himself was the Sun God Apollo, must have shuddered to the depths of his being when faced with his minister's ambitious mythological allu-

Maincy, Château de Vaux-le-Vicomte
Sculpture at the edge of a *broderie parterre*, one of the major design features of the Baroque garden 1620–1720.

Maincy, Château de Vaux-le-Vicomte
View from the castle of the extensive garden landscape

Maincy, Château de Vaux-le-Vicomte
Fountain, pool, and ramp in the rear area of the garden (at a distance from the castle)

sion. Taken all in all, there is undoubtedly only one emotion that he could have felt: the bitterest envy. And there was of course an inescapable suspicion: how could a minister of the crown, his minister, raise so much money to finance this vast garden? Could it be that his job as financial administrator had helped? There was a scandal. Only a few days after the glittering opening ceremony on August 17, 1661, with a concert, a stage play, and a ballet, and ending with brilliant fireworks, Fouquet was thrown into prison, where he was to remain until he died. It had rapidly become clear to the regent that the huge amount spent on the castle and garden could only have been raised by making a very deep dent indeed in the state coffers. Thus the owner of the castle only had a very brief opportunity of enjoying his splendid property.

The Palace Gardens of Versailles

Thus the history of the most famous palace and garden of them all began with the lavish opening festivities at Vaux-le-Vicomte and the abject disgrace of its master. In the very same year as the ceremony that had proved so fateful for Fouquet, Louis XIV began to develop the palace and park at Versailles. Le Nôtre, who had given undeniable proof of his abilities, was of course the clear favorite to be chosen as master architect for the garden. The now vacant post of minister of finance was filled by Jean Baptiste Colbert, who rapidly emerged as the most important and effective member of the king's staff. In 1665 the minister wrote the following lines to his lord:

"Your Majesty knows that in the absence of warlike activities, nothing can do more to display the greatness and spirit of a prince than architectural achievements."

The decision to develop Versailles systematically had been taken years earlier, as pointed out above, but these lines emphasize the king's need to intensify work at Versailles. Adjoining land was made fit for planting, and included in the conception of the garden.

Building work on the castle proceeded very rapidly. Finally, in 1666, the king with his court was able to hold the first festivities there, in the course of which, incidentally, Molière's *Tartuffe* was given its first performance.

Versailles, birds's-eye view of the palace and garden
Painting, oil on canvas, 115 x 161 cm (c. 45 x 63 in.), 1668
Pierre Patel
Versailles, Musée du Château

A painting by Pierre Patel (illustration above) dating from 1668 gives an imaginary bird's-eye view of the garden site and the castle. The observer feels as if he is floating above the earth. In front of and below him an extensive landscape opens up, fading away into the distance, to the west, in the blueish haze of a chain of hills, and framed, to the north and south, by gently undulating mountain ranges. But the garden site in its entirety cannot be made visible in this landscape panorama. It extends further than the hilly landscape and continues beyond the horizon. The garden is basically conceived in terms of three areas which have as their point of reference the castle, from which alleys radiate outward like a fan, or like the rays of the sun, into the surrounding space, where they branch out in multiple forms, thereby defining more and more new sections of the garden.

The first area is the Petit Parc, as it is today, which had been begun by the Sun King's father, Louis XIII, under the supervision of Jacques Boyceau. It figures in the so-called *Plan du Bus* dating from 1661 (illustration p. 192 bottom), the oldest known plan of Versailles. This parterre measuring *c.* 93 ha (230 acres), with the adjoining boskets, is bounded by the transverse alley which crosses the Apollo pool. The second area, the Grand Parc, as it is today, is ten times as large. In the above-mentioned painting it extends beyond the horizon, that is to say far beyond the channel. The third area, the former Grand Parc, measuring 6475 ha (16,000 acres), is the largest, the vast hunting grounds which include villages such as Saint Cyr, Rennemoulin, or Marly. A wall of 43 km (*c.* 27 miles) in length was needed to provide a boundary for this area, which was guarded at twenty-two gateways.

Versailles was not only intended to provide a refuge or a place of distraction and pleasure. It was at the same time understood as an image in

Château de Versailles
View, across floral and box parterre ornamentation, of the palace facade on the garden side, created 1668-78 by Louis le Vau and Jules Hardouin-Mansart.

ILLUSTRATIONS OPPOSITE
Versailles, palace gardens
Latona fountain 1668-86

***Plan de Bus* dating from 1661–2**
Paris, Bibliothèque Nationale

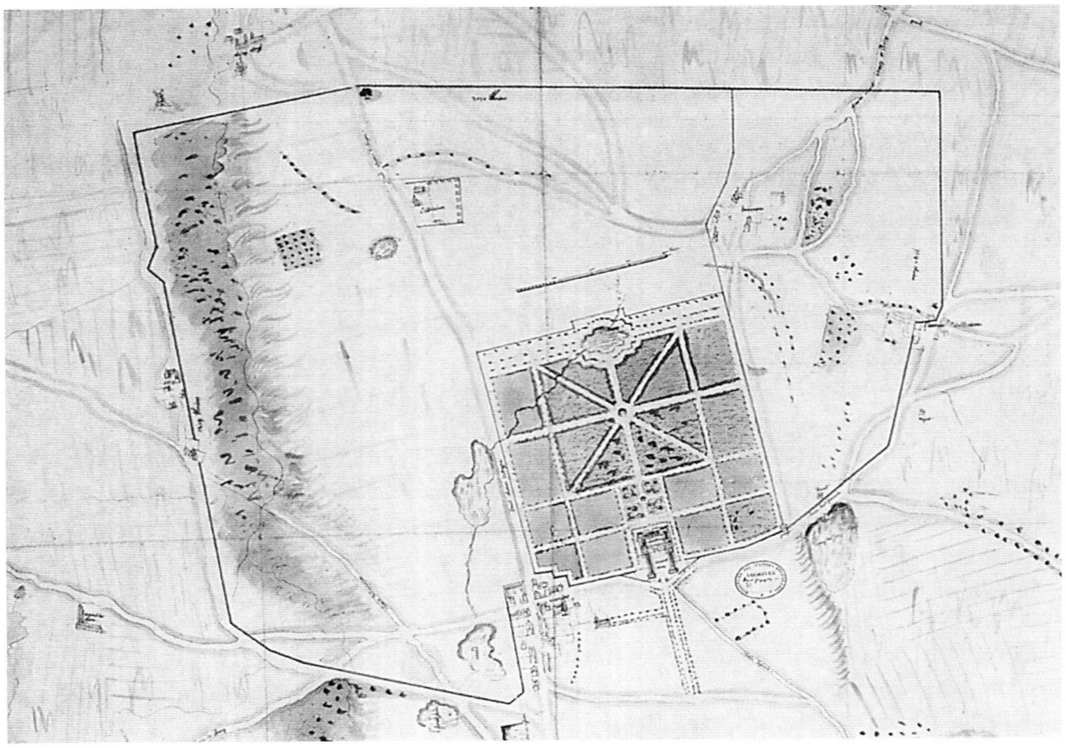

miniature of a new spatial organization, signifying a new political order, indeed a new world order. The equation of Louis XIV, the Sun King, with the Greek god Apollo was not only a mythological game, but also, and especially, a political strategy. As the leader of the Muses and the founder of a universal harmony, Apollo stood for Louis's political goal, his attempt to be seen as the new leader of a Christian world which had to be given peace and government. The garden thus reflected the principle of order providing the rules by which the power of the state operated, by which in its turn civilization was guided.

The iconography of the Petit Parc reveals what was important in order to understand the royal world order. Toward the end of his life, Louis drew up an itinerary for visiting the most important features of his park. If one walks through the Hall of Mirrors and out of the palace, one then finds oneself on the terrace of the Parterre d'Eau, where there are two pools, designed by Le Nôtre and constructed by Jules Hardouin-Mansart between 1683 and 1685. From there the eye is directed toward the central axis and roams over the Apollo pool and the channel to the horizon (see plan above). The world appears as ordered space, a world of sun and light. The surface of the water

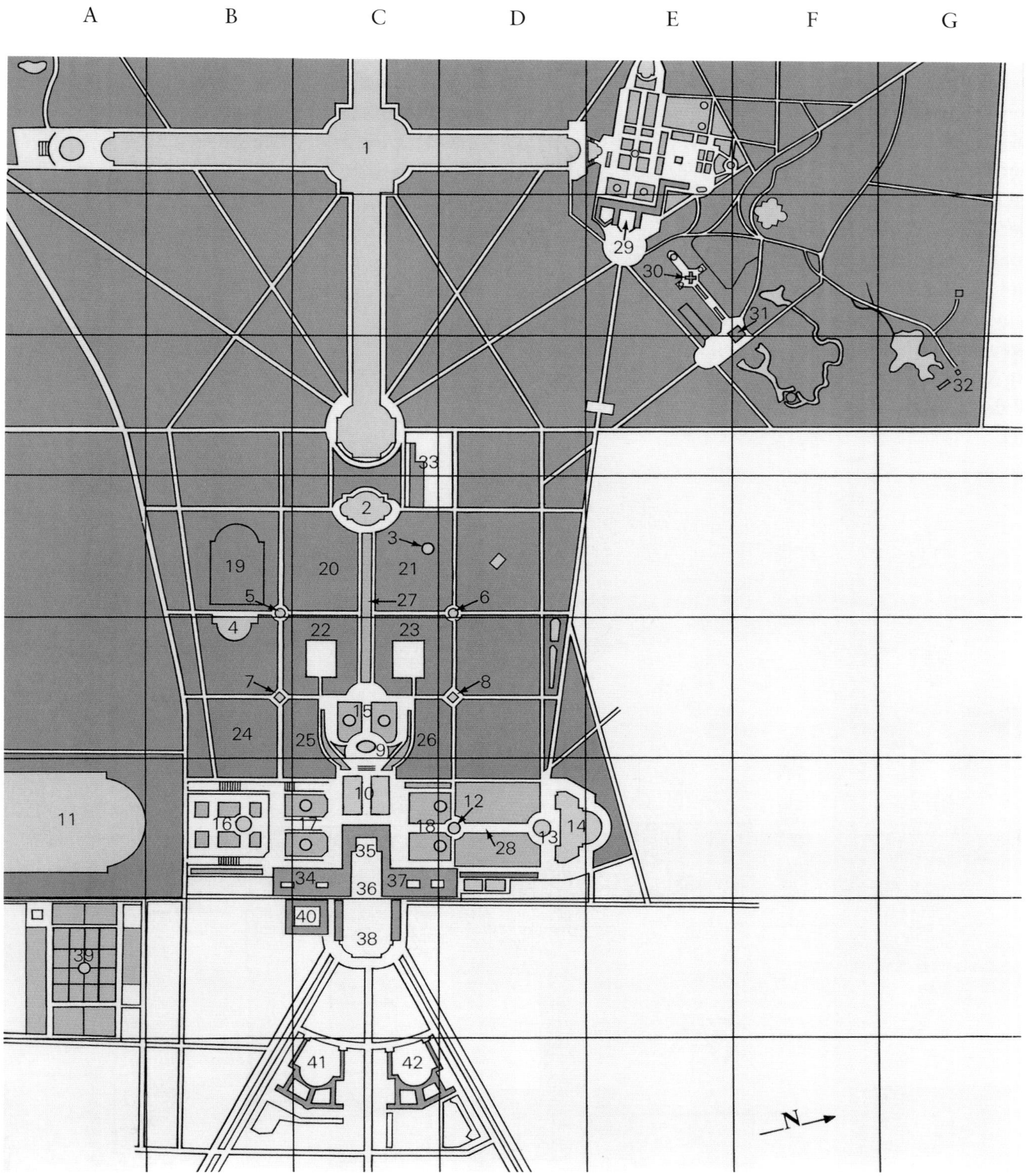

Plan of the garden layouts and Trianons

Pools

1	Great Channel	C1
2	Apollo pool	C4
3	Enkelados pool	C4
4	Mirror pool	B5
5	Winter pool	B4
6	Spring pool	D4
7	Autumn pool	B5
8	Summer pool	D5
9	Latona pool	C5
10	Water sites	C6
11	Swiss pool	A6
12	Pyramid and Nymphs' bath	D6
13	Dragon pool	D6
14	Neptune pool	D6

Parterres

15	Latona parterre	C5
16	Orangery parterre	B6
17	South parterre	C6
18	North parterre	C6

Boskets

19	King's bosket	B4
20	Colonnade bosket	C4
21	Cupola bosket	C4
22	South quincunx	C5
23	North quincunx	C5
24	Queen's bosket	B5
25	Seashell bosket	C5
26	Apollo's bath bosket	C5

Alleys

27	King's alley and Green Carpet	C4
28	Water or grotesque alley	D6

Courts and buildings

29–32	Trianon	
29	Grand Trianon	E2
30	Temple of Love	E2
31	Petit Trianon	F2
32	The Hamlet	G3
33	Little Venice	C3
34–38	Palace	
34	South wing	C6
35	Marble Court	C6
36	King's Court	C6
37	North wing	C6
38	Court of honor and minister's wing	C7
39–42	Minor buildings	
39	Kitchen garden	A7
40	Main counting house	C7
41	Small stables	C8
42	Large stables	C8

reflects the sky, and the mirrors in the Hall of Mirrors in the palace reflect this teasing image, as if they wished to gather the outside space into the inside space. Passing the bronze copy of a classical statue of Apollo, and the orangery, a masterpiece by Jules Hardouin-Mansart (1684–6), one comes to the maze with the Fountain of Animals and winding pathways, which is probably Le Nôtre's most imaginative creation (1666). According to an old description, it was said to be a pleasurable experience to lose one's way there. One passes twenty-five features, and experiences the world of nature and the spirit in mythological themes, panoramas, and in the growth of the plants.

The first major building phase lasted from 1661 to 1680 (see the chronological table on p. 208). During that period fifteen boskets were planted, bounded by alleys. Each bosket is a world of its own, architecturally shaped and with varied stereometric units. In the "wellspring bosket," laid out by Le Nôtre in 1679, pathways twist and turn between numerous streams, seeming to mock the strict symmetrical arrangement of the site as a whole. For Le Nôtre, order was revealed by giving shape to that which lacked order. It was probably for this reason that Mansart was commissioned in 1684 to "straighten" the bosket and add a colonnaded rotunda (illustration opposite).

ILLUSTRATION OPPOSITE
Versailles, Aerial photograph showing the palace and the gardens

In 1681 the king appointed Mansart to be the artist in charge. Garden design now developed in a classical direction. From now on, "built architecture" was distinguished more rigorously from "plant architecture." Mansart eschewed stone supporting walls, and had turfed embankments laid out instead. Where ingenious sytems of pathways were intended to twist and turn through boskets, Mansart often envisaged clearly articulated turf surfaces.

Versailles, palace gardens
Borghese vase at the Latona parterre

Sculpture in the Garden of the Palace of Versailles (illustrations p. 198)

The dominant sculpture group in the garden, which is at the same time an allegorical representation of the Sun King, is the famous *Apollo's Bath* by François Girardon from the period 1668–75. It was modeled on the classical Apollo Belvedere in the Vatican, which Girardon was able to study in detail on his trip to Italy. His Saturn or Winter Fountain (1672–7) is likewise one of the crowning glories of garden sculpture at Versailles. Antoine Coysevox was also decisively involved in the interior decor at Versailles. His most famous work is probably the stucco relief of Louis XIV on horseback in the castle's Salon de Guerre (1678). A particularly large number of works by Jean-Baptiste Tuby in the castle park have survived, including the Apollo fountain with the god on a horse-drawn carriage. It was created between 1668 and 1670. The gilded Flora or Spring fountain (1672–9), by Tuby, is regarded as a masterpiece. In addition to Girardon and Tuby, Gaspard and Balthasar Marsy created the Bacchus or Autumn Fountain (1672–5). The Marsy brothers also created the *Sun Steeds*, which can be seen in conjunction with the *Apollo's Bath*: while nymphs wash and anoint the god, his steeds are taken to be watered. Mention should also be made of the many allegories in strict classical style, such as the *Melancholic* by La Perdrix (1680) or the *Air* by Etienne le Hongre.

Water supply was a major problem. A horse-driven pumping system installed in 1664 conveyed

ILLUSTRATION OPPOSITE
Versailles, palace gardens
Detail view of the colonnades, 1684, created by Hardouin-Mansart

Versailles, palace gardens
River god, personification of the Rhône
1685, by Jean-Baptiste Tuby

ILLIUSTRATIONS ABOVE
Versailles, palace gardens
The Melancholic, 1680, by La Perdrix (left)
The Air, 1685, by Etienne le Hongre (center)
Ganymede, 1682, by Laviron (right)

Versailles, palace gardens
Apollo and nymphs (*Apollo's Bath*)
1666-75
by François Girardon
Marble and rocaille, life-size

ILLUSTRATION OPPOSITE
Versailles, palace gardens
Sun Steeds, 1668–75, by Balthasar

Versailles, palace gardens
Ceres or Summer fountain, 1672–9,
by Régnaudin
Lead, gilded

Versailles, palace gardens
Saturn or Winter fountain, 1672–7,
by François Girardon
Lead, gilded

ILLUSTRATION OPPOSITE
Versailles, palace gardens
Detail view of the Apollo fountain,
1668-70,
by Jean-Baptiste Tuby
Lead, formerly gilded

Versailles, palace gardens
Flora or Spring fountain, 1672–9
by Jean-Baptiste Tuby
Lead, gilded

ILLUSTRATIONS OPPOSITE
Versailles, palace gardens
Apollo fountain in the central vanishing line (top)
Orangery parterre and Swiss pool (bottom)

water from the Clagny pond. Later the Le Vau reservoir was also tapped. But stocks were soon insufficient for the huge quantities of water required by the castle and the park. Other springs were located, and in the 1680s windmills were set up to drive the pumps. Water towers were erected at the pools themselves to provide not only the basins but also the boskets with water. Between 1678 and 1685 ditches were dug and many small ponds and marshy areas around Versailles were drained. The water was conveyed to various ponds and thence via channels to several reservoirs. From there the water reached the castle and gardens. In Marly, which the King instructed Mansart to develop into a hermitage in 1676–86, a system of 257 pumps was installed, the famous *Machine de Marly* (illustration below) which brought water from the Seine over the hill to Versailles by way of an aqueduct.

The king probably soon tired of court life. He found a retreat in Trianon and in Marly. After the village of Trianon had been demolished, he had the Trianon de Porcelaine, the first European summer-house with Chinese décor, built there by Le Vau in 1670 for his mistress Madame de Montespan. With the rise of a new royal favorite, Madame de Maintenon, this pavilion had to give way, in 1687, to a new building, the Trianon de Marbre, built by Mansart and named after the reddish marble of its pilasters, later given the name of Grand Trianon. The parterre at the front was designed as a realm of Flora, a pure flower garden (illustration p. 204).

After the court had been established at Versailles in 1674, and Mansart's artistry, including garden design, had risen in the king's favor, Le Nôtre applied for leave and went on his trip to Italy. In Italy Le Nôtre encountered water features and the art of laying out cascades. Although he gave expression to the low regard in which he held the Italian type of garden, he could not help adopting motifs from the ornamental plant beds, and subsequently using them in France in a modified form. Moreover, the famous French gardener was not only a welcome guest in some of the villas of Italy, but also a sought-after advisor in matters of parterre design. Before turning back to Le Nôtre, let us for the moment pursue the continuing history of Versailles.

After the death of Louis XIV in 1715, Louis XV took over the care of the gardens, which had changed considerably during the past few decades. By then the trees in the boskets had grown so tall that it was no longer possible to trim them

Aqueduct and *Machine de Marly*
Painting, oil on canvas, 115 x 161 cm (*c.* 45 x 63 in.), 1724
Pierre Denis Martin
Marly, Musée-Promenade de Marly

Versailles, palace gardens
Trianon de Marbre, also known as the Grand Trianon, with flower parterre, created by Hardouin-Mansart in 1687

ILLUSTRATION OPPOSITE
Versailles, palace gardens
Ha-ha alley in the garden of the Grand Trianon

horizontally. For Louis XV the Trianon was an ideal retreat. He had a menagerie built there with indigenous, economically useful animals. The idealization of country life now took on specific form in the pre-Romantic pastoral image. The garden gradually changed, taking on the form of the English landscape garden. In the years between 1763 and 1767 the king had the Petit Trianon built by Jacques-Ange Gabriel (illustration p. 207). After the death of Louis XV in 1774, his successor Louis XVI made over the little castle to his wife Marie Antoinette, who enjoyed in this more private spot the carefree pleasures of country life until the French Revolution.

Toward the end of the 18th century the English garden became increasingly popular, so that an eager lookout was kept for gardeners from across the Channel. What was now desired was unspoiled nature, enhanced by set pieces such as rocks, waterfalls, or river banks with an unchecked growth of vegetation. The rustic aspect was brought in by building a mock village with eleven straw-thatched cottages, the Hameau de Trianon (illustration on p. 209). After the French Revolution the garden went to ruin. It was not until the reign of Napoleon was the Trianon taken care of again.

English Taste at Versailles

It is often said that the main characteristic of the landscape garden was the removal of the boundary between the garden and the open landscape. Some important aspects of this conception, which was first formulated in England at the beginning of the 18th century, are already to be found in the monumental Baroque gardens of André Le Nôtre and the ideas of the theoretician Antoine Joseph Dézallier d'Argenville, as will be seen in the next chapter. As a result, the French were already receptive to the ideas associated with the English landscape garden.

Around the mid-18th century some parts of the huge garden site at Versailles gradually changed. The boskets which had been planted decades previously had grown into dense clumps of tall trees. In the Regency years and under Louis XV

there was a lax approach to tree pruning. It became increasingly rare for the gardeners with their unusually high scaffolding carts to tackle the trees, with the result that the branches of limes and elms spread beyond the former prescribed boundaries. Little by little the predominantly geometrical layout of the site became blurred.

In those years a new relationship with nature developed. People preferred to spend their time out of doors, in the woods, they sought the solitude of lawns edged with bushes, and in summer they liked to be in the shady areas where a river ran. Back at the beginning of the century Antoine Watteau and François Boucher portrayed such scenes as these in their pictures.

This new feeling for nature can be described in terms of the idealization of country life or the concept of the pastoral. In the neighborhood of the Petit Trianon (illustration below), Louis XVI's gift to his wife Marie Antoinette, this pastoral idyll was staged as a *tableau vivant*. A peasant family from Touraine moved into the farm in the *Hameau* (hamlet). A farmhand, a cowherd, and a maid looked after the animals. This idyll, which in no way reflected the social and political conditions of the time, evolved in the garden area, which from 1774 onward was shaped in the English landscape style. Antoine Richard, who had studied Stowe and Kew Gardens while on a trip to England a short time previously, submitted plans in the Anglo-Chinese style which – after being modified by several other garden architects – were implemented under the queen's critical supervision.

The most urgent task, to begin with, was to give the garden an English orientation: an irregular network of pathways leading across modeled hill formations, ruins of classical temples and Chinese pavilions and pagodas (the latter were not built, however). Finally, from 1783, the *Hameau de*

Illumination of the *Rocher* and the *Belvedere* in the garden of the Petit Trianon at the fête given for Joseph II of Austria
Painting, oil on canvas, 60 x 74 cm (*c.* 24 x 30 in.) 1781
Claude-Louis Châtelet
Versailles, Musée du Château

Versailles, palace gardens
Forecourt facade of the Petit Trianon created 1762–4 by Jacques Gabriel

ILLUSTRATION OPPOSITE
Versailles, palace gardens
The Temple of Love in the garden of the Petit Trianon created in 1777–8 by Richard Mique for Marie Antoinette.

Trianon, the pastoral hamlet, was created beside an artificial lake (illustration opposite). Thus it was possible to stroll along the shores of the lake and look at the separate buildings, which Châtelet drew in 1786: the dairy sheds and the tower for the fishermen, the billiards house, which was linked by a pergola to the Queen's house, and the mill.

At first sight there appears to be a glaring contrast here: the most famous Baroque garden in Europe evolved almost harmoniously into the first distinctly English landscape garden on the Continent. The geometrical garden had not, as one often reads, exhausted its potential. Quite the contrary. Since the Baroque garden was conceived, both actually and symbolically, as a model landscape, the new Rousseau-esque feeling for nature was easily able to give the impetus for its transformation. The only strange thing is that England took this path to the landscape garden long before the French – but not in any way without the French. The "open interior space of an exterior space," as Dézallier d'Argenville described the garden at the beginning of the 18th century, needed various design elements which would allow interplay with the surrounding landscape. Relative proportions had to be determined for this *situation naturelle*, in order to match the height of the hedges, alleys, or boskets to the neighboring terrain. The garden had to have a boundary, but this must not be conspicuous. The ha-has proposed by Dézallier d'Argenville were first used not in France but in England, for example at Stowe in Buckinghamshire.

Chronicle of the Versailles gardens

1623 Hunting lodge built
1638 First garden laid out by Jacques Boyceau
1661 Development of park and palace
1662 Parterres and boskets laid out by Le Nôtre
1666 First festive event: première of Molière's *Tartuffe*; Maze created
1668 Palace extended by Le Vau; village at Trianon demolished
1670 Trianon de Porcelaine built (demolished 1687)
1671 Bosquet du Théatre d'Eau by Le Nôtre
1674 Court established at Versailles
1675 Maze replaced by the Bosquet de la Reine
1676 Jules Hardouin-Mansart's Marly hermitage (until 1686)
Machine de Marly built (water conduit and pumps)
1678 Palace extended under Hardouin-Mansart. At times 36,000 workmen were employed in the palace and the garden.
1679 Swiss Pool constructed
1680 Great Channel completed (begun 1667)
1681 Bosquet des Rocailles and amphitheater
1682 Official seat of the French court
1683 Parterre d'Eau by Hardouin-Mansart
1684 Orangery built by Hardouin-Mansart; second bosket planting phase
1685 Colonnade (Hardouin-Mansart) and Marly-Versailles aqueduct built
1687 Trianon de Marbre (later Grand Trianon) built
1699 Court chapel built to plans by Hardouin-Mansart
1700 André Le Nôtre dies
1708 Jules Hardouin-Mansart dies
1715 Louis XIV dies
1722 Louis XV, known as "*Bien-Aimé*," takes over the care of the gardens
1750 Menagerie of economically useful animals at Trianon
1761 Display and plant-breeding garden laid out at Trianon
1762 Petit Trianon built by Jacques-Ange Gabriel along the main axis of the garden; utility garden removed
1774 Boskets cleared and replanted (until 1776)
1775 Theater built in the Jardin Français
1779 Botanical Garden laid out, with a pastoral emphasis and very closely modeled on the English landscape garden
1783 *Hameau de Trianon* (rustic village complex) built
1789 French Revolution, all work stopped
1793 Louis XVI executed. Park grounds split up, some parts ravaged
1795 *Ecole Centrale* founded. Versailles opened to visitors
1798 Tree of Liberty put up
1805 Trianon made into private residence by Emperor Napoleon I
"Petit Trianon" and *Hameau* restored
1860 Boskets planted under Louis XVI cleared and replanted
1870 Park ravaged by Prussian troops
1883 Boskets replanted
1889 Centenary of the opening of the *états-généraux* in 1789 celebrated

ILLUSTRATIONS OPPOSITE
Versailles, palace gardens
Hameau de la Reine, created by Richard Mique for Marie-Antoinette from 1783
Queen's house (top)
Mill (bottom)

Château de Chantilly
Castle and garden with large pool

Château de Chantilly

In 1663, shortly after drawing up the initial designs for the Versailles parterre, Le Nôtre was summoned to Chantilly to design the gardens for Prince Louis II Condé (*Le Grand Condé*). In those years the splendid castle was created, and extended in accordance with plans drawn up by the master architect Jules Hardouin-Mansart. The castle was destroyed during the upheaval of the French Revolution, but was rebuilt *c.* 1830 in the neo-Renaissance style by the master builder Honore Daumet, who was commissioned by the Duke of Aumale. Let us return to the history of the garden. Le Nôtre envisaged a monumental system of channels similar to that at Versailles. The "Grand Canal" ran parallel to the castle frontage and led to a large pool into which, from a basin situated higher up, the water from the little River Nonette flowed via a cascade. In the middle the Grand Canal expands to become a broad transverse basin pointing toward the castle situated to the side (illustration above). This pool is flanked by two water parterres with fountains. The *Grand Condé* garden was made as a channel and pool layout with an abundance of water. This work showed Le Nôtre to be an artist with a wide spectrum of design possibilities at his disposal. Whereas at Vaux-le-Vicomte and Versailles he gave prominence to water as a significant factor but subordinated it to the quarters and compartments, at Chantilly he inverted the relationship between the parterre and the channel. Here the design of the plant beds, the tree-lined alleys, and the lawns served as a framework for the pools and channels.

Château de Chantilly
One of the channel bridges in the castle garden

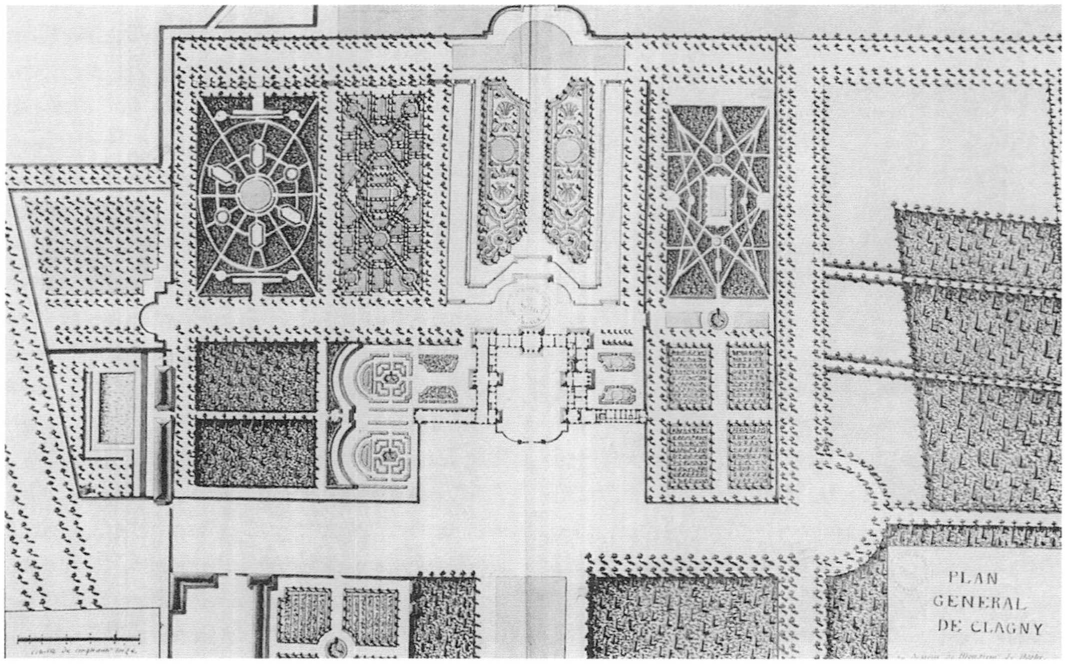

Clagny, plan of castle and garden after André Le Nôtre
Little remains today of the Baroque site which was so typical of the artistry of Le Nôtre's garden designs.

Overall view of Marly castle and pavilions
Painting, oil on canvas, 296 x 223 cm (*c.* 117 x 88 in.), 1724
Pierre Denis Martin
Versailles, Musée du Château

Marly and Clagny

In 1676 Louis XIV decided to have a refuge built at Marly, close to Versailles. He chose Jules Hardouin-Mansart and his own garden architect André Le Nôtre for the task. Work on the project was largely finished by 1686. Today it is scarcely possible to tell what was Le Nôtre's and what was Mansart's share in the work. The entire site nestles in a dell. The terrain slopes downward from south-east to north-west and is marked by a water axis (illustration below). Water plunges down from the top at the south-east, on the rear side of the castle, via the cascade known as La Rivière, into the valley. In front of the castle there are four large pools with adjacent alleys. Beyond each of the main alleys six pavilions were erected, arranged to match the twelve signs of the zodiac.

The mythological program again revolves around the theme of Apollo, and hence around the symbolism of Louis XIV as ruler, who saw himself as embodied, like the sun, in the Greek god of revelation. At the same time this group of buildings is conceived as the outer boundary of the two garden quarters designed by Le Nôtre. He was probably also the creator of the great water stairway, the Rivière cascade, a feature probably inspired by many comparable cascades in Italy.

Neither in Versailles nor in Marly can André Le Nôtre's typical "signature" be discerned. In Vaux-le-Vicomte, where he had worked when he was still unknown as an artist, he had been able to present his new conception of the garden for the first time. The layout had been unmistakably conceived in terms of the effect of distance, and had brought the artist to the attention of the king. With the same determination and with comparable resources, Le Nôtre also tried to implement this conception in Clagny. The little castle of Clagny situated to the north-east of the town of Versailles, was demolished as early as 1769 because renovation work appeared too expensive. Jules Hardouin-Mansart's building for the royal mistress Madame de Montespan was completed in 1680 and included a spacious garden. Because nothing remains of all this, we are obliged to use our imagination, helped by the plan of Clagny (illustration above), to visualize how it was at that time. From the garden terrace in front of the large salon of the main pavilion, we can see that in Clagny Le Nôtre relaxed the rigorous system which he had applied at Vaux-La-Vicomte, without giving up the effect of distance. One gazes across a main parterre, situated lower down in a hollow, along an extension of the main axis of the garden, at a lake. In the middle of the lake an islet rises up, creating a *point de vue* and underlining, as it were, the effect of distance in the garden layout (not shown

on the plan above). To the side of the main parterre, at the level of the castle, boskets are laid out with diagonal pathways. Walking through these copses one is again and again surprised by interesting vistas. Sometimes a section of the main parterre appears, sometimes the castle, or the lake with its island in the distance. Whereas in Vaux-le-Vicomte an austere and effective conception had been carried out, in Clagny Le Nôtre's desire was for a layout full of variety, dedicated more to private enjoyment than to political symbolism.

It is very difficult today to assess the extent to which André Le Nôtre's artistry influenced Baroque garden design in Europe. One reason for this, among others, is that there has been insufficient research into the work and the personality of this French garden architect. At the same time the gardens can today only be reconstructed, and in many cases only very fragmentarily at that, since hardly any more plans, sketches, or financial details are to be found. One may, however, assume that Le Nôtre's artistry, admired throughout Europe during the 17th century, continued to be influential in France into the second half of the 18th century.

If one wishes to summarize briefly what was special about Le Nôtre's artistry, one might use the concept of perspectivism. He was indeed at pains to combine the near and the distant, to include the horizon as a tangible design feature in his plan. For this garden architect, closeness and distance were two means of seeing to which he wished to give shape. He translated the system of lines of sight into alleys and channels in order to give shape to as large a section of the landscape as possible and render it suitable to look at. His gardens were like theatrical stages on which court society acted and could observe itself acting, from close up and from a distance. But there is another aspect, which is important with regard to Baroque culture as a whole: the art of illusion. Fittingly, Le Nôtre was a great lover and collector of paintings by the French landscape painter and etcher Claude Lorrain (1600–82). After his death Lorrain's pictures became the property of the king, and they can today be seen in the Louvre.

Domaine de Marly
Alley and ornamental trees at the large pool

ILLUSTRATION OPPOSITE
Domaine de Marly
The sculpture of a rearing horse, at the old watering trough at the edge of the garden, recalls Marly's brilliance in the 17th century.

Domaine de Marly
View from the autumnal alley of the row of ornamental trees and the large pool

Lorrain used unusual resources regarding composition and color to dissolve the perspectives of a landscape in a warm, hazy evening light. He expanded space by portraying distance as an indefinable dimension, in contrast with the faithful detail and measurability of what was close up.

To understand this way of looking at Le Nôtre's artistry it is helpful to take another look at the painting by Patel (illustration p.191). The bird's-eye view, artificially contrived but which cannot actually be experienced, presents the garden of Versailles as the motif of a picture, not in order to document an architectural description. The difference is a decisive one, for this idealizing presentation undoubtedly drew inspiration from the compositional approach and use of color in Claude Lorrain's paintings. The utopian implications of the subjects of Lorrain's pictures – the longing for a peaceful and ordered world – was to be transposed to Versailles as a model of the new world order of Louis XIV. Anyone standing today on the garden parterres of Versailles or Vaux-le-Vicomte, with the setting illuminated by a gentle evening light, might think that Le Nôtre wished, with the help of his artistry, to give shape to a painting by Lorrain as a natural phenomenon. It is as if he had intended to give the court the illusion of walking through a painting.

What could follow Le Nôtre? Apart from a series of gardens of similar design, probably only the landscape garden, which was already prefigured in Versailles. It comes as no surprise that as early as 1779 the Botanical Garden in Versailles was laid out with an unmistakable pastoral emphasis, and very closely modeled on the English landscape garden. Le Nôtre undoubtedly created both the climate for the way of looking at this new kind of garden and the readiness to accept it.

Paris, Parc de Saint-Cloud
Great Cascade from the 17th century

The park at Saint-Cloud goes back to the Gondi family, who acquired the site in 1577. Le Nôtre created the Baroque layout for the Count of Anjou. He included the cascade in his design. The architect Antoine le Pautre began work in 1667. François Mansart completed the imposing site thirty years later. Because the gradient was too slight to operate the fountains, and, moreover, there was not enough water available for the cascade, it had to be brought via aqueducts measuring several kilometers in length, and conveyed to the individual fountains by means of a network of water conduits.

Manoir d'Eyrignac

The garden at Eyrignac is one of the surprises of Perigord (illustrations pp. 218–223). The reason for this may be that it is very difficult to find. The way to it leads via narrow little roads like field paths, and dark, narrow, twisting and turning forest tracks. But perhaps it is also the case that Eyrignac, to the north of Sarlat, does not catch the eye as a garden because the idyllic surrounding landscape itself seems like a garden. Be that as it may, the garden at Eyrignac certainly seems to be a mysterious, paradisial spot.

The garden site and the country house go back to Antoine de Costes de la Calprenede, who as the First Consul of Sarlat had been obliged to defend his territory against the encroachments of the "*Grand Condé*." His grandson, Louis Antoine Gabriel, Marquis de Costes de la Calprenede, laid out the garden in the obligatory Baroque style. In the 19th century the garden was overtaken by the same fate that befell almost all French Baroque gardens. It was transformed into an English landscape garden.

From 1960, however, the garden changed once more under the supervision of the then owner Gilles Sermadiras de Pouzols de Lile. He was concerned to reintegrate aspects of the geometrical garden into the most picturesque site that Eyrignac enjoys.

The results of this redesigning are impressive to see. The box gallery with its elegant curve, the little cabinets with cut-out windows, and the elegant Renaissance pool flanked by box tubs, give one a hint of the Baroque parterre. The gravel paths, laid out ornamentally, lead from one section to the next. The parterre immediately in front of the little castle can be considered a special achievement in itself: the ornamental box hedges laid out in the Baroque manner, along with the conical box trees and the gently ascending steps, lead to a copse and via a gravel path on to a terrace situated higher up, where yet another parterre of Baroque design becomes visible.

The Eyrignac garden gains its vitality from its surprises and its perspectives, whether one stands directly in front of an 18th-century fountain, its water collected in a Merovingian sarcophagus, or steps out of the window rondel, crosses a broad, unshaped lawn, and looks down a long, extended alley of curved box hedges.

Salignac, Manoire d'Eyrignac
View of the manor

OPPOSITE
Parterre of the manor

Pages 221–222
Alley of hornbeams

Page 222
Pond and hedge
Sculpture recesses (top)
Box rondel (bottom)

Page 223
Little garden house

Albi, Palais de la Berbie
Terrace layout with box and flower parterre

ILLUSTRATIONS OPPOSITE
Albi, Palais de la Berbie (top)
Detail views (bottom)

Albi, Palais de la Berbie

The Palais de la Berbie in Albi was built around 1265 as a bishop's residence directly adjacent to the 12th-century cathedral. "Berbie" comes from *bisbia*, bishop. A garden was laid out beneath the inner tower, which was transformed into a Baroque pleasure garden in the 17th century. It has kept its geometrical character and its unique charm, especially in the statues of Bacchus and of the Four Seasons, down to the present day. The appeal of the garden undoubtedly lies in its unique relationship with the River Tarn and with the old town of Albi, which can be seen in its entirety from the upper terrace.

One may be reminded here of the medieval *hortus conclusus*, the secluded garden. Grassy seats, arbors, plant bed zones surrounded by rose bushes, gravel paths, and herb beds at the outer edges of the garden site – these were all part of the customary design at that time. Possibly a *Hortulus* of this kind preceded the Baroque pleasure garden.

Nîmes, Jardin de la Fontaine

The Jardin de la Fontaine (illustration on pages 226–227) was laid out in the 18th century by the army engineer Jacques-Philippe Mareschal. The terraces extend from the Nemausus spring, which was already known in classical antiquity, via the hills of Mont Cavalier to the Tour Magne, a unique *point de vue*.

Mareschal had the garden planted with deciduous trees and pines, along with cedars. He edged the pathways with balustrades, and put colorful blooming flowers in smaller beds. The spring water is collected in a pool and flows down via small basins to the large channel.

The three large gateways to the garden, with filigree wrought-iron work, date from *c.* 1750. So do the vases, and the statues representing Endymion, Diana, and Flores. Even in Roman times this area (recognized as a sacred area) was used as a town reservoir and for bathing. Remains of a 2nd-century temple to Diana were probably part of a larger temple complex.

Nîmes, Jardin de la Fontaine
Since the 18th century a Baroque garden has enclosed the area of the spring. Rain water accumulates in the fissured cliffs of the Garrigue and emerges here at the spring. In classical antiquity the whole area was treated as sacred.

The Garden Theory of A.J. Dézallier d'Argenville

Vaux-le-Vicomte
View of the parterre from the château (detail)

"On the other hand there is nothing more pleasurable and agreeable in a garden than a good view of a fine landscape. The pleasure of catching sight, at the end of an alley, or from a mound or a terrace, of the many villages, forests, rivers, hills, meadows and other things that are part of a fine landscape, for four or five miles around, surpasses anything that could be said about it here; these are the kind of things that one must see for oneself if one is to form a judgement of their beauty."

This statement could refer to Pierre Patel's picture of Versailles (illustration p. 191) or to a painting by Claude Lorrain, for it presents the garden as a vantage point from which to experience the landscape. But the words are actually those of Antoine Joseph Dézallier d'Argenville, a French gentleman scholar who devoted himself, as an amateur, to the art of garden making. It is to him that we owe one of the most important treatises on the theory and practice of Baroque garden design. The work, *La Théorie et la Pratique du Jardinage*, appeared in 1709, just ten years after the death of André Le Nôtre, and was translated into German a few years later.

For Dézallier d'Argenville a pleasure garden served one single purpose: to give pleasure. In his Introduction he deplored the fact that previous garden theoreticians such as Jacques Boyceau de la Barauderie or André Mollet had paid insufficient attention to this aspect. He identified a total of five points which in his opinion were fundamental when laying out a garden: 1. good light, 2. quality of the soil, 3. water, 4. view of the landscape, and 5. comfort. The statement quoted above referred of course to the fourth of these design points.

In order to be actually able to let the eye roam beyond the garden terrain into the distance, anything that might obstruct the view, such as walls, grilles or hedges, was to be avoided. To this end Dézallier d'Argenville proposed that the garden site should be bounded by fixed ditches (illustration opposite). To designate them, he chose what is one of the strangest terms in cultural history, but which has nonetheless found a permanent place in garden terminology:

"Nowadays, openings in the walls are made, called Ha-Has (clairesvoies, appellées des ah, ah'). These are situated at the level of the alleys, without ironwork, with a wide and deep ditch beneath them, walled on both sides to retain the soil, so that nobody can climb up. This takes the approaching observer by surprise, making him exclaim 'ha ha!', from which the name is derived. Such openings obstruct the view less than railings do."

Such ha-has later occupied an important place in the English landscape garden as a means of preserving the continuity between the garden and the adjoining landscape. The English theoretician Stephen Switzer drew a similar ha-ha with only one wall, giving a very vivid illustration of how it worked (illustration opposite, lower).

For Dézallier d'Argenville it was important to include the *situation naturelle* in the design. He saw a garden as the open interior space of an exterior space, as a spatial entity within nature, which should always be perceptible as such. For this reason he attached particular importance to the dimensions and design of hedges, alleys, and bowling greens (sunken lawn areas giving an unobstructed line of vision or a particular view.) A popular design feature with regard to pathways was the *patte d'oie*, the "goose foot," that is, alleys

Versailles, view of the Apollo Pool and the Great Channel
Painting, oil on canvas 260 x 184 cm (*c.* 102 x 72 in.), 1713
Pierre-Denis Martin
Versailles, Musée du Château

laid out like a fan; these alleys break through the hedges planted in a half-moon shape as recommended for parterre boundaries.

Dézallier d'Argenville gathered his knowledge and experience in the gardens of his time. In some respects, his recommendations and explanations already point in the direction of the landscape garden. The open landscape itself was not as yet subject to the designer's hand, but being a visible area, it was to be integrated into the design. A few years after his treatise was first published, the theoretician modified his arguments to give a clear emphasis to the relationship between art and nature. In the 1713 edition we read:

"If one wishes to lay out a garden it must be borne in mind that one must stay closer to nature than to art. No more should be borrowed from the latter than may serve to reinforce nature."

Art becomes the handmaid of nature. It's role is to highlight and further the essence of nature, namely the growth and welfare of plants. For this reason, according to Dézallier d'Argenville, stair-

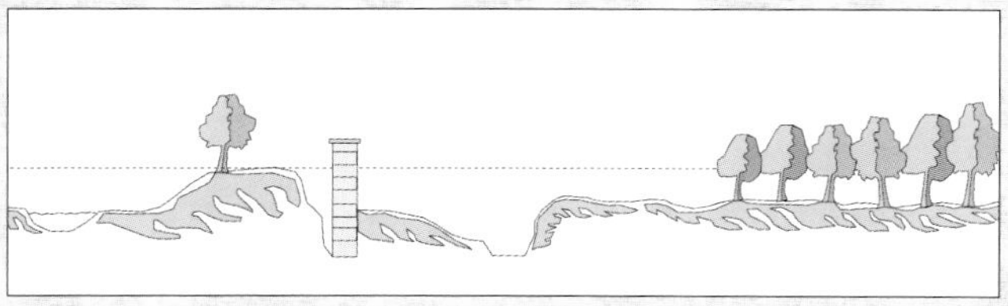

Versailles: Palace garden
Ha-ha alley in the garden of the Grand Trianon (above)
Ha-ha wall and ditch at the end of the alley (left)
Diagram of a ha-ha after Stephen Switzer (bottom)

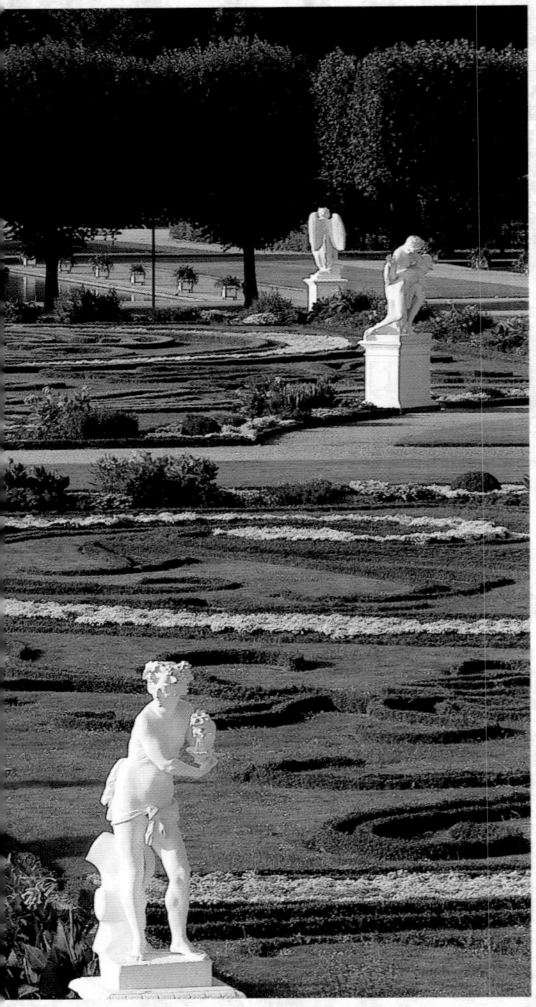

ways, luxurious adornment of fountains and walled boundaries were to be repudiated, because "...here one sees the hand of man rather than of nature."

Dézallier d'Argenville regarded parterres and boskets as the most important parts of a garden. They should be arranged so that they are always contrasted with each other, that is to say "...a bosket and a flower bed compartment, or a sunken lawn (bowling green), and not all flower beds on one side and all shrubs on the other; or a sunken lawn opposite a fountain, contrasting different heights."

In order to illustrate his ideas Dézallier d'Argenville presented pattern designs from which the overall structure and the arrangement of the various compartments can be seen (illustration right). On stepping out of the castle into the garden, one would catch sight of the parterres. They are to be *broderie parterres*, arranged to one side of the main axis. Then comes the first transverse axis, edged with yew trees, with a pool at the point where it intersects with the central alley. Then, after smaller segments of lawn, there is an adjoining semicircular bosket zone with diagonal pathways. The bosket hedges have recesses for sculptures. This first part of the garden ends with a wide channel running across the site. Further on there is a large bosket quarter divided

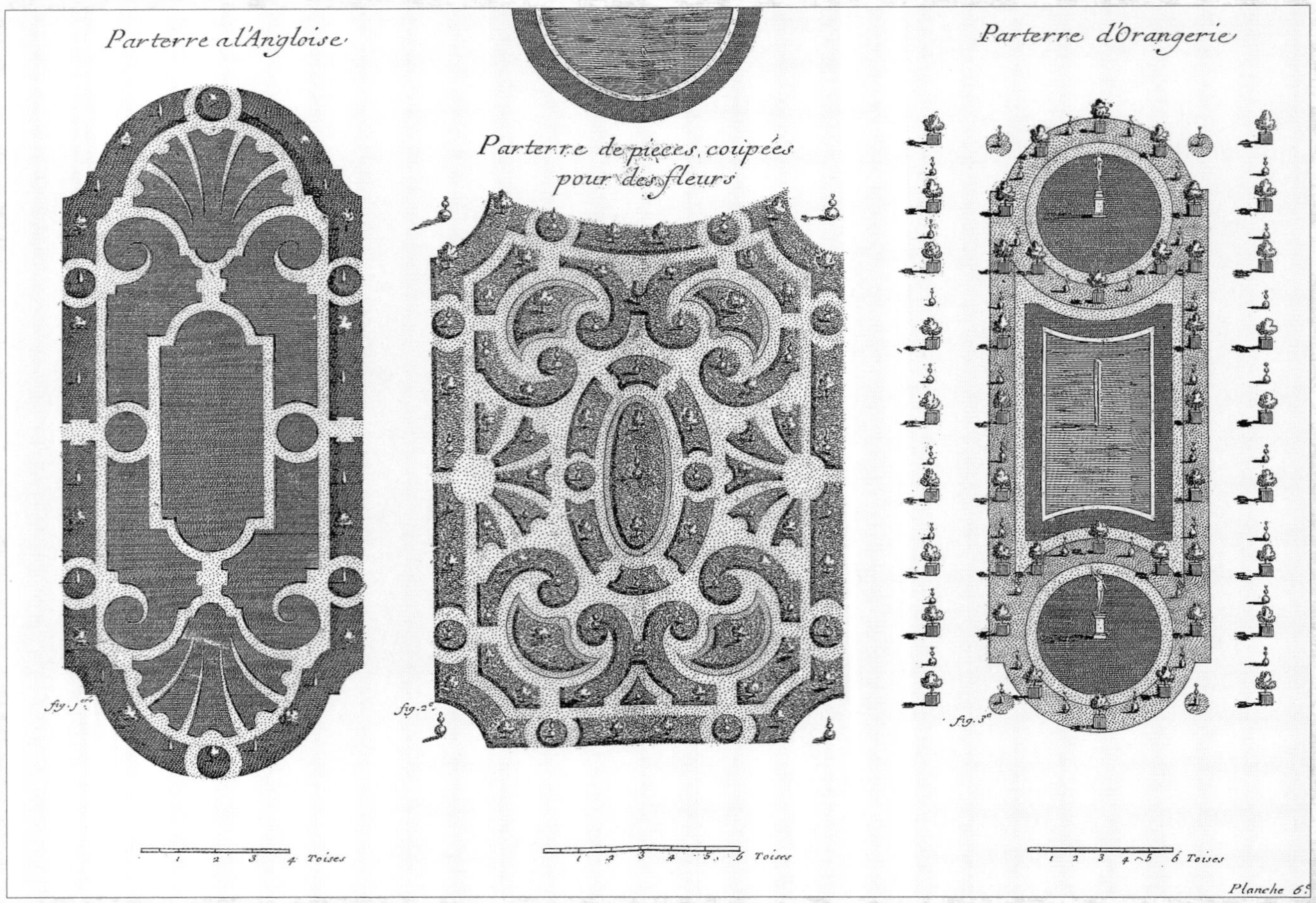

Herrenhausen, Great Garden
Detail view of the parterre site with sculptures

A.J. Dézallier d'Argenville
First pattern design, 1709
(top right)

Parterre forms:
Parterre à l'Anglaise, Parterre de pièces coupées pour des fleurs, Parterre d'Orangerie

ILLUSTRATION OPPOSITE
Brühl
Augustusburg Castle

by the central alley. A *point de vue* is there, provided by a Triton fountain in the extended middle section of the channel.

In this pattern design, Dézallier d'Argenville was concerned with the distribution of light and shade. The light parterre zone immediately adjoining the castle contrasts with the low-growing bosket compartments which end at the channel. The taller boskets planted on the other side of the water create sharper contrasts, with the result that the more distant part of the garden comes visually closer and appears to be more closely connected with the quarters situated in front of it.

The parterres are the most important design feature, since most of them are directly adjacent to the garden frontage of the castle. Dézallier d'Argenville distinguishes four types: first comes the *broderie parterre*, with strips of lawn and dwarf box trees for ornamentation. This is followed by the compartment parterre composed of symmetrically arranged borders and sections of lawn, with their inner areas filled with sand; a fountain is envisaged at the center. The English parterre, also called a lawn parterre, is a section of lawn with pathways showing an ornamental design. Finally, the flower parterre, the *parterre de pièces coupées pour des fleurs*, consists of symmetrically arranged flower borders in small sections enclosed by low box hedges (illustration opposite, bottom). At the corners or in curved gaps topiaries are often found, that is box or yew trees cut in geometric shapes, known in French as *arbrisseaux* (see also pp. 346ff.). The flower parterre was especially popular at small castles or in less central areas of the garden, such as the *giardino segreto*.

During the 18th century Dézallier d'Argenville's treatise, which at the time was called the "Bible of garden design," appeared in many editions and translations. In essence, the author's advice, recommendations, and the designs which he had worked out, were already known from Le Nôtre's work in garden design. But here the designs and layouts of that garden maker of genius were set out for the first time in a book of rules, with theorems that could henceforward be followed or modified by later generations of gardeners.

It may even be supposed that Dézallier d'Argenville's emphasis on the landscape factor and his commitment to nature provided some of the initial impetus for the adoption of the English landscape garden.

Baroque, Rococo, and Classicist Gardens in Spain and Portugal

Seville, garden of the Alcazar
Plant beds beneath the arcade gallery

Spain

We left the Moorish gardens in Spain when the Christians arrived and redesigned some of the existing gardens while destroying and replacing others. From the mid-12th to the mid-16th centuries we encounter the phenomenon of the Mudéjar, the art of Islamic builders and artisans under Christian rule. One of the most important examples of this style was the Alcazar in Seville, which Pedro the Cruel, King of Castile and Leon, had laid out by Moorish builders between 1350 and 1369. At the beginning of the 16th century, under Charles V, the gardens were extended in the Italian style.

To obtain an idea of the Baroque site, one should stroll beneath the 17th-century arcade gallery through the terraced gardens with the pools (illustrations left and opposite). Hedges clipped to a regular shape draw attention to a maze which likewise goes back to models from Italian Renaissance art. The pavilion of Charles V, the Pabellón de Carlos V, which rises up close by is crowned by an imposing cedarwood cupola.

Until well into the 18th century further parts were added to the garden, and old areas were substantially altered, making it difficult for us today to assess the extent to which the Moors were involved, and thereby to determine the typical Mujédar style. No unambiguous artistic tendency or specific stylistic rhetoric can be identified in Seville. Here one looks in vain for the lighthearted touch of the Italian Renaissance garden or the grand, lavish layout of the Baroque garden. What predominates is rather the mood, sometimes gloomy, of a secluded medieval monastery garden.

For the gardens of Italy and France distinct artistic profiles can be produced, for the Renaissance just as for the Baroque period. For Spain one looks in vain for this clear line, which is such an aid to understanding. The reasons for this are, however, not only political. Although Italy and Spain are geographically located at approximately the same latitude, and hence, as typical Mediterranean countries, share a common climate, they differ in one respect which is crucial for the development of a garden culture: the ground is fundamentally different. Italy has been praised since antiquity as a fertile country. Dense, soft layers of topsoil cover the lower strata of slate and clay. The lovely hilly landscapes, covered with olive or pine groves, merge gently into one another. The valleys display their enchanting colors in the mild Mediterranean light. As we have seen from many examples, there is a connection between the gardens and this ambience.

Over large areas Spain is an infertile country. In many parts of the country the ground is hard and arid, the vegetation sparse. Even the few green areas are often dried out by the summer sun. If one visualizes Spain's landscapes as paintings, one is faced with pictures with sharp, harsh shadows. The middle ground is often a gap. The foreground seems to merge directly with the horizon. The tendency to create a paradisial alternative world, a garden isolated from the neighboring countryside, is understandable. As former desert peoples the Moors were masters at obtaining water and artists when it came to creating a flowery island amid barren surroundings. The Alhambra to this day bears witness to this mastery.

But, on the other hand, the cultural and political differences between the two countries must also be taken into account in order to understand the contrast in the evolution of gardens. Whereas in Italy, with the development of humanism, the basis was created for a new European cast of mind, Spain for a long time remained intellectually, and especially as regards religion, tied to the Middle Ages. It was the numerous princely courts of Italy which produced the outstanding cultural achievements. Since Ferdinand and Isabella, Spain had been a centrally governed kingdom. Minor courts were not tolerated. Scientific speculation and humanistic discussion were condemned out of hand by the Inquisition and enlightened thinking was persecuted. The attempt by the Habsburg Emperor Charles V to bring, at last, the Iberian peninsula also under the sway of the spirit of the Italian and the Flemish Renaissance was a brief and almost wholly unsuccessful venture. There were no multipliers, as we would put it today, no social class prepared to reshape the new cultural imports as a cultural tradition of its own. In Spain the descendants of an ancient knighthood confronted a peasantry which eked out its existence on the verge of destitution. There were no

municipal communities, no flourishing guilds, let alone princely courts, that might have been active in promoting the arts and sciences.

The Gardens of the Escorial

Except for the private gardens of Philip II, the garden of the Escorial, one of the first great gardens of the modern age in Spain, was conceived as a secluded medieval monastery garden. Philip II, the son of Charles V, founded the Escorial not only as a residence with a church and a royal sepulcher, but also, and especially, as a monastery. After defeating the French army at the battle of St. Quentin on St. Lawrence's Day, August 10, 1557, he resolved, out of gratitude for this victory, to establish a monastery dedicated to St. Lawrence. With this victory over France, Spain consolidated its position of preeminence in Europe while at the same time spearheading the Counter Reformation. By devastating the Ottomans in the sea battle of Lepanto in 1571, by taking over Portugal when the royal dynasty died out there, and by combating – at that time still successfully – the aspirations of the Netherlands for independence, Spain secured its preeminence not only in the Mediterranean area but also in northern Europe.

The foundation stone of the Real Monasterio de San Lorenzo del Escorial – to give it its full name – was laid in 1563. The design by the master builder Juan Bautista de Toledo, who had trained under Italian architects, envisaged a monumental rectangular block. The facades, framed by corner towers, are articulated with a reticence which creates an impression of monastic austerity. The block includes a church, built, after the death of the master builder Bautista in 1567, by Juan de Herrera as a central building with a central cupola and barrel-vaulted cross members. Herrera laid

Seville, garden of the Alcazar
Pools edged with hedges

San Lorenzo de El Escorial
Overall view of the layout built in 1563–84 by Juan Bautista de Toledo and Juan de Herrera

out the gardens together with the master garden builder Marcos de Cordona, who had been appointed by Philip. The monastery garden is laid out in the Patio de los Evangelistas, within the largest cloister in the world. On its central axis an octagonal temple rises up, along with four square pools, with recessed figures of the four evangelists. Their emblems, the so-called apocalyptic beings, that is the lion, the bull, the angel, and the eagle, keep the pools supplied with water. The ornamentation of the compartments anticipates the manner of the 18th century. Low clipped box hedges form arabesque patterns. Box hedges and conical box trees frame and accentuate the gaps left by the crisscross system of footpaths.

The monastic residence included a further set of gardens laid out around the king's private apartments, which were situated to the east of the main chapel. They were huge *giardini segreti*, accessible only from the royal apartments. Today the design of these gardens is similar to that of the cloister garden. But it may be supposed that at that time the flower beds were ornamented in the Italian Renaissance style and framed by low box hedges. In the 18th century a park with a summer-house, the Casa de Abajo, was laid out beneath these gardens.

Philip probably inherited his liking for gardens from his father, Charles V. It is also to be seen in the new design for the royal palace in Madrid, on which he began in 1556, at the very beginning of his reign. The south wing was given a splendid Renaissance facade of the kind familiar from Italian palaces. To the northeast of the Alcazar he had new gardens laid out which were destroyed along with large parts of the palace during the fire of 1734, and not subsequently restored. The fire also destroyed an intimate *giardino segreto* that the king had had laid out on a terrace adorned with fountains to the southwest, below the Torre d'Oro. Here he had his collection of busts of Roman emperors, which had been given to him in 1561 by Cardinal Ricci da Montepulciano.

Back in the period of Charles V, the present day castle park, the Campo del Moro to the west of the Palacio Real, and the Sabatini gardens situated to the north, were used as extensive hunting grounds. The Habsburg emperor is reported to have brought crows with him from his Flemish homeland to nest in the trees and become a native species. From

San Lorenzo de El Escorial
Detail view of one of the court gardens

Madrid, Palacio Real
Campo del Moro

ILLUSTRATIONS OPPOSITE
Madrid, El Buen Retiro
View through the garden looking toward the Casón del Retiro (top)
Garden façade of the Casón del Retiro (bottom)

Madrid, El Buen Retiro
Garden sculpture

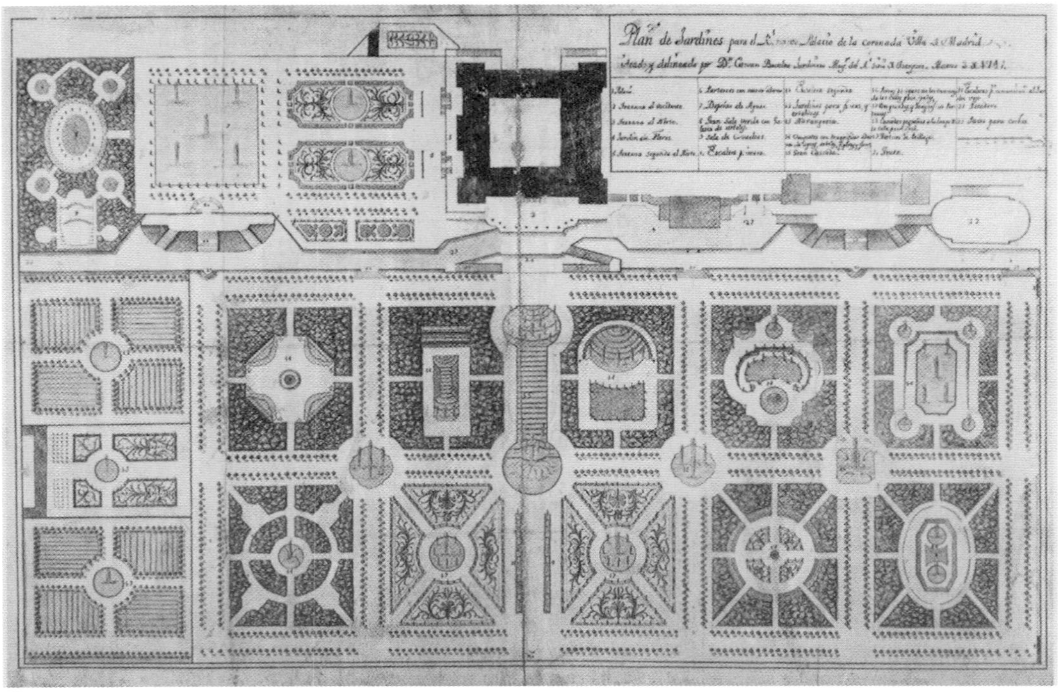

Madrid, Palacio Real
Plan of the gardens of the Palacio Real by Esteban Boutelou, the chief gardener in Aranjuez, 1747

here the king's Bridge leads across the River Manzanares to an extensive park area, which Philip had enlarged in 1558 as a park for wild animals with fishponds, aviaries, and compounds for wild animals.

El Buen Retiro in Madrid

Hardly any traces of the Baroque gardens of Madrid still exist. Only the extensive park areas recall the dimensions of the grand former site. Nor can the old Baroque garden any longer be discerned in the Buen Retiro park, situated to the east of the town center, the last of the Spanish Habsburg gardens. The Florentine Cosimo Lotti, who had previously been employed on the terracing of the Boboli Gardens in Florence, was commissioned in 1628 by Duke Olivárez, Philip IV's minister, to lay out the garden. After the King's death in 1665 it went to ruin.

During the regency of Philip IV and of the last Habsburg monarch, Charles II, who reigned from 1665 to 1700, the Spanish empire that had occupied such a dominant position in Europe went into decline. The policy of decentralization carried out under Duke Olivárez led to insurrection in Catalonia and especially in Portugal. There, the dukes struggled vigorously for independence, which they finally gained in 1668.

Ultimately the Spaniards were so exhausted by Portugal's struggle for independence and by the Thirty Years' War that in the Peace of Westphalia of 1648 they were also compelled to acknowledge the independence of the Netherlands. Charles II, the last Habsburg monarch to occupy the Spanish throne, died without an heir. The marriage policy laid down in his will also failed in its objectives. That Charles envisaged as his successor Phillip of Anjou, the grandson of his stepsister, who was married to Louis XIV, provoked the Habsburg Emperor Leopold I, who attempted to prevent, by force, the implementation of the will. The War of the Spanish Succession (1702–14) affected the entire country. After peace had been concluded Spain lost many of its possessions as well as the Habsburg crown. The Bourbon Philip V became King of Spain.

In these decades of confusion the gardens of Spain fell into disrepair, as might be expected. After the peace agreement of 1714, Buen Retiro in Madrid was to be laid out anew by the Paris garden architect Robert de Cotte. He drew up a grandiose design, which, however, was rejected as being far too expensive. Only a small octagonal garden area in the French Baroque style was laid out as a *parterre de broderie*.

In 1767 the Spanish King, the Bourbon Charles III, presented the park to the public. A hundred

years later the former site of Buen Retiro became the property of the city of Madrid.

Today it is one of the most popular inner-city tourist attractions. In the south, in the Chopera, one can walk in the shade of the old trees, and looking at the well-tended flower beds in the northern area called "*El Parterre*," one can still detect a hint of the artistry of French Baroque gardens. Numerous little temples, fountains, and statues contribute to the lively overall effect of the garden. On the shore of the great lake, the 19th-century monument to Alfons XII catches the eye. Not far off is the Palacio de Cristal, a palace built with iron and glass filigree work, also dating from the 19th century (illustration p. 238, top). Quite nearby a delightful garden landscape opens up with a grotto and a pool. There, in that garden, it should undoubtedly be possible to detect the garden atmosphere that prevailed in the period of "sentimentality" *c.* 1800.

ILLUSTRATIONS OPPOSITE
Madrid, El Buen Retiro
Glass palace (top)
Two fountains (bottom)

Aranjuez, castle garden
Fountain with putti and dolphins

The Castle Garden in Aranjuez

From the following Bourbon period, that lasted until the Spanish Wars of Liberation against Napoleon (1808–14), two significant gardens have survived: Aranjuez and La Granja.

The garden of the royal summerhouse in Aranjuez, *c.* 65 km (*c.* 40 miles) south of Madrid, dates back to the 16th century, when under Charles V and his son Philip II the hunting lodge situated there was converted into a summer residence with extensive gardens.

Around 1562 Dutch and Flemish master garden architects laid out this famous garden on an artificially created island in the Tagus. They arranged the compartments at right angles to symmetrically laid out alleys. Sixty years later the Florentine garden architect Cosimo Lotti drew up a new plan for this site, shortly before being summoned to Madrid by Duke Olivárez in 1628 to work on the Buen Retiro garden. A bosket was laid out on the island with many fountains of striking design. Even the entrance to the garden betrays the architect's origin. There we encounter a variant of the Fountain of Hercules familiar from the Boboli Gardens: from a large pool a small rocky island rises up, which is crowned by a fountain basin in which Hercules stands brandishing a club. Strolling through the garden one is repeatedly reminded of the Florentine model which inspired it. The points where the alleys intersect form round or octagonal areas on which fountains stand (illustration above).

The most famous, and probably also the most popular, was the Triton fountain, which today, however, is to be found in the garden of the Royal Palace in Madrid. From anywhere in the garden, according to 17th-century accounts, walkers could see five or six fountains adorned with sculptures. It

Aranjuez, Palacio de Aranjuez
Built in 1748 and 1771 by Santiago Bonavia and Francisco Sabatini, main facade with side wings

ILLUSTRATIONS OPPOSITE
Aranjuez, castle garden, Jardin de la Isla and view of the Tagus (top)
Vase in the Jardin del Parterre (bottom left)

was to the plentiful supply of water from the Tagus that the garden also owed its unusual water features, such as jets of water which came pouring down out of tall trees taking startled visitors by surprise, or hidden amoretti on an artificial mound throwing water at animal sculptures climbing up to a statue of Diana.

At the beginning of the 18th century Philip V had the famous island garden transformed into a Baroque French garden (illustrations opposite and p. 242) Many of the older waterworks and fountains have fortunately survived down to the present day. The king had elms planted in Spain for the first time. The hornbeams shaped into hedges were also new to Spain. Many pathways were roofed over by treillages, that is lattice-work trellises, so that there were repeated opportunities for the walker to seek out shady spots.

From 1763 the later King Charles IV had the Prince's Garden on the banks of the Tagus redesigned in the style of an English landscape garden. He also had a botanical section set up on the site and a suitable greenhouse built for it.

Although the gardens were substantially redesigned in the 17th and 18th centuries, the southern area, the Jardin de las Estatuas, may perhaps still convey Philip II's special interest im garden design. There too, as in Madrid, he indulged his liking, acquired in Italy and brought back from there, for putting up artistic monuments. King Philip mainly preferred busts of emperors from antiquity and wanted to have large numbers of them put up in the garden. Suitably, his own statue was later likewise positioned in this part of the garden.

The Bourbon monarch's building activity and devoted concern for the garden had a stimulating effect on the grandees of the country, awakening their interest in art. They quickly realized that the garden adorned with an abundance of sculpture was inspired by Italian Renaissance and Baroque gardens. This made them covetous.

The Duke of Alcalà, who was at the same time the viceroy of Naples, was to make good use of his connections with Italy and, with diplomatic skill, achieved the transfer of many antiquities from

Naples and Rome to Spain. In his garden in Seville, now known as the House of Pilate, busts of emperors were put up, a Janus Fountain installed and classical tablets were fixed to the garden walls. This zeal for collecting was perpetuated by many of the Spanish dukes, and was partly responsible for giving the gardens their unmistakable stamp of the Renaissance.

Under Bourbon rule the French garden became established in Spain. The gardens laid out in the Italian style under the Habsburgs, especially Charles V and his son Philip II, were transformed into French parterres.

Spain never developed a distinct type of garden of its own. Only slight traces of the old Moorish gardens remained. Even the garden in Seville designed in the Mudéjar style, which would have had the greatest likelihood of establishing itself as a Spanish garden type, was altered soon after its completion, and hence it did not create any specific Spanish tradition. The various foreign influences over the centuries proved to be too dominant for the country to withstand.

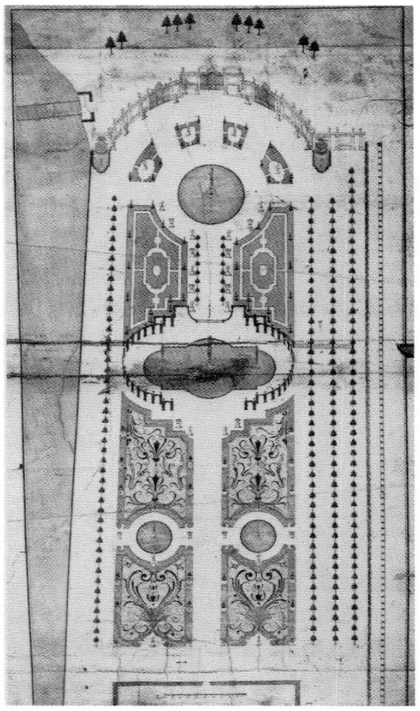

Aranjuez, section of parterre
Drawing by Marchand, *c.* 1730

Aranjuez, castle garden
Fountain of Apollo (top)
Sculptures in the Jardin de la Isla (left)

ILLUSTRATION OPPOSITE
Aranjuez, castle garden
Small circular temple by Juan de Villanueva, 1784

The Castle Garden of La Granja

Although Spain did not develop a garden type of its own, it is interesting to note that a Spanish garden, La Granja de San Ildefonso near Segovia, was nevertheless the model for one of the greatest Italian gardens. The connection is admittedly of a political rather than an artistic nature. In 1714, following the Spanish War of Succession, Philip was made King of Spain. He was the grandson of the Sun King Louis XIV, and, in memory of his carefree childhood days at the French court, he decided to have a garden modeled on the Versailles gardens laid out at the foot of the Sierra de Guadarrama at a height of almost 1,200 m (*c.* 4,000 ft.). To this end, he commissioned, in 1728, plans from two French garden architects, René Carlier and Etienne Boutelou (the latter was also employed in Aranjuez).

In 1735 Philip's son, as the second born, took over the Kingdom of Naples and Sicily from his father. He ruled there as King Charles IV, and starting in 1750 created the monumental garden layout with the grand castle of Caserta, probably not only to remind him of his Spanish homeland but also to surpass his father's summer residence in brilliance and grandeur (illustrations pp. 182–183)

La Granja, the "Spanish Versailles," occupied some 146 ha (360 acres) of land. Cliffs had to be broken out of the massif in order to lay out the cascades. Here, unlike Versailles, the water flowed in abundance from the mountain springs in the immediate vicinity. This is vividly apparent in the innumerable fountains and pools, and of course the elegant cascade along the central axis of the castle, which gathers the water at its highest point for it to come gushing down the steps (illustrations opposite and below).

In contrast to Versailles, the layout at La Granja is not dominated by a main axis and a parterre. A central axis in conjunction with two rectangular plant bed compartments leads to a semicircular pool, with a delicate Fountain of Amphetrite which can be hardly discerned from a distance. Behind this the marble cascade begins, crowned by an

La Granja de San Ildefonso
The Cascada Nueva

ILLUSTRATION OPPOSITE
La Granja de San Ildefonso
Parterre, cascade fountain and garden facade of the hunting lodge built by Filippo Juvarra and Giovanni Battista Sacchetti in 1734–6

octagonal garden house with a Fountain of the Graces situated in front of it. To the east of the palace another garden axis was laid down, leading via stepped ramps to a parterre on a lower level which is bounded on one side by a channel. The view across the terraced pools to the distant mountains is undoubtedly more spectacular than the panorama to be seen from the central axis of the castle. To the east there is another adjoining parterre where the subject of Andromeda is represented in a vigorous sculptural ensemble. A little maze is hidden away in the neighboring bosket. From the Patio de la Herradura, the castle's Court of Honor, another alley leads to a side parterre which is divided up by fountains. In the middle of this layout the Renaissance motif of Mount Parnassus familiar from Italy soars up. It is shaped out of rock and topped at its peak by the allegorical figure of Fama riding on the back of the winged horse Pegasus.

It must surely have been the king's second wife, Isabella Farnese, with her Italin origins, who inspired the Fama fountain. Pegasus has already risen up, and is preparing to leap forward. In the myth we are told that Pegasus made the river Hippocrene well up by tapping his hoof. On his back, Fama triumphantly holds up her trumpet to proclaim the fame of the Spanish royal house. From it the fountain pipe rises up, sending a jet water vertically into the air. The distant gleam of this column of water can be seen as far away as the city of Segovia 10 km (*c.* 6 miles) away. The fountain jet at La Granja is considered to be the highest in all Europe.

The manifold variety of the layout, its surprising perspectives, and the spectacular fountain ensembles make La Granja appear as an unusual Spanish garden, it is true, but hardly as a typical one. There is no unified overall design such as distinguishes the garden of the Palace of Versailles, for example, along with the Italian variant of La Granja, Caserta castle, and its gardens.

We are left, therefore, with the summary given above, that is that the gardens of Spain reveal a great variety of foreign influences: fragments of the Moorish garden, waterworks and fountains from Italy, and parterres from France. But it did not prove possible there to fuse these elements and shape them into a unified national type. The variety of design in Spanish gardens, so lavishly adorned with sculptures, can, on the one hand, it is true, be singled out as a typical characteristic, but, on the other hand, the variety can also be regarded as a symptom of this very lack of indigenous expressive forms.

La Granja de San Ildefonso
Poseidon fountain

ILLUSTRATION OPPOSITE
La Granja de San Ildefonso
Vases, sculptures and fountains in the castle garden

The Maze at Horta

In 1794 the Italian architect Domenico Bagutti began to lay out a hedge maze made of cypresses in the grounds of the Villa de Horta in Barcelona. It was commissioned by Juan Antonio Desvalls under the inspiration of the amorous literature of the age, which often revolved around the motif of a labyrinth of love.

The maze is somewhat small: a rectangle measuring only 45 x 50 m (*c.* 148 x 164 ft.). Cascades, water basins, romantic grottoes, and stairways in the grounds are arranged so as to point the way, so to speak, to the maze. In this area of the garden, sculptures are encountered again and again illustrating the wide variety of guises in which love appears.

Finally, an alley of cypresses leads to a large pool with a surrounding balustrade. Here too is the noble classicist pavilion, the cupola of which can be seen from far away.

At the entrance to the maze, with a double stairway leading down, there is a marble tablet showing Ariadne giving Theseus the thread that is so important for his return.

But at the center, it is not the dreaded minotaur that is to be found but Daphne, who has fled into the maze for fear of Apollo's pursuit of her. Curved apertures have been cut into the high growing hedges situated at the center, some of which, depending on one's vantage point, frame the columns and the cupola of the pavilion.

Barcelona, Horta maze
Round temple and maze (left)
Sculpture at the center of the maze (above)
Sculpture inside the round temple (bottom)

Barcelona, Horta maze
Romantic waterfall in miniature

ILLUSTRATION OPPOSITE
Barcelona, Horta maze
Fountain and double stairway with grotto

Benfica, Palácio dos Marqueses de Fronteira
Detail of decorative tiles in the Royal Gallery

Portugal

It is often thoughtlessly said of Portuguese gardens that they absorbed design motifs from everywhere, be it from the Arabs in the neighboring country, from the Italian Renaissance garden, or the French Baroque parterre. That may be correct, but the Portuguese have succeeded in giving their gardens a profile of their own. They were more willing than the Spanish to concentrate on their own indigenous design resources, and integrate them into the tradition of garden making. There are various reasons for this.

On the one hand, the country is more fertile and less rugged than Spain. It has wide rivers with an abundance of water, navigable all the way into the interior of the country. Trade was more intensive, the exchange of goods was easier to manage. The stately mansion, with its grounds and garden, was always at the center of the country's economic life. In Portugal's cultural history it plays as important a part as the churches and palaces. Portugal's early overseas orientation strengthened its economic power, and contributed to its largely stable political evolution. Throughout its history Portugal remained independent and autonomous, except for the brief Spanish intermezzo under Kings Philip II, III, and IV. In this respect Portugal existed in isolation from the rest of Europe and was able to develop a culture of its own which had sufficiently strong roots to be able to absorb foreign influences and render them fertile for the country itself.

What is the significance of this for the development of the Portuguese garden? A brief note may illuminate the difference between Portugal and Spain, for example. In Spain, gardens were laid out for Habsburgs or Bourbons, in Portugal it was for the kings of the original Portuguese House of Bragança. Thus a national character was guaranteed from the outset.

There are three elements of garden design which constitute the specifically Portuguese quality of the Portuguese garden: Azulejos, that is ornamental or representational tiles, terraced pools, and finally a special kind of box parterre design.

The Garden of the Palácio dos Marqueses de Fronteira in Benfica near Lisbon

One of the first Baroque gardens in Portugal illustrates very clearly the manner in which foreign stylistic features were integrated and transformed into an indigenous form of garden design. It is the garden of the Palácio dos Marqueses de Fronteira, which was begun as a hunting lodge in 1669 to the order of the Marquês de Fronteira, João de Mascarenhas (illustrations pp. 252–257). The Marchese Corsini from Florence visited in the same year and gave an enthusiastic account of it:

Benfica, Palácio dos Marqueses de Fronteira
Palace and formal garden

Benfica, Palácio dos Marqueses de Fronteira
Garden layout with the Royal Gallery in the background (above), sculpture and painted tiles at the pool beneath the Royal Gallery (left).

"The residential building is in the process of being built, systematically and tastefully, and there is an adjoining garden with various parterres, statues and bas-reliefs. There are five splendid fountains, along with a few smaller ones of different heights, on different levels of the garden."

His enthusiasm is understandable in view of the Italian master builders and architects who had been engaged by the marquês. But it may also have been elicited by the unaccustomed new sights which met the marchese's eyes, for those eyes, pampered with Italian culture, now saw voluminous box hedges arranged in very dense geometric patterns, with very beautiful half-height boxwood cones, adjoining a large pool which in turn is bounded by a wall a bare 5 m (*c.* 16 ft.) high. This wall is subdivided into fifteen arches, twelve of which are designed as blind arches with tiled panels showing a horse and rider in the style of paintings of horses by Velázquez. Three of the arches open into spacious grottoes.

Then, to the side of the wall, stairs lead to the so-called Royal Gallery with recessed figures, flanked by two pavilions. In the center of the gallery above the balustrade there is an open rectangular stone portal with a broken scrolled pediment framing the view of the palace facade across the parterre (illustrations p. 253).

The vigorous box ornamentation, the balustrade adorned with flower pots, the figures on their high pedestals, the surface of the water in the pool reflecting the vivid blue-and-white tile pattern of the blind arches, and the Royal Gallery, likewise decorated with tiles, all combine to create a visual

Benfica, Palácio dos Marqueses de Fronteira
East facade of the terrace leading to the Chapel ("Gallery of Arts"): allegory of poetry with statues of Apollo and Marsias at the sides (above)
Bench with multicolored decorative tiles (right)

ILLUSTRATION OPPOSITE
Benfica, Palácio dos Marqueses de Fronteira
East pavilion at the end of the Royal

Benfica, Palácio dos Marqueses de Fronteira
Tiled bench and wall encrusted with seashells and pieces of porcelain

ILLUSTRATION OPPOSITE
Benfica, Palácio dos Marqueses de Fronteira
Terrace on the way to the chapel ("Gallery of Arts"): tiled walls of arcade and recesses, recessed marble figures, and enameled medallions in the manner of the Renaissance artist Luca della Robbia.

enchantment, which in this form is unique in European garden design. The Italian marchese, who was assuredly convinced of the quality of garden design in his own country, and who therefore thought in terms of systems of lines of sight, will have been surprised by the sight of this intimate garden layout which was at the same time such an effective *tableau*.

The Garden of the Quinta da Bacalhôa

Whereas in Frontiera the Italian Renaissance was already being transformed into a specifically Portuguese Renaissance style, at the Quinta da Bacalhôa no more than a cautious opening up *vis-à-vis* the Italian artistic ideal can be discerned.

Braz de Albuquerque, a son of the great seafarer and military commander, acquired the site on the peninsula of Arrábida to the south of Lisbon in 1528, and created an Italianate country villa and garden. An extensive tour of Italy had given him the inspiration for this. He had been fascinated not so much by architectural or visual detail, but rather by the conception of a villa and garden as a single whole, the openness of the building toward the garden and of the entire site toward the landscape. He had loggias built as part of the garden facade of the villa and of the pavilion facade in the direction of the large pool. In so doing he was going against the more secluded and austere character of the traditional country house.

With this new villa concept he was at the same time also giving expression to a new sense of life. Architectural details, such as the tondi in the spandrels of the loggia arches, or the rusticated gateway arches, suggest models taken from the early and high Renaissance in Italy. But the Portuguese component can be seen in the resolute retention of the tradition of the Azulejos, the traditional Moorish art of embellishing walls, balustrades, window frames, recesses, arches, or cornices with decorative tiles. There is a wide variety of motifs ranging from dignified representations of Portuguese kings via mythological themes to dainty ornaments and scenes from everyday life or bizarre roguery.

The Garden of the Palácio Nacional in Queluz

The impressive interplay of landscape, garden, and villa, which probably evolved for the first time in Bacalhoa and gave a new direction to the combination of manor house and garden, was from then on to determine the development of the Portuguese villa.

In the hilly countryside to the northwest of Lisbon, the Marquês de Castelo Rodrigo had a small hunting pavilion built for himself in Queluz at the end of the 16th century. After John

ILLUSTRATION OPPOSITE
Queluz, Palácio Nacional
Tiled wall and sculpture at the stairs leading up to a bridge over the channel in the lower area of the garden site.

Queluz, Palácio Nacional
Tiled walls with vases along the channel (left)
Busts and vases in the lower area of the garden site (bottom)

ILLUSTRATIONS OPPOSITE
Queluz, Palácio Nacional
Poseidon fountain with the so-called "Fachada de Cerimónia" of the Royal Palace in the background (top)
Formal garden with sculptures and views of the facade of the Don Quixote wing of the Royal Palace in the background (bottom)

Queluz, Palácio Nacional
Sculptures and busts in the upper area of the garden site

IV had acceded to the throne in 1640, making Portugal independent of Spain, the site was confiscated in 1654, and then extended to create a residence for the Infantas. The decisive transformation of the building into a royal palace came about under Pedro III, who in 1747 entrusted the work to his master builder, Mateus Vicente de Oliviera.

Ten years later Jean-Baptiste Robillion took over the design and planning of the garden, the Portuguese architect having had to proceed hurriedly to Lisbon to direct reconstruction work after the disastrous earthquake of 1755. Robillion drew his inspiration from Marly in France, the summer residence of Louis XIV with its surrounding forests.

Stepping out of the castle's great reception hall onto the terrace, one looks across two fountains to a lower-lying parterre. The groups of figures on the fountains (illustration opposite, top) have the myth of Poseidon and Thetis as their theme, the more charming of the two being undoubtedly the Fountain of the Nereids with Thetis. The nymph Thetis, with whom Poseidon has fallen in love, emerges from the sea on a dolphin's back holding up the charger with the jewelry which Hephaestus, the god of the forge, has made for the beautiful girl.

The gardens of Queluz delight the eye not only by virtue of their fountain figures with such a wide variety of motifs, but also because of the lavish site, reminiscent of the art of Le Nôtre and of Italian gardens. But the Portuguese element remains unmistakable. It can be seen on the walls bordering the Grand Canal, with their decorative tiles (illustrations pp. 258–259).

Oeiras, Palácio do Marquês de Pombal
Double stairway to the garden, tiled walls with painted mythological scenes

ILLUSTRATION OPPOSITE
Nymphs, detail from the *Fall of Icarus* on the right-hand wall of the stairway

The overall atmosphere of the site was caught by the English intellectual, writer, and art collector William Beckford.

Beckford was in Queluz in December 1818, and wrote enthusiastically in his diary of the waterfalls and fountains that he saw in full play, with a thousand capricious jets watering the luxuriant laurel and lemon trees, and widely dispersing their delicious fragrance.

Amid the thicket, which was partly illuminated by candles placed on the ground under opaque glass covers, the Infanta's servants flitted to and fro, looking like nymphs, and, following her example, visible at one moment and vanishing again the next.

After his stay in Portugal, Beckford went back home to Wiltshire in England and began to design what was a palace, Fonthill Abbey in collaboration with the garden architect James Wyatt (illustrations pp. 389–399). He was committed to the Romanticism of the English landscape garden, but the Baroque garden of Queluz had made an important impression on him.

The Garden of the Palácio do Marquês de Pombal in Oeiras

The architect Carlos Mardel had made a name for himself in Portugal in the first half of the 18th century with his contribution to the Águas Livres, the great aqueduct which ensured Lisbon's water supply. In 1737 he was commissioned by the Marquês de Pombal to build a palace in Oeiras. Mardel was attracted in equal measure to both French and Italian Baroque architecture. This applied in particular to the distorted perspectives which he had studied in Borromini's bizarre decorative designs. They reappear in the scroll-work above the ground floor windows, which only appears to tower far above the level of the facade, being in fact quite flat. Mardel was probably also responsible for the conception of the garden. The grotto, looking like the stage of a Baroque theater with rough-hewn boulders and dark vaults, may likewise be derived from the design of Italian grottoes. He laid a water pipe into the grotto vault in order to have water dripping from the ceiling.

The result was a mini biotope with mosses and ferns surrounding the form of a river god. But the beautiful tiles on the walls of the double stairway (illustrations pp. 262–263) are a special attraction. They tell, in many individual scenes, the story of Venus and Mars and – as a kind of counterpoint – that of Perseus and Andromeda: Venus frees the warrior Mars from his armor in order to seduce him, and thereby prevent him from fighting. Perseus, on the other hand, needs armor and a sword in order to free Andromeda and save her from the lustful monster. Such dual themes were particularly popular during the Rococo period as a means of illustrating the problematic relationship between heroism and love.

This alternative world of the Rococo is typical of 18th-century garden design. Mythology was more than a collection of stories; it was a repository of meanings for a sense of life governed by the Arcadian element. The garden and the associated villa were conceived as a pastoral ensemble, as they are described in contemporary pastoral literature.

The Rococo saw itself as a decorative style. The commissioning owner wanted fountains, grottoes, stairways, and balustrades to be regarded as architectural ornamentation. The basic pattern was rocaille – the origin, incidentally, of the term Rococo. This asymmetrical ornamentation based on a fluid triangular shape provided the dynamics of garden and villa decoration.

Oeiras, Palácio do Marquês de Pombal
Araucaria terrace with sculptures (opposite and above)

Double stairway adorned with vases, with the Palácio in the background (left)

PAGES 266–267
Oeiras, Palácio do Marquês de Pombal
Casa da Pesca (fish pavilion) de la Quinta da Cima, painted tiles with water scenes based on drawings by Joseph Vernet, *c.* 1770

The Garden of the Quinta dos Azulejos in Lumiar
In the Quinta dos Azulejos in Lumiar, a suburb of Lisbon, there is a unique ensemble of tiles covering outer walls, columns, benches, inner walls, and balustrades amid an enchanting garden ambience (illustrations left and above). The scenes depicted are based predominantly on pastoral themes. On the southern outer wall, the boundary of the garden where it adjoins the palace, religious themes may also be discovered, as for example the *Wedding at Cana*, which is being celebrated in a sumptuous palace. In harmony with the garden plants, the scene is framed by a dynamic, upward growing rocaille motif. The garden architecture and the Azulejos date from the mid-18th century, and must surely have been inspired by the surpisingly similar Neapolitan Chiostro delle Maioliche of Santa Chiara which had been created a short time previously.

Lumiar/Lisbon, Quinta dos Azulejos
Tiled bench and columns (left)

View of painted tiles representing the biblical scene of the *Wedding at Cana*

Coimbra, Botanical Garden
View of the garden with an aqueduct in the background

On the peaks of the Sintra mountains, which rise up over the Atlantic coast close to the most westerly point of Europe, is a beautiful landscape which has been celebrated by both Portuguese and English poets. Ruins of Moorish castles, medieval monks' cells, and 18th-century grand mansions along with exotic 19th-century villas, give a unique stamp to this cultural landscape. The grand mansions with their gardens should be explored on foot. Sometimes there are only narrow pathways leading out from the towns and villages to the country estates and their villas or palaces.

The Gardens of the Quinta da Piedade and the Quinta da Sáo Sebastião in Sintra

The Quinta da Piedade in Sintra merits attention, since at the beginning of the 20th century a garden site in the manner of the 16th century was re-created there. The mansion belonging to the Cadavale family was built in the 19th century.

The descendants of the family set about laying out a garden planted in a regular, symmetrical manner and with a sophisticated system of lines of sight which draw in in the surrounding landscape. The tiled walls and benches create a "Portuguese atmosphere." The pool, the plant beds enclosed with box, and the arcades of the pergola framed by tall cypresses, providing a stage for the valley, the villages, and the distant mountains, were probably inspired by Italian models.

The Quinta da Sáo Sebastião in the town of Sintra is one of the most elegant 18th-century palaces in Portugal. The mansion is situated above the town on a hill. The terrain in front of the garden frontage descends steeply, so that there is an incomparable view from the garden terrace down to the town.

The pavilion-like mansion, with its terrace doors and windows in the shape of pointed arches and the tondi with their classicist framing, is bounded by a parapet of filigree design with stuccoed ribbons. The frescoes in the dining hall were designed by the Frenchman Jean Pillement and his pupils and, following the fashion of the time, they depict ideal landscapes with pastoral motifs. Curtains along with a *trompe-l'oeil* arrangement of painted frames suggest that the wall opens out into the distance: a transformation of the painted illusion into the real landscape outside the building.

The present-day garden site of the Quinta da Sáo Sebastião still shows traces of the 18th century, for example the box-framed flower beds, the terrace walls with nasturtiums growing over them, or even the little round guardhouses.

The Botanical Garden in Coimbra

To the north of Sintra and joining the coast to the east at Prata, the Mondego valley cuts into the mountain. The cultural center of this mountainous coastal region is Coimbra. There has been a university in this medieval city since 1308. In the 16th century it developed into a center of Humanism, where scientists from Italy, France, and Salamanca passed on their knowledge. In 1772 the Marquês de Pombal had a botanical garden laid out below the university building, the old Royal Palace of 1540 (illustrations pp. 270–272). He had a laboratory and a botanical museum set

up there for the purposes of university study. For work on the garden he succeeded in engaging the Englishman William Elsden, who surrounded the entire garden site with high walls and between 1791 and 1794 built the Queen Mary Gate, which is still in existence today, the Coimbra Gate and the Valley Gate.

The garden was complete by 1807. But further architectural work was also carried out during the following years. The spacious Stairway of Honor was created in 1821, the Main Gate in 1842 and the great glasshouse in 1856. By 1862 the garden had reached its present size of 50 acres.

At a time when the English landscape garden had long since conquered the capital cities of Europe, Portugal was mindful of the scientific task of a botanical garden and resorted to a typical Baroque structure for it.

Standing on the upper terrace of the garden today one has an impressive view of the entire site. The main axis laid down between the Coimbra Gate and the Queen Mary Gate is marked at the center by a large pool with a fountain arising from it. The individual beds are arranged symmetrically along the axis, and they are framed by low box hedges with half-height boxwood cones (illustration p. 272).

Coimbra, Botanical Garden
View from the terrace along one of the garden's lines of sight

Coimbra, Botanical Garden
View of the fountain at the center of the garden site

ILLUSTRATION OPPOSITE
Vila Real, Casa de Mateus
Southern view of the mansion

The Garden of the Casa de Mateus near Vila Real
Another region with gardens and stately mansions is to be found in the Douro valley in the north of the country. The growing number of country villas in the 18th century must surely be the result of the growing importance of winegrowing. One of the most magnificent Baroque sites in Europe is that of the Count of Vila Real: the garden and the Mateus mansion situated about 3 km (*c.* 2 miles) southeast of the village of Vila Real. The palace was probably built in 1743, and the separate chapel in 1750, by the Italian architect Niccolò Nasoni, who did a great deal of work in Portugal during the 18th century (illustrations opposite and p. 274). Nasoni created a kind of Portuguese late Baroque style, giving the impression of a strange stylistic variant somewhere between high Baroque and strict classicist forms. The many banisters, the broken pediments, the wall areas decorated with coats of arms, and the elaborate scrolls contrast with the classicist columns, the strictly arranged window axes, and the clearly articulated wall surfaces.

The variety of architectural forms continues in the design of the garden terraces. Scrolls, curved edging, double circles, symmetrically arranged pentagons, or irregular quadrilateral shapes – these form the basic patterns of the parterres. The forms are made of box hedges on a base of white marble gravel, or else they frame flower and shrub beds. While the corners are emphasized by means of boxwood hemispheres, the beds have today been predominantly planted with red sage, orange African marigolds, and crimson lagerstroemia. The individual parterres are enclosed by tall, sweeping box hedges, artistically clipped (illustration p. 274 bottom). Thus the tightly framed beds have the effect of paintings, the box ornaments are like huge cartouches, and the boundary hedges are like the cornices or pediments of a castle. The elements and composition of the garden make a unique and unmistakable effect – a Portuguese effect. The frequent use of African marigolds is also part of this effect. Because of its penetrating scent and its use as an insect repellant it is more commonly to be

ILLUSTRATIONS OPPOSITE
Vila Real, Casa de Mateus
Fountain and hedge rondel with the northern view of the mansion in the background (top)
Formal garden layout with boxwood ornamentation (bottom)

Vila Real, Casa de Mateus
Formal garden layout with an arcade formed of cypresses

found in peasant gardens. This rustic touch is likewise one of the distinguishing features of late Baroque gardens in Portugal.

A special surprise awaits the visitor to the lower garden, where a gallery of cypresses has been clipped with such artistry that a green barrel vault has been formed (illustration above). On both sides of this artistic arcade of trees there are more small gardens, such as a modern water garden with a Japanese maple tree growing in it. Another garden is surrounded by an artistically clipped hedge reminiscent of French Baroque pattern books. Behind the hedge there is an intimate bosket bounded by an ornamentally decorated wall fountain. In front of the fountain the master of the house has planted a decorative Hinoki cypress. Whereas in Italy the decorative relationship between the garden facade and the parterre appears balanced, and in France architecture is emphasized as the means of conveying majesty and dignity, Portuguese architects and master garden builders have tried to create unusual, conflicting relationships between the garden and the architecture. Still under the impression created by the lavish variety of forms in the main facade of the Villa Mateus, one is surprised to notice the elevation of the garden facade, which is simple and extremely reticent in its decoration (illustration opposite, top). But here we are already in the midst of the exuberance of color and variety of forms in the flower and shrub beds, and the box ornaments. It is as if the architecture had magnanimously lent its adornments to the parterres.

Among the Baroque gardens of Europe there are hardly any tangible national types apart from those of Italy and France. Stylistic influences of Italian Renaissance and Baroque culture, and French elements from the incomparable parterre artistry of Le Nôtre, contributed to an overall European type with many variants. Only the Portuguese Baroque garden does not fit into this scheme of things. The rural touches with regard to planting, the particular boxwood ornamentation, the combination of pool and building, and the imaginative, indeed almost extravagant, use of tiles created an independent Portuguese Baroque garden. Surprisingly, it survived the passage of time, despite the fact that later garden designers throughout Europe took their cue from the England landscape garden.

Baroque and Rococo Gardens in Germany and Austria

Schleißheim, castle garden
Detail of beds in parterre area

Ulm, Joseph Furttenbach's garden,
1641

Joseph Furttenbach's Garden

Heinrich Schickhardt's orange garden in Leonberg dating from 1611 and Salomon de Caus's Hortus Palatinus in Heidelberg dating from 1614 were of major importance for the development of the German Baroque garden. Joseph Furttenbach, the municipal master builder in Ulm who, with his theoretical treatises, had determined the direction in which the South German Baroque garden was to develop, was inspired by Schickhardt's orange gardens in Leonberg and Stuttgart. Certainly, Schickhardt's Italianate plant bed patterns appear in the "*Fourth Noble Pleasure Garden*" of Furttenbach's *Architectura Recreationis*, which was published in 1640. For Furttenbach planting was of prime importance (illustration below). In another theoretical treatise, the *Architectura Privata* of 1641, he describes ornamental beds of this kind. At the center of the layout there should be a *corona imperialis*, an "Emperor's crown," followed by tulips "...with their more than a hundred different colors, including in particular those that are beautifully marbled, flaming, striped, fringed or spotted." This planting system, in various forms, was adopted for almost every garden project in South Germany. Furttenbach's theoretical writings have always been helpful in reconstructing the planting of Baroque gardens.

Following Furttenbach's instructions, many early Baroque gardens in Germany and Austria, which had long since faded away, are indeed being restored to their vivid colors, at least in the imagination. Design and planting of parterres did, however, change in the course of the 18th century, the main emphasis then being on large-scale boxwood ornamentation, the integration of mazes or boskets, and the installation and composition of pools, channels, and fountains.

Schönborn Gardens

The name of the Schönborn family, above all that of Lothar Franz von Schönborn (1655–1729), is synonymous with generous patronage and the development of Baroque splendor. He was the Archbishop of Mainz and an Elector, and in addition to his official duties as archbishop devoted himself to the planning of his gardens, especially in Gaibach, near Würzburg, in Franconia, and in Pommersfelden not far away.

Lothar Franz von Schönborn inherited the castle and estate at Gaibach in 1668. In 1677, at the age of twenty-two, following an extended Grand Tour of Europe, he designed the garden layout, which is preserved in an engraving by Salomon Kleiner. The garden extends lengthwise along the whole width of the castle, a forbidding fortified building surrounded by moats, and has a central axis running through it. A decorative *broderie parterre* is followed by a quarter with the so-called "oval lake," and a bed compartment richly ornamented with flowers. The "oval lake" was invented by the owner of the castle and was as yet unknown in either France or Italy. A broad broderie ring, tilted inward, is broken at four points by balustraded stairways leading down to a pool with a fountain, with jets of water issuing from the figures (illustration opposite, bottom).

The garden is elegantly bounded by a semi-circular orangery, in front of which, to the side, there are berceaux, that is trellised walkways made of latticework, in the shape of a quarter-circle. The Dutch garden in Het Loo may have provided the model for this staggered boundary. The sunken

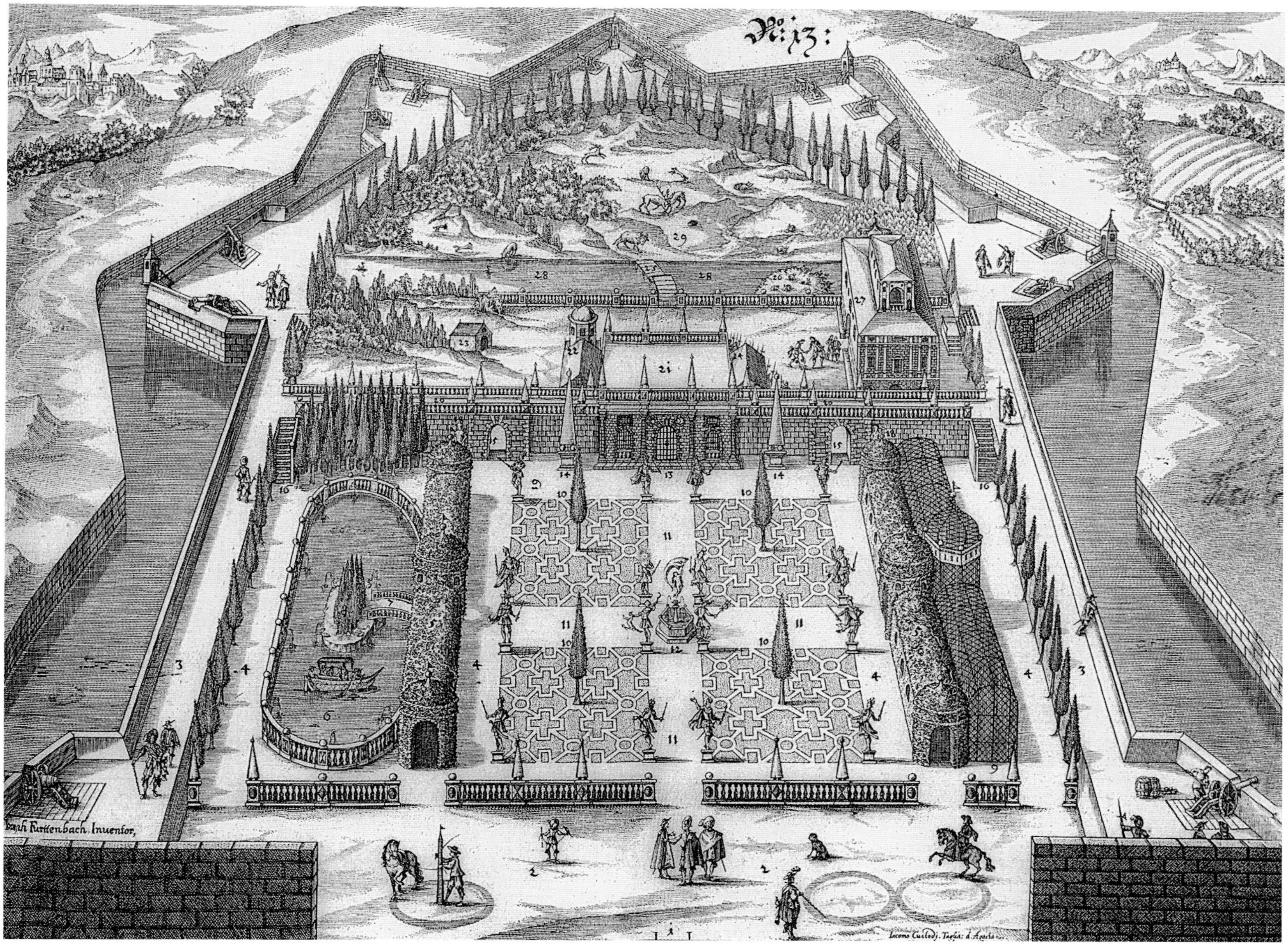

Princely pleasure garden and zoo
Joseph Furttenbach, *Architectura civilis*, 1628, Illustration 13

Gaibach, castle garden
Oval pool, engraving after S. Kleiner, 1728

Pommersfelden, Weißenstein castle
View of the castle and the castle garden from the southeast, engraving after S. Kleiner, 1728

oval pool is also frequently encountered in Dutch Baroque gardens (see illustration p. 330 bottom). Lothar Franz was thus receptive to the "world's taste," as he wrote in a letter to his nephew Friedrich Karl von Schönborn, the Imperial Vice Chancellor and later Prince Bishop of Bamberg and Würzburg.

What probably also interested Lothar Franz in Dutch gardens was the tendency on the part of both owners and gardeners to combine a utility garden and a decorative garden within a single quarter. The archbishop envisaged an unusual solution to the challenge of such a combination in the garden of his private castle at Weißenstein in Pommersfelden (illustration above). The garden was laid out according to a plan by Maximilian von Welsch between 1715 and 1723. In its upper third there is a chestnut rondel arranged in the shape of three concentric rings. The trees surround a sunken pool. There are utility gardens to the side of the rondel. This area, which is generally treated as part of the end of the garden, was often earmarked for utility gardens. The chestnut rondel, situated on the central axis of the garden, broke up the line of sight leading to a pavilion at the end of the garden. Unfortunately nothing has survived of this garden. It was brought into line with the modern "world's taste" as early as 1786, that is transformed into an English landscape garden which today is a deer park open to visitors.

The nephew, Friedrich Karl von Schönborn, had his residence in Vienna at the beginning of the 18th century, and conducted a lively correspondence with his uncle Lothar Franz. Between 1706 and 1711 he had a palace built by the famous Viennese master builder Johann Lukas von Hildebrandt. He wished to have two utility gardens for the annexes as well as a pleasure garden laid out by the rear facade of the palace.

There today's visitor finds a garden in the English style, albeit to some extent "romantically" overgrown. But in those earlier days the garden was famous for its tulip beds, where very rare species were to be seen. The proud owner of the site wrote to his uncle in Würzburg:

"Finally I must tell Your Grace of the wonderful beauty and variety of the tulips. I think I have already sent 2,000 of them to Court. I hear that there is nothing more beautiful in the world than the quality and diversity of the anemones and buttercups which are now in flower in my garden."

The filigree plant bed patterns of the main parterre can be seen in Salomon Kleiner's plan. Their ornamentation recalls Hildebrandt's decorative designs. This applies primarily to the knot structures and the inclusion of some asymmetrically designed beds within a symmetrical overall arrangement (illustration left).

The main building is flanked on both sides by the annexes, behind which there are large utility gardens running parallel to the pleasure garden. The bottom one ends with an orangery.

During the Baroque era there were very close political ties between the princely families of Germany and the Viennese Court. Their principal shared political goals were to combat Protestantism during the decades of the Counter-Reformation, to check the danger from the Turks, and to secure the Habsburg territories on the Rhine from encroachment by the French. There was also joint military involvement in the Spanish War of Succession.

Vienna, garden of the Palais Schönborn
Drawing by S. Kleiner, *c.* 1738

Schleißheim Castle

Between 1684 and 1688, the Bavarian Elector Max Emanuel had fought, with the Habsburgs, at the side of the famous "Ludwig of the Turks," the margrave Ludwig Wilhelm of Baden. He had emerged from the Turkish wars as a hero, and had been celebrated in Europe as a brilliant military commander. With an eye to his political ambitions, he married Maria Antonia, the daughter of the Habsburg Emperor Leopold I. It is possible that Max Emanuel, when he returned from his office of governor of the Netherlands in 1701, aspired to become king or emperor. The New Castle which he had built at Schleißheim was a particularly lavish residence, a "Bavarian Versailles," as it was soon being reverently called by his subjects. In 1701 he personally laid the foundation stone of the ambitious building, plans for which had been in hand since 1693. It provided a stately counterpart to the Lustheim hunting lodge, with its two dainty pavilions, which had been built previously. Between the two building complexes there was the huge garden area designed, along with the castle plans, by Enrico Zucalli (illustration above and p. 282 bottom). The architect planned a channel to flow around the garden and the ringed isle of Lustheim by which the site was bounded. The great channel and the ring channel are linked. These little waterways were used not only for pleasure trips but also for transporting cargo. The three-

Schleißheim, castle garden
View from Lustheim of the New Castle, across the spacious garden site.

Schleißheim, castle garden
Views of the parterre layout in front of the New Castle

part main parterre adjoining the castle is lower than the rest of the garden (illustrations right and below). The adjacent quarters on both sides of the central axis consist of six diagonally divided bosket compartments, of which the middle four are in addition joined together by radial paths. The parterre immediately adjacent to the castle did not follow Zucalli's plans, but was laid out by Dominique Girard in strict accordance with the French style from *c.* 1720, after Max Emanuel had sided politically with France.

Thus on both sides of the central axis the staggered fountains were created, one behind the other, and leading to a cascade, which, in its turn, creates a link with the higher level of the boskets. A central axis follows, the turfed alley for the game of pall-mall, and this extends as far as the Lustheim lodge.

Munich, Nymphenburg Castle
Overall plan, attributed to D. Girard, *c.* 1715–20

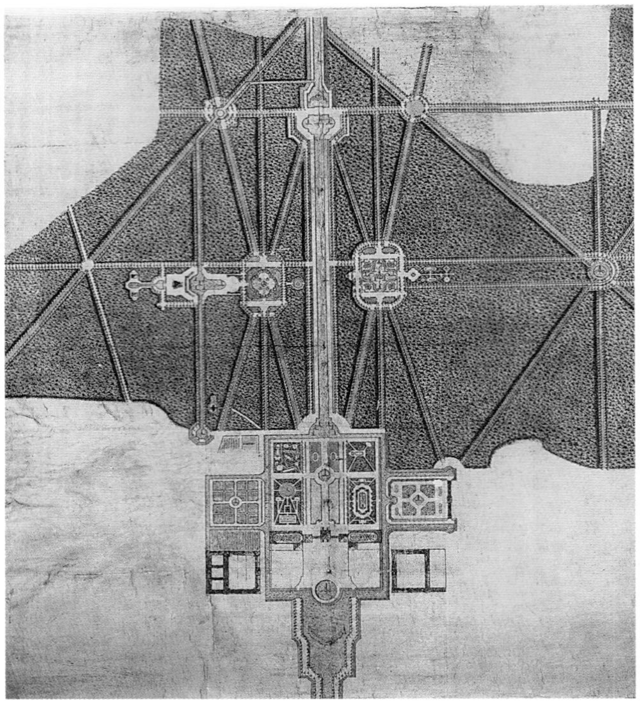

It should also be mentioned that the intimate little exclave of Lustheim was to a certain extent conceived as a wedding present from Max Emanuel to his wife Maria Antonia. The plans were worked out by Enrico Zucalli. The channel flowing in a circle around the castle grounds was intended to safeguard the married couple's privacy and to represent Cythera, the island of happiness and lovers (illustration below).

Nymphenburg Castle near Munich

In parallel with Schleißheim, Max Emanuel had another grandiose castle and garden site planned and implemented: Nymphenburg near Munich. The little castle, the "Castello delle Nymphe," had been built around 1662 for the young Princess Henrietta Adelaide, Princess of Savoy, the later mother of Max Emanuel. After 1701 the Elector had the country house, that had been built in the Italian style by Enrico Zucalli, transformed into a ceremonial castle, composed of staggered cubes (illustration opposite). The structure of the buildings is similar to that of Het Loo in Holland, which Max Emanuel might have studied during his period as governor. The Elector explicitly wished to have his ambitions regarding France, which by then had become very strong, reflected in his garden layout. He wrote to the Countess Arco in 1715 that the garden, with its boskets, channels, alleys, and pathways, could easily be in France.

It was probably once again the tried and trusted Dominique Girard who planned the garden in the style of Le Nôtre. He collaborated with Joseph Effner on the design of the site (illustration left). A painting by Canaletto conveys the harmonious interplay of water, garden, sculpture, and architecture. The painter chose his vantage point at the exit basin of the great central channel. Festively adorned barques and gondolas glide through the water. There is documentary evidence that Italian gondoliers were employed by the Elector as early as 1690 in order to provide pleasure trips with their masters.

Moving toward the castle, the main parterre comes next, dominated by a fountain at the point of intersection of the main axes. Guillielmus de Grof created this fountain, which he dedicated to Flora. The figures are formed from gilded lead castings. From the goddess' flower basket a jet of water shoots more than 10 m (*c.* 33 ft.) up into the air. In Canaletto's painting four compartments can be distinguished. Immediately adjacent to the castle frontage there are two broderie beds. Two lawn compartments with ornamentation in the style of ornamental fittings from the Low Countries, extend in the direction of the channel basin. The decorative beds are embellished by a number of gilded lead vases and charming groups of children, likewise the work of de Grof. The four smaller fountains depicted by Canaletto,

ILLUSTRATIONS OPPOSITE
Nymphenburg, castle garden
Grand parterre (top)
Statue of Jupiter from a model by I. Günther (1765) in the Grand Parterre (bottom)

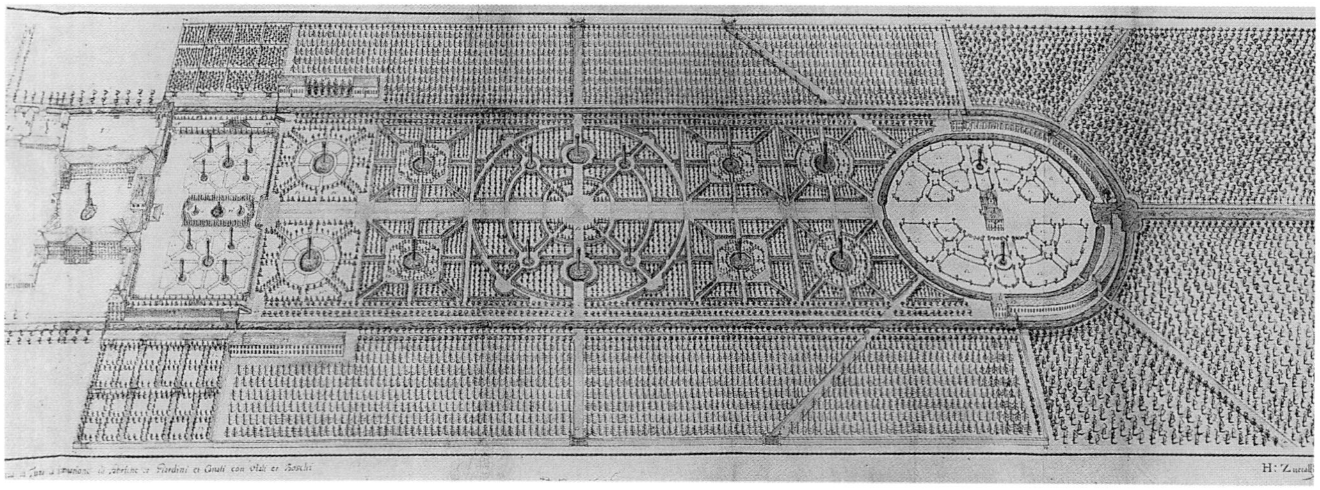

Schleißheim, castle garden
Detail from the overall plan by E. Zucalli, 1700

Nymphenburg, castle garden
Great cascade with personifications of the Danube and Isar rivers

surrounding the Flora Fountain, were not built. Today one can still wax enthusiastic over the sculpture with which the main parterre is lavishly adorned; it dates, however, from the second half of the 18th century. A few sculptures such as, for instance, the figure of Jupiter (illustration p. 283, bottom) are based on models by Ignaz Günther.

Apart from the main parterre, the most important features of the Nymphenburg garden site are the channels and boskets. One copse, for example, was laid out as an orange grove with a central pool; another included a small cabinet garden. The Elector's passion for outdoor sports was served by more boskets with bowling games and skittles. Summerhouses were erected at some of the playing areas, "where the ladies can watch the game protected from sun or rain," as a contemporary noted.

The site as a whole as shown in Girard's plan is an impressive one, and can easily be understood as a symbolic indication of the political stance of the Bavarian Elector.

The system of axes laid out along both sides of the central channel appears as a systematic repetition of the smaller parterre in front of the castle. Since the alleys themselves in their turn cross each other in water parterres, new areas of the garden are opened up and shaped, with pleasure buildings such the "Baden castle" and the "pagoda castle." More alleys branch off in the outer areas of the site, traverse again other alleys, and form rondels, which provide further starting points for laying out parterres and summerhouses or pavilions. The grounds are involved in a dynamic process of enlargement, entirely comparable to the political ambitions of the absolutist rulers.

Nymphenburg, castle garden
Figure of Pan playing his pipes in the woodland

Augustusburg Castle in Brühl

One of Max Emanuel's sons, the Archbishop of Cologne and Elector Clemens August of Bavaria (1700–61), had his father send Dominique Girard, who was by then an old man, to him at Augustusburg Castle near Brühl to submit detailed garden designs.

Work was probably begun by 1727. Girard's planning had to include an older area of the grounds, the zoo. Because this area was encircled by a water channel, Girard did not include in his "garden design as made here for Your Excellency" a cumbersome and expensive straightening of the irregular boundary. The channel was retained, with the owner's explicit approval. Clemens August was fascinated by the system of channels at Nymphenburg, but dispensed with a dominant central axis. Instead he planned a water crossing based on the Versailles model, but this was not carried out.

Today the garden site, which extends in front of the south frontage of the castle and is encircled by a broad channel, presents the visitor with a well-tended Baroque garden adorned with broderie beds and pools (illustrations opposite, top and bottom). Elegant box hedges form curves and loops and contrast strikingly with the light gravel. The beds are enclosed by floral borders, which are likewise framed by little box hedges. A large pool was laid out on the central axis.

At the side, tree-lined alleys separate the parterre from the boskets which, like Nymphenburg, have fountains at the points of intersection of the diagonal pathways. The plans for the garden at Brühl were Dominique Girard's last piece of work.

One cannot fail to see how closely it resembles Schleißheim and Nymphenburg. This was also partly the result of the Elector's family ties. The fact that Girard made use of many garden design features taken from the French garden architect André le Nôtre, should be seen not as plagiarism but rather as the result of an emphatic recommendation by his employer.

Augustusburg Castle, Brühl
View from the castle of the two-part broderie parterre

ILLUSTRATION OPPOSITE
Augustusburg Castle, Brühl
View of the garden facade of the castle across the western part of the parterre

Augustusburg Castle, Brühl
Flower beds and ornamental dwarf trees

Clemenswerth Castle near Sögel

One of the most important Baroque master builders in the region ruled by the Elector of Westphalia was Johann Conrad Schlaun. Between 1736 and 1745 he was commissioned by Clemens August, the Elector and Archbishop of Cologne, who was enamored of riding to hounds, to build the Clemenswerth hunting lodge at Sögel near Osnabrück. As his basic model Schlaun chose the pagoda castle in the grounds of Nymphenburg castle. He was also inspired by studying Marly-le-Roi and the Bouchefort hunting lodge near Brussels. But his project outstripped these models. The two-story lodge in red brick is built to a cruciform ground plan. It marks the center of a large circle which has seven pavilions and a chapel built on its periphery. They were positioned at the angles of the star-shaped alleys leading up to the castle. The effectiveness of the site lies in its clear structure. The wide, undesigned lawn areas and the dignified tree-lined alleys are in line with the style of the building. The articulation of the walls is simple and almost devoid of superfluous ornamentation. Schlaun thereby underlined his early classicist leanings at a time when Germany was dominated by the fashionable decorative approach of the Rococo. The free landscape design of the castle area is also a surprise in comparison with the gardens at Brühl and Nymphenburg. The structuring of the site using alleys and the idea of the circular pavilions presumably ruled out the Baroque parterres that were obligatory at the time.

Clemenswerth Castle, Sögel
Central axis of the monastery garden

ILLUSTRATION OPPOSITE
Clemenswerth Castle, Sögel
Aerial photograph of the whole site with the monastery garden in the background

The Great Garden of Herrenhausen

The Great Garden of Herrenhausen in Hanover is considered to be one of the most famous Baroque gardens in Germany.

The French garden architect Martin Charbonnier was commissioned by the Electress Sophie of Hanover in 1696 to plan and lay out the garden (illustrations pp. 290–295). The work was completed by 1714. There are obvious parallels with French gardens: the central axis of the garden is at the same time the central axis of the castle, and ends at a round patio. The composition of the boskets and parterres is as indebted to the classical French Baroque garden as are the *giardini segreti* situated to the side of the castle building. But the eye is also caught by other features that are not necessarily of French origin.

In 1696, shortly before planning began, Charbonnier had made a trip to Holland in order to gather informatiom in, among other places, Nieuwburg, Honslaerdyck, and Het Loo. It is quite possible that this trip gave him the idea of the channel enclosing the garden area. The orchard with its triangular fields enclosed by box hedges indicates Dutch influences. Charbonnier was able to fuse all these elements into a unified whole, thereby creating a type of garden that has become typical of the north German lowland plain (illustration below).

Herrenhausen, Great Garden
Large parterre with vase
Der Sommer ("Summer") by Ch. Vick

Overall view of the castle and the garden, engraving by J. van Sasse, *c.* 1720

ILLUSTRATION OPPOSITE
Herrenhausen, Great Garden
Corner pavilions by Remy de la Fosse

PAGES 292–293
Herrenhausen, Great Garden
The newly designed parterre

This new type of garden was conceptualized by Hennebo by analyzing its various evolutionary variants and their origins. The strict axial structure led to a thinning out of the compartments, which are particularly conspicuous in the parterre and bosket zones. This may have its origins in Dutch traditions, but it may also be derived from the French Renaissance garden. On the other hand one is also struck by design features which could be taken from the Baroque pattern books of Dézallier d'Argenville. There already it was a matter of the schematic arrangement of beds and parterres and of a structure for ordering the overall design. In accordance with the inclination of the Electress toward the implementation of a contemporary design, which would take its bearings from the classical French formal canon, Charbonnier studied the relevant plans with a view to harmonizing them with his studies in Holland.

If one looks today at the overall design of the parterre one can detect traces of the ideas and images of Dézallier d'Argenville – but only traces. When the garden was reconstructed in 1966 the aim was probably not so much to follow the historical plans that the Electress Sophie had preferred, but rather to produce a pleasing design in the manner of 19th-century neo-Baroque bed plans.

The garden of Salzdahlum castle, belonging to Duke Anton Ulrich of Braunschweig-Wolfenbüttel, was created at almost the same time as Herrenhausen. In 1697 the Electress, later Queen Sophie Charlotte, the daughter of Sophie of Hanover, had the garden of Charlottenburg castle in Berlin laid out. Planning was the work of Siméon Godeau, a pupil of the famous André le Nôtre.

ILLUSTRATION OPPOSITE
Herrenhausen, Great Garden
Detail: view of the Great Cascade

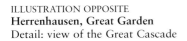

Herrenhausen, Great Garden
Low German flower garden with sculpture *Die Wahrheit* ("Truth") by Evermann

The Gardens of August the Strong

Having, in the course of extensive travels, become closely acquainted with the splendor of the courts of kings and princes in France and Italy, August the Strong, the Saxon Elector and King of Poland, was seized with a desire to outdo this pomp and ceremony. Under his rule, the ceremonial traditions of Saxony flourished and expanded to a hitherto unknown splendor. Baroque festivities could last for several days, with many attendant activities such as equestrian ballets, operas, fireworks, display banquets, or stage plays. The Elector therefore set the greatest store by a garden design which would take these festivities into account. In 1694 he even himself produced a sketch for the redesign of the areas designated for festivities and tournaments between the old castle and the fortified Zwinger in Dresden. He wanted a spacious, separate area for festivities, architecturally unrelated to the castle. The architecture of the court was to provide a dignified and ceremonious boundary for the area. He gave orders "that this Zwinger garden is to be created in accordance with the approved ground plan as a separate entity not symmetrically related to the castle." His architect, Matthäus Daniel Pöppelmann, carried out these instructions with almost slavish fidelity. Building work on the Zwinger was finished by 1728. A wooden gallery on the side nearest to the Elbe, later to be demolished, was not removed until 1847. It was replaced in 1854 by the gallery built by Gottfried Semper. Pöppelmann was able to report to his Elector: "For apart from the various large rooms for amusement, games, and dancing...the entire plan encompasses an oblong/round area so substantial that all manner of public tournaments, pageantry and other courtly entertainments can be put on there."

In 1717, a few years after building work on the Zwinger had begun, August the Strong acquired the Japanese palace in Dresden Neustadt. When the Zwinger was complete, the Elector had the palace extended by Pöppelmann in order to use its rooms to house his large collection of Chinese, Japanese, and Meissen china. The result was an imposing building with four wings and corner pavilions that had elegantly curved roofs in the Japanese style – hence the name of the palace.

The ground plan of the garden was to be similar to that of the Zwinger. Thus here too exedra-like bulges came into being on the long side. The parterres were adorned with many statues and surrounded with small clumps of trees which could be followed up to the exedras. The central section which sloped down gently to the bank of the Elbe incorporated the river landscape almost in the

Dresden, the Zwinger
Gallery and pavilion with bulwark by Matthäus Daniel Pöppelmann, 1662–1736

ILLUSTRATION OPPOSITE
Dresden, Great Garden
View of a vase with sculpted female figure (Corradini vase) and the palace in the background

Dresden, Pillnitz castle
The Water Castle with a large stairway leading to the Elbe

Bird's-eye view of the castle and the garden Engraving showing how it looked between 1725 and 1731

manner of a brochure. On the bank a stairway was built which extended down into the water, and could thus be used as a landing stage for gondolas.

From 1715 the Great Garden (illustration p. 297) was enlarged for the Elector by Johann Friedrich Karcher. The garden palace, which had been built to plans by Johann Georg Starke between 1678 and 1683, thereby came to be situated at the middle of the crossing point of the system of alleys. As in Marly, the central zone of the garden is separated from the boskets by pavilions and trellised paths.

Pillnitz castle belonged to Countess Cosel between 1708 and 1718. August the Strong acquired the estate after the countess had fallen out of favor at the court, and had it developed into a summerhouse for festivities on land and water. Pöppelmann was involved in the project from 1720 to 1730. Along the bank of the Elbe he planned an extensive building with curved roofs in line with the Chinese fashion of the time. This so-called Water Palace (illustration opposite, top) was followed four years later by its companion piece, the Mountain Palace (illustration right). A spacious court precinct came into existence, in which the pleasure garden was laid out. Above the Mountain Palace the elector had the Great Garden of the castle laid out. Here, at the regent's wish, games were to be indulged in. To this end a large lawn was created at the center, framed by alleys

Dresden, Pillnitz castle
The Mountain Palace seen from the south

Garden layout at Großsedlitz
The "Silent Music"

PAGES 300–301
Garden layout at Großsedlitz
View of the orangery parterre and the lower orangery

Garden layout at Großsedlitz
The "Ice pool"

and smaller pools. As the area was also used for shooting practice, a bullet trap had to be set up. One was devised in the form of a grotto installed on the narrow side of the lawn.

If Großsedlitz had been completed it would have been one of the most magnificent of gardens. Even as things are, the grandiose overall plan is visible in what can still be seen (illustrations pp. 299–302). The elector acquired the site in 1723. At that time there was the little Friedrich Castle, which was demolished in 1871, and the Upper Orangery with the greenhouse. Comprehensive alterations were planned, but work was unfinished. What remains are two parallel gardens extending from the hill across a dell. The Upper Orangery was an architectural point of reference for one of the gardens. Its central axis points toward the opposite slope where the water gushed over a cascade into a valley pool; neither still exists. The central axis of the adjoining part of the garden to the east points toward the Lower Orangery. The axis runs across two narrow channels with fountains – Vaux-le-Vicomte may have provided the inspiration – to the "Silent Music," a picturesque stairway adorned with Cupids making music, and framing a pool.

The Karlsberg in Kassel-Wilhelmshöhe

Landgrave Karl von Hessen-Kassel had become acquainted with the most important Renaissance and Baroque gardens during an extended trip to Italy in 1699–1700. The absorption with which he studied the details of garden design may be seen in his *Diarium Italicum*. He was delighted with the "wonders of Frascati," but he was also enthusiastic about the famous Palazzo Farnese in Rome, where he studied the statue of Hercules. He communicated this and many more impressions to Giovanni Francesco Guerniero, who immediately began planning a monumental garden site on the Wilhelmshöhe in Kassel. Work was in progress from 1701, and in 1705 he submitted to his landgrave a preliminary bird's-eye view of the projected overall site, at that time still named Karlsberg. A cascade passing over several terraces was to link a splendid castle on the mountain with a palace in the manner of an Italian country villa at the foot of the mountain. With insufficient financial resources, by 1718 only one third of the project had been carried out. Nevertheless, the present-day visitor is amazed by the site (illustration above). High up, an octagonal central edifice rises, crowned by a pyramid on which

Kassel-Wilhelmshöhe, Karlsberg
Overall view of the Karlsberg with octagon and cascade

Weikersheim, castle garden
View of the castle from the parterre
Sculpture of Artemis in the foreground

stands the towering replica of the Farnese *Hercules*, 9.2 m (*c.* 30 ft.) tall, created by Johann Jakob Anthoni in 1713–17. The cascade runs down over three terraces to the castle in the valley. The lower cascade, with two narrow tributaries, measures 250 m (*c.* 820 ft.), the longest section. Three transverse basins with fountains give shape to the play of the splashing water, which pours into the Neptune basin on the lower terrace.

Weikersheim Castle

The town of Weikersheim is situated in the picturesque Tauber valley, and is considered to be the hereditary seat of the Hohenlohe dynasty, the Lords of Weikersheim, of whom there is documentary evidence back to 1135.

In the market square of this little provincial capital, the so-called Baroque circular buildings catch the eye, with lavishly designed trellis pathways leading to the almost concealed Renaissance castle gateway. Weikersheim occupies a special position in the history of garden design in southwest Germany. The castle (illustration left), seen from the garden side, offers the visitor the view of a magnificent ceremonious building with three pediments adorned with scrollwork.

In an initial building phase between 1586 and 1603, Count Wolfgang von Hohenlohe had what was a medieval castle surrounded by water transformed into a splendid Renaissance castle. The tower with a staircase, the south wing, and the frontage, extended on the ground floor by arcades, give a vivid image of the nature of southwest German Renaissance architecture. This applies especially to the monumental coffered ceiling of the Knights' Hall, designed by Elias Gunzenhäuser. Ceiling panels are decorated with hunting scenes and pictures of animals, as the owner wished it to be. The height and width of the hall doorway must allow him to ride into his living room mounted on his horse.

Behind the hall, the garden opens up, preceded here by a gilded statue of Count Carl Ludwig von Hohenlohe on horseback where it remained until the 19th century.

Exploring the castle grounds is a pleasure. It is peopled with stone figures representing court fools, idlers, lady's maids or drummers (illustration opposite), portraying the life of the servants at court. Princely dignity finds expression in figures of Greek gods, in the allegories of the Winds, the elements, or the continents.

Little remains of the one-time Baroque garden, but the complex set of figures is almost complete. Daniel Matthieu designed the garden, and had it extended in three phases between 1707 and 1725. The basic idea is simple. A rectangular parterre is divided by paths which cross, into four identical beds. At the center there is a round basin with a fountain, and a transverse basin was laid out in front of the main parterre, pointing toward the garden frontage of the castle. Everything evidently revolved around the figures, for which the garden seems to have been specially created. Johann Jakob Sommer, a sculptor from Künzelsau, made most of them in 1708.

Weikersheim, castle garden
Gallery of dwarfs on the balustrades by the castle moat

Details of the dwarfs: master cellarer (far left), court gardening girl (left)

The garden was given its final companion piece to the castle building in the orangery in two parts (illustration on the right), built to a plan by Johann Christian Lüttich between 1719 and 1723. The garden was completed two years later.

The selection of images is intelligently arranged. It seems as if the garden site represents the entire cosmos in relation to the House of Hohenlohe. The four outer corners of the main parterre are occupied by the allegories of the Four Winds. The four elements follow, in the front area, followed by the gods and demigods of Greek Olympus. But the central axis of significance ran from the garden hall of the castle via the gilded statue of Count Carl Ludwig von Hohenlohe on horseback and the front garden terrace, flanked by *Hercules* and *Zeus*, and on to the central fountain with the figure of *Hercules*.

It comes to an end at the semicircle of the final orangery with *Europe* positioned at its center. To the side are *Asia* and *Africa*. In order to mitigate somewhat the solemnity of this all-inclusive view of the world as seen by Count von Hohenlohe, the castle staff have gathered on the front garden terrace, led by the *drummer* and the *policeman*, who have taken up their positions directly in front of *Zeus* and *Hercules*.

Weikersheim, castle garden
Orangery, detail of the east wing (above) and Fountain of Hercules (left)

ILLUSTRATION OPPOSITE
Weikersheim, castle garden
View of the orangery from the castle across the parterre

ILLUSTRATION OPPOSITE
Potsdam. Sanssouci, castle garden
Terraced vineyards and castle

Two Terraced Sites

Unfortunately little remains today of the Baroque garden of Sanssouci castle in Potsdam, as the site was transformed into a romantic landscape garden by Peter Joseph Lenné in 1822. But the unique feature of this garden, the terraced site, can still be seen (illustration right). With this site a new type of garden was created. Work was carried out between 1744 and 1764. The king, Friedrich the Great, provided sketches which his master builder, Georg Wenzeslaus von Knobelsdorff, was expected to follow meticulously. No direct models for the castle, the terraces shaped like exedras, or the parterre and the ramps to the side, are to be found in the Renaissance, nor in the Baroque. The king had the Great Fountain, surrounded by marble statues, positioned at the foot of the vineyard and on the central axis of the castle and the terraces.

It is interesting to note that another terrace garden was created at around the same time (1740–50), at the former Cistercian monastery of Kamp on the lower Rhine (illustration below). The parallels with Sanssouci are surprising, especially as any mutual influence can be ruled out. It can at most be a question of shared models, which one would have to seek in the exedras and theater architecture of ancient Rome. But pragmatic reasons may also have played a part. Handbooks on garden design point out, for instance, that concave terraces are favorable for catching sunlight and distributing warmth.

Kamp Lintfort
Terraced garden
View across the parterre of the terrace layout

Bayreuth, Sanspareil cliff garden
Flower and box parterre in front of the Oriental Building

ILLUSTRATIONS OPPOSITE
Bayreuth, Sanspareil cliff garden
Ruins and grotto theater (top)
Bears' Cave (bottom left)
Diana's Grotto (bottom right)

The Cliff Garden of Sanspareil near Bayreuth
Sanspareil near Bayreuth, situated at the foot of Zwernitz Castle, could be desribed either as one of the last German Baroque gardens or as the first German landscape garden. It is very difficult to make a clear distinction here, since the little Rococo castle, of which unfortunately only a small rectangular building with the elegant dining hall survives, was given a picturesque location in a beech grove. A wall was even built around one tall beech tree in order to incorporate it into the building. The garden parterre, solitary and isolated from the castle, adjoins the grove, and is bounded by the kitchen building. The layout was created by Countess Wilhelmine, the wife of the margrave, Frederick the Much Loved, who at the time was indulging in an affair with the Countess Burghaus. In 1744, heartbroken, she withdrew into solitude and, in the impassable low-lying area of Zwernitz at the foot of a cliff, discovered a cave to which she gave the name "Calypso's Grotto." Having turned her back on the world, she transformed the grove into the island Ogygia, named after the loving goddess. Inspired by reading Fénelon's *Adventures of Telemachus*, she created for herself a place that had no equal, that was "*sans pareil.*"

The life of solitude in the forest soon changed. The grotto was decorated with colored stones. The countess soon found further suitable places by the cliff where she had various grottoes hewn out. Then views were painted on parts of the cliff in order artificially to enhance the effect of nature. The Nature Theater, built of heavy tuff, was like dilapidated stage architecture from antiquity (illustration opposite, top). The auditorium was designed like a rock cave. The islet of sentimental literature, that remote poetic world, lasted for only a few years. After the countess's death in 1758 the park was neglected, and eventually went to ruin. In 1838 Sanspareil was sold to be demolished.

After more than 200 years of neglect, the Nature Theater, conceived from the beginning as a ruin, makes an even more fantastic impression than the countess probably ever imagined.

Benrath, castle garden
View of the garden in front of the main building of the summerhouse

The Garden of Benrath Castle

In 1746 the Elector Karl Theodor gave a commission for his castle to be rebuilt and a garden to be laid out in Benrath. He chose as his architect the tried and trusted Nicolas de Pigage, with whom he was also acquainted from Schwetzingen.

What Karl Theodor had in mind was a rural summerhouse, but one which was to have all the trappings necessary for the ceremony and brilliance of court life. He had the castle built with a central section and two wings, arranged in a semicircle around a pool. The elegant single-story building resembling a pavilion has a central section projecting some considerable way on the garden side. Pigage had an ingenious idea for the position of the house relative to the garden. The private apartments located to the side of the central section adjoin a garden area which is separate from the main garden. The main axis starts at the great garden hall and is indicated by a channel which extends as far as the main bosket. A narrow channel flows round the bosket, whose most striking feature is its twisting paths. The Elector set particular store by the design of the main parterre. Pigage chose paths crossing in a star-shaped pattern, ending at a circular alley in the upper garden area.

It is interesting to observe the combination of a system of paths within the bosket, which almost approaches the English landscape garden, and the unmistakable Baroque design of the main parterre. The elector's lordly demeanor demanded pomp and ceremony – following the French model, of course. But due attention was also to be paid to the new ideas about gardens which were gradually taking root, on the continent also, during the second half of the 18th century. And to some extent this is what did happen.

The Veitshöchheim Garden

Anyone looking for a typical Rococo garden will be sure of finding it in Veitshöchheim near Würzburg. This applies particularly to the sculptures by Ferdinand Tietz with which it is adorned and which make a decisive contribution to the carefree atmosphere of this garden.

The history of the garden goes back to the 17th century, when, *c.* 1682, Prince Bishop Peter Philipp von Dernbach from Würzburg had a little summer house built. It formed the nucleus of the later castle. To its side a tree garden came into being, which was extended *c.* 1702, under Prince Bishop Johann Philipp von Greiffenclau, to become a sumptuous garden layout.

Finally, Prince Bishop Adam Friedrich von Seinsheim is considered to have completed the site. As is clear from the perspective plan (illustration below) drawn by Anton Oth *c.* 1780, the garden consists of three areas. The castle is embedded amid twelve parterres of varying measurements arranged symmetrically around the central axis. Along the central axis there follow two adjoining rondels enclosed by hedges and trees. The larger garden area, situated to the east of the castle, is divided by a central alley into two zones, the southern zone being dominated by the Great Lake (illustration p. 314). A "Circus," that is a rondel surrounded by a trellised walkway, was laid out in the upper area as a companion piece.

Tietz's figures, created between 1765 and 1768, were intended for the lake zone and the boskets. In that particular place, amid the dense foliage of the boskets, the figures seem as if they were from a painting by Antoine Watteau. Sometimes it is a putto swinging his cape on a rocaille-shaped

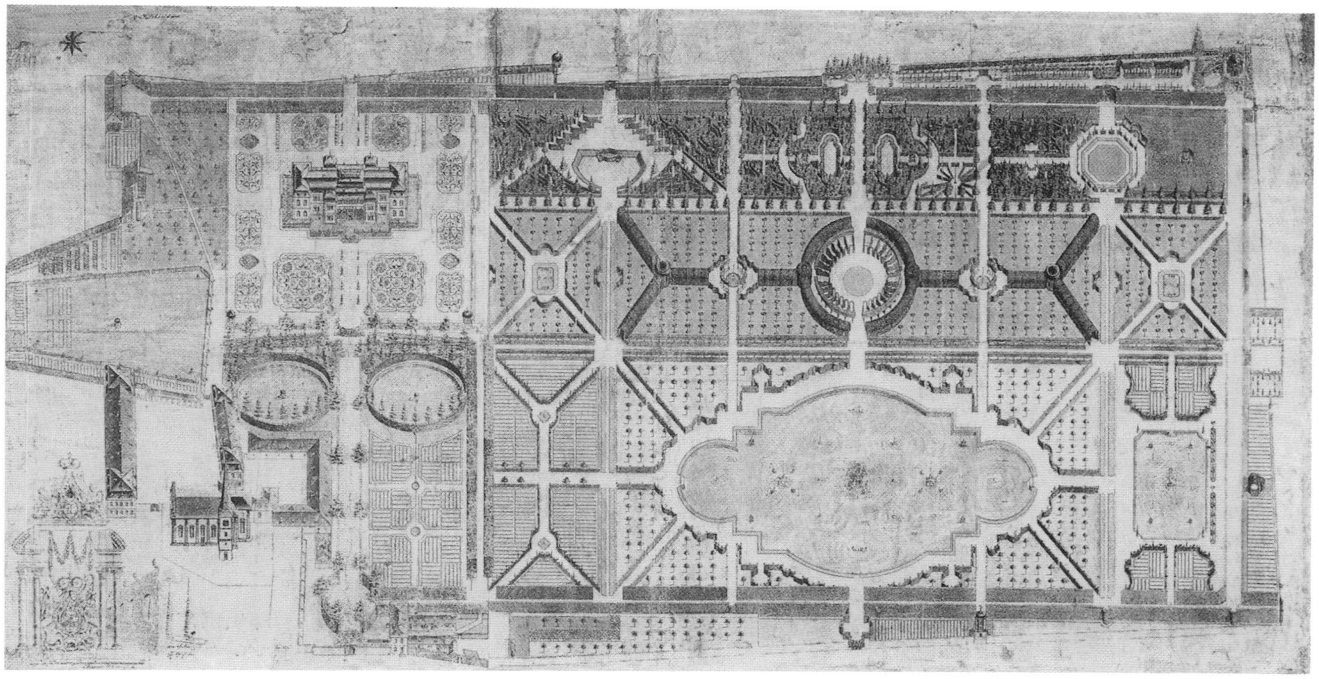

Veitshöchheim, Rococo garden
Sculpture by Ferdinand Tietz

Perspective plan of the entire site by J.A. Oth, *c.* 1780

pedestal, sometimes the figure is a dancing lady curtsying elegantly.

In addition to the allegories there are scenes from Aesop's fables, for example, the Fox and the Stork; a pair of musicians in shepherd's costume also make an appearance, so that it is as if one were seeing the repertoire of the *commedia dell'arte* distributed over the entire garden. Today the playful Rococo world still exerts its charm and magic in this garden.

At the time, however, the aims went further than this effect. The creation of a "sentimental" counter-world had come into fashion along with the beginnings of the Enlightenment. Man opened his heart to nature, to discover there a reflection of his own feelings. Whereas the day-to-day political life of the rulers was dictated by reason, a pastoral atmosphere was meant to develop man's sensitivity and thoughtfulness. Animal fables, shepherds making music and dancing, or allegorical scenes from Greek mythology, combined with the entire inventory of nature which expressed the yearnings and hopes for a ideal world.

The Romantic garden, derived and developed from the Baroque concept, often provided the model for the ideal views and panoramas that began to appear at this time.

Veitshöchheim, Rococo garden
The Great Lake with Parnassus, the Mount of the Muses (left); one of the numerous sculptures around the Great Lake (bottom)

Veitshöchheim, Rococo garden
Pavilion in the Chinese style in the woodland (left)
Grotto house (opposite)

The Castle Garden in Schwetzigen

The building of the castle park in Schwetzingen brings the art of the Baroque garden in Germany to an end on a final chord. At the same time the new strains of the English landscape garden can be heard, accompanied to an even greater extent, at least in Germany, by historical motifs.

In 1720, shortly after turning his back on his old capital city of Heidelberg in order to create, on the drawing board, the new commercial metropolis of Mannheim, Count Palatine Carl Theodor sought refuge in Schwetzingen in order to escape, at least during the hot summer months, from the gigantic municipal building site on the Rhine. From 1742 he was an Elector, and resolved to develop this location as his summer residence. Between 1753 and 1758 the court gardener of the Palatinate Elector, Johann Ludwig Petri, designed a new garden. The rotondas by Ferdinando Galli-Bibiena which made up the castle determined the structure of the parterre (illustration opposite). Around the crossing point of two axes, rectangular and pediment-shaped compartments with obelisks and pyramids were laid out. At the center of the crossing, pediment-shaped plant beds surround a pool. Tree-lined alleys and boskets accompany the large rectangular compartments, which are framed by box-edged flower borders. In 1970–5 the parterre was sensitively recreated from Petri's

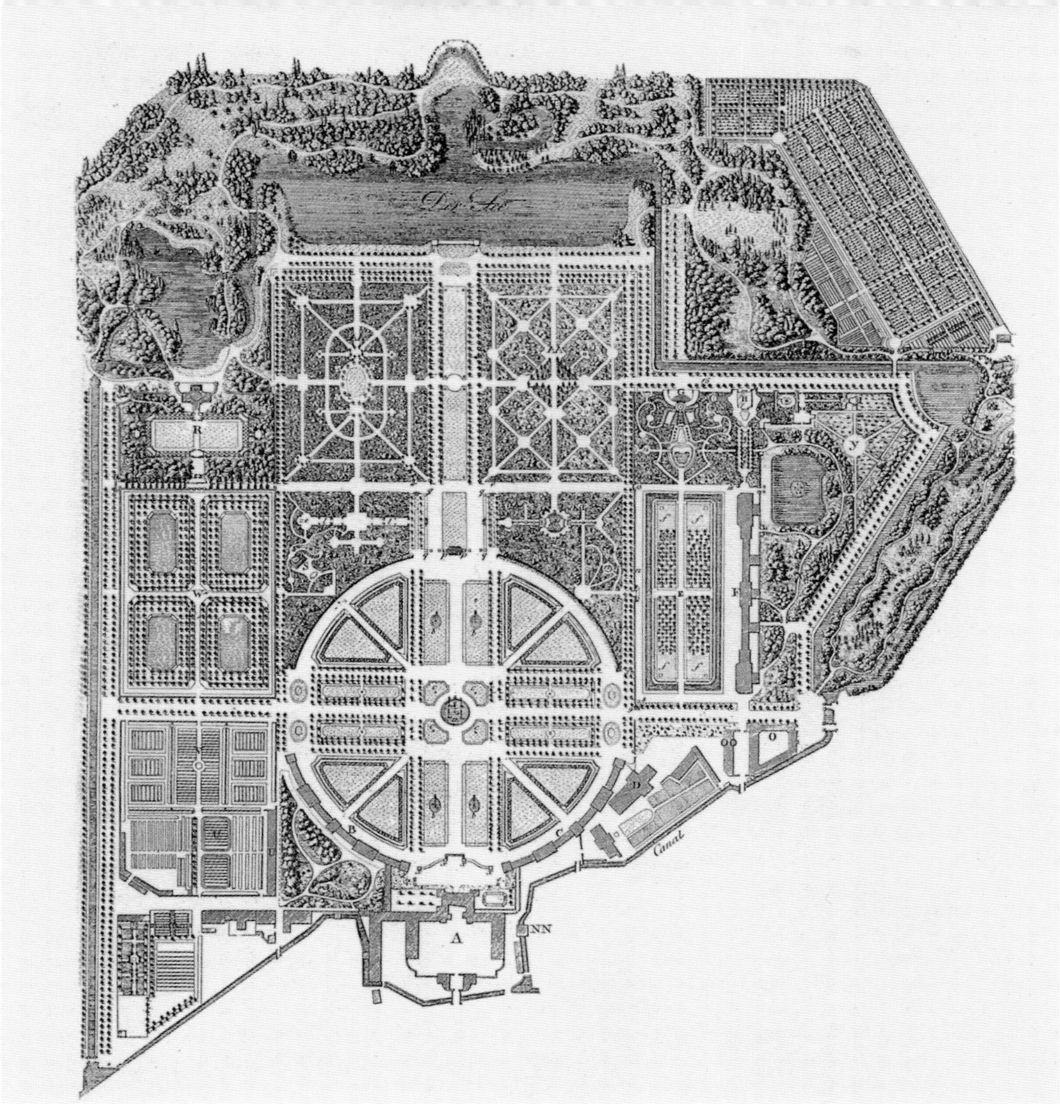

Schwetzigen, castle garden
Plan of the entire site after G.M. Zeyher (1809) (above)
Nature theater and view of the Temple of Apollo (left)

ILLUSTRATIONS OPPOSITE
Schwetzigen, castle garden
Southern rotonda and circular parterre (top)
Main axis and parterre (bottom)

Schwetzigen, castle garden
Temple of Mercury

ILLUSTRATION OPPOSITE
Schwetzigen, castle garden
The "Telescope." The picture of the idyllic river landscape at the end of the trellised walkway is by Wilwert, the Mannheim court painter.

plans, so that today we can still form a precise picture of this Baroque site.

From 1761 the appearance of the garden gradually changed as a result of its extension by Nicolas de Pigage from 1761. The bosket areas were enlarged, a channel was added, and in the northern area an orangery with an orangery garden was laid out. In some bosket sections a new element of playfulness is detectable in the maze-like tangle of paths in the garden.

The new buildings, such as the bathhouse with the Chinese tearoom (1769–73) and the Temple of Botany (1776–9) reinforce the exotic element, and enhance the experience of the garden for the visitor. Then (1776–9), the Roman water castello – an artificial ruin with an aqueduct and an obelisk – was added, along with the Temple of Mercury (1784–7), also designed as a ruin (illustration above), and the famous mosque. The "Roman ruins" are intended to symbolize the realm of the gods, nymphs, satyrs, Muses, and heroes. As regards these decorative buildings, the intention may possibly have been to design "concrete images," or a theatrical space for aristocratic festivities such as were typical of late Baroque illusionism. Models were provided by the paintings of Johann Heinrich Schönfeld from Biberach, who had spent many years in Rome, and made detailed sketches of the ancient ruins there. His themes were popular at the time and may have provided inspiration for the work of garden designers.

The "Telescope" (illustration opposite) may serve to illustrate the extent of the concern in Schwetzingen with the fluid boundaries between architecture, garden design and painting. It creates a point of view from which one looks across the castle grounds to a monumental view with an idyllic landscape, which was intended to strengthen the pastoral element in the grounds.

This ensemble of decorative buildings and views amid intimate bosquets, with accompanying mazes or orangery gardens, marks a fundamentally new phase of garden culture, namely the historical garden of the late 18th and early 19th centuries.

Schönbrunn, garden side
Oil on canvas, 1758–61
Bernardo Bellotto, known as Canaletto
Vienna, Kunsthistorisches Museum

The Palace Garden of Schönbrunn, Vienna

The pre-Baroque history of Schönbrunn can be traced back as far as the 16th century. By then the mayor of Vienna, Hermann Bayer, had had a fortified mill, the so-called "Katterburg," extended to make a stately home with a pleasure garden. But the actual name of the place goes back to the Emperor Mathias, who while out hunting discovered a spring to which he gave the name "*der schöne Brunnen*," the beautiful wellspring. He commissioned a little castle to be built there, but it was destroyed by the advancing Turks back in 1683. Schönbrunn as it is today only took shape under the Emperor Leopold I. Johann Bernhard Fischer von Erlach planned a modest but elegant mansion and garden. Building work began in 1696 but was not completed until the regency of the Empress Maria Theresa. Expansion and rebuilding were in the hands of Nicolas Pacassi until 1749.

The large-scale park came into being while Fischer von Erlach was still working on the castle. Following the completion of the central section, Emperor Leopold I commissioned the French garden architect Jean Trehet to plan and create the park. Trehet had a thousand young trees transported from Paris to Vienna along with the model of an irrigation machine. It is reported that hunting took place and the first festivities were held in the spacious grounds of Schönbrunn as early as 1700.

The decisive redesigning of the park, as far as its present-day appearance is concerned, was carried out in the period 1750–5. A star-shaped system of alleys was laid out, taking the older paths and alleys into account. The plan envisaged that the castle should be integrated even more emphatically into the center of the entire site. Even when in their festive apartments, and even more so of course when on the terrace, the emperor and his family were to experience the park as their own special piece of landscape. At the end of the western diagonal axis, Nicolas Jadot de Ville-Issey planned to have a circular menagerie with an octagonal pavilion. The menagerie was divided into thirteen sections, each with a small parterre and a pool. In 1755, in order to increase the stock of animals, the emperor sent the botanist Nicolaus Jacquin on an expedition to the West Indies. Later there were expeditions to South Africa, St. Helena, and even to Brazil. An obelisk was chosen as the optical end point of the eastern diagonal alley.

For his next major building task the emperor tackled the orangery. The building was designed by Pacassi and was 200 m (*c.* 656 ft.) long. For heating he installed a hypocaust which still functions today. The sensitive plants were taken into the orangery in winter, and its buildings were sometimes even used for festivities and theatrical performances. Finally, all that was lacking was the crowning building on the slope of Mount Schönbrunn. In 1772 the architect Johann Ferdinand Herzendorf was commissioned to design a reservoir to be reached by a twisting path with eight fountains. In 1775 it was at last possible to celebrate the completion of work by building the viewing pavilion known as the "Gloriette." Following the death of Maria Theresa, work on the Great Parterre, which stretched as far as Mount Schönbrunn, was completed by *c.* 1780, as can be seen in the painting by Canaletto in the Kunsthistorisches Museum in Vienna (illustration opposite). The thirty-two garden figures located beside the hedges embody gods of classical antiquity, characters from Greek mythology and heroes from Roman history. At the end of the 18th century there was a fundamental stylistic change to the design of the garden. Hetzendorf worked out plans which were heavily indebted to the concept of the English landscape garden. Around 1780 the Roman Ruin and the Obelisk fountain were built along with the Gloriette. The Fountain of Neptune was added in the form of a monumental cliff landscape peopled by mythological figures.

The Garden of the Palais Liechtenstein in Vienna

Shortly after 1700, Prince Adam von Liechtenstein requested plans for a garden palace. Johann Bernhard Fischer von Erlach produced the first plan. Later, the Italian Domenico Martinelli worked out more plans. The building was finished by 1704. The somewhat raised central section with five axes is flanked by wings with four axes.

The splendid garden area adjoining the rear facade is unfortunately no longer in existence. But a mid-18th-century painting by Canaletto gives a very vivid picture of the one-time parterre (illustration pp. 324–245). The central axis with a fountain leads from the entrance up to the terrace of the former garden Belvedere by Johann Bernard Fischer von Erlach. It was pulled down in 1873 to make way for a new building in a historicizing style. The bed compartments, with different ornamentation and planting, lead off from the central axis. Box trees, yews, and cypresses are to be seen, along with knot and spiral ornaments.

The garden site was adorned with numerous sculptures. Figures from classical mythology are to be seen on high pedestals, along with charming allegorical scenes such as that of Apollo and Daphne. The sculptures alternate with richly decorated vases.

Vienna, Schönbrunn castle garden
Sculptures by the parterre (above) the "chamber garden" with a view of the castle (left)

Liechtenstein summer palace in Vienna, garden side
Oil on canvas, 1758–61
Bernardo Bellotto, known as Canaletto
Vaduz, Fürstlich Liechtensteinische Sammlungen

The Belvedere Castle Garden in Vienna

In 1693 the victorious Field Marshal Prince Eugen acquired several pieces of land outside the gates of the city of Vienna, in order to have a palace with a large garden designed and built. By 1706 the prince had conceived the first plans for the Lower Belvedere which was built by Johann Lukas von Hildebrandt from 1714. Even at this early stage Hildebrandt was laying out the first terraces for the garden. Work on the single-story lower pavilion, which stretched out lengthwise, proceeded apace and was finished by 1716. The building rises up behind a trapezoid Court of Honor; only its central section has a second story. Then work on the garden began.

The art of garden design in Austria undoubtedly culminated in the layout of the Belvedere garden. The slightly sloping terrain was exploited to create, between the more intimate little castle of the Lower Belvedere and the stately Upper Belvedere, built later (illustration opposite), an incomparable garden, which was recorded in its original form in the engraving by Salomon Kleiner (illustration right). In 1717 Prince Eugen succeeded in engaging the Bavarian architect Dominique Girard, who had previously worked at Nymphenburg and Schleißheim, to work on the Belvedere castle garden.

Vienna, Belvedere castle garden
Lower parterre with view of the cascade and the Upper Belvedere

The garden is divided into two terraces by way of an embankment with steps at the side, which provides a transverse axis, and a central cascade. This cancels out the difference in height between the two palaces (illustration above). On the lower terrace a hedged garden with stereometrically shaped trees was laid out. Flower beds and waterworks were envisaged for the upper terrace. The similarities with Versailles are unmistakable, but this garden is not by any means an imitation. The design of the bosquets, which are divided up by means of a system of diagonal paths, can be found in Dézallier d'Argenville's gardening treatise, which was published in 1709, and this treatise became the most important guide for 18th-century garden designers.

Even while work on the garden was still in progress, the prince had plans for a crowning glory at the highest point of the site. He resolved that a stately building was to be erected. Work on the Upper Belvedere began in 1721. In front of the roofed central pavilion with the marble hall there is the staircase and a vestibule with a rounded pediment. Each wing ends with two octagonal pavilions crowned with round cupolas, which take up and bring to a conclusion the rhythm of the different story heights. The garden terraces extend lengthwise, their movement being brought to an end with a touch of genius in the architecture of the Upper Belvedere. The wings are "phased," that is to say each of the lateral sections which extend outward from the central pavilion has its height increased at the first five axes, thereby rising higher than the pediment of the vestibule. Behind them the central pavilion with its roof rises up like the crown of the entire building. There is scarcely any comparable garden site in which architecture and garden design are so harmoniously coordinated.

The uniqueness of the Vienna Belvedere lies in several features. On the one hand it is a matter of the interplay of architecture, nature shaped by human hands, and the landscape. On the other hand it is Hildebrandt's brilliant achievement in planning and creating it.

The Lower Belvedere, of somewhat modest dimensions, but most sumptuous as regards the details of its design, provides a prelude to the unusual but fascinating dialog between the garden terraces and the roof landscape of the Upper Belvedere. A well thought-out system of lines of sight such as was customary in Baroque garden design, seemed unnecessary here, since the layout of the garden and the architecture of the palaces combine to provide a homogenous aesthetic experience in which the complex visual relationships are subsumed.

ILLUSTRATIONS OPPOSITE
Vienna, Belvedere castle garden
Sphynx and parterre in front of the Upper Belvedere; in the background the Lower Belvedere and the city of Vienna (top)

Bird's-eye view of the overall layout of the castle buildings and gardens, etching by S. Kleiner, 1731 (bottom)

Mirabell Castle Garden in Salzburg

The Baroque garden of Mirabell in Salzburg goes back to the Archbishop of Salzburg, Prince Wolf Dietrich von Raithenau, who had the site laid out in 1606 for himself and his consort Salome Alt and their children. At that time the site was called Altenau Castle. Markus Sittikus of Hohenems, the cousin and successor of the Prince Archbishop, renamed the castle "Mirabell." During the Thirty Years' War the Italian Santino Solari built comprehensive fortifications in Salzburg which affected Mirabell to a certain extent. The pleasure garden was enclosed by the city ramparts. At the end of the 17th and the beginning of the 18th centuries, the two most famous Baroque architects in Austria, Johann Bernhard Fischer von Erlach and Johann Lukas von Hildebrandt, took over the development of the castle and the garden. In the garden two parallel axes directed toward the Hohen-Salzburg fortress were established. A large fountain with over-lifesize figures was positioned at the center of the main parterre. Franz Anton Danreiter, inspector of court gardens in Salzburg, developed the garden further from 1728. This affected the small parterre, the orangery garden and a newly created area on the large rampart. From 1811, when the castle was the residence of the Crown Prince of Bavaria, the garden was transformed by Friedrich Ludwig von Skell into a landscape garden, except for a small area, which he left as a geometric site.

Salzburg, Mirabell castle garden
Fountain of Pegasus (top)
Bird's-eye view of the overall layout after F.A. Danreiter, *c.* 1728 (left)

ILLUSTRATION OPPOSITE
Salzburg, Mirabell castle garden
View across the garden of Hohen-Salzburg fortress

Baroque and Rococo Gardens in the Netherlands, England, Scandinavia, and Russia

Het Loo, palace garden
Lower garden with Globe Fountain

Baroque Gardens in the Netherlands

Along with the outstanding French gardens, Dutch gardens also provided considerable inspiration, whether it was for the Nymphenburg in Bavaria or for Herrenhausen in Lower Saxony. They flourished in particular in the context of political developments during the period from *c.* 1670. After the liberation from Spanish rule and the Peace of Westphalia in 1648, Holland was dominated by the urban patrician class. This bourgeois elite appropriated the traditional symbols of the ruling class, and incorporated them into its public image. For its part, the government set store by courtly manners as a way of emphasizing its political dignity.

Heemstede

The statesman Diderick van Veldhuysen from Utrecht acquired land in Heemstede near Utrecht in 1680, and had a huge garden laid out there in the French style. Daniel Marot, a French Huguenot who had gone into exile in the Netherlands, was probably involved in the planning. This can be clearly seen in the parterre and the ornamentation of the beds, which reveal features of garden design that were favored by Louis XIV.

At the center of the layout there is an octagonal castle surrounded by water, with polygonal corner towers which give it a touch of the exotic.

French models must surely also have suggested the axis-symmetrical division of the quarters and the lines of sight with the tensions which they create. The ornamentation of the beds can probably also be traced back to the relevant French pattern books. Information on this point is provided by the watercolors painted by Isaac de Moucheron *c.* 1700 (illustration right). The "*gout français*" was taken into account by way of treillages, galleries, bosket walls, boxwood obelisks, and mazes. But the rectangular grid of channels and alleys is a typical Dutch motif, which reflects the appearance of the landscape. More so than in France, where garden sites are bounded by hills or mountains, the Heemstede site is open as far as the horizon. It is scarcely possible to say at what point the garden merges with the surrounding man-made landscape.

The Park of Het Loo Palace

In 1685 the ruler of the Netherlands, later King William III of England, had a garden laid out adjoining his palace at Het Loo, for which the plans were produced by Daniel Marot (illustrations opposite and pp. 332–3). Contemporary engravings and the descriptions of the king's personal physician, Walter Harris, still convey a precise image of the garden, which ran wild *c.* 1800 and was not re-created until 1978.

The basic design is French, inspired by Versailles. This applies to the upper garden, which is spaciously laid out with a system of pathways radiating outward from a central axis. The lower garden adjoining the palace, by contrast, is typically Dutch in appearance. It is divided into separate, independent units, the whole site being structured by the tree-lined alleys and hedges that are so typical of the Dutch landscape.

The system of channels which was of such importance for the Dutch garden, and later also for

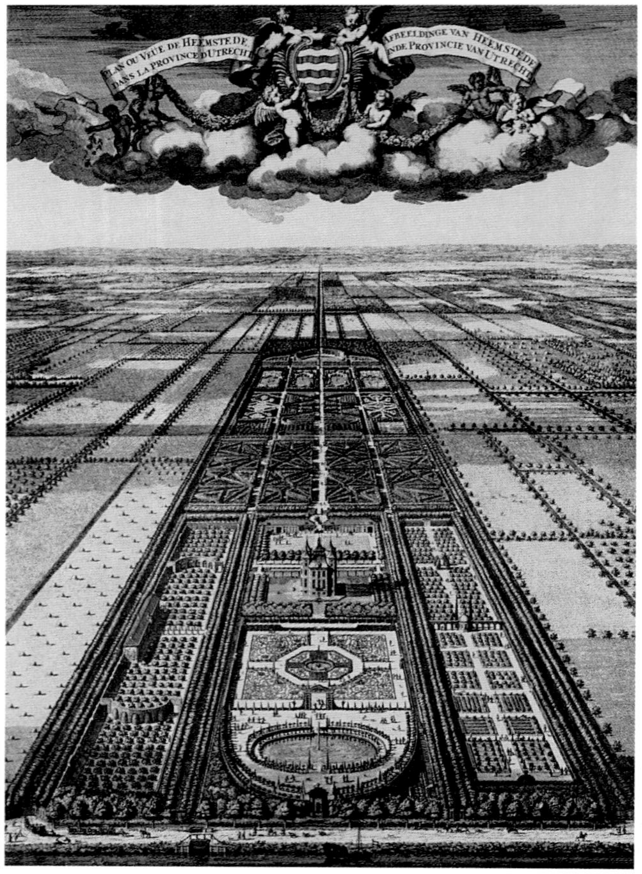

Heemstede
Bird's-eye view of the entire site
Engraving by D. Stoopendaal after
I. de Moucheron, *c.* 1700

Het Loo, palace garden
View of the parterre from the palace
The main fountain at the center of the parterre is dedicated to Venus and Cupid.

Nymphenburg and Schleißheim, goes back to the garden of Honslaerdyck in South Holland, to the south of The Hague, which Prince Frederik Hendrik had laid out from 1621. The huge site, along with the palace, was surrounded by a channel, joined for part of the way by tree-lined alleys.

In Het Loo one can to this day trace the transformation of French bed ornamentation from the age of Louis XIV into a specific Dutch variant. The reason for this is the design "handwriting" of the Frenchman Daniel Marot, who had already worked at Heemstede previously. At the time Marot was considered to be the most important artist in the sphere of ornamentation. His parterre designs are included in the voluminous reference book, which is almost on the scale of an encyclopedia, bearing the title *Oeuvres de Sieur Daniel Marot*, which was first published in 1703. He worked out the ornamentation of the parterre in conjunction with the Dutch sculptor and architect Jacob Roman. Although Marot was heavily indebted to Le Nôtre's style, he varied the latter's structures and arrived at a symmetrical form which, in comparison with French examples, makes a sober, almost austere impression. The Dutch, with their particular mentality, could easily identify with patterns such as these. For the inner structure of the parterre, Marot resorted to an unusual device. He laid out strips of lawn linking the ornamental zones of the borders. Strips of this kind were a recurrent feature of his ornamentation, and he also used them for the outer frame and as a means of accentuating the crossed axes. One is also struck by his use of the colors of flowers. His flower borders were intended to frame beds or quarters, while at the same time adding brightness to the general green coloring within boxwood arabesques.

Marot's efforts survive to this day in the planting and design of Het Loo, for example in the *broderie parterre* of the Queen's Garden (illustration p. 332), the main parterre in front of the palace (illustration above), or in the layout of the upper garden (illustration p. 333).

The so-called Green Cabinet in the Queen's Garden, with its pavilions formed with great artistry out of boards covered with creepers, or the elegant trellised pathways which traverse this area of the garden, sprang from Marot's imaginative world of ideas, and had been anticipated in his reference book.

ILLUSTRATION OPPOSITE
Het Loo, palace garden
Part of the parterre, with vase and sculpture, old trees in the upper garden

Het Loo, palace garden
Parterre with box ornaments, ornamental trees and berceau in the Queen's Garden

In addition to these typical Dutch aspects, visitors again and again find their attention drawn to purely French features. The lower garden, adjoining the palace, is flanked by terraces which give a view of the layout, making the structure of the parterre visible, with its criss crossing pathways and the central fountain. These terraces may have been a good place for spectators when dramatic festivities took place. The lords and ladies were able to follow the spectacle from the garden terrace of the palace. Such terraces were not particularly common in Holland, since because of the topography of the country the excessively costly design and creation of hilly zones tended to be regarded as unnecessary. In France, by contrast, such terraces accompanying the main parterre are frequently to be found, for example in the Tuileries in Paris.

Whereas the lower garden at Het Loo is clearly structured and unequivocally associated with the palace building, the upper garden, which was added later, proves to be a vast layout intended to express spaciousness and boundlessness. Here too there was a continuing influence of the French garden ideology of Louis XIV, who wanted Versailles, for example, to be a vivid symbol of his boundless property.

London, Hampton Court Palace
Palace garden
View of the Privy Garden with river landscape in the background

England

It cannot really be said that the English garden evolved entirely independently of continental developments, although English Baroque gardens differ in many details from French gardens. In architecture one can identify distinctive developments that were specifically English, but as regards gardens the prototypes of the Italian Renaissance and the French Baroque and Rococo appear to have been adopted and modified in an abundance of variations.

Hampton Court is a good example of how French concepts were taken up and put into practice. The alleys leading outward from a rondel in the shape of a star to structure the park or garden site were popular and easy to lay out. The pathways often provided interesting views of distant church steeples or of fountains installed within the garden area.

The history of Hampton Court gardens goes back to the reign of King Henry VIII, who succeeded in acquiring the site from Cardinal Wolsey at the beginning of the 16th century. The garden took on a more distinct form in the 17th century during the reign of King Charles II. Around 1660 he had the Grand Canal added, which proceeded from the palace as a central axis corresponding to the alleys leading outward in the shape of a star from the area in front of the palace. This clear adaptation of French garden layouts is underlined by Charles' preference for the artistry of the neighboring country on the continent. He sent his gardener, John Rose, to Paris to study the garden design work of André le Nôtre. Indeed, he even had inquiries made at the French court as to whether Master Le Nôtre could come to Hampton Court in person to design the parterre there. Flattered by this suggestion, Louis XIV is reported to have indeed given his gardener permission to go to England. But there is nothing on record of Le Nôtre having spent any time at Hampton Court.

The golden age of Hampton Court falls in the reign of King William and his wife Mary. They planned the expansion of the palace and the garden to create a permanent residence for themselves at Hampton Court. Christopher Wren, the most famous architect in Europe at the time, was commissioned in 1689 to extend the palace, that beautiful Tudor building, following the model of Versailles. A semicircular ornamental garden was created in front of the east wing of the palace. The alleys and the canal were pushed back. Gravel paths interspersed with rondels and fountains, as extensions of the alleys and the canal, now cut through the semicircular main parterre as far as the garden frontage of the palace. This area was adorned with thirteen larger and smaller fountains along with numerous sculptures, so that even then people spoke of the Great Fountain Garden. The much sought-after Daniel Marot provided the ornamentation of the parterre.

The older gardens on the site, including the water garden, also known as the Pond Garden, have survived down to the present day, with planting in the Renaissance style. Only the old Privy Garden, the private garden of Henry VIII with the artificial mound and the viewing pavilion, was redesigned. King William had the mound demolished, and parterre beds laid out. Finally, the French craftsman Jean Tijon provided the site with beautiful iron railings with twelve gates. Unfortunately this splendid piece of craftsmanship was removed in 1865, and transferred to the South Kensington Museum. But at the beginning of the 20th century its extraordinary effectiveness as a piece of garden art was remembered, and it was restored to its rightful place.

King William's garden planning came to an end with the transformation of the old orchards of the northern area into the so-called "Wilderness." William chose the French bosket as his model, but avoided its artificial design and gave the woodland a system of winding pathways. This was a foretaste of features of the English landscape garden. The French bosket, a popular source of shade in the summer, a place for lovers to spend time, and an intimate setting for their trysts, was unsuited to either the English temperament or the English weather. Places with plenty of shade were sought in the airy alleys rather than in constricted and secluded bosket cabinets.

Blenheim Palace, Oxfordshire
Box tree ornaments and pools with artistically sculpted corners together form a kind of water parterre landscape. The formal gardens adjoining the palace, imitations of both Italian and French gardens, were created in the 20th century.

Blenheim Palace

The foundation stone of Blenheim Palace was laid on June 17, 1705. Five days later the dramatist and architect Sir John Vanbrugh wrote to his master, the Duke of Marlborough, that terracing of the

London, Hampton Court Palace
Palace garden
Eastern garden layout

garden had begun that same day, along with building work on the ducal palace. He wanted to have the garden laid out and planted within a year. That could not, of course, be done. The final plan of the layout, signed by Charles Bridgemann, is dated 1709. It shows the so-called Military Garden with its bulwarks, the kitchen garden with its defensive wall, and the alleys planted with elms to the north and east.

Henry Wise was in charge of the planting and maintenance of the gardens. The unusual idea of having fortifications for the garden probably goes back to Vanbrugh. In 1719 the Duke of Marlborough was at last able to move into his palace and walk in the gardens, but unfortunately not for long. He died a few years later, in 1722, at Windsor.

Chatsworth Garden, Derbyshire

Bess of Hardwick was a remarkable woman. She was widowed by the age of thirteen and outlived her last husband, the fourth, by many years. She had only one passion: building and laying out castles and gardens. For her this passion was the elixir of life, for a gypsy had prophesied that she would stay alive for as long as she was building. She was almost a hundred years old when she died. Bess, a member of the landed aristocracy, was born in 1520. She married, of course, exclusively within her own social class, acquired a substantial fortune, and – more importantly as far as her building mania was concerned – came into the possession of large estates. She was involved in planning and consultation at, among other places, Hardwick Hall and Welbeck Abbey. But her first and most important achievement was Chatsworth, from the period of her marriage to Lord Cavendish. Work on the stately home began in the second half of the 16th century, and over the following centuries it was subject to considerable modification. It is even said that one of the earliest typical Renaissance gardens was laid out at this time. But no traces of this are still in existence today.

From 1687 the duke commissioned Henry Wise and George London, the most important garden designers of their day, to lay out the garden. Wise was Queen Anne's chief gardener and was considered to be an adherent of the French style, which he converted into an unmistakably English Baroque style. He managed to integrate mazes into an artificially designed wilderness as at Hampton Court, and to lay out strictly symmetrical alleys of elms as at Blenheim. It was important to his

Chatsworth Garden, Derbyshire
Salisbury Lawns

ILLUSTRATIONS OPPOSITE
Chatsworth Garden, Derbyshire
Broad Walk and Blanche's Vase (top)
The maze (bottom)

Chatsworth Garden, Derbyshire
View from the Great Cascade of the house and the adjoining hilly landscape

Plan for the redesigning of Chatsworth Garden
Drawing by William Kent

ILLUSTRATION OPPOSITE
Chatsworth Garden, Derbyshire
The Cascade House

masters that there should be a clearly perceptible French element in the garden, but without its English character being neglected.

Wise and his partner London were commissioned by the duke to design a garden for Chatsworth in the manner of Versailles. This referred to size and splendor, but not necessarily to the ornamentation of the beds of the structure of the parterre. The hill which rose gently behind the garden facade offered a wealth of opportunities for geometric design, and of course for the concept of a dominant watercourse. To this end the duke, in 1694, invited a Frenchman and pupil of Le Nôtre to come to England to construct a cascade. The Cascade House at the end of the cascade (illustration opposite) is by Archer.

The garden was redesigned again under its new owner, the fourth Duke of Devonshire. In 1760 he engaged Lancelot "Capability" Brown, who began to redesign the site completely as a landscape garden. Fortunately Brown left the cascade untouched. Today it still bears witness to the former Baroque garden.

Melbourne Hall, Derbyshire
Anyone who regrets the loss of the splendid Baroque garden laid out by Wise and London at Chatsworth, is compensated by Melbourne Hall. The site, in Derbyshire, is one of the few examples in England where the layout has to a large extent survived from the 17th and 18th centuries. The agreement between the two garden architects and Thomas Coke, Queen Anne's Vice-Chamberlain, dates from 1704.

At that time there was evidently already a Baroque garden in existence, conceived in strict geometrical terms following the example of Le Nôtre. Wise and London took over this concept but extended the garden area. They performed a minor miracle by planting a tunnel of yew trees 90 m (*c.* 300 ft.) long, the longest in Europe. The tunnel was located to the south of a row of terraced lawns leading down to a large pool surrounded by tall cypresses. To the south of this is the adjoining bosket with yews and beeches, and with alleys running through it. Where they intersect, Wise and London installed fountains, water jets and sculptures. Not far from this area a grotto was constructed which included a fountain emitting mineral water. The arbor known as the "birdcage" is unique in English gardens. It was made out of wrought iron, with an elegant design and great artistry, by Robert Bakewell in 1706. It is situated to the east of the lake. The birdcage served the lords and ladies well as a distant "point of view," and was separated from the Hall by the lake and an extended alley of yew trees (illustration opposite).

From the upper terrace there is a long view across the alley, the pond, and the wonderful birdcage to the rising terraced lawns and more alleys, as far as the horizon.

Melbourne Hall, Derbyshire
Sculpture of Mercury in the French Garden
To this day the gardens of Melbourne Hall show clear indications of the French style.

ILLUSTRATION OPPOSITE
Melbourne Hall, Derbyshire
View of the Hall from the wrought-iron "birdcage," across the pond

Hillerød near Copenhagen, Frederiksborg Castle
View of the castle across the castle garden pond

Scandinavia

Like the other countries of Europe, Denmark also has a long tradition of garden making to look back on. Following the Middle Ages, when the monks laid out the monastery gardens, the Danish garden had been, to begin with, primarily a utility garden rather than an ornamental or pleasure garden. It was not until the Danish King Frederik IV (1699–1730) became acquainted with the gardens of André Le Nôtre during a trip to France, and was filled with enthusiasm for their splendor, that Denmark developed a garden culture of its own. Around 1700, when Frederiksborg Castle was built in Hillerød near Copenhagen (illustration above), work began on the terracing of the garden in the French Baroque style. The design submitted by the Swedish architect Nicodemus Tessin in 1699 was rejected by the king as too costly. Instead, he commissioned Hans Hendrik Scheel to plan and carry out the work.

A few years later, in 1717, the king decided to have another castle built for ceremonial purposes at Fredensborg to the north of Copenhagen (illustration right). The Italian architect Marcantonio Pelli collaborated with Johann Cornelius Krieger in drawing up plans for the garden. They were implemented between 1759 and 1769. But the financial resources of the court ran out rather quickly, with the result that it proved impossible to construct the costly marble terraces and cascades that had been part of the plan. Instead, less expensive possibilities were examined, for example earthen ramparts covered with vegetation. Expensive pools with fountains were replaced by ponds strengthened with wood and boulders. Thus, not only was a Danish variant of the European Baroque garden created, but also a first step was taken in the direction of the landscape garden. The gardens of the castle now

Fredensborg Castle (Denmark)
Castle garden with earthen ramparts covered with vegetation, and view of the castle.

Drottningholm Castle on an island in Lake Malar to the west of Stockholm
Castle garden with fountain site in the castle's central line of sight

appeared more intimate, more pleasing, and not as ostentatious as in France or Italy.

In Sweden garden culture developed in a similar way as that in Denmark. It was French monks who laid out herb and pleasure gardens in the monasteries in the mid-12th century. The Order of St. Bridget of Sweden kept a monastery garden at its abbey in Vadstena which can still be visited today.

In Sweden the development of the Baroque garden was not so much influenced by French gardens, but rather by the Hortus Palatinus of Salomon de Caus in Heidelberg (illustration p. 133). Under the Vasa kings the medieval fort in Stockholm was rebuilt as a Renaissance palace. Gustav II Adolf, the king of Sweden and the great antagonist of the imperial supreme commander Wallenstein, secured Swedish rule over the Baltic in the early years of his reign, until Sweden entered the Thirty Years' War in 1630. In these years between 1611 and his military campaign, he evidently became acquainted with the plans of the castle and garden at Heidelberg. We only have precise knowledge, however, of the building activity of his daughter Christina, after the end of the Thirty Years' War. She invited the Frenchman André Mollet to Stockholm, where he published his influential book *Le Jardin de Plaisir* in 1651. Mollet began to put his ideas into practice by modernizing the Royal Garden in Stockholm, where he created a large *broderie parterre*. To this end he had plants imported and built orangeries.

One of the most splendid garden layouts in northern Europe was created in Drottningholm (the Island of the Queen) on an island in Lake Malar to the west of Stockholm (illustration above). The late medieval castle was rebuilt under Queen Hedwig Eleonora from 1661. The garden was laid out at almost the same time. The plans produced by Nicodemus Tessin were based on Mollet's parterre patterns, and as regards its dimensions and structure the layout was inspired by the plans of Le Nôtre, with whom the Swedish

St. Petersburg, Petrodvorets (Peter's Court)
Double cascade in front of the palace

architect was in personal contact. The site has survived almost unchanged down to the present day. The bronze figures in the garden are by Adrian de Vries. This exquisite collection came to Sweden as war booty from both Prague and the Danish castle at Frederiksborg. The royal family has lived at Drottningholm Castle since 1981.

Russia

It is not until the 18th century that it is possible to speak of a specifically Russian garden culture. It is true that by the 17th century there were summer residences in the surroundings of Moscow, but little is known concerning them. In all probability it was a matter of wooden buildings which were at risk of damage by fire, and consequently had frequently to be renewed or rebuilt.

Not until Peter the Great appeared in the first third of the 18th century, and St. Petersburg was founded, were gardens included when palaces and residences were built. The czar studied architecture and garden design on his extended journeys through Europe. He drew much inspiration from Holland, England, and Germany. His summer palace on the Admiralty Island in the River Neva, which has now unfortunately vanished, had a splendid parterre. It contained sculptures, fountains, and various summerhouses and the like, along with a bosket modeled on the example of Versailles, and also a grotto with water features. The master builder Andreas Schlüter from Berlin was engaged to build and install the grotto with water features.

In 1715 the czar decided to have a summer residence built facing his city on the south coast of the Gulf of Finland. The location was favorable, as the terrace for the palace rises some 12 m (*c.* 40 ft.) above sea level at this point, and slopes quietly down to the sea in gentle undulations. Petrodvorets (Peter's Court), named after the czar, was to be built in the style of French Baroque residences with their adjoining gardens.

In 1716 a pupil of Le Nôtre, the French architect and master garden builder Jean-Baptiste Alexandre Le Blond was brought to St. Petersburg to plan and build the palace and the gardens (illustrations left and opposite). The garden extended from the palace terrace down to the sea. Difficulties arose not so much with the earthworks as with the planting of the terrain. To this end the czar had trees and plants brought in from all over Europe. Over 40,000 elms and maple trees from Russia, fruit trees from Italy, and many other exotic plants from the Near East were transported to the castle on long journeys. It is reported that the new plants thrived, despite the long and severe Russian winter.

The crowning glory of the entire layout is still there to be admired today: the double cascade on the two sides of a grotto, which descends via seven steps made of colored marble, edged with gilded figures into a large pool (illustration left). There an artificial cliff towers up, with a mighty Samson forcing open the lion's mouth to allow a jet of water to spurt out of it. From the pool a canal edged with water jets flows quietly toward the sea. Here a small harbor made it possible for the regal ships to dock comfortably.

Czar Peter the Great learned the art of lines of sight in Versailles. Following the motto: "Possess all that the eye can see!" he organized the positioning of the palace, the cascade, and the canal. Up on the castle terrace the observer sees a wonderful panorama.

The eye is directed via the cascades to the canal and from there farther across the coast and the sea to the golden domes of the city of St. Petersburg. This visual demonstration of power is repeated in the capital itself when one stands on Decembrists' Square behind the monument to Peter the Great designed by Etienne Maurice Falconet. The horse leaping up with the czar from a huge block of

St. Petersburg, Petrodvorets
Fountain and large pool in the palace garden

St. Petersburg, Petrodvorets
Marly Pavilion in the lower area of the palace garden

granite directs one's gaze across the square and the Neva into the distance in the direction of the sea and Petrodvorets. This aestheticized gesture of power, a political topos of absolutism, was a design feature not only of gardens but also of town planning. Town and garden were not necessarily integrated, but there was a long-distance visual relationship between them. It was a question of implying distance in order to assert a claim to power beyond visible boundaries.

Seen in this light, the description of Petrodvorets as a "Russian Versailles" did less than full justice to its intention. The Sun King's garden continent was intended to be seen as a model for a structured and organized sphere of power. St. Petersburg and Petrodvorets, on the other hand, were merely corner points in an all-embracing territory that stretched out in every direction, whose boundaries, even beyond the sea, had to be redefined again and again.

A few decades later, after the czar's death, it was decided to level and extend large parts of the site. The intention was to obey the latest fashion and transform the entire garden area into an English landscape garden.

Topiary: the Art of Shaping Trees

The art of cutting trees and hedges to particular shapes was described by the Roman encyclopedist Pliny the Elder as "*opus topiarium.*" He was referring to garden design in general, which was primarily a matter of giving a particular form to nature. Thus in ancient Rome landscape gardeners or those who tended gardens were called "*topiarii.*" They were mainly slaves from Greece, who sometimes acquired extraordinary skill, and achieved considerable recognition. Their names were even immortalized on gravestones. Later the concept took on a more limited meaning. In theoretical treatises on garden design the various forms of clipped trees and hedges came to be called *topiari* (French *topiaire*, English *topiary*).

These hedge and tree shapes first became famous through Francesco Colonna, who published illustrations of a collection of topiary in his *Hypnerotomachia Poliphili* of 1499. It included not only trees in the shape of rings, spheres, or mushrooms, but also imaginative shapes such as circular temples adorned with birds, or human figures holding up ornamental gateways (illustration p. 43).

Francis Bacon, the English philosopher and founder of empirical science, published various treatises on the layout and care of gardens. In his essay "On Gardens" of 1625 he took a skeptical view of the use of topiary:

"For the ordering of the ground within the great hedge, I leave it to variety of device, advising nevertheless that whatsoever form you cast it into, first it be not too busy or full of work. Wherein I, for my part, do not like images cut out in juniper or other garden stuff: they be for children."

He may possibly have been alluding to the particularly lavish topiary at Hampton Court near London which was created during the reign of Henry VIII.

Chatsworth Garden, Derbyshire
Ring pond, hedge layout with inset sculptures and ornamental trees

Enghien (Belgium)
Garden site with great variety of topiary
Engraving by Romain de Hooghe, *c.* 1687

ILLUSTRATION OPPOSITE
Het Loo, palace garden
Detail view of the *broderie parterre* with ornamental trees

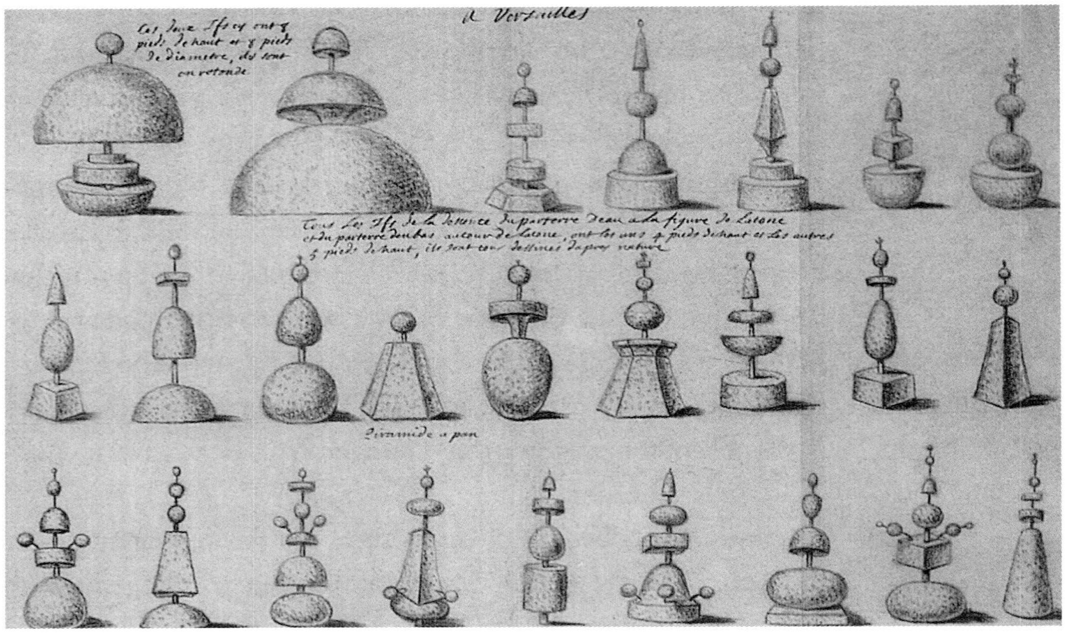

Sheet of patterns with numerous variants of topiary shapes for the trees by the ramps in the Latona parterre of the garden of Versailles Palace

Francis Bacon, in contrast, recommended simple hedges, clipped into round shapes in some places, with a few pretty pyramids and in other places beautiful pillars supported by lattice work. This was probably the earliest recommendation in Baroque garden design that architectural forms such as pillars, architraves, or colonnades should be cut from trees and hedges.

In his treatise *La Théorie et la Pratique de Jardinage* of 1709, the French garden theorist Antoine Joseph Dézallier d'Argenville, who has already been mentioned a number of times, also described architectural topiary of this kind. This treatise, which soon became famous as the "bible of garden design," was reprinted and translated many times and became the standard work on 18th-century garden design. D'Argenville compared the alleys and pathways of a garden to the system of roads in a town. The design of this system contributed decisively, he argued, to the appearance of a garden. He suggested interspersing the trees lining the alleys to the side of the parterre with so-called *parapette*, that is hedges *c.* 130 cm (*c.* 50 in.) in height, to indicate the end of a row of trees, while at the same time giving a view of the adjoining area of the garden. If these hedges were to grow taller, little window-shaped gaps to look through could even be added. On the other hand, however, Dézallier d'Argenville also stressed the independence of the hedges and bushes and envisaged clipping them to a variety of architectural forms. He produced a kind of catalog of clipped hedges which were soon to be seen, in a modified form, in many European gardens, and which inspired other garden theorists or architects to design similar patterns (illustration left). In the 17th and 18th centuries numerous books of topiary patterns were published, including one by the German master garden builder Matthias Diesel with the title *Erlustierende Augenweide in*

Manoir d'Eyrignac (southwest France)
Yew tree pillars and small spherical trees in the formal garden of the manor

Vorstellung hortlicher Gärten und Lustgebäude ("Entertaining Delights for the Eye in Images of Gardens and Buildings for Pleasure"), published in 1717, in which he presented ingenious tree and hedge figures composed of stereometric structures.

Topiary went out of fashion during the period of the English landscape garden, and was regarded by many English garden lovers as an example of bad taste. But when, *c.* 1800, gardens began to be adorned with period or rustic architecture, clipped trees came back into vogue, and were used effectively as an ornamental feature. In small private gardens, yews clipped to the shape of spheres or cones actually never did go out of fashion. John Ruskin and William Morris, who in the 1860s revitalized arts and crafts and gained greater respect for them, also envisaged decorative design possibilities for "cottage gardening" and helped topiary to a new, albeit low-key recognition. It was, however, primarily a matter of individual clipped plants decoratively arranged in the garden or in front of the building. In this function topiary acquired particular importance in *art nouveau*. But the Baroque ensembles of plant architecture, the imaginative facades composed of hedges and trees, were unable to maintain their place in 20th-century gardens and can now only be admired at sites where Renaissance and Baroque garden designs have been lovingly reconstructed and are continuously maintained. In these gardens the artistic shapes of the clipped trees and hedges are still the principal objects of attention.

Chatsworth Garden, Derbyshire
The maze, with a wide variety of topiary

PAGES 350–351
Wivenhoe Park, Essex
Painting, oil on canvas, 56 x 101 cm (*c.* 22 x 40 in.), 1816
John Constable
Washington, National Gallery of Art, Widener Collection, USA

The English Landscape Garden

Rousham Park, Oxfordshire
Lead sculpture of Bacchus by John van Nost

Stowe, Buckinghamshire
Stowe was one of the first English landscape gardens. It was laid out *c.* 1730 and decisively influenced the future development of this new type of garden (illustrations pp. 352–8). Stowe had been the property of the Temple family since 1593 and was extended between 1715 and 1726 by Richard Temple, the first Viscount Cobham. The principal garden architect was Charles Bridgeman, who was something of a key figure in the early development of the English landscape garden. Bridgeman held the post of royal gardener under George II and Queen Caroline. He worked at Hampton Court, in St. James's Park, Hyde Park, and Kensington Gardens, being responsible for the Round Pond and the Serpentine. The royal gardens made few demands on him, his job being mainly to preserve their traditional structure. This situation changed when he began to receive private commissions, especially from the viscount at Stowe, where Bridgeman began to work as early as 1713.

Initial plans show a layout similar to that of a French Baroque garden. One can clearly detect the closeness in time to the garden designs of André Le Nôtre. Apart from the irregular boundaries, Bridgeman's approach was to create his own variant of this parterre structure. In order to make the adjacent open landscape visible, he constructed a ha-ha, that is a walled artificial ditch, according to the instructions of Dézallier d'Argenville (illustrations p. 229). It was only under the leadership of William Kent, the "enemy of straight lines" as he was mockingly called by his contemporaries, that the garden changed, starting in 1735, into a picturesque, idyllic reflection of nature. The Elysian fields were created, a little valley with small temples in the Palladian style, twisting pathways, and clumps of trees. Kent was also called in to plan the landscape garden at Holkham Hall in Norfolk, where he likewise attempted to structure the spacious meadowlands by means of clumps of small trees, as can be seen from a pen-and-ink drawing by him (illustration opposite, bottom).

The so-called garden revolution in England was not quite as spectacular as is often claimed. Nor was the English landscape garden a consequence of the supposed demise of the Baroque garden, which in some places survived for a long time and was cultivated and encouraged in parallel with the landscape garden. The Stowe plan drawn by Bridgeman, which was published in 1739, still shows a structure determined by axes, with geometric parterres extending outward from the house. A long alley stretching far out into the landscape connects the more distant and incomparably larger landscape park with the viscount's own site (illustration below). Furthermore, a contemporary description by Lord Percival, who visited the site in 1724, reads more like an account of an Italian Renaissance garden. He writes of fountains and transverse pathways ending at colonnades, statues, and arches, and of hidden pathways leading through the boskets. But there was one design feature to which the viscount

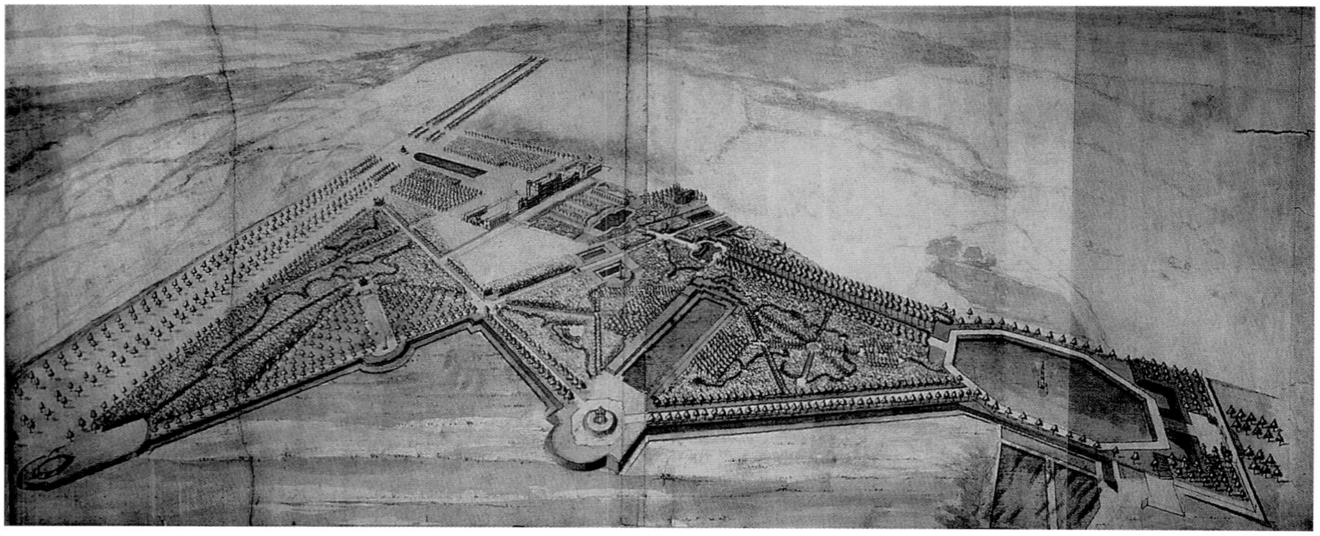

Plan for Stowe
Drawing by Charles Bridgeman, *c.* 1720
Oxford, The Bodleian Library

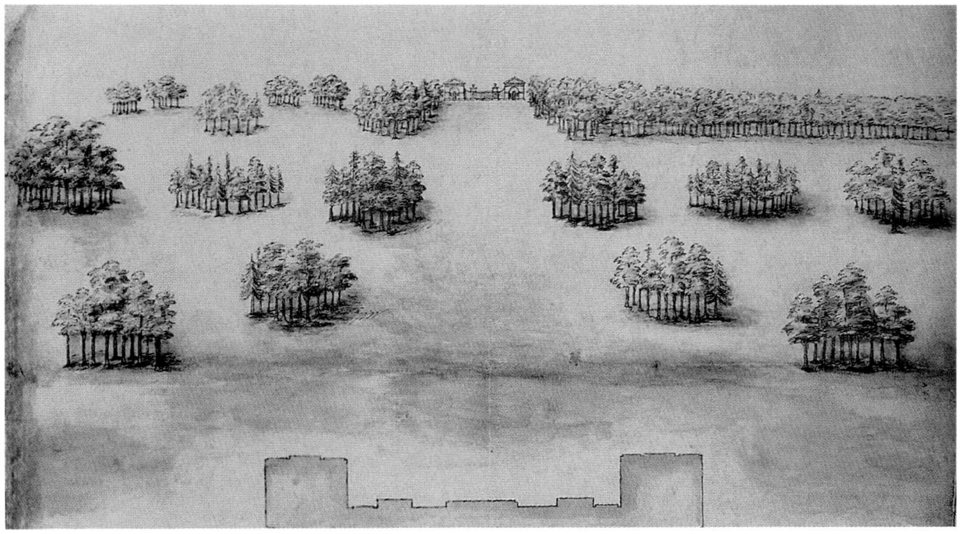

Stowe, Buckinghamshire
View of the two lakeside pavilions

Planting plan for the park at Holkham, Norfolk
Pen-and-ink drawing by William Kent

Stowe, Buckinghamshire
Elysian Fields with William Kent's "Temple of Ancient Virtue"

ILLUSTRATION OPPOSITE
Stowe, Buckinghamshire
Gothic "Temple of Liberty" by James Gibbs, 1741

PAGES 356–357
Stowe, Buckinghamshire
Palladian bridge

appears to have paid special attention. Lord Percival noted that the beauty of the garden was further enhanced by the fact that it was bounded not by walls but only by a ha-ha, giving an unimpeded view of a beautiful wooded area while disguising the length of the alley with its tall trees.

This rather austere pattern was gradually modified by Bridgeman, in collaboration with Kent, and replaced by pleasing earthen shapes and curving pathways. What factors brought about this change in the conception of an English garden layout? To begin with, social and political factors need to be scrutinized. From the end of the 17th century the English landed aristocracy was attempting to offset the consequences of the Civil War and the ensuing economic depression by acquiring land and bringing fallow land into cultivation. Large estates came into being, which could be put to intensive agricultural use. The aim was to create a countryside which would enhance the quality of life of the people. This led to a new attitude toward nature. A picture painted by Joseph Wright in 1780 retrospectively sums up this new view of nature. The English painter portrayed the young Sir Brooke Boothby lying thoughtfully, in a melancholy pose, on the grass in a forest glade. To judge by his dress and bearing – though without hat or shoes – he could also be lying on a couch in a room of his country house. But his realm is nature, to which he feels a closer affinity than to architecture. The book which he has just been reading is by – who else? – Jean-Jacques Rousseau.

From then on many Englishmen changed their attitude toward the French garden, in which nature, with its promise of prosperity, was clipped and straightened, in short: violated. The French garden as a symbol of absolutism could not find favor in England. Following the "Glorious Revolution" of 1688 and the Declaration of Rights a year later, which together prepared the basis for modern civil society, England rose to become the world's leading trading nation and economic power.

Versailles and other French gardens were regarded more as a kind of catalog from which the aristocracy, when designing their own gardens, borrowed this or that detail, such as mazes, boskets, parterres, or ha-has, in order to arrange their own variants of them in the vicinity of the main building. This was not meant in a derogatory sense. It was more the absolutist symbolism of the gardens of France, along with the associated political arrogance of its rulers that Englishmen despised. The veneration of Le Nôtre and his artistry, in contrast, remained unalloyed into the first half of the 18th century. English garden designers adopted a different approach, directed toward the dynamic processes of nature, which was to be cultivated, but not organized or turned into geometric shapes. As early as John Milton's epic poem *Paradise Lost* of 1667, the primal image of a garden is presented as an ideal image of the world. It has features of a landscape park, whose essence is to be found in the self-revelation of nature.

However, the embourgeoisement of the English landed aristocracy and the conception of the landscape as an indicator of progress and prosperity, were not the only reasons for the changes in garden design. England's far-flung trading links with the whole world encouraged another strand in its cultural history: exoticism, the cult of the foreign (cf. pp. 389). China was particularly involved here. Travelers' reports from the first half of the 18th century told of wonderful gardens which were like

Stowe, Buckinghamshire
"Temple of British Worthies" by William Kent

miniature landscapes, with their menageries, twisting paths, artificial mounds, and watercourses with elegant arched bridges. This Chinese variant of the English garden soon became a major feature of many European landscape gardens *c.* 1800. China came to be regarded as an inexhaustible source of decorative ideas, and use was made of it accordingly. In 1757 the English architect Sir William Chambers published a collection of drawings of Chinese architecture, containing predominantly garden buildings, under the title "Designs of Chinese Buildings." He noted with exuberant enthusiasm:

"The art of laying out grounds after the Chinese manner is . . . liable to as many variations, as there are different arrangements in the works of the creation.'

In addition to exotic imports from China, Englishmen on their Grand Tour were also gripped, in Italy, with enthusiasm for ancient Rome. They traveled via Tuscany to Rome in order to look with amazement at the legacy of classical antiquity. They continued via Latium to the Gulf of Naples and along the Amalfi coast to Paestum. Italy was the Promised Land for enlightened minds. However, the educational aspect of the tour was usually limited to collecting objects of real historical value, and sketching the antiquities. Along with the souvenirs, the overwhelming impressions made by the tour were eventually to contribute to the adornment of the park landscape. Garden architects had become accustomed to Italian taste by way of the Palladian architecture which had already, at an earlier stage, attracted the attention of Inigo Jones. They now began, on the urgent recommendation of their patrons, to place little round temples or temple facades, antique busts and statues, along with Chinese pagodas, pavilions and arched bridges in various areas of the garden, like pieces of theatrical scenery.

However, the English, with their enthusiasm for nature and classical antiquity, will hardly have seen in Italy any pastoral landscapes with temples or senate halls topped with cupolas, with passing shepherds and sheep. On the other hand, they were able to look at sensitive and almost meditative landscapes in the paintings of Claude Lorrain, Nicolas Poussin, or Gaspard Dughet in the Villa Doria Pamphili in Rome, or at home in the National Gallery in London. There the spectrum

Hagley Hall, Worcestershire
Landscape park with mock ruined castle *c.* 1747

Hagley Hall, Worcestershire
Landscape park with Temple of Theseus, 1758

ranged from the concrete experience of the landscape of Campagna to the vision of a supposedly paradisial way of life in antiquity. But these Utopian landscapes constituted a direct presentation of a model which vividly showed how idyllic landscape and sublime antiquity could be combined. This model then had to be converted to reality in the landscape park. Unlike in the case of Le Nôtre, who in his gardens wished to suggest the long-distance effect of a painted landscape, it was now a limited section of landscape – a particularly attractive subject for painters – that became the yardstick for a garden layout.

Hagley Hall, Worcestershire

Hagley Hall in the West Midlands is a special case among English landscape gardens. The picturesque element that Lorrain had made so popular was enriched by a poetic variant. George, the first Lord Lyttleton and nephew of Lord Cobham of Stowe, was a successful politician, who also supported the Scottish James Thomson, whose poem *The Seasons* had been enthusiastically received by the English landed aristocracy. Published in 1730 with illustrations by William Kent, the poem depicts country life in impressive imagery. It aimed to teach people how to rediscover their English homeland with its idyllic landscape. In addition to powerful verbal descriptions of landscapes, it was also his didactic ambitions which were highly esteemed by English landscape painters.

Lord Lyttleton designed the spacious park toward the middle of the 18th century. The two architects Thomas Pitt and Sanderson Miller gave him their support with the architectural components. Miller designed a castle ruin *c.* 1747 with battlements and a Gothic window wall (illustration opposite). Pitt constructed a bridge in the Palladian style. Later, the architect James Stuart was commissioned to build a Greek temple, a replica of the Temple of Theseus below the Acropolis in Athens, at the top of a wooded hill (illustration above). This building laid the foundation for Classicism. The nexus of relationships between the classical ideal and the Romantic image of medieval chivalry created the pastoral atmosphere of a painting by Lorrain, and established new ways of looking at the English landscape. Over and over the visitor is surprised by the vista across the Malvern Hills or the Black Mountains of Wales.

Rousham Park, Oxfordshire
Formal area of the garden by the dovecote near Rousham House

Rousham Park, Oxfordshire

The landscape garden of Rousham House in Oxfordshire is probably the only garden by William Kent which, in its entirety, has survived the passing of time almost unchanged down to the present day. The layout was largely complete by 1738, and at the time was considered in England to be a unique example of a country estate that had been converted into a landscape park. The English poet and critic Alexander Pope, who even at the beginning of the 18th century had been vehemently opposed to the formal garden in the French manner and in favor of the natural garden, saw his desire fulfilled at Rousham. There, as the poet put it, the landscape is presented as a piece of shaped nature. Furthermore, he said, the park was laid out in such a way that the surroundings formed an integral part of the conception. He praised the park as a most beautiful place, where there were waterfalls, small rills, and ponds to admire, and where hills covered with shrubbery along with wooded zones stretched out into the distance.

There is a drawing by Kent of the so-called Venus Vale. A bridge made of natural stone crosses over cascades which pour down into a pond from which a jet of water spurts upward. People gather, individually or in groups, beneath tall trees and on spacious lawns. The Watteau-esque atmosphere must have been intended by Kent in order to emphasize the pastoral ambience. The garden designer also, of course, supplied the appropriate ornamental buildings.

A circuit of the garden led from the Venus Vale across the upper bridge with the statue of Venus across to the Temple of Echo, a central building designed and built by William Townesend fronted by a Roman portico (illustration opposite). A little farther on, beneath the Temple of Echo there is a statue of Apollo. In addition to the classicist statue and the ornamental building William Kent envisaged a neo-Renaissance building, a seven-

Rousham Park, Oxfordshire
Detail view of the Praeneste arcade

ILLUSTRATION OPPOSITE
Rousham Park, Oxfordshire
"Temple of Echo" by Kent and Townesend

arched arcade, the so-called Praeneste arcade, by which the lily pond is bounded (illustration p. 360). The medieval aspect was also taken into account, the neo-Gothic rotunda with the elegant lantern and the dormer windows served at the time as a dovecote (illustration p. 360). In 1750 the gardener John Maccalary described, in a letter, a circuit of the site which took him to the most notable viewing points, and included the ornamental buildings along with the ponds and their bridges. It emerges from his description that Rousham had initially been conceived as a *ferme ornée*, a garden put to agricultural use. This is, of course, also suggested by the dovecote. The park itself was intended to be separated from the garden by evergreen plants in conjunction with a ha-ha.

Today the spaciousness of the park, the many idyllic or heroic views across the garden site, along with the picturesque placing of the ornamental buildings and sculptures, still make this site one of the most desirable and frequently visited cultural monuments in England.

ILLUSTRATIONS OPPOSITE
Rousham Park, Oxfordshire
A Lion Attacking a Horse
Peter Scheemakers, 1741 (top)
Sculpture of Venus at the upper cascade in the Venus Vale (bottom)

Rousham Park, Oxfordshire
Grotto of Neptune with lead sculpture of Neptune

Coast View of Delos with Aeneas
Oil on canvas, 100 x 134 cm (*c.* 40 x 53 in.), 1672
Claude Lorrain
London, National Gallery

Stourhead, Wiltshire
Close-up view of the Pantheon by the lake in the landscape garden

Stourhead, Wiltshire
View across the lake of the Bristol Cross and the Church of St Peter.

Stourhead, Wiltshire

Stourhead in Wiltshire was, and still is today, probably one of the most famous gardens in England, and certainly the most romantic. The owner, who commissioned the building, was the London banker and lord mayor, Henry Hoare, who in 1721 had a country house built by Colen Campbell, modeled on the Venetian villas of Andrea Palladio. The large garden site stretches out to the side of the great house and is arranged around an irregular chain of lakes. The garden is designed in accordance with William Kent's ideas. But the owner himself planned the layout and had it created by gardeners. The curved lakeside repeatedly provides surprising vistas of temples, waterfalls, or bridges. Rhododendrons – which, however, were not planted until later – surround a Roman Pantheon (illustration opposite, bottom). From there one looks down to the old village church and the Temple of Flora. Henry Hoare is said to have been so enthusiastic about his garden that he called it "a charming Gaspard picture," that is a painting by Gaspard Dughet, also called Poussin. Indeed, these nature paintings in the manner of Poussin, Dughet, or Lorrain are still worth a visit today. It is conceivable that before designing the Stourhead landscape setting, Hoare studied Lorrain's painting *Coast with Aeneas on Delos* in the National Gallery in London (illustration opposite, top).

At this point, at the latest, it must be admitted that it is very difficult to make a clear distinction between a garden and a park. One often hears the view that a landscape garden should be called a park. Did gardens undergo a transformation into parks in the first half of the 18th century? The genesis of the Petit Trianon in Versailles might suggest this, since there the geometric parterre structure turned into a twisting tangle of paths and tracks laid out over the hills. The plan of Stowe which Bridgeman had produced earlier was similar. In Stowe, however, there was one striking difference. The Baroque garden that had been transformed into a landscape garden had, to a large extent, to dispense with straight alleys, whereas in the most distant landscape park a large-scale composition of alleys laid out in the shape of a star was envisaged. The English garden theorist William Gilpin in his *Dialog upon the Gardens* made an explicit distinction between gardens and parks, noting:

"The park, which is a species of landscape little known, except in England, is one of the noblest appendages of a great house."

Stourhead, Wiltshire
View of the Pantheon across the turfed bridge and the lake

Leasowens, Shropshire
View of the lake in the landscape park

Of course, Gilpin also envisaged that parks would be artistically designed, but only in such a way that nature, growing wild, was perfected by the gardener. Gilpin used the term "garden" to describe a "pleasure-ground" situated closest to the actual house. Flower borders and gravel paths adorn a garden, and trees and bushes should be planted in its outer areas in order to connect it with the park.

Leasowens, Shropshire

Along with Stourhead, Leasowens in the county of Shropshire in the Midlands was one of the most famous romantic landscape gardens of its day, which no longer hovered between the traditional parterre and park design. Its owner, William Shenstone (illustration right) designed the site during the years 1745 to 1763 (illustration above). Shenstone was a poet and a garden theorist. In his essays he described – though not explicitly – the difference between a garden and a park. He divided garden work into three areas which he denoted as "kitchen-gardening, parterre-gardening, landskip- [sic] or picturesque gardening." By picturesque landscape garden he probably meant a

Portrait of William Shenstone
From R. & J. Dodsley, *The Works in Verse and Prose of William Shenstone*, Vol. I, London 1764.

park. He stressed that this part of the garden (or park) should surprise visitors with its spaciousness, beauty, and diversity. The topography of the site was very varied, with wooded valleys, fast-running streams, arched bridges, cascades, and even the ruins of an old abbey.

There were points of view which brought the surrounding countryside, with its striking uplands such as Clint Hills or Frankley Beeches, into the idyllic scene.

This garden not only belongs unequivocally to the picturesque or romantic type, it is also a "*ferme ornée*," that is, an ornamental farm. This term relates to a similar phenomenon which we have already seen at Versailles in the Hameau de Trianon, namely the theatrical staging of country life. In England, however, and especially at Leasowens, the site that was put to agricultural use was to be included in the garden area, a typical indication of the English attitude toward nature and of the estate owner who thought in terms of economic profitability.

The idea came originally from Stephen Switzer, who, in his pamphlet *The Nobleman, Gentleman, and Gardener's Recreation* (1715), wrote that the useful and profitable aspects of gardening should be combined within a garden site in a practicable and successful manner. But Shenstone was the first to introduce, in 1745, the term "*ferme ornée*" using, strangely enough, a French term. He distinguished between this term and the "*parc orné*," by which he meant a geometrically designed parterre. He left it open, however, in what direction the "*ferme ornée*" was to evolve: into farmland designed like a garden, or into a park put to agricultural use.

Hence the term soon disappeared again from garden literature, as only a very few estate owners were either able or indeed willing to devote themselves to agriculture in combination with the artistic design of park landscapes. Only in Rousham was an attempt made to combine these two elements and to harmonize the two different areas of garden and park.

Leasowens became a meeting place for gentlemen with literary and philosophical aspirations. Louis-René Girardin, Vicomte d'Ermenonville, also visited Leasowens in 1763, the year in which William Shenstone died, and reacted enthusiastically to both the landscape garden and the concept of the "*ferme ornée*."

In his pamphlet on the landscape garden, which was published in Geneva in 1777, his aim was likewise to combine the picturesque features with the areas put to meaningful agricultural use. He had a monument to William Shenstone put up in Ermenonville – in the immediate vicinity, incidentally, of the grave of Jean-Jacques Rousseau, who had spent the last two months of his life on the Vicomte d'Ermenonville's estate (illustration p. 441).

ILLUSTRATIONS ABOVE AND BOTTOM
Bristol – Henbury, Avon
Blaise Hamlet with so-called "*cottages ornés*" by John Nash, 1811

Warwick Castle, Warwickshire
View of the Avon and the Victorian boathouse

ILLUSTRATION OPPOSITE
Warwick Castle, Warwickshire
Castle situated in the landscape garden

The Work of Lancelot "Capability" Brown

Horace Walpole, the fourth Earl of Oxford and youngest son of Sir Robert Walpole, the first English prime minister, became well known through his essay *On Modern Gardening*, written between 1750 and 1770. Walpole described William Kent as the founder of the picturesque landscape garden. He gave John Milton's sensitive verses and Claude Lorrain's utopian landscape visions as the sources of inspiration. This reference makes little sense, since for his own little garden at Strawberry Hill, Twickenham, with a picturesque view of the Thames, Walpole preferred straight alleys, which for William Kent were definitely bad gardening practice. Nor was his judgment always reliable when describing or assessing other garden layouts and their creators. For example, this garden theorist said of Warwick Castle in 1751:

"It is well laid out by one Brown who has set up on a few ideas of Kent and Mr. Southcote."

By a few years later Walpole had probably realized, with profound regret, to whom he had referred to as "a certain Brown." For this was a well-nigh intolerable disparagement of the man who at that time was the most famous gardening personality in England: Lancelot Brown, also known as "Capability" Brown. The nickname referred to Brown's ability to see the garden design potential ("capability") of almost any landscape. Brown was born in 1716, and when he died in 1783 Walpole pasted into his notebook the following words from an unidentified newspaper:

"His great and fine genius stood unrivalled, and it was the peculiar felicity of it that it was allowed by all ranks and degrees of society in this country, and by many noble and great personages in other countries.""

Who was Lancelot Brown? His career began modestly, first as a gardener's assistant, then as a kitchen gardener at Stowe where he gave the English aristocracy conducted tours of the garden, thereby making the acquaintance of his future patrons. He produced his first designs under William Kent's guidance, and during the years *c.* 1750, under the guidance of his patron Lord Brooke, he created the garden at Warwick Castle in Warwickshire, which made him famous (illustrations left and opposite). The medieval castle rampart was razed to the ground, and the terrain reshaped. Then clumps of trees were planted, including cedars of Lebanon and Scots pines. The site was laid out in relation to the castle hill, and designed in such a way as to produce, again and again, picturesque vistas of the castle and the Avon valley.

In 1750, while working at Warwick Castle, Brown designed the stately house at Croome Court, Worcestershire, in the Palladian style for Lord Deerhurst. He also laid out the landscape garden. He created a summerhouse in the classicist style on the little island in the lake, and even built a tunnel under the main road so as to be able to design the

Twickenham, London, Strawberry Hills
Neo-Gothic country house, 1749/50–76
Built by Horace Walpole and others
View from the south with garden

neighboring terrain also as a garden, and link it with the main site.

Brown now traveled continuously in England, designing landscape gardens for the nobility and planning stately homes. He was indefatigable, changing his location almost every year.

In 1767 he was appointed master gardener at the Royal Court, and was given Wilderness House to live in as part of his contract. He was frequently to be seen strolling with King George III in the gardens of Hampton Court, where he had only a few alterations made. He worked principally on Old Park in Richmond, which is today part of the Royal Botanical Gardens.

During these years Brown was occupied with designs for the gardens at Langley and Blenheim, Oxfordshire. The garden at Blenheim had been begun back at the beginning of the 18th century. Bridgeman later designed parts of the site, including the kitchen garden and a so-called Military Garden with bulwarks, which, however, had to make way for Brown's designs.

Brown's plans for changes at Blenheim Park for the 4th Duke of Marlborough date from 1764. The work was to keep him busy for ten years. First it was necessary to dam the River Glyme, and remove earth to create two lakes. Brown envisaged a great cascade in the western area at the furthermost lake banks, to replace Sarah's Cascade which

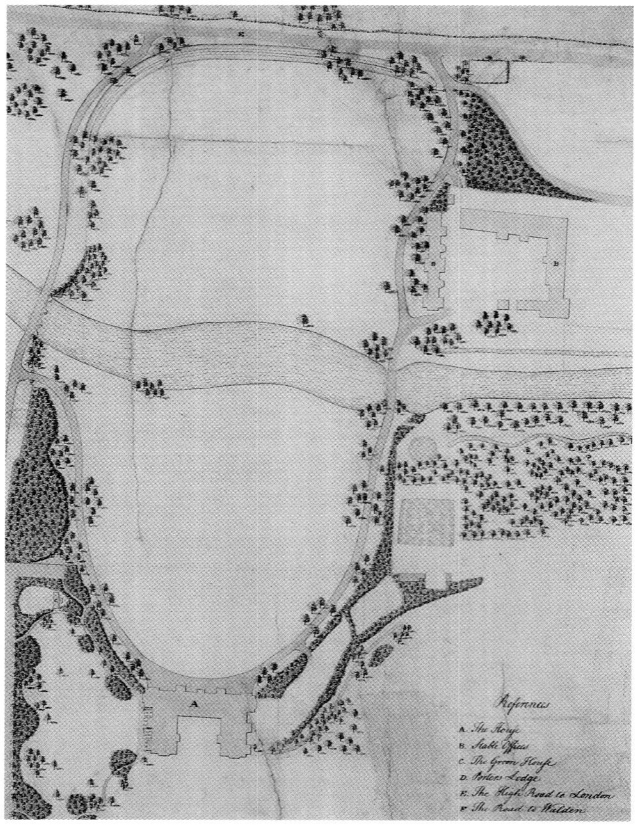

Audley End House, Essex
Plan by Lancelot Brown, *c.* 1762

Blenheim Palace, Oxfordshire
Landscape garden designed by Lancelot Brown in the mid 18th century

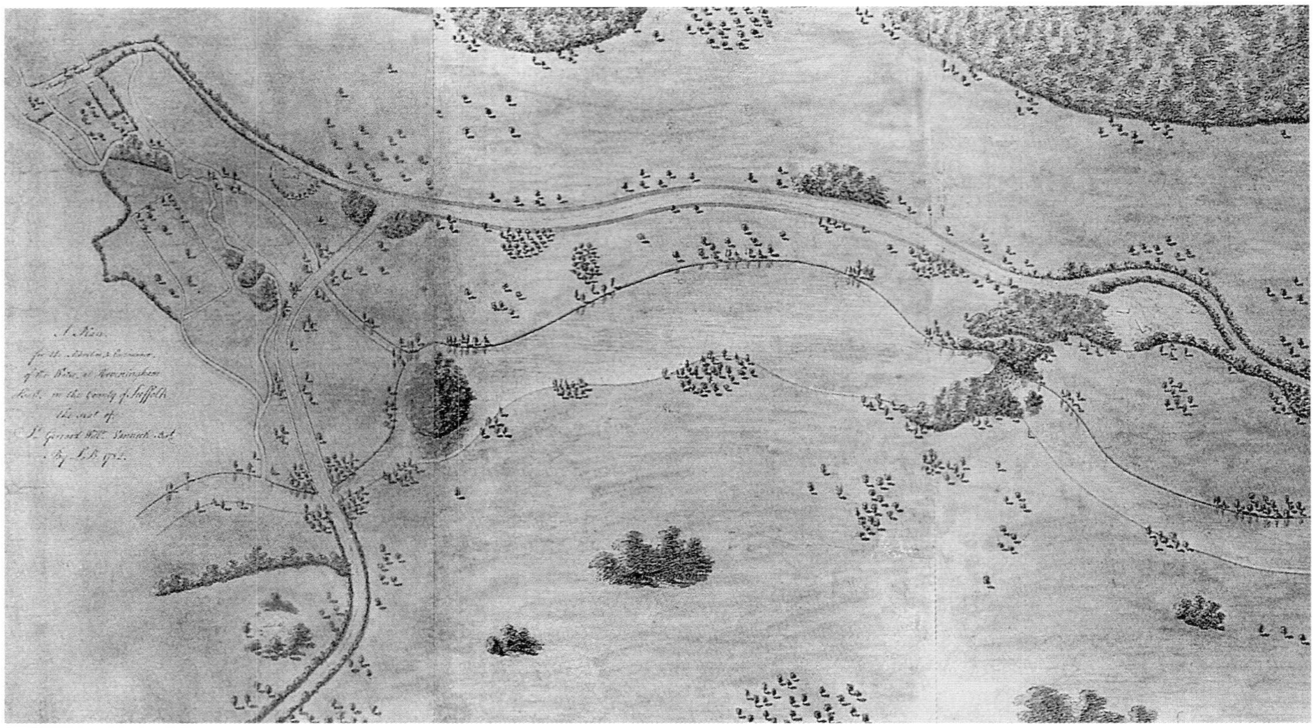

Heveningham, Suffolk
Plan by Lancelot Brown 1781

had been created by the widowed Duchess Sarah in 1720.

The abundance of water at Blenheim survived into the 20th century – but with an almost ironic reinterpretation. Around 1930 the 9th Duke of Marlborough engaged the French garden architect Achille Duchêne, and he redesigned the site by laying out three water terraces in the style of the Versailles *parterre d'eau.* His father, Henri Duchêne, was a gardener and had made his name by transforming English landscape parks into classical Baroque gardens.

Lancelot Brown died suddenly and unexpectedly of a stroke in 1783. None of his three sons was a suitable successor for him. The extent of his activity was exceptionally wide. It is interesting to note that, if the square miles of garden designed by him are added together, the result is many times more than the area occupied by the gardens created by André Le Nôtre.

How, then, did Brown's creations differ from those of other English landscape gardeners? His dictum that a garden must be laid out with the feelings of a poet and the eyes of a painter, must surely apply to many other garden designers also. Yet this axiom seems hardly to have mattered to Brown. He deliberately avoided color contrasts. One rarely finds ancient buildings integrated into nature, at least not to the high degree which is a conspicuous feature of other landscape gardens. Brown designed no settings in the manner of either Lorrain or Poussin. What mattered to him was harmony of line as embodied in gently undulating hills or winding river valleys. Buildings and statues tended to be seen as an intrusion. Brown used artistic resources very sparingly, as can also be seen from his plans. The plan for Heveningham in Suffolk, dated 1781, at first sight depicts an extremely bare setting (illustration above). The clumps of trees are distributed over extensive lawns, and an uncomplicated system of main paths runs in long curves through the site, which includes a lake laid out in serpentine form and complete with a wooded island.

Brown did nothing less than change the face of the English landscape garden. He designed entire landscapes, but was less concerned with expressing closeness to nature than with producing a harmonious appearance, without any intention of concealing its artificiality.

Horace Walpole took Brown's creations as an occasion for singing the praises of the English landscape garden in highly patriotic language. England had achieved perfection, he said, and had given the world a model of true garden artistry Other countries, he went on, might imitate and adulterate English taste, but in England itself it should reign on its green throne, original by virtue of its elegant simplicity. England, he said, did not take as great a pride in any other art as in this, which had succeeded in mitigating the severity of nature and in imitating its charming play.

Sheffield Park

In 1776 John Holroyd, first Earl of Sheffield, decided to create a large landscape park of 40.5 ha (100 acres) in the county of Sussex. He succeeded in engaging two of the most famous English garden designers for the task, "Capability" Brown and

ILLUSTRATION OPPOSITE
Sheffield Park, East Sussex
Vegetation growing on the banks of the Ten Foot Pond

Humphrey Repton. The latter worked on the garden from 1789 and was responsible for laying out a chain of small lakes up to the house. Brown laid out the two lakes, which were known as Woman's Way.

No further work was done on designing the garden until 1883, when the third Earl of Sheffield extended the lakeland area. The company of Pulham and Sons was contracted for the work. James Pulham had become famous in England as a rock sculptor. He was the first person to use cement to create artificial rock landscapes. The cascades between the lake terraces were probably also Pulham's work. Conifers and rhododendrons were planted during this period.

At the beginning of the 20th century the garden became the property of Arthur Soames, who from 1909 to 1934 used the lakeland area to plant many different sorts of trees and bushes intended to give a special coloring to the foliage in autumn (illustration left).

The so-called Queen's Walk was created recently; it leads through the lake area and at one particular point gives a very beautiful view of Sheffield Park House (illustration above). The building was erected in 1887 to mark the 50th anniversary of Queen Victoria's enthronement. The park was later taken over by the National Trust, which opened it to the public. The ban on decorative buildings, which English garden purists had been demanding since the mid-18th century, was controversial and was disregarded in many landscape gardens.

Sheffield Park, East Sussex
Long-distance view from the landscape garden of Sheffield Park House (above)
Vegetation on the banks of the Middle Lake (left)

Tatton Park, Cheshire
Italianate garden with Fountain of Neptune, laid out by Joseph Paxton in 1859

ILLUSTRATIONS OPPOSITE
Tatton Park, Cheshire
Views of the Japanese garden, 1910

Tatton Park

Even in the 17th century, as can be seen from the engravings in the *Britannia Illustrata*, the English landed aristocracy favored gardens divided up by tree-lined alleys. Alleys with beech or lime trees were not only chosen as driveways leading up to the house, but were also used in the inner areas of the garden. Tatton Park near Knutsford in Cheshire is famous for its beech alleys radiating out in many different directions. One of the alleys led from the geometrically arranged late Baroque garden to the house, which was built shortly after 1700. Humphrey Repton advised the owners to demolish the alleys in order to plant clumps of trees, and lay down twisting paths. This, he told them, would accord with the landscape garden ideal. But fortunately his plans were resisted. The alleys remained, and are still there today.

During the period *c.* 1814 Lewis Wyatt designed a flower garden, of which the alcoves, Lady Charlotte's Arbor and the elegantly shaped fountain have survived. An orangery was added to the garden ensemble in 1818. Sir Joseph Paxton, the famous architect of the Crystal Palace in London that was built in 1850 for the Great Exhibition, also went to Tatton Park in that same year to design the park terraces in the Italian style. He laid out large stairways, sketched a central fountain basin, and distributed elegantly curved flower vases among the balustrades (illustration above). From there a landscape garden situated some distance away could be reached, where the Golden Brook was to be found, an enchanted garden lake with a Shinto temple. This area, designed as a Japanese garden, was laid out in 1910 (illustration opposite).

It was in Knutsford that the English writer Elizabeth Cleghorn Stevenson, born in 1810, underwent her spiritual crisis. She later married the Reverend Gaskell, and became famous under that name. Tatton Park provided the setting for *Wives and Daughters*, in which she rechristened the site "Cumnor Towers." She was referring to the country house which the architects Samuel and Lewis Wyatt had built in the classicist style for William Egerton *c.* 1800.

Tatton Park is a vivid example of the extent to which approaches to garden design are a matter of tradition. Rococo culture, that was so receptive toward exoticism, was a significant source of inspiration for garden designers *c.* 1900. That was why there was a revival of interest in exotic decorative buildings, of which the Shinto temple in Tatton Park is an example.

ILLUSTRATION OPPOSITE
Castle Howard, North Yorshire
Long-distance view of the Mausoleum, built by Nicholas Hawksmoor, 1726–9

Castle Howard, North Yorkshire
"Temple of the Four Winds" by Sir John Vanbrugh, 1725

Castle Howard

Castle Howard in Yorkshire might make the onlooker think of an "English Versailles." In 1699 Charles Howard, 3rd Earl of Carlisle, and the naval officer and author of comedies John Vanbrugh, were considering the possibility of building a huge castle which would surpass everything that had ever been built in Britain. Vanbrugh drew up plans for a vast castle complex; the viscount had it built. Vanbrugh rapidly rose to be the most important of architects. No other secular building in England had a larger dome than that of Castle Howard. The castle, with a protruding central section, wings with nine axes, and corner pavilions, was surrounded by a spacious garden which soon showed all the characteristics of a later landscape garden. Although still influenced by the Baroque ideal, people wanted spacious and sublime vistas, and created them by means of winding paths, rivers, and bridges. But on the main parterre, where the monumental Fountain of Hercules stands today, there were manneristic hedge figures, mock buildings, obelisks, and arched gateways. It is uncertain whether this Baroque site was actually completed or whether it remained unfinished when attention turned to the new ideal of the landscape garden. To the east of the castle the English garden theorist Stephen Switzer laid out a copse, Ray Woods, with twisting paths and trellised walkways leading to glades with pavilions, and to fountains and cascades. This area of the garden now gave the new English landscape garden its first definite stamp. Switzer noted proudly:

"This incomparable Wood is the supreme peak that will ever be attained by either natural or gallant garden art."

The "terrace walk" leading southward provides magnificent landscape vistas. The path leads above an artificial lake to the Temple of the Four Winds, a free variant of Palladio's Villa Rotunda (illustration below). Vanbrugh built it in 1725. The mausoleum, built by Nicholas Hawksmoor in 1729, is a classical round temple with a shallow cupola, and makes a powerful impression (illustration opposite).

Duncombe Park

The small town of Helmsley in Yorkshire is dominated by a romantic castle ruin which provides a panoramic vista of the landscape down into the valley of the River Rye. The castle was acquired by Sir Charles Duncombe, the banker to the London goldsmiths, at the end of the 17th century. It was not merely a decorative building, but an actual medieval building.

But Sir Charles soon came to prefer a castle built by Sir John Vanbrugh around 1710 together with a spacious park. From the castle one proceeds via a spacious lawn to a sundial which is being set by Saturn, the father of Time. The sculpture is by the Flemish sculptor John Van Nost (illustration below). A terraced path leads walkers past the winged Saturn and in a wide concave curve from the Tuscan Temple across to the Ionic Temple, allowing them to enjoy a splendid view down into the valley of the River Rye (illustration opposite). Below the Ionic Temple built around 1718 there is a ha-ha wall, which later appeared at Stowe in a similar form.

Like Castle Howard, Duncombe Park is also one of the early landscape gardens of England. Vanbrugh must be singled out as a pioneer of this type of garden. His success may also have been due to the fact that he had no formal training either as an architect or as a gardner. He intuitively grasped the potential for creating relationships between a natural landscape and an artificially laid-out main parterre. One of his fundamental ideas was to have

ILLUSTRATION OPPOSITE
Duncombe Park, North Yorkshire
View of the landscape from the Ionic Temple

Duncombe Park, North Yorkshire
Sundial with sculpture of Saturn by John Van Nost with a view of the Ionic Temple

the main alley running parallel to the castle facade. This made it possible to look from the House into and across the garden and far out into the landscape. This new "English style" of seeking the proximity of nature in the garden or park was probably put into practice for the first time at Duncombe Park and, more or less simultaneously, Castle Howard.

Studley Royal

Describing the ruins of Fountains Abbey in North Yorkshire, near the little village of Aldfield, the writer and politician Benjamin Disraeli wrote of the ruins of the great abbey, spread over no less than 4 ha (10 acres), its masonry encrusted for the most part with moss where once the residential and agricultural buildings of the former owners had stood with their extensive terraced gardens. Amid these ruins, he wrote, one of the noblest works of Christian art was still standing, that is the abbey church, damaged, but still admirable in its form and shape, its only roof in summer being the vaulting ribs, and with nothing remaining of its magnificent windows except for the symmetry of their great arches and a few motley fragments of the fantastic tracery.

The ruins date back to a Cistercian monastery built in the 11th century (illustrations pp. 386–7). But they owe their appeal entirely to John Aislabie, who acquired the site at the beginning of the 18th century and, from 1722 until his death twenty years later, transformed it into a delightful water garden. He channeled water to the site from the River Skell, laid out a large lake, and designed grotto springs and the famous Moon Pools, one of them in the shape of the full moon, the others as crescent moons. Toward 1728 he designed the classicist Temple of Piety, which was built by Richard Doe (illustration opposite). Above the water garden he laid a pathway up the hill to an octagonal neo-Gothic temple which was begun shortly before his death. From here the peak of Tent Hill can be reached, with an unforgettable view across the channel and the cascades of the River Skell to the ruins of Fountains Abbey.

The most impressive view of the water garden is from a raised plateau opposite the Temple of Piety. Studley Royal, together with Fountains Abbey, is probably one of the special cases in English garden design. The romantic ruins that were obligatory for a "sentimental" garden already existed. The combination of a ruined monastery and classicist architecture, within an extensive landscape park with lakes, ponds and canals, is probably unique.

ILLUSTRATION OPPOSITE
Studley Royal, North Yorkshire
Sculptures in the water garden

Studley Royal, North Yorkshire
Temple of Piety, *c.* 1730

ILLUSTRATION OPPOSITE
Duncombe Park, North Yorkshire
View of the landscape from the Ionic Temple

Studley Royal, North Yorkshire
Fountains Abbey, former abbey church
Nave leading eastward

Exoticism

In the 17th and 18th centuries some of the countries of Europe such as France, Holland, or England, succeeded in extending their colonial power to the Pacific, the Far East, and South and Central America. Overseas trade prospered and brought to those countries goods which had never been seen or tasted there before. In addition there were illustrated travel descriptions, often imaginatively written, with accounts of unbelievable animals, plants, and human races. Chinese products in particular, such as vases or fabrics, soon became increasingly popular. At the courts of European kings and princes, artists began to copy foreign ornamentation, and to integrate it into traditional court art as a new kind of decorative style. Before long, exotic buildings such as Moorish temples or Chinese bridges and pagodas were adopted as decorative features. The attempt was made, particularly in English landscape gardens, to create a perfect illusion of remote parts of the world. A recurrent feature of exotic garden design was the Chinese pagoda, which the English architect Sir William Chambers introduced for the first time in 1763, at Kew Gardens (illustration opposite). Pagodas subsequently appeared at Het Loo, Sanssouci, and the English Garden in Munich.

Exoticism in garden design is undoubtedly dominated by so-called Chinoiserie. This applies not only to Chinese pagodas or bridges but also to the décor of country villas and castles, using mirror and porcelain cabinets and Chinese rooms. But Indian and Moorish cabinets also made their presence felt. In Wörlitz landscape garden Chinese decorative buildings are to found alongside Egyptian features. Turkish or Moorish motifs in architecture and decor are to be found, for example, in Stockholm, Schwetzingen, and at the Wilhelma Botanical and Zoological Gardens in Stuttgart. Such eclecticism, the combination of different (usually contrasting) stylistic features, paved the way for the historicism of the second half of the 19th century.

Chinese pavilion
Illustration from Le Rouge, Cahier XII of *Détails des nouveaux jardins*, 1784

ILLUSTRATION OPPOSITE
London, Kew Gardens
Chinese pagoda, 1763, by Sir William Chambers

Heale Garden, Wiltshire
Japanese bridge in front of a teahouse

Whereas the vogue for China soon evolved into an established feature of Rococo style, the less common decorative motifs of the exotic Orient and India were treated as curiosities. Arabian mosques with slender minarets, Turkish tents, or Indian temples with broad arches and richly figured facades – in the wide spaces of a landscape garden they featured as aesthetically acceptable foreign bodies which were intended to exercise their exotic charm as eye-catchers at the end of an alley or concealed amid a clump of trees. And so for the most part these variants of exoticism remained isolated features, which could not be integrated to any great extent into the decor of Chinoiserie.

Exoticism in garden design was not by any means universally popular, it also provoked criticism. As early as 1748 William Gilpin, in his *Dialog upon the Garden*, wrote that the vogue for China lacked truthfulness and taste, and that it made it impossible to create the effect of Arcadia, which after all had to be measured against the Greek idea of the Elysian fields.

Chinese pavilion
Drawing by Sir William Chambers from *Designs of Chinese Buildings*, 1757

Cassan, formerly an 18th-century park
Chinese pavilion

English Garden Theories in the 18th and 19th Centuries

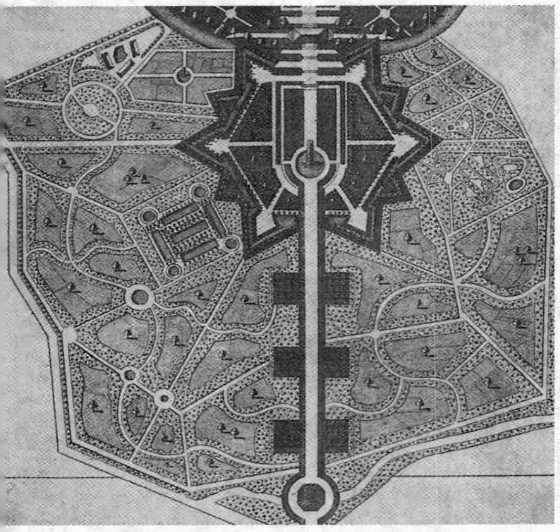

The manor of Paston
Site plan after Stephen Switzer

English garden theories draw an interesting picture of garden practice. Often theory did not precede practice, but vice versa. Gardens and parks frequently gave rise to theoretical conceptualizations of their design features. Stephen Switzer (1682–1745), a practicing gardener, was probably the first to bridge the gap between the French Baroque garden and the nature-oriented landscape garden. His work *Ichnographia Rustica*, in three volumes, was published in London in 1718. He demanded that garden design should combine useful and pleasant features, but decisively repudiated French garden geometry. This is surprising, since in 1718 he followed the French model when laying out his ideal garden. It is true that there is no specifically French bed ornamentation. But the structure, with geometrically designed compartments on both sides of a regularly enclosed pond, is quite clearly derived from the traditional Baroque garden (illustration left). The close connection with agriculture desired by Switzer led to the construction of fenced ditches, the so-called ha-has, to prevent cattle from straying into the areas of the pleasure and utility gardens. Switzer took up many ideas from the writings of Dézallier d'Argenville and reshaped them in an English spirit, thereby introducing the first theoretical ideas concerning the landscape garden.

Close contact with landscape painting was made a subject for discussion for the first time by Thomas Whatley, a Tory member of parliament, in his work *Observations on Modern Gardening Illustrated by Descriptions* (London, 1770). He praised the value of garden design, which he regarded as superior to landscape painting, the original always being preferable to a copy. This is an interesting comparison, for it drew attention to the fact that the garden designer is able to shape nature, in contrast to the painter, who is only able to imitate it. Whatley, with his pronounced aestheticism, saw gardening not so much as a craft, but rather as an art requiring inspiration. For this

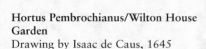

Hortus Pembrochianus/Wilton House Garden
Drawing by Isaac de Caus, 1645

This is what garden layouts at stately homes looked like, in England also, in the mid-17th century, before the new type of English landscape garden brought a distinct change to the picture from the first half of the 18th century.

reason he was not concerned with listing tasks for the gardener to take into account and carry out, but with integrating garden design into the broad field of the liberal arts. Therefore a painting should never be a model for a garden design, since the garden designer works to his own aesthetic rules derived from the study of nature. Stowe, Stourhead, and the gardens of Lancelot Brown were Whatley's models. In them he discovered the aesthetic structures which he organized and summarized in his writings. It would not even be wrong to describe Whatley's observations as the theoretical counterpart to Brown's concrete creations. He had a particularly powerful and lasting influence on the continental landscape garden in Germany.

Whereas Whatley, in line with Brown's garden design practice, favored an almost purist landscape design, the London architect Sir William Chambers (1723–96) was interested in exotic garden design. His journeys to China awakened an intense interest in Chinese decorative features for the landscape garden. In contrast to Brown, he paved the way for the "sentimental" garden that was intended to have a primarily emotional appeal. In fact both types of garden managed to coexist in England, but their supporters were firmly divided into two camps behind Chambers and Brown. In Germany and other continental countries, on the other hand, Chambers' ideas were taken up rather than Brown's gardens being imitated.

The distinction between a park and a garden in the theoretical writings of William Gilpin (1724–1804) has already been dealt with. His emphasis of the painterly element led to a way of looking at gardens which was similar to analyzing a picture. For Gilpin, who was a clergyman in Boldre, Hampshire, and a friend of Horace Walpole, a garden was a three-dimensional, dynamic painting, as can be seen in his *Remarks* of 1791. In this essay he used watercolors to demonstrate the correct and the incorrect way of designing the edge of a forest or a clump of trees. In order to enhance the picturesque quality of a landscape garden, Gilpin suggested creating systems of lines of sight with the aid of decorative buildings. Thus tree-lined avenues starting at a pond or a basin were to lead to a distant ruin. The ruin itself did not necessarily have to be architecturally constructed, but could be painted

Heale Garden, Wiltshire
South terrace in front of the stately home from the 17th and 19th centuries

Perspective view of an avenue
ending at the ruins of an old building in Roman style
After Langley, 1728

Incorrect (upper) and correct (lower) combination of vertical and horizontal forms
From Humphry Repton, *Sketches* (1840 edition)

on a screen, or represented by a brick wall with cement rendering. Gilpin elaborated a way of looking at the English landscape garden which emphasized its painterly qualities. In the emerging industrial age he contributed decisively to a way of seeing things which eliminated certain aspects of practical life.

Like Gilpin, Humphry Repton (1752–1818), who from 1788 worked exclusively as a garden designer, also made a distinction between a park and a garden. For gardens laid out close to the house he demanded a strict geometric, architectural design, but for the park situated at a greater distance from the house he envisaged the principle of giving an artistic shape to nature. Repton drew up different sets of design rules in order to demonstrate the aesthetic interplay of the garden, the grand house, and the park. Like Gilpin, he distinguished between correct and incorrect design approaches. In his *Sketches and Hints on Landscape Gardening* (London, 1795) he analyzed the possible combinations of vertical and horizontal forms. This referred to the positioning and clipping of deciduous trees or conifers in the proximity of the house (illustrations left). A building with historical features, such as stepped gables, vertically structured and flanked with turrets, needed to be contrasted with the broad, widely spreading tops of deciduous trees which would frame the building, together with an ensemble of low-growing shrubbery. For a house in the classicist style, on the other hand, with its emphasis on horizontal lines, tall spruces, contrasting by virtue of their height with the elevation of the house, were suitable.

Much as Repton emphasized the painterly qualities of park, garden, and house in these examples, he was obviously not exclusively concerned with picturesque effects. In the *Sketches* he wrote:

"I have discovered that *utility* must often take the lead of *beauty*, and convenience be preferred to picturesque effect in the neighborhood of men's habitation . . . In whatever relates to man, propriety and convenience are not less objects of good taste, than picturesque effect."

ILLUSTRATION OPPOSITE
Bath, Somerset
Prior Park, view from the castle across the landscape park with the Palladian bridge

Sheffield Park, East Sussex
Vegetation on the banks of the Middle Lake

John Claudius Loudon (1783–1843), the son of a Scottish estate owner, brought about a change of direction in the artistic and social assessment of the English landscape garden. This can be traced in his voluminous writings on the theory and practice of garden design. Although Loudon to a large extent followed Repton's ideas, he lost no opportunity of demonstrating errors and weaknesses in the system of the older man (older, indeed, by a generation). He reverted to talking about gardens, not parks. He argued that the picturesque garden should extend right up to the house and provide proof of the owner's taste. Later he set the geometric garden on an equal footing with this type of garden – without any acrimony, incidentally, toward the traditional architectural or Baroque garden. He expressed these opinions in many writings in the early 19th century. In the 1830s, however, Loudon, writing in the eighth edition of the *Gardener's Magazine* (1837) introduced a new term. He wrote:

"The gardenesque style . . . is calculated for displaying the art of the gardener."

He was concerned with the arrangement and clear placing of systems of pathways and clumps of trees. Trees and shrubs were now regarded as individual entities in order to emphasize their aesthetic forms, in complete contrast to the picturesque style, where the eye concentrated on clumps of trees or groups of bushes while neglecting their individual design.

With the concept of the "gardenesque," geometric forms became increasingly important. Within a system of curving paths, trees, bushes, and circular beds that were easy to plant were to be arranged in groups (illustration below). It was important, Loudon suggested, to plant each bed with one single kind of flower or shrub only. Furthermore, they should be separated from the pathway and from one another by a least *c.* 1 m (3 ft.). A few years later, when designing a "suburban residence," he converted this model to a strict geometric pattern (illustration right). In front of the dwelling house there are kitchen gardens with an alley of fruit trees between them leading to the entrance frontage. The rear garden frontage is taken up by a sunken garden in the style of the English Renaissance garden, divided by a single large ornament. A square encloses a circle containing beds in various forms such as semicircular arches, bulbous shapes, or rectangles, with different planting. The paths are paved in order, as Loudon tells us, to economize on maintenance costs.

Loudon consistently trod the path from the English landscape garden to the historicizing or eclectic garden. His ideas had a positive echo because he took into consideration less privileged social groups, for whom he produced the idea of the townhouse garden, which of course could not possibly be laid out as a landscape garden.

The decisive step from the landscape garden to the geometric garden was taken by the bookseller and bookbinder Shirley Hibberd (1825–90), at least in his theoretical statements. In his writings he followed in Loudon's footsteps and announced the demise of the landscape garden. Hibberd wrote explicitly for "plain people," the poor, and proceeded from the assumption that everybody had taste and hence also a certain degree of artistic skill. And so he tried to instruct people in the art of gardening so that they could cultivate their souls as they cultivated the flowers in their gardens. He wrote that of all the places in the world, the gloomy towns needed the presence of flowers to call us back now and again from the hectic bustle of business and remind us of our childhood, our parental home, our first love, our first ramble, our mother's smiles and kisses, the Eldorado that a meadow of buttercups was for us then. The romantic idealism of this social attitude was intended to contribute to the improvement of morals, since although nature was out of reach for the town dweller, a microcosm of it could be set up in the living room or on a small plot of land outside the front door.

Seen in this light, the old-style English garden was proclaimed as the new, modern garden, providing a counterweight to the industrialized towns. The models were consciously taken from older pattern books from the Renaissance or the French Baroque. This could be illustrated by comparing Hibberd's geometric garden with a design by Dézallier d'Argenville. The garden boundary was, once more, to stand out prominently – a clear repudiation of the old landscape garden ha-ha.

This approach to garden design was undoubtedly justified in the decades of social utopias. But how was it possible for the landscape garden to be defamed, in view of increasing urbanization and a society alienated from nature by industrialization? For Hibberd this type of garden symbolized the privileges of the landed aristocracy, in which the greater part of the population could have no share. Hence something like a miniature landscape garden, outdoors or indoors, had to serve as a substitute for nature. For this type of garden the geometric form was to a certain extent the obvious choice.

Suburban residence in the geometric style
From *Gardener's Magazine*, 1841

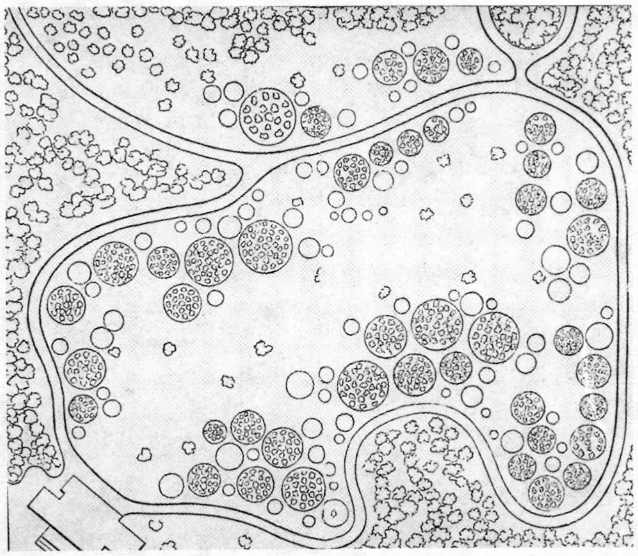

Circular bed layout
Garden design proposal by John Claudius Loudon for gardeners who are not artists
From *Gardener's Magazine,* 1835

William Beckford and Fonthill Abbey

William Beckford (1760–1844)
Portrait of the Romantic eccentric as an aesthete

Fonthill Abbey was for the English landscape garden what Bomarzo was for the Italian Baroque garden – an eccentric example of its genre. It is not a case of the monstrosities of Bomarzo appearing in their corresponding variants at Fonthill, but the anecdotes which grew up around its creator William Beckford were as curious as the fantastic creatures in the Italian garden. The anecdote that was probably the most typical of the master of the house was reported by Hermann Prince Pückler-Muskau in his *Briefe eines Verstorbenen* (Letters of a Deceased Man). The eccentric Beckford is said to have surrounded his estate with a wall *c.* 3.5 m (12 ft.) high in order to keep out unwanted visitors. A prying lord from the neighborhood managed to get over the wall with a tall ladder and suddenly found himself face to face with William Beckford. The latter very politely offered to show the intruder his house and garden. After the tour William Beckford said goodbye to his guest and wished him a pleasant day. When the lord found the way out locked and asked the servant to open it for him, the latter repeated his master's command that the guest should go out the same way he came in.

The Prince begins his anecdote with the question: "Have you ever heard of the eccentric Beckford, a kind of Lord Byron in prose...?" It was in fact Lord Byron himself who described William Beckford (1760–1844) as the richest man in England, whose fortune enabled him to turn his romantic visions into reality (illustration on the left). Beckford had his first garden laid out in Portugal in the Sintra hills which, as he wrote, was a "Claude-like place" – meaning that it was a garden in the spirit of a painting by Claude Lorrain. Following his return to England in the 1790s, Beckford commissioned the architect James Wyatt to build the neo-Gothic abbey at Fonthill near Salisbury in the county of Wiltshire. It curiously combines a medieval belfry, a high Gothic nave, castle-like wings and towers edged with battlements – a theater of architecture on whose stage one man alone, namely the master of the house himself, directed and acted at the same time (illustration on the right).

Who was Lord Beckford? His immeasurable fortune had been left to him by his family, who had become rich through the slave trade and sugarcane plantations in Jamaica. When he was five years old he had the privilege of piano lessons from Wolfgang Amadeus Mozart. The watercolorist Alexander Cozens initiated him into the art of drawing. When the young William Beckford celebrated reaching adulthood on Christmas 1781, the rooms of his father's country residence, Fonthill Splendens, were transformed into a fairytale illusion with transparent moving pictures – illuminated by colorful lighting and accompanied by the singing of the most famous castrati in Europe. In those years Beckford worked on his novel entitled *Vathek*, a work of gloomy Gothic romanticism which places the Faust theme in an oriental setting. Lord Byron called this book his bible. This promising start to a literary and political career came to an abrupt end when rumors spread of Beckford's homosexual inclinations, and malicious campaigns forced him to flee abroad. He went to Portugal. He soon exchanged this self-imposed exile for the "exterritorial" Fonthill Abbey. Beckford called the building plans "diabolical." The central tower was said to loom up 84 m (275 $^1/_2$ ft.) into the sky, and the central nave to be almost as long as Westminster Abbey. Beckford said that never had so many building stones been used apart from in Babylon. There he could indulge his loneliness and melancholy – surrounded by a whole host of servants, a doctor from Strasbourg, and a Swiss dwarf by the name of Perro whose task it was to open the 10 m (*c.* 33 ft.) high oak door to the few

Fonthill Abbey
William Beckford's country residence created in the form of a medieval abbey

guests who came there. Later Beckford was to write that his sufferings were not inconsiderable on account of the appalling boredom and the loneliness of that grave of an abbey. The worse thing was that in that grave no rest could be found such as other graves offered.

The estate was surrounded by a wall 3 m (*c.* 10 ft.) high and 12 km ($7^1/_2$ miles) long and included a park – to some extent like a fairytale but otherwise gloomy – as well as the conglomeration of architecture. Beckford had a so-called American garden laid out when, in the second half of the eighteenth century, frost-resistant plants were imported from North America, for example rhododendrons or magnolias as well as cypresses or tulip trees which became popular. Below the abbey he created the artificial Bitham Lake. Broad expanses of lawn and long avenues of trees cross the grounds which are surrounded by trees, some of them native species, some of exotic origins. Beckford wanted a horticulturally controlled wilderness where animals, which outside the walls would have been mercilessly killed by lords mad on hunting, could be granted a paradisial refuge.

In 1799 the young J.M.W. Turner stayed at Fonthill for three weeks in order to make drawings and watercolors of the park and the abbey (illustration above). Beckford probably wanted to see his own visions realized in Turner's art, as one of his descriptions of Fonthill corresponds fairly accurately to a watercolor by the artist. He wrote that all the dark woods around the abbey were shrouded in radiant color from the setting sun under the loveliest blue from the sky. From these forests the castle of Atlas rose up with all its windows sparkling like diamonds. He said that he had never in his life seen anything approaching this one single vision, nothing so great in appearance or so magical in color. Beckford had taken the motif of the castle of Atlas, the magician floating in the air, from Ariosto's *Orlando Furioso*.

In 1807 the slave trade was abolished. The sugar prices slumped in the colonies in the West Indies and Beckford's income dwindled. The estate was expensive to maintain, and could no longer be financed. So in 1822 Fonthill Abbey had to be sold off at Christie's in London for £330,000. Beckford commented that he had got rid of that "holy sepulchre." When some years later the tall tower of the abbey fell down, he expressed himself in a similarly detached manner. He regretted not having being there to view it.

Joseph Mallord William Turner
Leeds Museum and Galleries
(City Art Gallery)

View of Fonthill Abbey from a quarry
Pencil, Indian ink, and watercolors on paper, 29.8 x 47.7 cm (*c* 12 x *c.* 19 in.), *c.* 1799

Landscape Gardens in Germany around 1800

The roots and the theoretical basis of the landscape garden are to be found in France, but it was, of course, in England that it developed into a specific type of garden. But how did the English landscape garden find its way back onto the continent? After all, it was the French King Louis XV who in the 1760s had the Trianon area laid out at Versailles in accordance with notions of pastoral romanticism. Toward the end of the 18th century the English garden became more and more popular and gardeners from across the Channel were always in demand. By this time the Baroque garden had come to the end of its development. What was wanted now was primal nature, enhanced by scenic features such as cliffs, waterfalls, proliferating vegetation by the waterside, and little classical temples.

Jean-Jacques Rousseau played a decisive part in propagating this new idea of a garden. His epistolary novel *La Nouvelle Héloise, ou lettres de deux amans, habitans d'une petite ville au pied des Alpes*, was first published in 1761, and had been translated into German by 1762. In it he outlined a new philosophy of life based on close contact with nature. His model was the garden, where he found nature, where people could find the way back to the sources of their own identity, to naturalness. For this reason there was no place in a garden for symmetry, orderliness or straight lines. Following the motto "Nature does not plant anything in straight lines," the natural growth of plants, bushes, and trees, and the character of the landscape, were to be encouraged.

The Landscape Garden at Wörlitz

The idea of the landscape garden based on Rousseau's philosophy spread particularly quickly in Germany. In the age of "sentimentality" and Enlightenment, the garden at Wörlitz soon acquired importance. It was created by Prince Leopold Franz von Anhalt-Dessau, completed *c.* 1790, and soon became one of the principal sights to see in Europe. Painters, philosophers, and writers were invited to visit Wörlitz. The prince regarded his garden as the model of an enlightened state. The realm of the garden was to be presented as the aesthetic center of an exemplary principality. The English landscape garden unmistakably provided the model. The English diplomat Charles Stewart, faced with the spacious layout of the park and the often surprising landscape vistas, is reported to have exclaimed enthusiastically "God damn, I'm in England here!"

Even as a young man, Prince Franz (illustration left) had devoted himself, starting in the 1770s, to the painstaking care of the landscape and the embellishment of his property. This was the result of several lengthy journeys to England to study the gardens there. He had been accompanied on these journeys by the architect Friedrich Wilhelm von Erdmannsdorff and the gardener Johann Friedrich Eyserbeck, who was made responsible for supervising the design of the Wörlitz garden. But the prince himself also tried his hand at planning and designing – often even going against the ideas of his own experts.

The prince succeeded to a certain extent in giving reality to his vision of a republic of letters. He was able to give a home in Wörlitz to the classical scholar and translator August von Rode. The Allgemeine Buchhandlung der Gelehrten und Künstler [General Scholars' and Artists' Bookshop] was established in Dessau in 1781, and by fifteen years later the "Chalkographic [that is Copper-

Wörlitz, landscape garden, view of the Temple of Venus

Prince Friedrich Franz von Anhalt-Dessau
Painting, *c.* 1766
Anton von Maron
Nuremberg, Germanisches Nationalmuseum

ILLUSTRATION OPPOSITE
Wörlitz, landscape garden
The castle or country house at Wörlitz was built in 1769–73 by Friedrich Wilhelm von Erdmannsdorff, based on Italian and English models (top).
Lake Wörlitz with the Amalia grotto (bottom)

Wörlitz, landscape garden
Lines of sight fanning out at the Golden Urn with views of the synagogue, the Church of St. Peter and the so-called Warning Altar

ILLUSTRATION OPPOSITE
Wörlitz, landscape garden
Temple of Flora

plate Engravers'] Association" was attracting important copperplate engravers. The educationist Johann Bernhard Basedow was working at the Philanthropium. But what was particularly popular was the specialist library in the Wörlitz park, which had been established especially for garden architects from all over the world. All this was achieved by the prince whom his powerful neighbor Friedrich II of Prussia contemptuously called a "princillo," a "princeling," but a prince who had been able to detach his territory politically from Prussia, and to declare his principality neutral. Friedrich Franz had to raise enormous sums of money to pay for this prudent measure, but for him the financial price was worth it, in order to come closer to the great goal of creating a republic of letters. In the middle of the lake he created Rousseau Island with a monument to indicate the intellectual origins of his philosophy, the germ cell of the Enlightenment, and his relationship with the French thinker with whom he had become acquainted in Paris in 1775.

The "English view," like a landscape allusion, finds unmistakable expression at Lake Wörlitz, when one strolls along its banks and suddenly catches sight of the Nymphaeum, picturesquely flanked by tall trees. This temple-like pavilion was designed by Erdmannsdorff in 1767–8 as a roofed garden seat. The park, with its wealth of allusions, is a repository for the prince's travel impressions. A visit to Naples led him to have the "Stone" island designed, so that even when at home he would be able to take pleasure in the landscape of the Campagna. Strawberry Hill, Horace Walpole's country seat just outside London, inspired him to build a comparable edifice in the neo-Gothic style. The Gothic House on the spacious lawn, surrounded by spruces, makes an alien, almost exotic impression in the context of classicist buildings (illustration below). The prince presumably discovered his liking for this style in England. In the second half of the 18th century, both classicist and historicizing, that is neo-Romanesque or, even more frequently, neo-Gothic architectural forms were to be seen there – which in the architectural sphere did not appear and spread in Germany until later. In Wörlitz the prince had grasped at an early stage how these architectural styles, that were formally speaking so opposed, could be combined by way of the art of garden design.

Wörlitz, landscape garden
Gothic house, built by Friedrich Wilhelm von Erdmannsdorff 1785–6

Weimar, park by the River Ilm
Goethe moved into the garden house situated at the edge of the valley in 1776. Duke Karl August had made him a gift of the house. The park by the Ilm, a river meadow surrounded by wooded slopes on the outskirts of the old inner city of Weimar, was begun in 1778. Goethe was involved in the project. Duke Karl August and Goethe had previously visited the Wörlitz landscape park, and found in it a model for the Weimar layout. A few park buildings were provided and the site is said at one time to have been marked by a "sentimental" atmosphere. The view shown above conveys a sense of this.

Hirschfeld's Theory of Garden Design

The writings of English garden theorists were also responsible for the overwhelming success on the continent of the English landscape garden. These were available in German translations by the 1770s and were studied closely when new gardens were designed. Along with these pamphlets, the garden theories of Christian Cay Lorenz Hirschfeld, professor of philosophy and aesthetics at Kiel University, very soon became popular. Although he had never had the opportunity of looking at English gardens in person, he subjected the landscape garden to analysis and drew up a list of its compositional elements and features. Unlike earlier theories, Hirschfeld, in his *Theorie der Gartenkunst* (Theory of Garden Design), published in 1779 (illustration opposite), distinguished, with regard to gardens, between different times of day and different seasons of the year. He also drew distinctions between sites in terms of the moods experienced during a visit. Thus he spoke of melancholy, cheerful, sentimental, and solemn gardens. For him a mood was created by the particular plants to be seen. Garden typology was extended for the first time in Hirschfeld's work. To the monastery, cemetery, academy, bathhouse, hospital, and castle gardens were added the people's garden. Hirschfeld's idea was that here the population of the town would enjoy "exercise, the pleasure of fresh air, recreation from work, and convivial conversation." In his opinion the structure of the garden should take into account both the English landscape garden that was popular at the time and the French Baroque garden, in order to create a specifically German garden. Hirschfeld not only rejected "artificiality," the French Rococo garden style, but also saw in the English landscape garden elements to be avoided, for example Chinese teahouses and other dainty decorative buildings. With these recommendations Hirschfeld wanted to give the garden the even more decisive quality of a landscape garden. He therefore took his cue from the "strict English line" represented, for example, by Lancelot "Capability" Brown. Hirschfeld's "Theory" was soon established as a standard work on German garden design.

"Both starting at the frontage of the arcaded house and behind it, the areas for walking spread out almost in the manner of an English garden. In front of the arcaded house there is a fairly substantial copse of oak trees, but with many large spaces in between them planted with various native and foreign species of flowers and bushes mixed with flowering shrubs. Hollows and mounds have been made to give variety to the walks and the views. Everywhere there are white benches, seats,

Theorie
der
Gartenkunst.
Von
C. C. L. Hirschfeld,
Königl. Dänischem würklichen Justizrath und ordentlichem Professor der Philosophie
und der schönen Wissenschaften auf der Universität zu Kiel.
Erster Band.
Leipzig,
bey M. G. Weidmanns Erben und Reich. 1779.

Christian Cay Lorenz Hirschfeld
Theorie der Gartenkunst (Theory of Garden Design)
Title page and vignette, Leipzig, 1779

and tables on the hills and in the vales. Beneath the tall oak and beech trees growing between them there are inviting places to rest in the shade."

These words of high praise by Hirschfeld referred to the Wilhelmsbad park in the vicinity of Hanau, near Frankfurt am Main. The comparison with the English landscape garden was not only justified in terms of visual appearance, but was also to be expected in view of the family relationships of the owner, the heir apparent Prince Wilhelm von Hessen-Kassel, whose mother was a daughter of the English King George II. The prince had had the site built between 1776 and 1784. The bathhouses, the Fountain Temple with the statue of Aesculapius, and a castle ruin in the medieval manner, along with smaller pavilions, were there for the entertainment of the visitors, who included garden experts such as Hirschfeld. The romantic ruin situated on an island (illustration below), which was *de rigueur* in almost every English landscape garden, was where Wilhelm lived, "...a half ruined Gothic tower in a truly deceptive style, built according to the prince's drawings," as Hirschfeld wrote in his notes on Wilhelmsbad. A special attraction was the temple-like merry-go-

Wilhelmsbad, landscape park
Castle ruin based on the ground plan of a Gothic pavilion (after an engraving by B. Lanley). The building was built in 1780 in its island location as a dwelling-place for the heir apparent Prince Wilhelm von Hessen-Kassel.

Wilhelmshöhe park and castle
Idealized view, painting, *c.* 1800
Johann Erdmann Hummel
Kassel, Staatliche Kunstsammlung

round with mechanically operated wooden horses. Today it can still be admired on a small mound in the park.

When Wilhelm moved to Kassel in 1785 to take over the reins of government as Landgrave Wilhelm IX of Hessen, work at Wilhelmsbad ceased. For a few decades a small number of visitors still came to take the waters, then this too came to an end. From a conservative point of view, the present-day visitor can be thankful that this fate befell the once so lively health resort, for the structure of the landscape garden has not been altered since.

Kassel, Wilhelmshöhe

In Kassel the new Landgrave of Hessen found one of the most sumptuous Baroque gardens in Germany. Landgrave Karl had been inspired by the gardens of Italy, which he had visited. From 1701 he had had a garden laid out in the Italian style on the eastern slope of the "Hawk's Wood." The *pièce de résistance* of this garden was, and still is, the famous cascade constructed by Giovanni Francesco Guerniero, 250 m (*c.* 820 ft.) in length and crowned by the memorable statue of Hercules, a monumental replica of the Roman Farnese *Hercules*, which was mentioned in an earlier chapter (see p. 303).

Immediately after his move, Wilhelm set to work on transforming the huge garden site into an English landscape garden. However, he retained important elements of the Baroque structure, as he had realized that although the landscape park had to be completely rethought, it could only gain from the integration of the dominant cascade axis (illustration above). In the upper third of the site the cascade, enclosed in stone, leads down from the uninhabitable castle crowned with the Hercules statue at the top of the mountain, to the oval Neptune Fountain. From there it flows picturesquely through a narrow woodland path via several intermediate stages down to the spacious area which is bounded by the semicircular classicist castle. The principal attraction of the Karlsberg, which was not renamed the Wilhelmshöhe until later, is the water jet which the landgrave positioned in the lower pool in front of the castle in 1790. To this day this spectacular sight can be observed during the summer months. The water flowing down from above creates so great a pressure that the jet of water spurts more than 50 m (*c.* 164 ft.) up into the air. The so-called "Weißenstein" and "Kirch" wings of the castle were begun by Friedrich Simon Louis du Ry in 1786 and 1788, and its block-shaped central

ILLUSTRATION OPPOSITE
Wilhelmshöhe (Kassel), landscape garden
Pond with water jet and Jussow Temple, 1817–18

Wilhelmshöhe, landscape garden
View of the castle from the Hell Pond

building with a middle portico was completed in 1798 by Christoph Jussow. Between the castle and the pool with the water jet, the landgrave had a so-called bowling green laid out. Despite its spaciousness and the relatively large distance involved, this sunken lawn created an ingenious visual foreshortening. The castle, the water jet, and the mountain looming up behind it with the cascade appear to move closer together, forming a self-contained ensemble with a romantic effect.

In 1803 the landgrave became the Elector Wilhelm I, and over the years further decorative buildings were added in the park, which had been afforested and given a complicated system of pathways. As well as Virgil's Grave (illustration opposite, bottom left) and the Temple of Mercury, the Egyptian Pyramid (illustration opposite, bottom right) and Socrates's Hermitage – an expression of the philosophical inclinations of the owner – can still be seen today. This sentimental setting was given the obligatory dab of exotic color in the form of a complete Chinese village, of which unfortunately only one pavilion survives (illustration opposite, top).

It can be said that the landgrave continued in Kassel the park-making work that he had begun in Wilhelmsbad near Hanau. What we admire today at the Wilhelmshöhe would probably have been carried out at Hanau if Wilhelm had not taken up office in Kassel. One is struck by the fact that the medieval ruin at Wilhelmsbad was further developed by him at Wilhelmshöhe into a sumptuously appointed knight's castle, the Lion's Castle, named after the heraldic beast of Hessen (illustration p. 413). Romantic emotions and sentimental inclinations could be devloped and indulged in the

Wilhelmshöhe, landscape garden
Chinese pavilion (top)
Virgil's Grave (far left)
Pyramid (left)

illusory medieval space. The castle was at the same time a dwelling-place and a burial place – as the elector wished it to be. The elector may well have been transported out of this world by the ambience of the surroundings, with the Wolf's Glen and the memorable Devil's Bridge (illustration opposite).

Whether or not, in his castle apartments or in Socrates' Hermitage, he reflected on the moral justification for selling his soldiers to the English, who in Boston and its surroundings were fighting against the Americans, desperately struggling for independence, remains uncertain. At any rate he used money raised by the trade in soldiers to finance the expensive park.

In 1805 the expansion of the site was interrupted for a few years. The elector was driven into exile by Napoleon, whose brother Jérome ruled at the Wilhelmshöhe, as the King of Westphalia, until 1815. Jérome preferred the brightly lit banqueting hall to the gloomy hermitage, and led a glittering life at court. His vassals, joined before long by the people, gave him the mocking nickname of "King Merry." His traces can still be found today in the Weißenstein wing of the castle museum.

Hirschfeld was restrained in the views he expressed regarding the Kassel site. On the one hand, he hoped to be given a post at court in Kassel. On the other hand, in order not to lose credibility, he had to dissociate himself from the absolutist power symbolized by the park with the Castle of Hercules. It went against the spirit of the Enlightenment to which the sensitive Hirschfeld felt profoundly committed. After a struggle, he came up with the following tactful assessment:

"Astonishing though this achievement is by virtue of its extraordinary audacity and grandeur, its effect has been nevertheless stripped of all those emotions which are aroused by old mountain castles and ruins on the top of cliffs. The Carlsberg is a miracle which appears as if created by a supernatural power. Its unusual size oppresses the onlooker, who soon comes to feel the pettiness and feebleness of other works of man."

Did Wilhelm understand this message – if he ever heard it? If so, the idea of offering the famous garden theorist a post in his service presumably never crossed his mind. Hirschfeld's words reveal that he had a different kind of garden architecture in mind, which could more readily have been achieved by a natural setting in the immediate vicinity of a medieval castle.

Wilhelmshöhe, landscape garden
Lion's Castle, 1791–9

ILLUSTRATION OPPOSITE
Wilhelmshöhe, landscape garden
Romantic Devil's Bridge by Christoph Jussow

Friedrich Ludwig von Sckell (1750–1820)
Portrait of the garden architect *c.* 1820
Sckell was the first professional garden architect of the new landscape style in Germany. As a leading exponent in his field he succeeded to an unprecedented degree in becoming independent of patronage.

The English Garden in Munich

Nor, we may assume, did Friedrich Ludwig von Sckell (llustration above) consider the layout at Kassel worth imitating. He felt a stronger affinity with Hirschfeld's views than with the late Baroque garden structures favored by the Elector of Hessen. It was entirely in Hirschfeld's spirit that he decided to design a garden which would, he proclaimed, "express the quality of German genius." But the garden in question was the English Garden in Munich, conceived on the one hand as a kind of pantheon for the great Bavarian regent, and on the other as a public garden to provide edification and instruction.

When the Elector Karl Theodor, under whose aegis the garden at Schwetzingen near Heidelberg had been created, moved from Mannheim to Munich in 1778, he had the city fortifications pulled down to make room for new residential areas, in line with the dictum: "Munich can henceforth no longer be a fortress." In the north of the city the so-called Schönfeld grounds were planned; they came into being along with the Carl Theodor Park, later to become the English Garden.

Sckell had a unique opportunity of putting the new ideals of garden design into practice as he saw fit, without being subject to the constraints of an existing Baroque garden. The elector, the new regent, was not greatly loved in Munich, and wanted to present the new garden to the people as a gift from their ruler. In 1789 he issued a decree which he hoped would make him popular with the people of Bavaria. His intention was "...to have the "Hirschanger" (Stag's Green) used for the people's pleasure in his capital city of Munich," and he made it known that he was graciously minded "no longer to withhold this most beautiful natural site from the public in its hours of recreation."

In this early example of a German public garden Sckell was able to put Hirschfeld's recommendations into practice. But during the early stages of planning and execution he was involved in disputes with Count Rumford, an American in the service of the Bavarian court, and his successor Count Werneck. When Sckell finally went to Munich in 1804 he was promoted by Maximilian Joseph, the new regent, to the rank of court superintendent of gardens. Now he was able to start on the task of transforming a huge piece of land, over 5 km (*c.* 3 miles) in length, into a harmoniously and rhythmically structured park.

The site consisted of four parts. The first area, the so-called Schönfeld meadow, was bounded by the court garden. Then came the Hirschanger wood, the area surrounding the Chinese Tower;

Munich, English Garden
Chinese Tower

Munich, English Garden
Kleinhesselohe Lake

the latter was reserved for the use of court society at the time (illustration opposite bottom). To the north the third area of the garden stretched out around the artifically created Kleinhesselohe Lake (illustration above). Finally came the Hirschau (Stag's Meadow) area leading to the Aumeister terrain. Sckell wanted to have a twisting panoramic pathway joining the first two areas in order to create a visual connection between the park and the city. He walked through the terrain in person indicating where the pathway should go, in order to be sure that walkers would be able to see "...the city of Munich in the foreground and the age-old Hirschanger wood in the background along with the other beauties of nature." Crown and countryside, the spheres of courtly and rural society, were to be linked by means of curving paths of this kind. Sckell imagined fluid transitions between the court garden and the park area of the village of Schwabing. However, he was unable to carry out his plan of linking the court garden with the English Park because the Palais Salbert, which had been built in the Palladian style in 1803 and was later to become the Prince Carl Palais, acted as a barrier between the two areas.

Following Hirschfeld's recommendations, Sckell wanted only such decorative buildings to be erected as were in the "good, pure style," that is the classicist style. He considered sentimental and exotic features, most especially the Chinese Tower that had been built back in 1790, to be out of place, and wanted them removed. But the Chinese Tower survived to become the best known landmark of the English Garden. After being destroyed during the Second World War, it was rebuilt in its original form.

This decorative building is a variant of the pagoda which Sir Williams Chambers designed in 1757 when Kew Gardens in London were being redesigned (illustration p. 338). The Chinese Tower was thus probably also meant as a gesture indicating an affinity with the English landscape garden. Sckell evidently had no objection to the so-called Rumford Room, a summerhouse adjacent to the pavilion. It had been designed by the architect Johann Baptist Lechner in the pure Palladian style, as was obligatory for decorative buildings in the English landscape garden. For Sckell, park buildings had to have not only a clear architectural form but also a particular political signficance. It was therefore important to him that the buildings should serve as a reminder of "worthy regents and meritorious men of the state." On the other hand he rejected any excessively prominent allusions to classical mythology, and, even more decidedly, any romantic glorification of medieval chivalry.

Sckell did not live to see Leo von Klenze's realization of his conception of decorative buildings in the "good, pure style." He died in 1823. One of the most imposing buildings is certainly the "Monopteros" built in 1838 on the artificial mound close to the court garden (illustrations left and below). Ludwig I had a memorial tablet to Karl Theodor and Maximilian I put up in this circular

Munich English Garden
Monopteros (garden temple), built by Leo von Klenze in 1837 (left)

View of Munich town center from inside the Monopteros across the park landscape (bottom)

Munich, English Garden
Waterfall, romantic area by the Eisbach stream

temple. On the bank of the Kleinhesselohe Lake, in the area of the actual public garden, the Sckell monument towers up (illustration opposite, left). Based on designs by Leo von Klenze, it was created and erected shortly after the death of the great garden architect. The inscription reads, in translation: "This memorial to the profound master of beautiful garden design, whose abundant contributions to the purest enjoyment of the earth were crowned by this park, was erected by his King, Max Joseph MDCCCXXIV."

To which of Hirschfeld's types does the English garden belong – the melancholy, cheerful, sentimental, or solemn type? Since it is essentially a matter of a public garden, the description "cheerful" would be the most appropriate. Neither the Monopteros (garden temple) nor the Chinese Tower give this garden either an aristocratic or a sentimental coloring.

Although in his pamphlet Hirschfeld called for a very sparing use of decorative buildings, either he or his successors must also have wondered whether merely giving a shape to nature was by itself at all sufficient to produce sentimental or melancholy moods. The sentimental garden draws its vitality from the yearnings of its owners or visitors. Then, it was almost always yearning for Italy or the past, only tapped by using suitable decorative buildings.

The challenge was therefore to find an alternative within the English conception. On the one hand, the nature that was on display in the park, within the urban ambience, required architectural fixed points. On the other hand, this selfsame nature must not be obscured by myths and fairy tales. Leo von Klenze's classicism led him to replace the decorative buildings by appropriate park architecture by means of which it was possible to elicit sublime thoughts and sentimental feelings.

Munich, English Garden
Sckell monument at the southwest end of the Kleinhesselohe Lake, erected in 1823, based on a design by Leo von Klenze

Munich, English Garden
Werneck memorial. Count Werneck was one of the creators of the English Garden, along with Rumford and Sckell.

Potsdam, New Garden
Kitchen building in the style of a Roman Temple of Mars (1788–90) and marble palace (1797) by Carl von Gontard and Carl Gotthard Langhans

The New Garden and Sanssouci Park

The New Garden to the north of the municipal district of Potsdam is a wonderful example of poetic/sentimental garden design. The garden was created in two stages. In 1790, during the first stage, Friedrich Wilhelm II summoned Johann August Eyserbeck, who was known as one of the group of artists in Dessau-Wörlitz. Eyserbeck embellished the lakeside area by the Holy Lake with numerous buildings, and was concerned to take long-distance effects into account in line with the English model. One of the most attractive vistas can be enjoyed in the area in front of the kitchen house with a temple ruin half sunk into the ground (left-hand building in the illustration above). From there a subterranean passage led to the king's summer residence, the Marble Palace (right-hand building in the illustration above), built by Carl von Gontard and extended in 1797 by Carl Gotthard Langhans, who built the Brandenburg Gate. Nearby there are also the redbrick houses of the Dutch Establishment, a group of gatehouses and servants' quarters with stables and coachhouses, along with a pyramid used as an ice cellar. This garden, with its abundance of unexpected points of view, displays a sophisticated complex of allusions. Anyone expecting to find a gravestone in the pyramid or a relic of the past in the Roman temple, will be surprised to see their practical functions. For strolling in the garden and enjoying the sentimental atmosphere, the decorative buildings and the romantic natural setting are indispensable prerequisites. But anyone who wants to enjoy living in this park will find the palace, the kitchen, and the ice cellar equally indispensable.

About twenty years later, during its second stage of development, the landscape garden was once again turned, by Peter Joseph Lenné, the widely traveled royal landscape gardener, into a place for poetic daydreaming. By then the park had become almost completely overgrown and had to

Peter Joseph Lenné (1789–1866)
Portrait drawing by Gerhard Koeber, *c.* 1830
The layout and redesign of the Potsdam gardens was the *magnum opus* of this versatile garden architect.

be cleared. Lenné had pathways cut to create lines of sight, and at the same time vegetation was also removed from the lakeside areas to create new views and vistas. He noted in a letter:

"My humble proposal is thus this: during the coming autumn, when the defoliated trees will permit the most interesting views and vistas to be ascertained, to determine the points of view both from the new garden and from Chancellor Hardenberg's country residence at Klein-Glienicke."

During those years Lenné was likewise occupied with the large park area adjoining the terraces of Sanssouci Castle, which he reshaped as a romantic landscape garden. An area at the foot of the terraced vineyards was laid out in a regular fashion. Further to the east, a small *jardin anglo-chinois* and a teahouse built by Johann Gottfried Büring in 1754, created the effect of an exotic pocket-handkerchief garden in the middle of a wooded area that has to a large extent run wild (illustrations pp. 422 and 423).

Lenné was commissioned by King Friedrich Wilhelm II to expand the park, and began work around 1816. He faced an almost impossible task. The cheerful Rococo style of the age of Friedrich the Great, in the shape of the ubiquitous terraced vineyards and the elegant castle, had to be harmonized with the new demands of the romantic landscape garden with its mock-historical or exotic decorative buildings. This meant that classical austerity had to be made to reveal a cheerful side, in order to combine the landscape garden, with its somewhat melancholy atmosphere, and the Rococo elements. Lenné began by laying out spacious lawns, and planting loose clumps of trees. The forest was thinned out, pathways were created, and finally, starting in 1825, there was further expansion in order to include the little Charlottenhof Castle in the overall plan of the site.

The crown prince, with his enthusiasm for Italy, wanted a Mediterranean villa in the modern, that is to say classicist style. It was designed by Karl

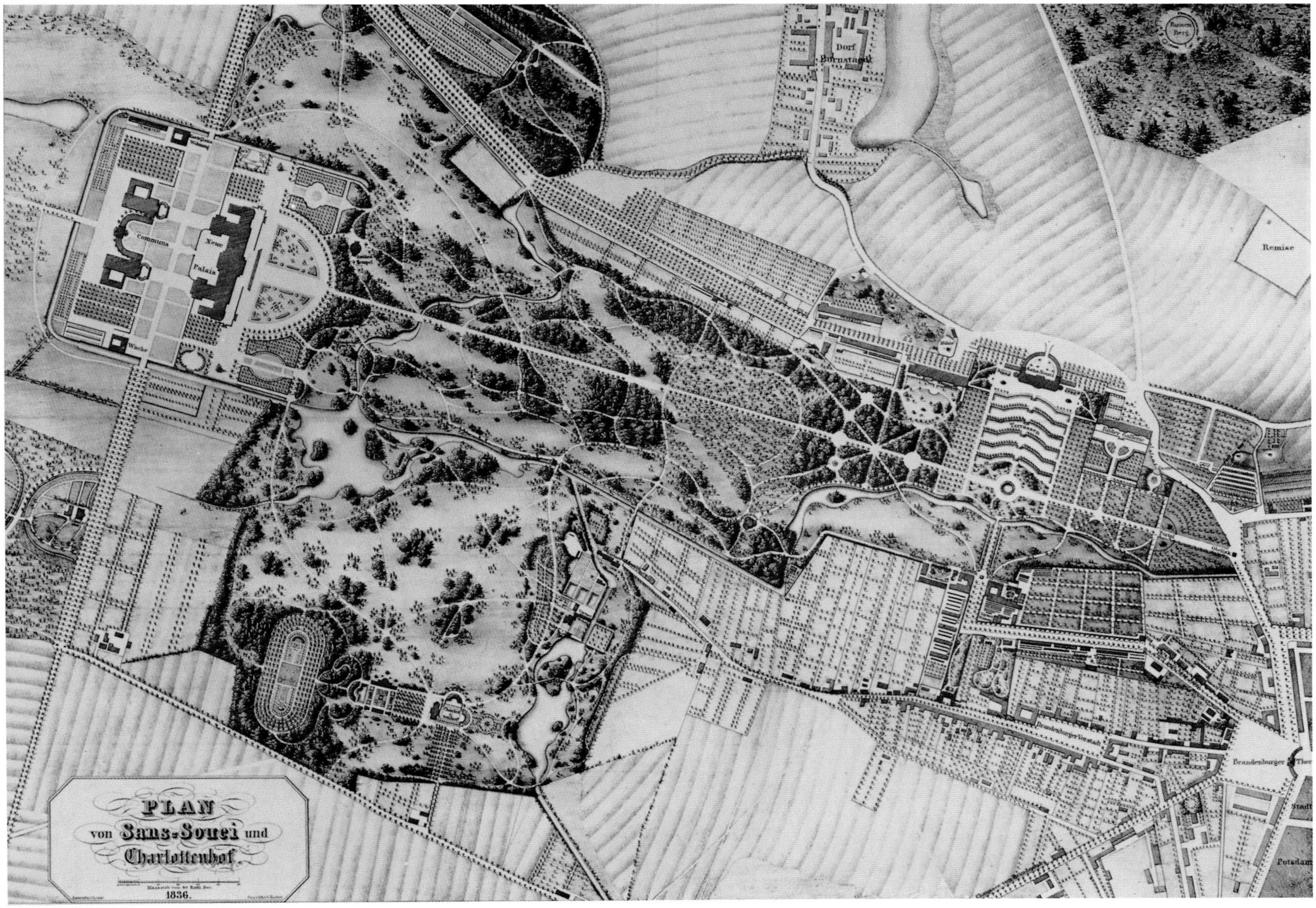

Plan of Sanssouci and Charlottenhof, 1836
The plan contains the extensions and alterations to the old garden carried out by Lenné.

Potsdam, Sanssouci Park
One of the ironwork pavilions adjacent to Sanssouci Palace

Golden suns symbolizing Enlightenment and humanity adorn the ironwork pavilions on both sides of the palace. At the same time they are an allusion to the secret society of Freemasons, to which Friedrich the Great belonged.

View from the Round Room of the Chinese Teahouse (left)

ILLUSTRATION OPPOSITE
Potsdam, Sanssouci Park
The Chinese Teahouse, built by Johann Gottfried Büring in 1754–5, is situated within the former deer garden to the south of the Great Alley.

Potsdam, Sanssouci Park
View of the Mount of Ruins fron Sanssouci Palace

ILLUSTRATION OPPOSITE
Potsdam, Sanssouci Park
Parterre region in front of the vineyard with view of a sculpture of Diana and the Great Alley in the background

Friedrich Schinkel, and built in 1826–9 (illustration p. 427, top). Thus the previous building, a simple 18th-century country house, became the new, elegant Charlottenhof Castle. Nearby was the Poets' Grove, planted with chestnut trees, with busts of famous German and Italian poets such as Goethe and Petrarch. Not far from the palace are the Roman Baths, also designed by Schinkel, again in the style of an Italian country house, and built in 1829–35.

In 1840 the crown prince came into his heritage and ascended the throne as Friedrich Wilhelm IV. He chose his Prussian Arcadia to be his summer residence and acquired the so-called Vogel vineyard to the east of the palace. There he intended to put his own ideas concerning garden design into practice, and at the same time to compete with the French model that was omnipresent in courtly matters. He called this new garden site the Marly Garden, in memory of Louis XIV's summer refuge. The garden was separated from the other zones by dense vegetation. In 1845 Friedrich Wilhelm instructed his master builder Ludwig Persius to build a church. The church, to which the king gave the name of Friedrichskirche, was intended both as a monument to his father's peace policy, and as a burial place for himself and his wife. Plans for the building were worked out jointly by the king and his architect. When he was crown prince he had visited Italy, and had taken such a liking to the church of San Clemente in Rome that he wanted a replica of it for his park. He wanted the eastern part and the steeple to be reflected in a lake, so Lenné transformed the little pond in the park area into a sizable lake. The flanking lake and the trees create an effective setting for the parts of the church, namely the neo-Romanesque belfry and the apse adorned with a dwarf gallery (illustration p. 427, bottom). It is a classicist landscape in the style of Jakob Friedrich Hadeerts.

In Germany the increased intellectual interest in the Middle Ages, the longing for Italy and the veneration of classical antiquity played a greater part than the use of chinoiserie or other exotic stage props. To begin with, it was fragments of classical antiquity which adorned the park as decorative buildings; then the patrons discovered their liking for the Middle Ages and requested plans for castles and castle ruins. From the court of honor of Sanssouci Palace one looks out over a valley at a hill on which remarkable ruins have been built. This so-called Mount of Ruins (illustration p. 424) had already been planned a hundred years previously by Friedrich the Great together with his master builder Georg Wenzeslaus von Knobelsdorff. Then, the ruins were imitations of ancient fragments, such as parts of an amphitheater or of an Ionic colonnade. Frederick Wilhelm IV who, in line with contemporary thinking, wanted the Middle Ages to be represented there too, commissioned his master builder Persius to build a medieval watchtower. Today, observers may see a remarkable contrast in the Ionic temple

Potsdam, Sanssouci Park
Sculpture in the parterre area in front of the vineyard
Personification of the element of water

Potsdam, Sanssouci Park
Rondel of the Muses

fragment and the medieval city wall ruin, framed by dense foliage and *vis-à-vis* a dainty little Rococo castle. At that time this strange seeming combination was an obligatory part of the make-up of a garden. Ancient ruins, a Romanesque basilica, or the Chinese teahouse, assembled from long ago and far away: these were by no means conceived as a homogenous ensemble. They were meant to be seen in the context of the park and its system of pathways, and to be felt as indicators of a particular educational intention.

The sentimental decorative buildings, which presented odd combinations of architectural themes and functions – such as, for example, the Egyptian pyramid used as an ice cellar at Potsdam – became increasingly popular *c.* 1800. This contradicted both Hirschfeld's theory and the approach to an English landscape garden in the style of someone like Lancelot Brown. The Greek temple standing next to the medieval castle ruin was felt by the kings and princes to be a sign of their enlightened cast of mind, even if contemporary poets and philosphers offered a different definition of that sentiment.

Potsdam, Sanssouci Park
Charlottenhof Castle, built by Karl Friedrich Schinkel 1826–36

Potsdam, Sanssouci Park
Friedenskirche (Church of Peace) built by Ludwig Persius 1843–8

Klein-Glienicke

Whereas in the New Garden Lenné had to introduce landscape elements into a predetermined site, in Klein-Glienicke he was able to convert an area that was predominantly in agricultural use into a landscape garden. That is to say, he was able from the outset to develop a fundamental concept of the garden. The owner was the Prussian Chancellor Karl August Prince Hardenberg. Lenné's first task in 1816 was to design the so-called pleasure ground (illustration p. 430, bottom), a type of English garden dating back to the Renaissance. In this type of garden the terrain is hilly, with spacious lawns, smaller ponds, and dense shrubbery, bounded by twisting gravel or sand pathways. Lenné laid out the garden in this form on three terraces. When the Crown Prince Carl, the third son of Friedrich III, acquired Klein-Glienicke in 1822, he realized its "poetic possibilities." After a lengthy visit to Italy he explained to his gardener and to the architect Karl Friedrich Schinkel that what he desired was a typical "*villegiatura*," a country life in a Mediterranean atmosphere where he could rest and recuperate. The two of them together achieved a unique interplay of shaped nature and architecture.

In 1824 Schinkel designed new facades in a clear, classicist style for Hofrat (Court Councillor) Mirow's old 18th-century Glienicke hunting lodge (illustration p. 430 top). A wonderful flower garden was laid out in the inner courtyard. Prince Carl used the walls of the "Cavaliers' House" situated opposite by studding them with the fragments collected during his travels in the countries of the ancient world, like trophies. Another specific

Potsdam, Klein-Glienicke landscape garden
Water jet with lion at Glienicke Castle, built in 1837, based on a design by Schinkel

Golden griffin at the main portal of Glienicke Castle

Potsdam, Klein-Glienicke landscape garden
Glienicke Castle, view from the south
The miniature castle was redesigned by Schinkel and Persius 1824–5. It was given a classicist facade in the process.

OPPOSITE
Potsdam, Klein-Glienicke landscape garden
Stibadium (semicircular roofed couch), built by Persius in 1840

reminder of Italy can be seen at the Lion Fountain in front of the southern castle frontage. An almost Baroque impression is created by the ensemble of lions on columns, balustrades, and an elegant circular basin (illustration p. 428–9). The unusually high water jet was operated by steam power provided by an engine installed somewhat farther to the north. Water from the plinth of the Stibadium also gushes out of lions' heads into small semicircular basins. On the driveway to the castle is the Stibadium, constructed by Ludwig Persius in 1840 following ancient Roman practice: a roofed couch with a fountain in front of it and a caryatid acting as the central supporting pillar for the arbor (illustration opposite). There the prince could indulge in his reveries as he gazed out across the park terraces and the River Havel to Potsdam.

At the lower tip of the park, directly in front of the present-day Glienicke bridge, the prince had the so-called "Große Neugierde" ("Great Curiosity") built, a roofed rotunda also providing a splendid view over Potsdam and the Pfingstberg ("Witsun Mountain") to Sacrow. In 1824, while still working on the castle, Schinkel set about redesigning the old Billiards House. He created a little gem, the summerhouse near the bank of the Havel, to which he gave an Italian pergola with vines. On the side facing the Havel a double flight of steps leads down into the garden, which is separated by a trellised walkway from the park and the river bank.

Work in the park was finished by 1860. In those decades Lenné planted no fewer than 25,000 trees, including some that were already fully grown, to give dignity to the park. A few years later its ignominious decline set in. The garden deteriorated, and was cut into pieces by broad alleys intended to link Potsdam with Berlin in the 1930s. A youth hostel was set up in the castle. But starting in 1979 attention turned once again to the old cultural heritage, and a start was made on restoring the park and the buildings. Today the incomparable ensemble can again be seen in its former splendor.

Potsdam, Klein-Glienicke landscape garden
The so-called "pleasure ground"

ILLUSTRATION OPPOSITE
Berlin-Wannsee
View of the Peacocks' Island from the Nikolskoje Block House

Berlin-Wannsee, Peacocks' Island
Little castle built by Johann Gottlob David Brendel 1794–7; iron bridge between the turrets 1807

Peacocks' Island

In 1685 the island known as "Pfauwerder" was used by the Great Elector for breeding rabbits – which was why it briefly bore the very unpoetic name of "Kaninchenwerder." The special appeal and beauty of the lonely wilderness was only discovered by Friedrich Wilhelm II. He acquired the island in 1793, and from 1821 had an exotic park laid out, within a mere three years, by the tried and trusted gardener Lenné. The island was adorned with summerhouse, a dairy farm, a kitchen house, and warden's quarters. Wilhelmine Encke, Friedrich Wilhelm's mistress, suggested giving the castle the form of a ruin (illustration below). She is said to have conceived the idea of this bizarre artifact while traveling in Italy. The gatelike building consists of two circular turrets joined by an incomplete middle section. The two turrets are connected by an elegant iron bridge.

The king died shortly before the completion of his castle. His successor, Friedrich Wilhelm III had a conservatory for palm trees built and 5,000 rose bushes planted. A steam engine shed provided the power for irrigating the garden.

Hohenheim, former castle park
"Three Columns of Thundering Jupiter" (top)
Village with a dairy farm and a Swiss cottage (above)
Colored engravings by Victor Heideloff

The Former Park at Hohenheim

How was it possible for Duke Carl Eugen of Württemberg ever to be regarded as an enlightened statesman, when he let the poet Christian Friedrich Daniel Schubart languish in Hohenasperg prison for ten long years, precisely because of his enlightened writings? The duke must have had an uneasy feeling about it.

After traveling to Rome in the company of his mistress, later to become Countess Franziska von Hohenheim, he made her a gift of Hohenheim Castle and its park, situated near Stuttgart. In 1781 the duke commissioned the master builder Reinhard Ferdinand Heinrich Fischer to expand the old castle, which was surrounded by water, into a sumptuous residence. Johann Caspar Schiller laid out a landscape park in the English style. For the first time a romantic park took shape in the Duchy, with its abundance of Baroque gardens. The duke set great store by the creation of a place of illusions at Hohenheim, to which he could escape with Franziska in order, amid flowers and watercourses, rural buildings and a Roman inn, to live the simple life of pleasure that was denied him in Stuttgart.

Perhaps he was able there to forget the imprisoned enlightener Schubart and to elaborate his own philosophy of Enlightenment. So he had a village built with a dairy farm and a Swiss cottage "on the ruins of ancient Rome." Of the approximately one hundred garden houses that were built only the gaming house built in 1788, the "City of Rome Inn," and the "Three Columns of Thundering Jupiter" have survived (illustration top left). Fortunately there are colored engravings recording the form of more of these strange looking buildings. Victor Heideloff, professor of art at the Carlsschule and a close personal friend of Friedrich Schiller, produced a total of forty-four engravings in order to present the duke with his dream landscape in a portfolio. Leafing through this work today, the duke's idea of a village on Roman ruins becomes clear. The dairy farm building, for example, is framed by an incomplete Ionic temple. The columns, which form an integral part of the building, tower up above the two-story house, and it is to be hoped that the incomplete architrave, which looks heavy and unstable, is not holding the roof up (illustration left). The monumental "Three Columns of Thundering Jupiter," with their composite capitals above short shafts and the incomplete architrave, tower up from a cornfield in which tiny figures of peasants can be seen bringing in the harvest. The scene, with its surrealistic effect, is bounded by a copse, with expressive banks of cloud beyond.

The duke, who died in 1793, did not live to see the completion of the castle and garden. For his successor, Duke Friedrich II, the former "mistress's residence" – Carl Eugen had married Franziska in 1785 – was of no importance. Franziska was driven out of Hohenheim, and spent the last years of her life on her widow's estate at Kirchheim unter Teck, where she died in 1811.

The English landscape garden at Hohenheim was a kind of foil for the decorative buildings that were installed there, which owed more to the duke's individual taste and the effects of his experience of Rome, than to consistent planning and professional execution. As Heideloff's engravings show, the duke wanted accessible pictures with subjects derived from his memories of travel and the resulting cultural awareness. The "nature" of the garden was an artificial nature, straitjacketed to provide a "view," in the way nature was subordinated to geometry in Baroque gardens. The dominance of the decorative buildings, including the mock-village, helped to reduce the landscape garden to a natural framework. By attributing artistic potential to landscape as a three-dimensional painting, this type of garden was deprived of its soul, which was the carefully tended natural landscape.

This danger was clearly perceived at the time. A balance had to be struck between laying out a pure landscape garden and putting up mock-historical buildings. At least one garden architect did achieve this, perhaps because he was self-taught, namely Prince Hermann Pückler-Muskau (illustration below). His approach seemed both simple and presumptuous: why put up decorative buildings when there is the opportunity of including existing buildings and villages in the landscape park? He set out his ideas in his *Briefe eines Verstorbenen* (Letters of a Deceased Man), which were widely read at the time.

Branitz, Prince Pückler-Muskau's landscape garden
Pergola and vase

Prince Pückler's Landscape Gardens at Muskau and Branitz

In the landscape gardens at Muskau and Branitz Prince Pückler created the crowning glory of this type of garden in Germany. He had a landscape garden of *c.* 600 ha (*c.* 1,500 acres) laid out on a former feudal estate in the Neiße valley which he inherited in 1811. Work began in 1815, and the garden was completed thirty years later. For him, the guiding lights of park design were the pathways, "the walker's mute guides," and water, "the eye of the landscape," as he was to write in his pamphlet *Andeutungen über Landschaftsgärtnerei* (Hints on Landscape Gardening), published in 1834. During the final stage of the Second World War bitter battles were fought out in Pückler's garden kingdom, largely destroying the site. As a result of the subsequent redrawing of the frontier along the River Neiße, there is today a German and a Polish part of the park, many areas of which have been restored.

Prince Hermann Ludwig Heinrich von Pückler-Muskau, *c.* 1835
Lithograph from a portrait by Franz Krüger of 1824
Prince Pückler-Muskau (1785–1871), garden designer and littérateur, made an unforgettable name for himself as the creator of the park grounds at Muskau, Babelberg and Branitz.

The prince had planned a "super-total art work," to use a phrase coined by Sedlmayr, the realization of which would entail transforming a landscape, along with villages and the town of Muskau, into a park. His aim was "to present a significant image of our family, or the aristocracy of our Fatherland, in the particular form of its development here, in such as way that this idea will develop of its own accord, so to speak, in the mind of the onlooker." His concept included a display of crafts and industrial processes which were already outdated at the time, for example in mining, distilling, or wax bleaching, for "every form of human development is honorable, and precisely because the form that in question is perhaps approaching its demise, it is once more beginning to arouse general poetic and romantic interest."

The prince had to sell his estate in 1845. He could no longer find the unimaginably vast financial resources which he needed in order to carry out his plan. It was also well known that his lavish lifestyle was swallowing up a large part of his means – he was vilified at the time as "Mad Pückler." Anyone wanting to explore the site today can make use of a network of pathways totaling 27 km (*c.* 17 miles), where he or she can roam for hours and even for days through an incomparable natural park. The pathways take the visitor to lakes, past the rebuilt Old Castle, through the Blue Garden or across the Oak Lake Weir, permitting one to experience the "ordered whole" favored by the prince as a romantic natural painting.

After selling his possessions in Muskau in 1845, the prince moved to Branitz, a village situated to the southeast of Cottbus. At the age of sixty he once again set about the task of converting the dilapidated property into a sentimental landscape garden. The prince employed over 200 workmen, including day-laborers and convicts, in order to achieve the desired shape of the terrain by means of large-scale earthworks. Then he had about 300,000 trees planted, including several thousand that were fully grown which were to form the park's skyline. At the center of the site of 70 ha (*c.* 173 acres) is the former Baroque castle that was rebuilt by Gottfried Semper in 1852 (illustration opposite). To the west is the flower garden embellished, with great artistry, by sculptures and with a blue rose arbor. For the prince, an indispensable component of the artistic effect of the garden was its separation from the park. The garden was related to the castle, and was seen by him as an "extended dwelling-place," whereas he interpreted the surrounding park area as "concentrated, idealized nature."

The earthen pyramids with their archaic appearance, which he had created after the death of his wife in 1852, are of an originality that could scarcely be surpassed, and certainly indicate their creator's extravagance. Prince von Pückler-Muskau had his grave prepared in the lake pyramid. He was buried there in 1871 in accordance with ancient Egyptian burial rites, as he had laid down in his will (illustration pp. 438–9).

Branitz, landscape garden
Group of sculptures "Bacchus and Faun" (above)
Monument to Henriette Sonntag (right)

Branitz, landscape garden
View across the Reed Lake of the Baroque castle rebuilt by Gottfried Semper in 1852

Branitz, landscape garden
The park, with a view of the smithy

Branitz, landscape garden
View across the pyramid lake of the earthen pyramid of 1871

Landscape Gardens in France, the Netherlands, Scandinavia, and Eastern Europe

Château de Canon, castle park
Castle outbuildings

France

During the 18th and 19th centuries the English landscape garden was adopted and modified in various ways in the different continental countries. In France the rustic aspects were emphasized at a very early stage, by creating a theatrical setting for agriculture, for example in the garden of the Petit Trianon at Versailles.

In Germany, on the other hand, the attempt was made to shape large areas of the landscape as spacious parkland. But, in contrast with England, there was no discussion in Germany of the pros and cons of decorative buildings to compare with the vehement disputes between supporters of Chambers and Brown. Hirschfeld, it is true, tended to prefer a pure form of landscape garden, somewhat in Brown's manner, but he found it difficult to avoid his patrons' romantic and sentimental predilections for chinoiserie or medieval castle ruins.

It is also possible to see a further variation in French design ideas regarding the so-called *ferme ornée*, the garden that was *de facto* put to agricultural use. The Marquis de Girardin's garden at Ermenonville, as mentioned earlier, was inspired by Leasowens in England, the work of William Shenstone. In 1766 the marquis acquired the land to the south of Senlis in the Ile-de-France. It is a site of *c.* 890 ha (2,200 acres), with forests bordering the area of Chantilly to the west.

Girardin divided the site into four parts: an agricultural zone on the plateau to the east of the village, a large park area by the lake to the south of the castle, a small park to the north of the castle, and the so-called "desert," a zone in which nature was to be left unrestrained. Bare hills, pines, and blocks of sandstone set their unmistakable stamp on the terrain. The valley was chosen to be the central axis of the whole layout.

From the north wing of the castle the Marquis had a view of the wide marshy landscape of the small park and delighted in the lovingly arranged Dutch scenery. A canal with flat bridges, a water mill, and a windmill, and a Gothic tower created a romantic ambience. Today only the canal and a mill have survived. Jean-Jacques Rousseau, who

Chantilly, castle park
In the eastern part of Le Nôtre's water garden is Le Hameau, a hamlet with wooden buildings (1774) which is older than the better-known Hameau in the gardens of Versailles Palace.

was deeply venerated by the marquis, spent his last years in Ermenonville, where he died in 1778. Girardin created Julie's garden, a little earthly paradise, the Bocage, to match the description in "La Nouvelle Héloise."

The southern area of the garden is of an unusually picturesque design. Ponds, twisting pathways, cascades, and a grotto create a sensitive atmosphere. It was certainly not out of pure unselfishness that the marquis allowed the villagers access to this area. He hoped that it would enhance the pastoral effect if the setting were populated by "genuine peasants."

From the windows of his castle facing south he could at least survey the entire site. At the end of the garden there is a fairly large lake with the Island of Poplars, where the philosopher's grave is situated (illustration above). In this monument the profound veneration for Jean-Jacques Rousseau was expressed by way of a garden design, an approach which was soon adopted in many other European landscape gardens, for example in Wörlitz, the Tiergarten (Zoo) in Berlin or in Arkadia in Poland.

Rousseau's philosophy, which revolves around regaining natural feelings in harmony with rational behavior, found a rare tangible form in Ermenonville. Julie's garden amid a pastoral setting may be seen as an early Romantic revolt against the Enlightenment.

Island of Poplars with the grave of Jean-Jacques Rousseau in Ermenonville
Painting. Oil on canvas,
53.3 x 64.8 cm (*c.* 21 x 26 in.), 1802
Hubert Robert
Privately owned?

Paris, Bois de Boulogne
La Bagatelle summerhouse by
François-Joseph Bélanger, 1777

One of the first English gardens in France, which could be seen as a kind of concentrated essence of Stourhead, was La Bagatelle in Paris. In the southern area of what is today the Bois de Boulogne, Marshal Victor d'Estrées had a country residence created in 1720, which Louis XV redesigned as a pleasure ground. When the Comte d'Artois, the brother of Louis XVI, took over the estate in 1775, he made a memorable wager with Marie Antoinette, who shared his enthusiasm for gardens. He intended to build the La Bagatelle summerhouse, and have water features and decorative buildings installed within sixty-four days (illustration left). But to win the wager the prince had to raise over a million pounds. In order to obtain the required building materials as quickly as possible he had all carts, with materials of all kinds, requisitioned outside the city gates. He thereby incurred the anger of the people. The gardens soon became known colloquially as the "Folie d'Artois," and this was presumably not meant just as an affectionate paraphrase for a prince's folly. The gardens were designed and laid out by Thomas Blaikie, a Scotsman, and François-Joseph Bélanger. The Frenchman had previously done a good deal of work in England in order to acquire experience for his Anglophile French patrons. He laid out a lake edged with rocks, a meandering river course, cascades, artificial cliffs, and bizarre decorative buildings (so-called *fabriques*). This term had been used since the mid-18th century to mean reconstructions serving purely decorative purposes. *Fabriques* first appeared in landscape painting (illustration below), then they became popular in English garden design, among other things as so-called "eyecatchers." *Fabriques* designed in the form of Chinese temples or miniaturized Egyptian

Carmontelle handing over the keys to Monceau garden to the Duke of Chartres
Painting
Carmontelle
Paris, Musée Carnavalet

pyramids were popular. In England, particularly bizarre forms which did not belong to any particular architectural category were called "follies." The Conolly Tower of Castletown in Ireland, which William Conolly had built in his garden at the beginning of the 18th century, is a famous example. This combination of a Romanesque arched building and an Egyptian obelisk later inspired many French garden architects to create similar *fabriques* or "follies." But almost all of them were destroyed in the upheaval of the French Revolution.

Seen in this light, the description "folie d'Artois" also denotes the type of garden, as Bélanger installed many more *fabriques*, such as, for example, the Philosopher's Grotto in the neo-Gothic style, the Chinese arched bridge, the obligatory island with gravestones, the temples of love, and finally the Pharaoh's Grave. All these follies no longer exist. Today La Bagatelle is merely part of the public park, the Bois de Boulogne.

Hubert Robert gave the Romantic landscape, as did no other 18th-century painter, a monumental and at the same time idyllic form (illustration p. 441). In 1783, shortly before the French Revolution, he was commissioned by Louis XVI to design and supervise the layout of the Rambouillet park to the south of Paris. The property, dating back to the time of Louis XIV, was converted into an English park while retaining the structures of the castle parterre and the system of channels with the large water basin. The king had one of the finest examples of pastoral architecture built by Charles Thévenin as a gift for Marie Antoinette: the Laiterie de la Reine, a dairy farm in the classicist style (illustrations above). The king also had a *ferme ornée* laid out nearby for breeding Merino sheep.

In French gardens from the second half of the 18th century a unique change in garden design themes may be observed. This applies not only to the almost abrupt transition from the formal to the romantic garden, but also to the entire thematic spectrum of garden design. The Rousseau-esque dimension, the "return to nature," is now intensified and becomes a kind of flight from the world. The *fabriques* and the "follies," the chinoiserie and other exotic leanings already

Rambouillet, castle park
Queen's dairy farm by Charles Thévenin, interior and exterior views (top)
Castle park in winter with castle in the background (above)

suggest the increasing loss of royal authority. Gardens such as these can be retrospectively seen as indicating the breakdown of absolutism, and heralding the rapid approach of the French Revolution of 1789.

The English landscape garden as modified in France moved far away from Le Nôtre's monumental works of art, and may be given the status of an independent type: the picturesque French garden. In some gardens, for example at Canon (illustrations opposite, right, and bottom), it only took over parts of the garden. The entire spectrum was explored, from pastoral, theatrical staginess to poetic, philosophical use.

The garden was at this time no longer perceived as a complex unity, but broke down into various zones with different designs and different themes. On the one hand, there was the tendency to rediscover nature and the contact with nature in country life. On the other hand, a need was felt for profound philosophical reflection with its resulting elegiac moods.

To bring the above observations to a point: rulers no longer made a grand display of their vast gardens, but preferred to occupy themselves breeding sheep, and reading Rousseau.

Seen through present-day eyes, these were entirely likable traits. But the late 18th-century bourgeoisie saw in them a clear weakness which they were resolved to exploit.

Château de Canon, castle park
Chinese pavilion (top)
Small classicist temple (left)

ILLUSTRATION OPPOSITE
Château de Canon, castle park
Chartreuse, arcade

PAGES 446–447
Château de Courances, castle park
Japanese garden

Holland

In the 18th century, Dutch garden design developed predominantly under the influence of the French. This did not, of course, preclude independent variants resulting from the very topography and flora of the country.

The most vivid and also the earliest example of a Dutch special development is Waterland near Velsen in North Holland. An Amsterdam merchant in 1720 laid out the first garden with a maze. He was evidently less concerned with a homogenous artistic parterre design than with picturesque elements such as clumps of trees, a Turkish tent, or a triumphal arch.

The Turkish tent was a popular piece of garden scenery which had reached England in the 1750s along with the vogue for China. From there it had also found its way into continental gardens (illustration p. 451).

The Dutch merchant, who had traveled widely, and had been inspired by many different cultures, also tried to create moving pictures – which was unique for northern Europe at that time. He created this illusion by means of a tunnel, the exit of which framed a scene with floating boats on a neighboring lake. Such ingenious artistry owed much to Netherlands Mannerism, that is to say it was more in tune with the Baroque era.

At Twickel near Delden in the Dutch province of Overijssel a geometric castle garden with a knot parterre along with a vegetable and fruit garden was laid out in the Renaissance style shortly before 1700. A channel edged with trees ran round the site. The design of the parterre and the boskets went back to Daniel Marot, who had produced a similar garden design for Kensington Gardens in London *c.* 1710.

Around 1790 the channel was widened into a lake and meandering watercourses were created. An idyllic “tree hermitage,” a fisherman’s hut, and a ferry were positioned in this zone. A little further away an artificial mountain was created, and a garden house, a chapel, and the obligatory ice house were built. A large deer park adjoined this area. On the one hand these features owed much to the English style, but on the other hand they were also derived from the picturesque approach of French gardens of the day. One might think of English chinoiserie and at the same time of the Ermenonville approach. The French influence became stronger *c.* 1800 as the political map of Europe changed following the appearance of Napoleon. The French emperor annexed the Netherlands almost silently in 1810 after his brother Louis had converted the country into a kingdom in 1806, but had ruled it unsuccessfully.

Twickel, castle garden
View of the castle across the lake

Then, after the fall of Napoleon, people were carefully concerned to remove every trace of the French. Jan David Zocher, the most significant Netherlands landscape architect of the 19th century, was commissioned to redesign the garden at Twickel. Zocher accepted the purist landscape principles of Lancelot Brown. He created a little world of water, meadows, and trees around Twickel (illustration opposite), favoring a harmonic line which he applied to the composition of clumps of trees, the watercourses, and the gently undulating meadowlands. His conception was taken over *c.* 1850 by the German Eduard Petzold, and only slightly altered. Petzold was a pupil of Prince Pückler-Muskau, and later became court gardener at Weimar.

For the parterre in the vicinity of the orangery at Twickel, a Frenchman was appointed, the widely traveled Edouard François André, who had worked in Russia, Italy, and England. His treatise, *L'art des jardins: Trité général de la composition des parcs et jardins*, was published in 1879, and it gives a detailed account of the history of garden design and its theories. The treatise also contains practical advice on design.

His guiding principle was to combine science and art in garden design. He therefore regarded concepts such as the *ferme ornée* as of little use, being the product of utopian ideas that could satisfy neither peasants nor art lovers.

During the era of industrialization the bourgeoisie was attracted to landscape settings. In Amsterdam the park at Vondel came into existence, named after the 17th-century Dutch poet Joost van den Vondel. The site was privately financed to a large extent, but was to be open to the public.

Jan David Zocher worked out the plans. The park was completed by 1877, and makes an unostentatious impression (illustrations top and right). A bandstand and a milk café were later added to the meandering watercourses and spacious lawns, with clumps of trees arranged in Lancelot Brown's manner.

Landscape parks had become established by the second half of the 19th century. Little use was made of purely decorative buildings. It became important that they were open to the public. The people were given a space within the town where they were free to pursue leisure activities or simply to relax. Citizens for whom the world of work was becoming increasingly demanding as a result of progressive industrialization, were calling for public amenities for their use in their free time.

Amsterdam, Vondel Park
View of the park in winter

Monument to the Netherlands poet who gave his name to the park, Joost van den Vondel (1587–1679)

Frederiksberg (Denmark), castle garden
Chinese tea pavilion

Scandinavia

In the Scandinavian countries such as Denmark or Sweden, landscape gardens followed the current European type. To start with there was the picturesque garden with decorative buildings, which changed in the course of the 19th century to a pure landscape park.

In 1699 the Danish King Frederik IV had the garden of Frederiksborg castle near Copenhagen initially laid out in the French style. Later, Johann Cornelius Krieger was appointed to develop the garden. He was able to incorporate some preliminary elements of landscape design.

The Danish nobility could not afford the material luxury of the French. Instead of marble, planks and boulders were used to enclose ponds and smaller lakes. Thus some sort of rustic approach was necessary in any case, making the transition to the landscape garden almost automatic. Frederiksborg was redesigned between 1785 and 1801 and given the typical trappings such as a Chinese teahouse (illustration above) and an Ionic temple.

Around 1840 Rudolf Rothe, one of the most prominent Danish landscape architects and the director of royal gardens in Denmark, turned his attention to the garden, and redesigned it yet again. The site is still in very good condition today, and worth seeing if only for the charming Chinese tea pavilion from the period *c.* 1800.

One of the first English landscape gardens with a Nordic element in Denmark was created in Liselund on the island of Møn. Ponds, cliffs, waterfalls, a lake, and twisting pathways leading to surprising views of the Baltic, created a romantic setting inspired by Jean-Jacques Rousseau.

In order to illustrate at least some areas of Rousseau's philosophical thought, the transitoriness of nature was made a theme. Artificial monuments and grave mounds are concealed beneath dense, dark foliage. But allusions to local culture were also to be included. Along with the Chinese pavilion a place was found for a Swedish house, the Norwegian cottage, and other buildings (illustration below).

One of the earliest and at the same time finest Baroque gardens in Denmark is to be found in Glorup on the island of Fyn. With its high mansard roof, the mansion, built by Philip de Lange from 1743 for Christian Ludwig Scheel von Plessen, dominates the garden, which dates back to the 17th century. Traces of the various phases in the evolution of its design can still be detected today. Indeed, every significant type of garden was created in Glorup, beginning with the late Renaissance ornamental garden, via the Baroque garden with its axis-determined structure, to the various forms of the landscape garden.

Fortunately Henrik August Flindt, an enthusiastic landscape gardener who from 1877 succeeded Rothe as director of the royal gardens, did not destroy the old garden structures when he was commissioned to renovate the Glorup garden. To the south of the house and at the end of a gleaming pool 200 m (*c.* 656 ft.) in length he planted, over the years, over 100,000 flowers for the park visitors. He converted the Baroque alleys into broad paths leading to the landscape garden in

Liselund on the island of Møn, landscape garden
Romantic setting with chapel

Leather tent in the Haga Park, Stockholm. Watercolor by Louis-Jean Deprez, 1787
The tent was erected for the guardsmen in 1785, and is an example of the oriental variant of the romantic exoticism of both utilitarian and decorative buildings to be found in many gardens *c.* 1800 (cf. also pp. 388ff.).

the English style. A special attraction is the remains of a neo-Gothic suspension bridge above an artificial boarded ravine.

English fashion also reached the kingdom of Sweden in the mid-18th century. It was principally a matter of adding chinoiserie to the royal gardens. The connections of William Chambers, the English architect and proven expert on China, with the Swedish royal family helped to bring about a lively cultural exchange.

Toward the end of the century it was the Swedish architect Frederik Magnus Piper, who was closely familiar with English landscape gardens, who was commissioned by King Gustav III to put the English concept into practice in Drottningholm and Haga.

The Haga park was redesigned in 1785 with all the usual props, such as a Turkish tent (illustration above) and a Chinese pavilion. Furthermore, the French architect Louis Deprez was commissioned to design a summerhouse in the classicist style. Work on this did not, however, progress beyond the foundations.

Like neighboring Denmark, Sweden was not able to establish a garden type of its own. The adoption of the English model was reinforced, if anything, by looking increasingly to the model of the German landscape garden.

In the early 19th century an attempt was made to bring at least a degree of order into the irregular natural layout by laying out symmetrical alleys in addition to the system of twisting pathways.

Eastern Europe

The English landscape garden also quickly became popular in Russia. This use of English garden design as a model was encouraged by the Empress Catherine the Great, who wrote to Voltaire in 1772 that she could only find diversion in a garden designed on the English model. She stressed the advantages of the curving lines of the landscape, of gently sloping hills and ponds looking like lakes. She firmly rejected straight alleys and fountains, which, as she put it, tormented the water and forced it to go in directions that were alien to its nature. Catherine went to unusual lengths in her enthusiasm for English culture. She ordered a table service from Wedgwood and Bentley consisting of 925 items and showing 1,244 views of Great Britain, including many landscape parks. The czarina sent her architect Vasily Ivanovich Neyelov on a six-month tour of England to look at the most important landscape parks. He adopted the design of the Palladian bridge in the park of Wilton House, and implemented it in Tsarskoye Selo (Pushkin Park). He also studied William Chambers' and John Halfpenny's plans and publications, and derived important ideas from them for his Chinese buildings. Years later the czarina invited the Englishman John Busch, who was of German birth, to St. Petersburg to work out plans for Pulkova. The czarina liked his designs and commissioned him to lay out the English landscape park at Tsarskoye Selo in collaboration with Neyelov. There is an extant plan by Busch,

Tsarskoye Selo, Pushkin landscape park
Palladian bridge

probably dating from *c.* 1790 showing the entire layout of this Yekaterinsky Park. It is divided into an older Baroque section, which was laid out anew for the Empress Elizabeth in the mid-18th century, and the English park with lakes, islands, hills, and twisting pathways. The plan also shows the buildings, including a ruined tower, Neyelov's Palladian bridge (illustration above), a triumphal arch, and smaller pavilions along with a classicist temple (illustration below). The layout of the park with its decorative buildings, lakeside zones, and forest paths is reminiscent of Stowe in England. One might even have the impression that the Russian park was competing with comparable English models, since a Chinese village, the largest of its kind in Europe, was built in what is today the Alexandrovsky Park. It was the work of Neyelov in collaboration with Charles Cameron, another English architect who had been working for the czarina since 1779.

The largest landscape garden in Russia, Pavlovsk, situated near St. Petersburg, encompassed some *c.* 600 ha (1,500 acres), and was also designed by Cameron. Its *pièce de résistance* was the temple, later named the Temple of Friendship, a central rotunda with Doric columns topped by a cupola (illustration opposite, top). In addition to other classicist buildings, including an aviary (illustration opposite, bottom), the Temple of the Three Graces (illustration page 455 bottom), and the Apollo colonnade, Cameron also built rustic buildings, namely a thatched dairy, a hermit's cell, and a charcoal burner's hut, in order to gratify the czarina's sentimental leanings.

Pavlovsk was probably the largest landscape garden in Europe. Large parts of it were destroyed during the Second World War, but were subsequently restored in an exemplary fashion, so that today one can take extensive and highly interesting walks in this Anglo-Russian example of the art of garden architecture.

Finally, mention should be made of another romantic landscape garden in eastern Europe, Arkadia in Poland.

Arkadia, 80 km (*c.* 50 miles) from Warsaw, was founded between 1778 and 1785 as a summer

Tsarskoye Selo, Pushkin landscape park
Grotto and other decorative buildings by the Great Pond

residence for the Radziwill family. The park, laid out by Szymon Bogumil Zug, Henryk Ittar, and Wojciech Jaszcold, developed the Arcadian themes of happiness, love, and death.

At the center of the park, the lake, surrounded by watercourses and pathways, was laid out with a little Rousseau-esque island. Ruins, rustic buildings, classicist temples, and an amphitheater are located close to the lake and along the watercourses and pathways, along with clumps of trees. Fortunately the park remained largely untouched by the turmoil of war. Today it is open to the public, who can thus enjoy the surprises provided by the site and its decorative buildings.

Horace Walpole, the proud English owner of a castle and garden, in his account, written in 1770, of the recent history of English gardens, wrote the memorable sentence: "We have given the true model of gardening to the world." At the time this dictum may have sounded a trifle presumptuous. But in the end it proved to be wholly true. The English model established itself very rapidly on the

Pavlovsk, landscape garden
Temple of Friendship by Charles Cameron, 1780–82

Pavlovsk, landscape garden
Classicist building of an aviary by the canal

Pavlovsk, landscape garden
Ring-shaped lake encircling the classicist palace built by Charles Cameron 1782–6

Sculpture in front of lilac bushes (bottom)

ILLUSTRATIONS OPPOSITE
Temple of the Three Graces (bottom left)
Sculpture of the Three Graces (bottom right)

continent, albeit in many different variants. And now every great city in the world has its municipal park or a castle and park in the English style. Whether in Mexico City, New York, Munich, or Paris, it is always the same type that we find: spacious lawns stretching out over gently shaped hills, with twisting pathways leading through the shade provided by clumps of trees and bushes to small lakes. Rills with arched bridges, concealed circular temples and pavilions – often housing a restaurant – enhance the idyllic setting.

Did the English landscape park, established for 250 years, remain the final stage in the development of European gardens, or did it bear within itself an artistic potential on which gardens and parks in the 20th century could draw?

Forms and Aspects of Gardens from 1850 to the Present Day

In the Renaissance and Baroque eras, inventive garden architects constructed greenhouses which could be put up in winter and taken down again in summer. Perhaps they were forerunners of modern prefabricated buildings: a special system of building blocks was devised for these mobile garden buildings. For the Renaissance garden in Stuttgart, the architect and garden construction engineer Heinrich Schickhardt even had a movable base for the fig houses produced and rails laid down so that the buildings could be pushed to suitable places.

In the 17th and 18th centuries orangeries in castle gardens came into fashion. These were hothouses for the cultivation and conservation of exotic plants.

The emergence of iron-and-glass architecture in the first half of the 19th century created a new, separate type of conservatory building: the winter garden. One of the first examples of this type is in England: the greenhouse at Downton Castle dating from 1815, built by Thomas Andrew Knight, who pioneered scientific research into garden making. Knight was the President of the Horticultural Society of London from 1811 until his death in 1838. Even the facade shows the iron ribs in the form of a quarter-circle that were used in later decades also. The rear wall was of brick. At the next stage of development space was to be increased without loss of light. The architects achieved this by means of a number of large glass vaults staggered one above the other. Other typical examples are the conservatories of the museum of natural history in Paris, designed by Christophe Rohault in 1833.

One of the most famous winter gardens constructed of iron and glass was at the Botanical Gardens at Kew in London, built by the architects Decimus Burton and Richard Turner in 1845–7 (illustration p. 458 top). Turner, an ironsmith from Dublin, worked not only for the English aristocracy but also for King Friedrich Wilhelm IV of Prussia. Burton, a successful building contractor

Brussels, Botanical garden
Classicist greenhouse in the form of a circular temple, built by François Gineste and Tilman-François Suys in 1826–9 (bottom)
Detail of figures on fountain in front of greenhouse (above)

ILLUSTRATION OPPOSITE
Laeken (Brussels), royal gardens, interior view of the Great Winter Garden, built by Alphonse Balat in 1876

London, Kew Gardens
Palm House, built by Decimus Burton and Richard Turner 1844–8

Vienna, Schönbrunn Palace garden
Palm House, built by Franz Xaver Segenschmid 1879–82

from London, had come to prominence back in the 1820s with the Colosseum which he built in Regent's Park in London.

Burton met the former gardener of Chiswick, Joseph Paxton, at Chatsworth. The Duke of Devonshire appointed the gifted Paxton as superintendent of Chatsworth Garden in 1826. He was instructed to design the Great Stove, that is the winter garden, in collaboration with Burton, who was undoubtedly more famous at that time. The work took from 1836 to 1840.

The duke was so impressed by Paxton's work that he sent him on a study trip to Switzerland, Italy, Greece, and Spain. On his return to England he devoted himself entirely to architecture and submitted an unsolicited design for an exhibition palace for the Great Exhibition in London. This building, the Crystal Palace in London, which was 600 m (*c.* 2,000 ft.) in length, soon acquired the status of an incunabulum of iron-and-glass architecture.

The new building materials could be used in a wide range of different ways. An exhibition palace could subsequently be used as a winter garden or a palm house. Concerts and theatrical performances took place in the Jardin d'hiver which was erected in Paris in 1847. Sometimes the upper echelons of society met there for festive balls. The winter garden soon underwent a metamorphosis into a versatile center of social life.

Barcelona, Parc de la Ciutadella
"Umbracle" – provider of shade – is the name given to the conservatory which was built for the international exhibition in 1888 by Josep Fontserè.

Paris, former Jardin d'hiver at the Champs Elysées
Built by H. Meynadier and Rigolet 1846–7 (destroyed 1852)

Anduze, Bambouseraie de Prafrance
The garden, which has been in existence since 1850 with nearly 200 kinds of bamboo, is a unique example of its kind in Europe.

Gardens in the South of France

Gardens in the south of France have not developed any special type of their own, since their design is dependent on Italian and French traditions (less so on the English landscape garden). But undoubtedly the climate, the landscape, and the properties of the soil have led to specific forms unrivaled in the spectrum of European gardens. A striking feature is the frequent and lavish use of palm trees, as for example in the Jardin Thuret.

Anyone who visits the Côte d'Azur expecting to find a paradisial landscape will have his expectations surpassed on sight of the magnificent layout of the garden of the Villa Ephrussi on Cap Ferrat. This applies to the lavish layout itself, and to the unique combination of a world of subtropical plants, Baroque design features, and the coastal scenery (see pp. 462–3).

The gardens of the south of France combine features of the traditional garden, with its pools, circular temples, and boxwood parterres, with examples of avant-garde art and architecture (illustrations pp. 464–5). The landscape garden, as a concept, is less important in this context, since the landscape element is provided by the stupendous natural spectacle (mountains and sea) of the landscape itself.

The Bambouseraie de Prafrance in Anduze is a European rarity. Almost 200 different kinds of bamboo are cultivated there (illustration left). The garden dates back to 1850 when a beginning was made in collecting kinds of bamboo that were able to withstand winter weather. Today the jungle-like areas of the garden, where the giant bamboo grows, are particularly impressive.

Villa Thuret

Gustave Thuret designed his garden in 1857 on the Cap d'Antibes, one of the most beautiful coastal regions of the Côte d'Azur, about 3 km (2 miles) south of the town. He followed the example of the English landscape garden, creating generous open spaces and lawns for exotic trees to be planted, and linking the separate areas by means of a system of twisting pathways. In addition to palm groves he set aside areas of the garden for, among other things, acacias and eucalyptus trees.

Today this garden is regarded as one of the most exotic in southern Europe. Over 3,000 plants, most of them of subtropical European origin, but in some cases from outside Europe, are to be found there. With the mild climate and the favorable location by the sea, the Jardin Thuret seems like a monumental orangery open to the heavens.

ILLUSTRATIONS RIGHT AND OPPOSITE
Cap d'Antibes, Villa Thuret
Palm groves, acacias and eucalyptus trees determine the image of this exotic garden, in which about 3,000 plant species from all over the world thrive.

Villa Ephrussi de Rothschild

Like the Cap d'Antibes, the Cap Ferrat also juts out into the sea like a peninsula. On the narrow ridge atop the cliff, the Baroness Béatrice Ephrussi de Rothschild implemented, *c.* 1905, an ambitious plan. She wanted to erect a monument to herself in the guise of a luxury villa with an adjoining garden. She undoubtedly succeeded. She invited many famous architects to submit designs, but was dissatisfied with everything that was forthcoming. Finally she took the work in hand herself and sketched a traditional building in a mock-historical style. The palace was built with four wings and a spacious arcaded courtyard in early Renaissance Italian style.

Inside, the building is decorated in French Rococo style. The decor was evidently also intended to harmonize stylistically with the Baroque parterre and the large pool. The Baroness refrained, however, from having geometrically ornamented beds.

The main garden, dominated by palms, cypresses, and other subtropical trees, is flanked by an Italian Renaissance garden with curved box hedges. Adjoining it are a Spanish garden and a Japanese garden. The main garden also contains a circular temple in mock-classical style with a statue of Venus, curving flights of steps with a small grotto beneath them, and intimate recesses with stone benches.

At a time when art, architecture, and to some extent garden architecture also, were in a state of upheaval, the Baroness created a highly personal garden complex which did not in any way accord with stylistic notions of the time.

Cap Ferrat, Villa Ephrussi de Rothschild
View of the garden facade of the villa across the central elongated rectangular pool (left). Double flight of steps (above)

the de Noailles family seems today like an early clarion call to transcend the boundaries of art by giving abstract form its own aesthetic value – in architecture, sculpture, and garden design.

The Sculpture Garden of the Maeght Foundation
Aimé Maeght arranged his collection of sculpture, including works by Joan Miró, Alexander Calder, and Pierre Bonnard, in a pine forest in St-Paul-de-Vence. In 1964 he had an eccentric museum built by the Catalan architect Josep Lluis Sert. The u-shaped, curving roofs, which seem almost to float in the air, above the Giacometti courtyard, contrast with the artist's elegant and elongated walking and stationary figures.

But in the pine forest all the magic of a sculpture garden unfolds. Alexander Calder's mobile sails with their garishly colored surfaces create a bizarre effect in the garden setting. Joan Miró was commissioned to design a maze, a task which he carried out with wit and imagination. Other artists positioned their monumental iron and steel figures in the forest or else put them up in conspicuous places like guardsmen. They were intended to reflect the unconventional architectural language of the museum building.

For his son, who had died young, the master of the house had a chapel built on the garden site. The building materials which he used included medieval masonry, a special way of cherishing the memory of his son.

Hyères, Villa de Noailles
Cubist garden layout by Gabriel Guévrékian

The Cubist Garden of the Villa de Noailles
In 1924 Charles and Marie-Laure de Noailles, well known as generous patrons of the arts, commissioned the building of a villa. They had chosen Robert Mallet-Stevens, the architect who, after Le Corbusier, was the most important architect in France at the time. The villa, which he created in harmony with the topography of the surroundings, constitutes a piece of Modernist architectural sculpture, a Cubist artifact incorporating the structures of contemporary modern abstract painting.

The de Noailles succeeded in engaging Gabriel Guévrékian to design the garden. He designed a Cubist garden. On a plane tapering to a point and leading outward from the villa, he laid out square bed boxes, which were staggered one above the other as they approached the tip. Planting was very sparing so as not to obscure the structure, which resembled a picture by Mondrian. The geometrically structured inside wall and the furniture consisting of pure cubes thus have their equivalents in the garden, which is reached directly from the living room. Together with the sculptures by Jacques Lipschitz, the villa-and-garden project of

St-Paul-de-Vence, Maeght Foundation sculpture garden
Museum building by Josep Lluis Sert and Giacometti courtyard

Standing in a boat, Monet punts his way through the famous water lily pond in his garden.

Monet's Garden in Giverny

The works of Claude Monet, who perfected Impressionist painting, can be divided into three groups. The first comprises the works which the young and restless Monet created, in all weathers, in the open landscape or in his workaday room. In them, he visually dissected his world and investigated the factors which made colors change with changes of lighting.

At the age of fifty Monet, now more sedate and calm, lingered before his subject, creating series of pictures to document the metamorphoses of a building or a section of the landscape brought about by the light.

Finally, the aged Monet stayed at Giverny, where he had found his paradise, in the garden that is so famous today. Here he took up the image of the water lily and created innumerable variations of it in his studio.

Monet and Giverny became as one in the aesthetic calculus of Impressionism. The imitation of nature dissolves in a welter of color which takes on direct artistic values of its own. The water lily image can be seen as a reproduction of part of a garden and at the same time as an independent color composition, whose artistic value lies not in imitation but in the creation of an independent artistic form in which a water lily is illustrated.

Whether Monet was moving, like Paul Cézanne, toward "abstract Impressionism" when he created the series of pictures of haystacks, cathedrals, or poplars, is a topic for speculation. Many of these pictures date from the early Giverny period. Monet moved to Giverny in April 1883 – in the same month when Eduard Manet died in Paris. He rented the property to start with. As he became better known and Giverny became a meeting place for the avant-garde, he gradually recovered from his financial situation, which until then had been difficult. He acquired a modest amount of capital which allowed him to buy Giverny in 1890.

During the following years he created his garden there. He set no store by any pre-existing garden design, but strove to achieve an atmosphere of

Giverny, Musée Claude Monet
Reflections of the weeping willows in the water lily pond in Monet's garden

blossoming and untamed proliferation. He was subsequently able to acquire more land on which he laid out a pond with water from the little River Epte, and crossed by a Japanese bridge.

His numerous letters and notes show that at Giverny Monet achieved his goal of observing nature in calm seclusion, nature which he shaped with his own hands. The garden provided him with a natural setting which he could study and sketch at any time of the day and in different lighting, and transmute into color in his studio.

Working in his studio was as important to him as sketching with brush and paint in front of the subject. His primary concern always, however, was to look at the real world. Images from the imagination or from memory were of no use to him in his creative process.

Previously, Monet had often complained about the way his subject appeared to change arbitrarily. The fishing boats at Etretat, he wrote, had been rearranged by the fishermen while he was painting them. He had had no choice, he said, but to scrape off the canvas everything that he had painted up until then, and begin his work all over again.

That could no longer happen at Giverny. Here his subject remained immutable. He could devote himself to what he described as the artist's real task, to discover, or reveal, what took place between himself and the object. He referred to it as "the beauty of the atmosphere," and also called it "the impossible."

Perhaps that is precisely what fascinates us today in the water lily pictures or the pictures of the garden at Giverny. We sense the crystallization of an atmosphere, an emotion captured in colors and forms. The reason why his water lily pictures were far removed from the reality of Giverny was precisely the evocation of that atmosphere between the subject and the canvas.

Monet's water lily pictures are often associated with the beginnings of abstract painting. This view is disputable, and disputed.

From *c.* 1890, Monet unquestionably moved, in his works, into the gray area between imitation and abstraction. However, he never lost contact with the "momentary impression" of beautiful things – the subject of his paintings.

Le Bassin aux Nymphéas, le soir (left-hand side of a diptych
Oil on canvas, 200 x 600 cm (*c.* 79 x 236 in.), *c.* 1916–22
Claude Monet
Zurich, Kunsthaus Zürich

PAGES 468–469
Giverny, Musée Claude Monet
Weeping willows and pond with water lilies in Monet's garden
The little "Japanese" bridge can be discerned in the background.

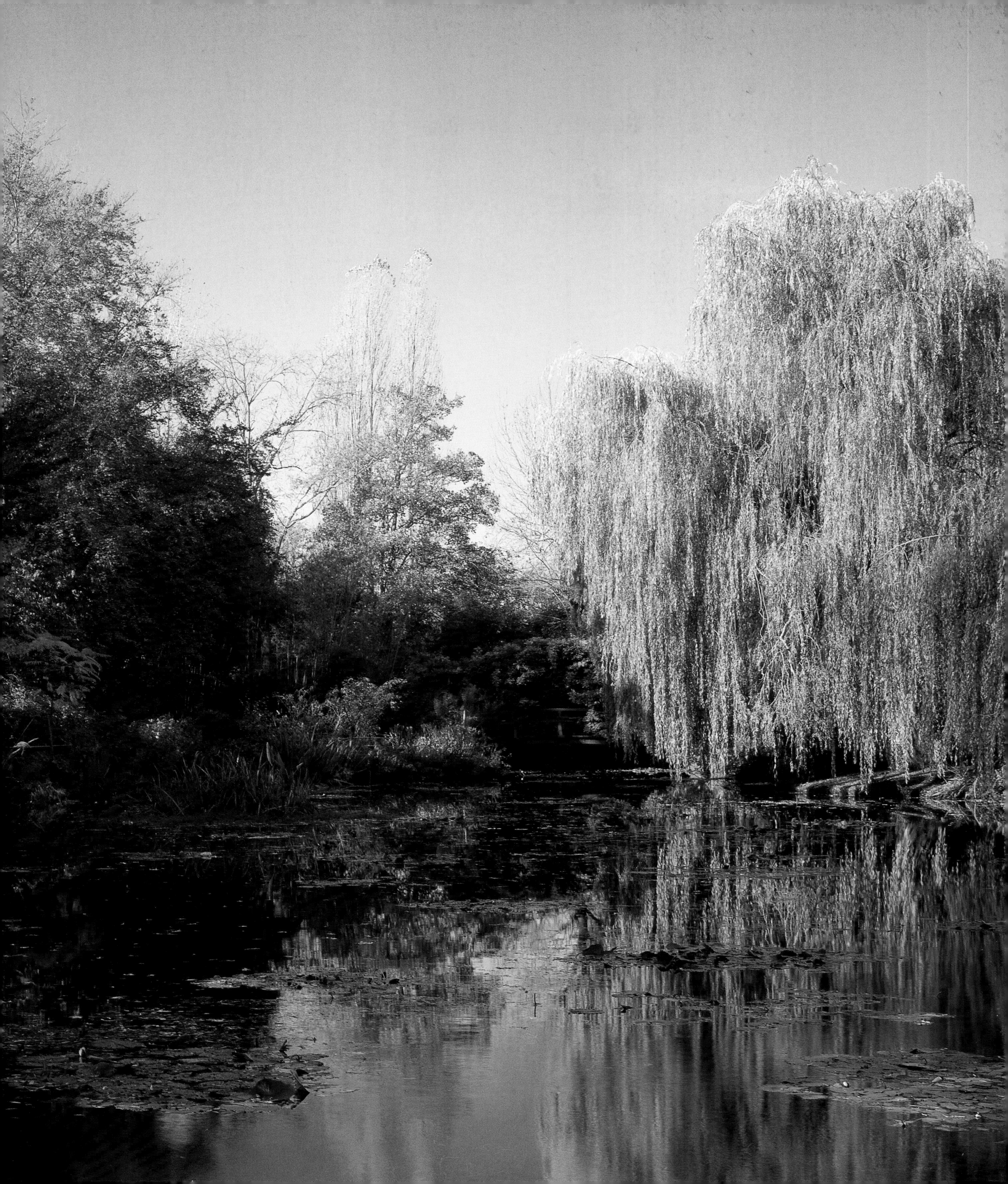

Gardens of Catalonia

Twentieth-century Catalonian gardens reveal a broad design spectrum. Along with the romantic garden of Santa Clotilde, laid out in the modern style above the bays of the Costa Brava, there is Antonio Gaudí's fairytale (and in some respects bizarre) "art nouveau garden" to be taken into account, namely the Parc Güell in Barcelona. The spacious municipal Parc de la Ciutadella – also in Barcelona – contrasts with the urban space of the Parc Joan Miró. In the one case we have the classic pattern of the 19th-century park, in the other a sober municipal park, given a lighter tone only by the playful language of Miró's imagery. More so than in previous centuries, the modern urban garden draws in architecture and art along with the everyday social life of the local people.

The Garden of Santa Clotilde

Some of the most beautiful coastal scenery in Spain is undoubtedly to be seen on the Costa Brava, to the north of Barcelona.

The Marquis of Roviralta had the Garden of Santa Clotilde laid out in the 1920s, at a time when this region was not as yet opened up to tourism to the extent that it is today. The site extends over the rugged Catalonian uplands of the Costa Brava not far from Lloret de Mar. Steep pathways and steps lead down from the Garden of Santa Clotilde to the beautiful Mediterranean bays of Los Fanales and Santa Cristina.

It was a costly project. In order to be certain that the garden would be adequately irrigated, many pipes had to be laid. Eventually it was also decided to blast holes in the cliff in order to plant trees of some size. A garden came into being with

Lloret de Mar, Garden of Santa Clotilde
Round pool with water jet below the villa (above)
The long flight of steps, edged with cypresses, leading down to the sea (right)

a resemblance to Italian Renaissance gardens (illustration opposite, top). This applies to the clipped hedges, the tall cypresses, as well as the many flowerbeds.

But what the marquis wanted was a picturesque garden layout which would incorporate the breathtaking panorama of the coastal scenery. For this reason he bought up neighboring land in order to keep the views from the terraces and steps unchanged. The picturesque is also combined with the romantic. Two marble statues, *Prudentia* and *Justitia*, the mythical guardians of the Elysian Fields, are to be found in a kind of ante-garden which is framed by four cypresses clipped to a cylindrical shape. From here, small steps and paths lead to the various garden terraces facing the sea. Another flight of steps framed by tall cypresses leads down to the Plaza de las Sirenas (illustration opposite, bottom).

The Parc de la Ciutadella in Barcelona

In the years between 1871 and 1881 the garden building engineer and architect Josep Fontserè created the spacious park on the site of the former citadel of Barcelona, where the Bourbon Philip V had the old stronghold built in 1716 in order to besiege the city. In 1869 the municipal authorities had the walls pulled down, thereby making it possible for the site to be artistically laid out.

At its heart is the great cascade, which has been restored in recent years. The young Antonio Gaudí was one of those involved in its creation. In 1888 the city of Barcelona hosted its first international exhibition. Unfortunately many of the buildings have since been demolished, but the "Umbracle" (the "sunshade"), a conservatory for exotic plants (illustration see p. 459), and the "Hivernacle" (the winter garden) have survived. These cast-iron constructions were designed by Fontserès.

Barcelona, Parc de la Ciutadella
Fountain with cherubs at play

The Parc Güell in Barcelona

In 1900 the manufacturer Eusebi Güell bought a site of *c.* 15 ha (37 acres) at Mont Pelat where he intended to create an exemplary housing estate in the manner of the English garden cities. But since the subsequent cost of the real estate would have been too high, he had a park designed by the architect Antonio Gaudí instead. Work on this fascinating project took fourteen years, and in 1920 Güell presented the park to the people.

However the style of the park is classified, it surprises the visitor with its unusual vistas, and delights him or her with its wealth of artistry. The roofs of the buildings, the park walls, and the benches are covered in colorful ceramic fragments. The ceiling of the "Hall of One Hundred Columns," originally planned as a covered market but looking like a temple maze, was decorated by Gaudí and his fellow designer Josep Maria Jujol with a visual collage of great artistry.

This is the point at which the so-called Trencadis technique, which subsequently became

standard practice for collage in the 1920s, should be mentioned. Gaudí pressed the ceramic pieces and fragments, which he was able to obtain for nothing from ceramics works, into the mortar while it was still wet. He took care to use fragments of tiles that were as colorful as possible, so that the yellow, green, and orange pieces would be dabs of color suggesting little flowers. His masterpiece is undoubtedly the walled bench with its broad curves, sections of which, at least, are reminiscent of the turf or flower benches of medieval gardens (illustration above, left). The buildings at the entrance, the office buildings, and the porter's lodge also create a fantastic effect with their raised edging at the windows, doors, and roofs.

Gaudí's formal language is unique. It is difficult to call the Güell Park an art nouveau park because its formal variety and its themes do not fit into the usual formal canon of this style. It is an expression of the Catalan "modernismo" in a new artistic heyday of *c.* 1900, and which can only partly be linked with the art nouveau of other countries.

Barcelona, Parc Güell
Barcelona's most famous park bench on the main square at the upper end of the park. Along with Antonio Gaudí, Josep Maria Jujol was also involved in its creation (top left).

Detail view of the so-called "Hall of One Hundred Columns" (above)

Promenade with leaning supports (left)

ILLUSTRATIONS OPPOSITE
Ceramic ornamentation (bottom)

LLUSTRATION OPPOSITE
Barcelona, Parc Joan Miró
Dona i Ocell (Woman and Bird). This sculpture is one of Miró's last works, which he created in 1984 for the park named after him.

Barcelona, Parc Joan Miró
Geometrically constructed pergolaI

The Parc Joan Miró in Barcelona

The Parc Joan Miró was created in 1984 as an "*espais urbans,*" an urban space, on the site of the former abbatoir in Barcelona. The strict geometric grid design was given its visual profile by means of plants on the one hand and architectural features on the other, for example the pergola shown below. The basic model for the park was provided by the paved piazza that is usually found in Mediterranean countries. This was then divided into play areas and quiet areas.

Because people living nearby felt the park to be chilly and lifeless, and protested at the urban concept, Miró was commissioned to design thirty sculptures for the piazza. Unfortunately only *Dona i Ocell* (Woman and Bird, illustration opposite) was actually created. It stands on a raised base in the middle of a rectangular pool.

The elongated cubic figure, which can be seen from far away, is covered with colored mosaics, giving it an elegant filigree effect. The building which extends along the sides of the pool, the Joan Miró Library, was built between 1988 and 1990. The library bears witness to the richness of imagination and delight in experiment of avant-garde Catalan architecture.

The central access area is flanked by ramps and leads to two columned halls, the entrances to the library. Below the protruding roof reproductions of various bronze statues by Miró are on display.

Hamburg, municipal park
Park lake with separate area for outdoor swimming.
The planetarium can be seen in the background.

Public or Municipal Parks in Germany

Leberecht Migge may be regarded as one of the first garden design modernists in Germany. Around 1900 he was working for Jakob Ochs as a garden architect in Hamburg. He then set up his own business in Worpswede. There he worked with, among others, the architect and urban visionary Bruno Taut. Migge proclaimed the end of traditional garden design, and regarded garden work as an applied art. This brusque assessment resulted from what he regarded as the unfortunate longevity of the romantic garden in the English style. His definition of the function of a garden in *Die Gartenkultur des 20. Jahrhunderts* (20th-Century Garden Culture), published in Jena in 1913, is succinct and to the point:

"A garden must be planned with a view to people's needs. Is that a lack of imagination? No, it is self-restraint, reflection, and self-restriction to the essentials. It is organization. But it is also – art."

Migge took the view that the content and the formal structure of a garden for the people, that is a public or municipal park, must be determined by the people's needs. It must not, as was still the case in Germany, be used as a means of enhancing the city's prestige. What was needed were above all sports facilities, plus shady areas for walking and, as he put it, "for looking at beautiful and edifying plant life." Migge did not have much to say regarding the layout of such gardens, but he did produce numerous designs for municipal public parks with indications of formal structure. Just as the new architecture of the Bauhaus derived an aesthetic model from the functional aspect of living, and accordingly designed plans and elevations with irregular positioning of the windows and asymmetrical relationships between the living areas, so Migge planned large grassy areas bounded by alleys, with intimate garden zones. As regards private gardens, he regarded the utilitarian aspect as paramount and therefore proposed a geometric structure: "I desire the architectural garden on economic and social, as well as ethical grounds."

Migge accepted the principle of practicality in conjunction with aesthetic ideas. In this he was very close to the theories of New Functionalism and, of course, to the new architectural ideas proclaimed by Walter Gropius. The architectural garden with its geometric structure, which had to meet people's social as well as their emotional needs, was intended to constitute a decisive repudiation of the English landscape garden. The Hamburg municipal park on the site of the newly wooded area known as the "Winterhuder Geest" was the first park of any size on the continent to turn its back decisively on the romantic garden. It was planned as a place for people from the densely populated districts of Hamburg to rest and recuperate. Beginning in 1912, following the outcome of a competition in 1908, it was laid out as a public park of some *c.* 182 ha (450 acres) based on plans drawn up by Fritz Schumacher, the head of the municipal building authority, and in accordance with the needs of city-dwellers. Otto Linne was responsible for planting. Along a central axis, and using basic geometric shapes, he laid out a wooded park, a grass area, and a flower garden around a lake. The former water tower at the western end of the axis is the point of reference for the individual areas of the park. Today it serves as an observation tower, with a planetarium in the dome. The tower was conceived as a kind of hinge between the neighboring district of Winterhude and the park (illustration opposite).

The function of the public park, as called for by Migge, namely of giving people the opportunity for physical and mental recuperation, increasingly became the main consideration when public gardens were laid out. In 1926 Martin Wagner, who had worked together with Migge in Worpswede, became a member of the Berlin city council with responsibility for construction matters. In 1938 he was appointed as a professor at Harvard University. He concentrated on the health aspect, which for him constituted the sole usefulness of a garden. Thus the sole *raison d'être* of the garden, or park, was to be a place where the air was stored and improved. Wagner presented these ideas for the first time in 1915 in his dissertation on *Das sanitäre Grün der Städte* (The Health-giving Green of the Cities). Like Migge he was in favor of public parks – urban open spaces, as he called them – which should be laid out for sport, games, and rambling. Hence he was not interested in aesthetic categories, but tried to produce medical proof of the physiological value of physical exercise. This utilitarian rationalism, which could already be detected in Migge, removed the garden not only from its traditional romantic and mock-historic conception, but also from any of its artistic ambitions. Wagner evidently did not consider it necessary to present medical evidence that the soul can also be fortified by the pleasures of the eye.

Even though the healthy effects of a garden, as called for by Wagner, later became widespread – in this connection compare the so-called "keep-fit tracks" of the 1970s and 1980s – gardens and parks did not develop solely in this direction during the 20th century. But significant changes did occur: the turn away from gardens as a source of prestige, from the romantic park landscape, and from the installation of a mock-historical theatrical stage in gardens. Is this also true in the case of England, the country in which the landscape garden originated?

Hamburg, municipal park
Detail of beds in autumn colors

Hamburg, municipal park
Rondel with fountain

Hidcote Manor, Gloucestershire
View of the garden with clipped trees

ILLUSTRATIONS OPPOSITE
Hestercombe Garden, Somerset
Views of the Edwardian Garden, a square sunken garden (bottom) bounded by two canal terraces at the sides (top)

Two Formal Gardens in England

Around the turn of the century, in both town and country, the Victorian garden with its densely planted beds and mock-historical features occupied a dominant position. Lawrence Johnston was one of the first garden architects in England to create an architectural garden, which he did from 1907 at Hidcote in the Cotswolds in the county of Gloucestershire, near the little town of Chipping Campden. Johnston went on many journeys and expeditions to South Africa and China, and brought exotic plants back with him to England, where he grew them. He was so successful that he was soon able to export his plants to many of the countries of Europe.

Along the longitudinal axis of his country house Johnston laid out a spacious lawn, from which a long alley edged with clipped beech trees led away at a right angle across the ridge of the hills. In the angle between the lawn, which he called the "Theatre Lawn," and the alley he created smaller geometric areas of the garden, related to one another but self-contained, which he defined in terms of themes. Adjoining the country house, for example, he laid out the White Garden surrounded by yew hedges. Crossed pathways divide the garden into four compartments planted only with white flowering species. A mighty cedar of Lebanon towers up with its wide-spreading branches above the garden like a shield (illustration left). The gardens positioned in the vicinity of the house and the alley are in strictly geometrical forms, though without producing a symmetrical overall layout. But beyond his Long Walk, the beech tree alley, Johnston designed a picturesque garden, the Stream Garden – an act of homage to the English landscape garden tradition. Here, a rill edged with luxuriant vegetation meanders through the terrain.

Many more comparable English architectural gardens could be listed here, such as, for example, Hestercombe Garden to the north of Taunton in

Hidcote Manor, Gloucestershire
Line of sight with pavilion

the county of Somerset. The property, which dates back to the 18th century, was redesigned by Edwin Lutyens and Gertrude Jekyll in the first decade of the 20th century. The central core of the layout is a terraced parterre in the manner of the Italian Renaissance garden. The parterre, the "Great Plat," was also conceived as a sunken garden with steps at the corners in the shape of quarter-circles (illustrations above and left).

The English evidently had no difficulty in taking leave of both the Victorian prestige garden and the romantic landscape garden. The 20th-century English gardens revert again more strongly to geometric models, while at the same time encouraging the natural growth of plants. The Italian Renaissance garden came back into view, not only because of its architectural approach to design, but also because of the ingenious system of lines of sight. The impressive – if somewhat Manneristic – Renaissance layout of the Villa Lante with its splendid vistas became a model, at least for Hestercombe, for incorporating the surrounding landscape into the structure of the garden as a visual, hence aesthetic, element.

Copenhagen, Tivoli
Pagoda roof of the Chinese Tower

ILLUSTRATION OPPOSITE
Vienna, Prater
Ferris wheel, by the engineer Walter Basset

Amusement Parks

The development outlined above from the landscape garden to the public park and thence to the amusement park is visible in a unique way at the Tivoli in Copenhagen. In 1843 the area in the vicinity of the main railway station was conceived as a landscape garden to provide a place of rest and recuperation for the townspeople. Alleys, a lake with twisting paths and gently undulating hills, Chinese teahouses and Moorish buildings, along with an amphitheater, were traditional adornments to the park. The basic structure and many of the buildings have survived down to the present day. In 1943, two years before his death, the Danish landscape architect Gudmund Nyeland Brandt laid out a parterre close to the lake.

In the 1950s Eywin Langkilde constructed a hanging garden and a sculpture garden as a children's playground. By then the Tivoli was already famous as an amusement park (illustrations left and below).

In the following years and decades amusement parks sprang up all over Europe, at first on the sites of public parks. The park provided the formal structure, to which the "machine inventory" was adapted. Later the element of amusement and entertainment became independent, for example in Disneyland, which was imported into France, or the German Europa Park at Rust. They were to a large extent detached from the idea of a park or garden. Many of the old amusement parks with restaurants, merry-go-rounds, shooting galleries, and Ferris wheels that were less important than the park as such, still exist today, such as the Tivoli in Copenhagen or the Prater in Vienna with its famous Big Wheel (illustration opposite).

In this type of garden the idea of social improvement to everyday life, which was in favor at the beginning of the 20th century, lives on. Citizens who had to bear the increasing burden of mechanical work were to be provided with areas where they could spend their leisure time and recuperate from their everyday working lives.

Copenhagen, Tivoli
Lake with pleasure steamer-restaurant

28
24

ILLUSTRATIONS ABOVE AND OPPOSITE (TOP)
Paris, Parc de la Villette
Iron construction and surfaces of reflecting glass interspersed with greenery dominate this modern public park by Bernard Tschumi.

ILLUSTRATION OPPOSITE
Futuroscope, technological theme park near Poitiers

Architectural and Technological Theme Parks

A few years ago Bernard Tschumi designed the Parc de la Villette, to the northeast of the city center of Paris, a multi-purpose park on the site of the city's former cattle market.

The restored Grande Halle, a 19th-century construction of iron and glass, houses a restaurant and rooms for cultural events. Nearby there is a spacious grassy area which the people who live nearby are fond of using for sporting purposes. Adjoining this there is a long avenue lined with plane trees.

By the nearby Canal de l'Ourq various so-called theme gardens have been created over the years, such as, for example, a bamboo garden, an exceptionally lively water garden, and an espalier garden which the sculptor Jean-Max Albert adorned with his sculptures.

At the northern edge of the park an unusual and almost futuristic building catches the eye, the spherical "La Géode." This is a cinema which constitutes an addition to the area of the park as a whole that is given over to pleasure and entertainment. But education and information are also on offer. Alongside the Music Museum, the Cité de la Musique, near the avenue of plane trees, a Museum of Science and Technology has also been built.

This idea of combining play, information, and entertainment was taken up at an imaginative and fascinating theme park, the Futuroscope near Poitiers. There, an audio-visual technology park has developed since 1987, on a site of about *c.* 53 ha (130 acres), with pavilions, water features, 3D movie theaters, and movie theaters with huge screens. The size of the park increases each year. In 1998 there were 2.7 million visitors. There is probably no other park in the world where avant-garde architecture – one can even speak of architectural experiments – is integrated in this way into a unified park concept with twisting paths, hills, spacious lawns, small boskets, and a lake.

Futuroscope may be the prelude to a new kind of park or garden design (illustration opposite). The park provides not only entertainment but also information about the potential of audio-visual technology. Furthermore it is a pleasure to stroll through the park and discover the bizarre futuristic pavilions and wide-screen cinemas from one new angle after another. On the threshold of the 21st century, architecture, technology, and garden design come together in a unity that is both harmonious and exciting.

Futuroscope may possibly have taken up an idea which arose in Germany toward the end of the 19th century and after the Second World War, developed to an unusual degree of popularity: the garden show. The first show of its kind was the international garden show in Dresden in 1887. After the Second World War the first national garden show took place on the Killesberg in Stuttgart in 1950. Later its younger sister, the provincial garden show, made its first appearance. A garden show is often characterized by a particular theme, for example the "Garden of Delights" organized by Horst Antes at the 1967 national garden show in Karlsruhe.

At the Baden-Württemberg provincial garden show "Grün 99" in Weil on the Rhine, in contrast, experimental architecture was on display. Zaha M. Hadit exhibited a snake-shaped building of layered concrete and glass, with a glass ramp bridging the building and giving a view of the interior.

Heale Garden, Wiltshire
Landscape garden with a view of the River Avon

Gardens and parks have developed in a variety of directions in the 20th century. Dominant types have undoubtedly been the recreational park, the amusement park, and the designed urban space. With individualistic, romantic or bizarre and fairytale-like layouts, the actual task of garden making has receded into the background. A garden should not be regarded as a substitute for nature, but as an artistic means of bringing human beings into closer contact with nature. A public park can only fulfill this task to a limited degree, since in it nature is used merely as a place of recuperation and diversion – necessary and welcome though this undoubtedly is. But more is involved in a garden. There one comes to grips with the essential forms and dynamics of nature. For this reason, plant arrangement requires scientific knowledge and at the same time artistic ability. This combination of art, science, and nature, which can be perfectly harmonized in a garden, has always been the driving force of civilization.

Appendix

Glossary

Amphitheater Area of the garden laid out in the form of an ancient amphitheater. Known as a garden motif since classical antiquity. In the Baroque garden the amphitheater was often used for stage performances.

Arboretum A separate area of the garden where exotic trees were cultivated for scientific purposes.

Arcadia A longed-for landscape in which Man is at one with nature. There was a fondness for describing parts of the English landscape garden as Arcadian areas. Arcadia, a mountain plateau of the Peloponnesus, was originally thought of, not as an Arcadian region, but as a landscape of death.

Belt walk A path or track leading round the garden or park. Found with particular frequency in the English landscape garden with the purpose of leading visitors to the points of view.

Belvedere Architecturally designed point of view in gardens and parks. Synonymous with the French term Bellevue.

Berceau Since the 18th century a trellised walkway constructed of lathes and wire. Hedges or bushes, and sometimes smaller trees, are arranged around it. Dézallier d'Argenville also used the term "berceau de treillage" denoting a combination of "berceau" and "treillage."

Border Long, narrow bed of decorative plants alongside pathways, lawns, walls, or espaliers.

Bosket The wooded area of a garden. The trees are clipped to a regular shape in order to create spaces such as "cabinets," "cloîtres," (q.v.) or "salons."

Botanical Garden The first botanical gardens were laid out in Italy in the 16th century, predominantly for scientific purposes. Following the development in Europe in the 18th century of interests in overseas territories, many exotic plants found their way to Europe, and were cultivated in orangeries and botanical gardens.

Bowling green Sunken lawn, often to be found in the parterre area.

Broderie parterre Plant beds ornamentally designed as if engraved, using mainly boxwood. The name is derived from the similarity with embroidery patterns. The most important design feature of the geometric garden from 1620 to 1720.

Cabinet An oval or rectangular open space within a bosket, often surrounded by clipped hedges. Larger spaces of this kind are known as "salons" or "salles."

Chinoiserie Toward the end of the 17th century Chinese products began to arrive in Europe. At court they were associated with a cheerful and carefree way of life, and in the course of the 18th century their forms were integrated into the Rococo world, at first in France, then in England, and eventually in Germany also. Chinese pavilions were popular in landscape garden areas.

Cloître Area within a bosket lavishly adorned with fountains, trellised walkways, and pools.

Clumps Groups of trees planted on spacious lawns in the English landscape garden.

Compartment Larger plant bed unit consisting of a symmetrical ornament made up of gravel paths, individual beds, and imaginative patterns made with flowers.

Dairy farm Complex of agricultural buildings within a landscape garden, intended to create a mood but not usually serving any utilitarian purpose. Compare Village, Ferme ornée

Decorative buildings Architecture developed especially as a monumental decorative element for landscape gardens. In line with contemporary taste, use was often made of past stylistic periods, exotic models, or so-called follies ("architectural craziness"). See also Romantic ruins, Chinoiserie, Folly.

English parterre or **Parterre à l'Anglaise**. Also known as lawn parterre. Ornamentally designed lawn. Often framed by floral borders.

Ferme ornée The 18th-century park or garden included an area used for agricultural purposes. Term first used by the English garden theorist Stephen Switzer in 1715. Compare Village.

Folly A particular form of decorative building of an intentionally irregular conception as regards its proportions and design. Examples are the Rometta in the Villa d'Este in Tivoli – a copy of a panoramic view of the city of Rome, in the form of a stage backdrop – or the Mannerist garden in Bomarzo. Imaginative follies are occasionally to be found in English landscape gardens, for example the Conolly folly of Castletown House in Kildare, Ireland.

Gardenesque This term was coined by John Claudius Loudon in 1832 to describe the free and natural growth of plants. It later came to denote the aesthetic evolution of the garden through its decorative flowers.

Garden/Flower Show In England, a horticultural fete was held at Chiswick in 1829. Today The Royal Horticultural Society shows include the famous Chelsea Flower Show and The Hampton Court Palace Flower Show. There are many others fine shows up and down the country, and throughout Europe. In Germany, the first such show was the International Garden Show in Dresden in 1887. After the Second World War, the first national garden show was held on the Killesberg in Stuttgart in 1950, followed later by its "little sister," the provincial garden show.

Giardino segreto A secret garden. Usually adjoining the bedchamber or private apartments of the palace or castle. In other cases the secret garden was situated in secluded areas of the garden to which access was difficult. It was often screened by tall hedges or walls. A speciality of the Italian Renaissance garden.

Geometric garden Beds and parterres laid out in regular geometric patterns. Mainly in Renaissance and Baroque gardens. The geometric garden was ousted by the landscape garden.

Gloriette Temple or pavilion of honor, often designed in the manner of a Greek circular temple. Found mainly in landscape gardens.

Grotto Artificial cave in Renaissance and Baroque gardens. In the 18th century, garden rooms were decorated as grottoes, with seashells, snails, moss, and rocks.

Ha-ha In order not to disturb the visual transition from the garden to the landscape by boundary walls or embankments, wide ditches were dug with sunken walls. The first description of a ha-ha was given by the Englishman Stephen Switzer in 1715.

Hameau A hamlet, or small village.

Hermitage Secluded and concealed area of the Baroque garden, often designed as a grotto. Retreat for court society.

Hortulus A poem of twenty-seven verses by Walahfrid Strabo dating from the first half of the 19th century. Probably the first comprehensive statement regarding garden making in Christian civilization. It refers to the monastery garden at St. Gall.

Hypnerotomachia Polyphili Allegorical novel by Francesco Colonna. First published in Venice in 1499. The woodcut illustrations show different kinds of clipped trees, topiary (q.v.), and bed ornaments.

Knot ornament Typical Renaissance plant bed patterning. First appears in a pronounced form in Sebastiano Serlio's tract at the beginning of the 16th century. The forms go back to the *Hypnerotomachia Polyphili* (q.v.).

Landscape garden A type of garden which evolved in England in the mid-18th century, which encouraged plants to grow naturally, and was rigorously opposed to the geometric approach of the French Baroque garden. The results were spacious meadows and shady clumps of trees, rivercourses, lakes, and a multitude of decorative buildings.

Lawn parterre See English parterre.

Menagerie Zoo in the Baroque park and the 18th-century landscape garden.

Monastery garden Consists of various sections such as the physic garden, the kitchen garden, the planted graveyard, and the quadrangle. In the physic garden roses and lilies were also found, the flowers symbolizing the Virgin Mary that were indispensable for a monastery garden.

Orangery Area of the garden away from the castle or palace where the orange trees were put up in the summer. It included a building for growing the oranges. In the Renaissance garden wooden arbors were often erected which in the winter were pulled over the orange trees using rollers.

Parterre Arrangement of beds divided by a simple system of paths laid out directly in front of the garden frontage of the palace or castle.

Parterre d'Orangerie Lawn or bed complex directly in front of the orangery.

Patte d'oie or Goose's Foot: system of alleys in the outer park or garden area fanning out in three directions. From a common starting point the alleys or pathways spread out until they reach a semicircular path, thereby harmoniously marking the end of a particular area of the garden.

Physic garden Also called a "herbularius." Found in medieval monasteries behind the complex of doctors' and apothecarys' buildings. The herbs planted included sage, rue, caraway, fennel, and lovage.

Pleasure ground Area of lawn directly in front of the castle or villa, adorned particularly lavishly with sculptures. Usually separated by a pool from the rest of the garden.

Point of view A point from which a sculpture, a fountain, or a decorative building appears at the end of a line of sight.

Quarter or Quarreaux A quarter comprises several compartments. It is separated from another quarter by pathways or alleys. Several quarters together make up a parterre.

Quincunx Five trees planted in the pattern of the number five on dice. It describes a so-called perpendicular square grid with a fifth tree placed in the middle of each square. When walking past a bosket of this kind, tree-lined alleys are seen in every direction, leading away either diagonally or at a right angle to the line of sight. The resulting effect is one of continuous rhythmic change.

Romantic ruins In landscape gardens a decorative medieval ruin often features as a sentimental image of the bygone splendor of chivalry and national greatness.

Salon See Cabinet

Salle See Cabinet

Topiary The art of clipping trees and bushes, first described in detail in the agrarian literature of antiquity and in Pliny the Elder. "Topiaria" means "artistic gardening" in Latin. Many examples of topiary which served as models for Renaissance or Baroque gardens are to be found in the *Hypnerotomachia Polyphili* (q.v.)

Treillage Trellised walkway made of latticed strips of wood, often interspersed with wooden pavilions. Dézallier d'Argenville also employed the term "berceau de treillage" to denote a combination of "berceau" and "treillage."

Tumulus A grave mound in classical antiquity. Artificially created in landscape parks to provide a sentimental view or, at Branitz, made by and for Prince Pückler-Muskau as a burial place.

Village In the Baroque or Rococo garden, rural buildings were arranged in the form of villages in order to simulate country life. Also known as "Hameau" or "hamlet;" cf. Ferme ornée.

Bibliography

Adorno, Th. W., "Amorbach," in *Ohne Leitbild*, Frankfurt am Main 1967

Andreae, B., *Am Birnbaum. Gärten und Parks im antiken Rom, in den Vesuvstädten und Ostia*, Mainz 1996

Baudy, G. J., "Adonisgärten," in *Beiträge zur klassischen, Philologie 176*, 1986

Baumann, H., "Die griechische Pflanzenwelt," in *Mythos, Kunst und Literatur*, Munich 1986

Baumgardt, U., and Olbricht, I. (eds), *Die Suche nach dem Paradies. Illusionen. Wünsche. Realitäten*, Munich 1989

Baumüller, B., Kuder, K., Zoglauer, U. (eds), *Inszenierte Natur. Landschaftskunst im 19. und 20. Jh.*, Stuttgart 1997

Beazley, M., *Gardens of Germany*, London 1998

Bianca, S., *Hofhaus und Paradiesgarten. Architektur und Lebensformen in der islamischen Welt*, Munich 1991

Böhme, G., *Für eine ökologische Naturästhetik*, Frankfurt am Main 1989

Börner, K. H., *Auf der Suche nach dem irdischen Paradies. Zur Ikonographie der geographischen Utopie*, Frankfurt am Main 1984

Brodersen, K., *Die Sieben Weltwunder. Legendäre Kunst- und Bauwerke der Antike*, Munich 1996

Brunner-Traut, E., *Die alten Ägypter*, Stuttgart 1981

Buttlar, A. von, *Der Landschaftsgarten*, Munich 1980

Buttlar, A. von, *Der Englische Landsitz 1715–1760 – Symbol eines liberalen Weltentwurfs*, Mittenwald 1982

Buttlar, A. von, *Der Landschaftsgarten. Gartenkunst des Klassizismus und der Romantik*, Cologne 1989

Carroll-Spillecke, M. (ed.), *Der Garten von der Antike bis zum Mittelalter*, Mainz 1992

Carroll-Spillecke, M., *Kepos, Der antike griechische Garten. Wohnen in der klassischen Polis III*, Munich 1989

Carvallo, R., *The Gardens of Villandry, Techniques and Plants*, Joué-lès-Tours 1991

Chambers, D., *The Planters of the English Landscape Garden*, London 1993

Clifford, D., *Geschichte der Gartenkunst*, Munich 1966

Cohen, R. (ed.), *Studies in Eighteenth-Century British Art and Aesthetics*, Los Angeles 1985

Correcher, C. M., and George, M., *Spanische Gärten*, Stuttgart 1997

Curtius, E. R., *Europäische Literatur und lateinisches Mittelalter*, 9th imp., Berne, Munich 1978

Eisold, N., *Das Dessau-Wörlitzer Gartenreich*, Cologne 1983

Ermann, A. (ed.), *Die Literatur der Ägypter*, Leipzig 1923

Fahlbusch, H., "Elemente griechischer und römischer Wasserversorgungsanlagen," in Garbrecht, G. *et al.*, *Die Wasserversorgung antiker Städte. Geschichte der Wasserversorgung 2*, Mainz 1987, pp. 135–63

Fröhlich, A. M. (ed.), *Gärten. Texte aus der Weltliteratur*, Zurich 1993

Fleming, J., *The "Roman de la Rose" – A Study in Allegory and Iconography*, Princeton 1969

Friedlaender, L., *Darstellungen aus der Sittengeschichte Roms*, 4 vols, Leipzig 1919

Gerndt, S., *Idealisierte Natur*, Stuttgart 1981

Gillen, O. (ed.), *Herard von Landsberg, Hortus deliciarum*, Landau 1979

Glaser, H., *Industriekultur und Alltagsleben. Vom Biedermeier zur Postmoderne*, Frankfurt am Main 1994

Gothein, M. L., *Geschichte der Gartenkunst*, 2 vols, Jena 1926, rep. 1988

Günther, H. (ed.), *Gärten der Goethezeit*, Leipzig 1993

Hajós, G., *Romantische Gärten der Aufklärung. Englische Landschaftskultur des 18. Jahrhunderts in und um Wien*, Vienna, Cologne 1989

Hajós, G. (ed.), *Historische Gärten in Österreich. Vergessene Gesamtkunstwerke*, Vienna, Cologne, Weimar 1993

Hajós, G., *Die Schönbrunner Schlossgärten*, Vienna, Cologne, Weimar 1995

Hamilton Haziehurst, F., *Gardens of Illusion – The Genius of André Le Nôtre*, Nashville, Tennessee 1980

Hammerschmidt, V., and Wilke, J., *Die Entdeckung der Landschaft. Englische Gärten des 18. Jh.*, Stuttgart 1990

Hannwacker, V., *Friedrich Ludwig von Sckell. Der Begründer des Landschaftsgartens in Deutschland*, Stuttgart 1992

Hansmann, W., *Gartenkunst der Renaissance und des Barock*, Cologne 1983

Harten, H. C., and E., *Die Versöhnung mit der Natur. Gärten, Freiheitsbäume, republikanische Wälder, heilige Berge und Tugendparks in der Französischen Revolution*, Reinbek 1989

Hartman, G., *Die Ruine im Landschaftsgarten. Ihre Bedeutung für den frühen Historismus und die Landschaftsmalerei der Romantik*, Worms 1981

Heinemann, E., *Babylonische Spiele. William Beckford und das Erwachen der modernen Imagination.* Dissertation, Berlin 1996

Hennebo, D., and Hoffmann, A., *Geschichte der deutschen Gartenkunst*, 3 vols, Hamburg 1965

Hennebo, D., *Gärten des Mittelalters*, Zurich 1987

Heyer, H.-R., *Historische Gärten der Schweiz*, Berne 1980

Hobhouse, P., *Gardens of Italy*, London 1998

Hirsch, E., Dessau-Wörlitz, *Zierde und Inbegriff des 18. Jh.*, Leipzig, Munich 1985

Hirschfeld, Chr., C., L., *Theorie der Gartenkunst*, 5 vols, Leipzig 1985

Hoepfner, W., Schwandner, F. L., *Haus und Stadt im klassischen Griechenland. Wohnen in der klassischen Polis 1*, Munich 1994

Hoffmann, A., "Gärten des Rokoko: Irrendes Spiel," in *Park und Garten im 18. Jahrhundert*, Heidelberg 1978

Irrgang, W., *Bemerkenswerte Parkanlagen in Schlesien*, Dortmund 1978

Jashemski, W. F., *The Gardens of Pompeii, Herculaneum and the villas destroyed by Vesuvius*, 2 vols, New Rochelle 1979, 1993

Kluckert, E., *Der "hängende Garten" der Apollonia. Renaissance-Gärten in Württemberg*, Schwäbische Heimat, 3, 1986

Kluckert, E., *Heinrich Schickhardt. Architekt und Ingenieur*, Herrenberg 1992

Kluckert, E., *Vom Heiligen Hain zur Postmoderne. Eine Kunstgeschichte Baden-Württembergs*, Stuttgart 1996

Kluckert, E., *Auf dem Weg zur Idealstadt. Humanistische Stadtplanung im Südwesten Deutschlands*, Stuttgart 1998

Koenigs, T. (ed.), *Stadt-Parks. Urbane Natur in Frankfurt am Main*, Frankfurt am Main, New York 1993

Koopmann, H., "Eichendorff und die Aufklärung," in *Aurora 1988, Park und Garten im 18. Jh.*, Heidelberg 1978

Kuhnke, R. W., *Die maurischen Gärten Andalusiens*, Munich 1996

Kuterbach, J., *Der französische Garten am Ende des Anciën Régime*, Worms 1987

Lablaude, P.-A., *Die Gärten von Versailles,* Worms 1995

Lazzaro, C., *The Italian Renaissance Garden*, London 1990

Le Nôtre, A., "Bericht über das Schloß und die Gärten des Trianon an den schwedischen Architekten Nikodemus Tessin, 1693," in Mariage, Th., *L'univers de Le Nôtre*, Brussels 1990

Mader, G., and Neubert-Mader, L., *Italienische Gärten*, Stuttgart 1987

Maurer, D., "Pilgrime sind wir alle, die wir Italien suchen. Das Italienerlebnis deutscher Schriftsteller vor und nach Goethes italienischer Reise," in Göres, J. (ed.), *Goethe in Italien*, Mainz 1986

Mayer-Solgk, F., and Greuter, A., *Landschaftsgärten in Deutschland*, Stuttgart 1997

Mayer-Tasch, P. C., and Mayerhofer, B. (eds), *Hinter Mauern ein Paradies. Der mittelalterliche Garten*, Leipzig 1998

Mosser, M., and Teyssot, G., *Die Gartenkunst des Abendlandes. Von der Renaissance bis zur Gegenwart,* Stuttgart 1990

Müller, U., *Klassischer Geschmack und Gotische Tugend. Der englische Landsitz Rousham*, Worms 1998

Niedermeier, M., *Erotik in der Gartenkunst. Eine Kulturgeschichte der Liebesgärten*, Leipzig 1995

Paracelsus, *Vom Licht der Natur und des Geistes. Eine Auswahl*, Stuttgart 1976

Pizzoni, F., *Kunst und Geschichte des Gartens,* Stuttgart 1999

Pückler-Muskau, H. Fürst von, *Andeutungen über Landschaftsgärtnerei*, Frankfurt am Main 1988

Pückler-Muskau, H., Fürst von, *Briefe eines Verstorbenen*, Frankfurt am Main, Leipzig 1991

Schneider, K., *Villa und Natur. Eine Studie zur römischen Oberschichtkultur im letzten vor- und ersten nachchristlichen Jahrhundert*, Munich 1995

Stoffler, H.-D., *Der Hortulus des Walahfrid Strabo*, Sigmaringen 1996

Taylor, P., *Gardens of Britain*, London 1998

Taylor, P., *Gardens of France*, London 1998

Thierfelder, W., *Gärten und Parks in Franken*, Würzburg 1990

Vérin, H., "Technology in the Park: Engineers and Gardeners in Seventeenth-Century France," in Mosser, M., and Teyssot, G. (eds), *The Architecture of Western Gardens*, Cambridge, Mass. 1991, pp. 135–46

Weiss, A. S., *Miroirs de l'infini – Le jardin à la française et la métaphysique au XVII. siècle*, Paris 1992

Weitzmann, K., *Late Antique and Early Christian Book Illumination,* New York 1977

Wenzel, W., *Die Gärten des Lothar Franz von Schönborn 1655–1729*, Berlin 1970

Wiebenson, D., *The Picturesque Garden in France,* Princeton 1978

Willis, P., *Charles Bridgeman and the English Landscape Garden*, London 1977

Wimmer, C. A., *Geschichte der Gartentheorie*, Darmstadt 1989

Wiseman, D. J., *Nebuchadrezzar and Babylon*, Oxford 1985

Woods, M., *Visions of Arcadia. European Gardens from Renaissance to Rococo,* London 1996

Index of Persons

Index of Place Names

Picture Acknowledgments

Abbreviations:

The publishers and the editor wish to thank the museums, archives, and photographers for making the original pictures available and for giving permission for them to be reproduced. In addition to the museums and institutions mentioned in the captions, thanks are also due to the following in respect of particular pictures:

AKG, Berlin: 156, 350–51

Andreae, Bernard, Rome: 16

Artothek, Foto: Joachim Blauel: 9

Artothek, Foto: Blauel/Gnamm: 21

artur, Cologne, Foto: Klaus Frahm: 420, 427 top, 427 bottom

Ashmolean Museum, Oxford: 136

Bassler, Markus, Dosquers (Girona): 2, 10, 236 bottom, 237 top, 237 bottom, 238 top, 238 bottom left, 238 bottom right, 239, 241 top right, 241 bottom, 242 top, 242 bottom, 246 top left, 246 top right, 246 bottom left, 246 bottom right, 248, 249 top, 249 bottom, 250, 251, 252 top, 252 bottom, 253 top, 253 bottom left, 253 bottom right, 254 top, 254 bottom, 255, 256, 257, 258, 259 top, 259 bottom, 260 bottom left, 260 bottom right, 261 top, 261 bottom, 262, 263, 264, 265 top, 265 bottom, 266–7, 268, 269, 270, 271, 272, 273, 274 top, 274 bottom, 275, 459 top, 470 top, 470 bottom, 471, 474, 475

Bastin, Christine, and Evrard, Jacques, Brussels: 12 top, 15, 23 top, 23 bottom, 32 top, 39, 152 bottom, 182 bottom, 182–3, 232, 233, 335 top, 456, 460 top, 472 top, 472 bottom left, 472 bottom right, 473 top, 473 bottom, 482, 483 bottom

Bednorz, Achim, Cologne: 25 top, 25 bottom, 26 top, 26 bottom, 27 top left, 27 top right, 27 bottom, 32 bottom, 33, 34 top, 34 bottom, 35, 36–7, 38 top, 100, 101 top, 102 right, 103 top, 104–05, 106–07, 108 top, 108 bottom, 109, 110, 111, 112–13, 114, 115, 116 top, 117 top, 118, 119, 120–21, 122, 123, 126 bottom, 132 top, 151 top, 184–5, 186 top, 190 top, 190 bottom, 197 top, 203 top, 203 bottom, 211 top, 211 bottom, 213, 214, 215, 218, 219, 220–21, 222 top, 222 bottom, 223, 224, 225 top, 225 bottom, 227, 228, 348, 390–91, 407 bottom, 440 top, 440 bottom, 443 top, 443 bottom, 444, 445 top, 445 bottom, 446–7, 460 bottom, 461, 466 bottom, 468–9

Bildarchiv Preußischer Kulturbsitz: 421

BPK, Foto: Jörg P. Anders: 129

Bollen, Markus, Bergisch Gladbach: 11 bottom, 18 top, 18 bottom, 19 top, 19 bottom, 42, 43 bottom, 44, 45 bottom right, 47, 51 bottom, 55, 62 bottom, 63 bottom, 64, 65 top, 65 bottom, 66, 67 bottom, 68–9, 70, 74 top, 75, 77 top, 78 top, 78 bottom, 79 bottom, 80 top left, 80 top right, 80 bottom, 88 top, 88 bottom, 89, 92, 93, 94 top, 94 bottom left, 94 bottom right, 95 top, 95 bottom, 96 top, 96 bottom, 97 top, 97 bottom, 98 top, 98 bottom, 144 bottom, 145 left, 145 right top, 145 right bottom, 147, 148 bottom left, 149, 154 bottom, 155 top, 155 bottom, 157, 158 top, 158 bottom, 161 top, 161 bottom left, 161 bottom right, 162 top, 162 bottom, 165 bottom right, 170, 171, 180, 181 top left, 181 top right, 181 bottom left, 181 bottom right

Bridgeman Art Library, London: 29, 137, 399

British Library, London: 152–3, 392 bottom

Claßen, Martin, Cologne: 41, 76, 79 top, 82–3, 84 top, 84 bottom, 85 top, 85 bottom, 86–7, 99, 165 bottom left, 168, 169 top, 169 bottom

© Crown Copyright: 11 top

Dagli Orti, G., Paris: 216–17

Das Fotoarchiv, Foto: Jörg P. Meyer: 342 top

English Heritage Photo Library: 372 left

Helga Lade Fotoagentur: 342 bottom (BAV), 344 (E. Bergmann), 345 top (Eicke), 450 bottom (Egon Martzik), 476 (Connor), 477 top (Connor), 477 bottom (Keres), 483 top (Dieter Rebmann)

Hinous, Pascal, Paris: 124, 125 top, 125 bottom, 126 top, 127

Könemann Verlagsgesellschaft mbH, Cologne/ Foto: Adam Bednorz: 24, 148 bottom right, 150, 188–9, 192 top, 193, 196, 197 bottom, 198 top left, 198 top middle, 198 top right, 198 bottom, 199, 200, 201 top, 201 bottom, 202 top, 204, 207 bottom, 209 top, 209 bottom, 234, 235 bottom, 240, 243, 244, 245, 247, 260 top, 296, 298 top, 299 top, 299 bottom, 303, 308, 413, 442 top, 462–3, 463 right, 464 top, 464 bottom, 465 top, 465 bottom; **Foto: Gerald Zugmann:** 481

Magnus Edizioni, Fagagna: 48–9, 52 top, 54, 56-7, 58, 59, 60–61, 73, 159, 160, 163, 166, 167, 174, 175, 176, 177, 178–9

Monheim, Florian, Meerbusch
Bildarchiv Monheim.de: 6–7, 128 top, 130 bottom, 131, 134 top, 139, 140, 142, 143, 230 top left, 231, 276 top, 279, 280, 281, 283 top, 283 bottom, 284, 285, 286, 287 top, 287 bottom, 288, 289, 290, 291 top, 292–3, 294, 295, 297, 298 top, 299 top, 299 bottom, 300–01, 302, 304, 305 top, 305 bottom left, 305 bottom right, 306, 307 top, 307 bottom, 309, 310, 311 top, 311 bottom left, 311 bottom right, 312, 313 top, 314, 315, 316, 317, 318 top 318 bottom, 319 bottom, 320, 321, 323 top, 323 bottom, 326 top, 327, 328, 330 top, 331, 332, 333, 334, 335 bottom, 336 top, 336 bottom, 337, 338 top, 339, 340, 341, 346, 349, 353 top, 354, 355, top, 369 top, 369 bottom, 370 top, 370 bottom, 371, 372–3, 376, 377, 378, 379 top, 379 bottom, 380, 381, 382, 384, 386, 387, 393, 395, 396, 400 top, 400 bottom, 401 top, 402–03, 404, 405, 406, 408, 410, 411 top, 411 bottom left, 411 bottom right, 412, 414 bottom, 415, 416, 417, 418, 419 left, 419 right top, 419 right bottom, 422 top, 422 bottom, 423, 424, 425, 426 top, 426 bottom, 428, 429, 430 top, 430 bottom, 431, 432, 433, 435 top, 436 top, 436 bottom, 437 top, 437 bottom, 438–9, 448, 449 top, 449 bottom, 457 top, 457 bottom, 478 top, 478 bottom, 479 top, 479 bottom, 484

Monheim, Florian; von Götz, Roman
Bildarchiv Monheim.de: 358 bottom, 359, 388, 458 top

© The National Trust: 138, 139, 140, 142, 143, 364 bottom, 365, 366–7, 375, 376, 377, 395, 396, 478 top, 478 bottom, 479 top, 479 bottom

Opitz, Barbara
Bildarchiv Monheim.de: 138, 329 top, 347 top, 352 top, 362 top, 362 bottom, 364 bottom, 365, 375, 383, 385, 389 bottom, 458 bottom

Polidori, Robert, Paris: 194, 205, 206, 228 top, 228 bottom

Puschner, Christoph/laif: 345 bottom

R. M. N., Paris: 153 bottom, 191 (Foto: Gerárd Blot), 202, 207 top. (Foto: Arnaudet), 212 bottom, 228 bottom, 442 bottom

Scala, Florence: 13, 14, 50 top, 62 top, 72, 144 top, 156, 172 bottom, 173

Schmid, Gregor M., Munich: 452 top, 452 bottom, 453 top, 453 bottom, 454–5 top, 454 bottom, 455 bottom left, 455 bottom right

Stockholm, Royal Academy of Fine Arts: 451

Tony Stone Images, Foto: Tony Craddock: 480 top

Zanetti, Fulvio/laif: 343, 450 top, 480 bottom

Zurich Foto, © 2000 by Kunsthaus Zurich, all rights reserved: 467 top